CONVERGENCE AND PERSI
CORPORATE GOVERNANCE

D ─────── ⌐OR RETURN

Corporate governance is on the ⌐orm al world. How will
global economic integration aff var tional systems of
corporate ownership and gover e Ang American model of
shareholder capitalism destined to become standard or will sharp differences persist? If there is change, which institutions will converge? Which will persist? This volume contains classic work from leading scholars addressing these questions as well as new essays. In a sophisticated political economy analysis that is also attuned to the legal framework, the authors bring to bear efficiency arguments, politics, institutional economics, international relations, industrial organization, path dependence, and property rights. The Enron-induced corporate governance events and reforms in the United States heighten the importance of this inquiry. Will Enron hold up a convergence that was in the works? *Convergence and Persistence in Corporate Governance* sets up the issues for study and analysis.

JEFFREY N. GORDON is the Alfred W. Bressler Professor of Law and Co-Director of the Center for Law and Economic Studies at the Columbia Law School, where he teaches corporate law, mergers and acquisitions, comparative corporate governance, and a course on regulation. His recent publications include "What Enron Means for the Management and Control of the Modern Business Corporation: Some Initial Reflections," 69 *Univ. of Chicago Law Review* 1233 (2002), "Controlling Controlling Shareholders," 152 *Univ. of Pennsylvania Law Review* 785 (2003) (co-author), and "An American Perspective on Anti-Takeover Laws in the EU: A German Example, in *Modern Company and Takeover Law in Europe* (2004). He is a co-author of the forthcoming book, *Foundations of the Regulatory State.*

MARK J. ROE is the Berg Professor of Corporate Law at the Harvard Law School, where he teaches corporate law and bankruptcy. His publications include *Strong Managers, Weak Owners: The Political Roots of American Corporate Finance* (1994), *Political Determinants of Corporate Governance* (2003), and academic articles such as "Delaware's Competition," 116 *Harvard Law Review* 588 (2003), "Corporate Law's Limits," 31 *Journal of Legal Studies* 233 (2002), "Political Preconditions to Separating Ownership from Corporate Control," 53 *Stanford Law Review* 539 (2000), and "Backlash," 98 *Columbia Law Review* 217 (1998).

In Memoriam: David Charny, 1954–2000

CONVERGENCE AND PERSISTENCE IN CORPORATE GOVERNANCE

Edited by

JEFFREY N. GORDON AND MARK J. ROE

CAMBRIDGE
UNIVERSITY PRESS

PUBLISHED BY THE PRESS SYNDICATE OF THE UNIVERSITY OF CAMBRIDGE
The Pitt Building, Trumpington Street, Cambridge, United Kingdom

CAMBRIDGE UNIVERSITY PRESS
The Edinburgh Building, Cambridge, CB2 2RU, UK
40 West 20th Street, New York, NY 10011–4211, USA
477 Williamstown Road, Port Melbourne, VIC 3207, Australia
Ruiz de Alarcón 13, 28014 Madrid, Spain
Dock House, The Waterfront, Cape Town 8001, South Africa

http://www.cambridge.org

First published 2004

Printed in the United Kingdom at the University Press, Cambridge

Typeface Minion 10.75/12.75 pt.   *System* LaTeX 2_ε [TB]

A catalogue record for this book is available from the British Library

ISBN 0 521 82911 9 hardback
ISBN 0 521 53601 4 paperback
1004905882

CONTENTS

v

FIGURES

vii

TABLES

CONTRIBUTORS

Lucian Arye Bebchuk, William J. Friedman and Alicia Townsend Friedman Professor of Law, Economics, and Finance, Harvard Law School

David Charny, late David Berg Professor of Law, Harvard Law School

Ronald J. Gilson, Marc and Eva Stern Professor of Law and Business, Columbia University, and Charles J. Meyers Professor of Law and Business, Stanford University

Jeffrey N. Gordon, Alfred W. Bressler Professor of Law, Columbia Law School

Henry Hansmann, George T. Lowy Professor of Law, New York University School of Law

Gérard Hertig, Professor of Law, Swiss Institute of Technology (ETA Zürich)

Reinier Kraakman, Ezra Ripley Thayer Professor of Law, Harvard Law School

Curtis J. Milhaupt, Fuyo Professor of Law and Director, Center for Japanese Legal Studies, Columbia Law School

J. Mark Ramseyer, Mitsubishi Professor of Japanese Legal Studies, Harvard University

Mark J. Roe, David Berg Professor of Law, Harvard Law School

Charles F. Sabel, Maurice T. Moore Professor of Law and Social Science, Columbia Law School

Reinhard H. Schmidt, William Merton Professor of International Banking and Finance and Dean of the School of Business and Economics, University of Frankfurt

Gerald Spindler, Professor of Law, University of Göttingen

ACKNOWLEDGMENTS

We thank the Alfred P. Sloan Foundation, which supported the Columbia Law School Corporate Governance Project for several years. Many chapters in this volume were first presented at a conference organized by this Project or trace their lineage to research support that the Foundation provided. We particularly appreciate the support and helpful engagement over the years of Ralph Gomery and Gail Pesyna. Several deans at Columbia and Harvard Law Schools – Lance Liebman and David Leebron at Columbia, and Robert Clark at Harvard – encouraged and supported this work.

Jeffrey N. Gordon and Mark J. Roe

Introduction

JEFFREY N. GORDON & MARK J. ROE

Corporate governance is on the reform agenda all over the world. The remarkable political economy of the post-Cold War era has made both democracy and market-oriented capitalism ascendant, even if not inevitably linked. Competition among radically different economic systems – communism vs. capitalism – has abated. States are withdrawing from ownership of the means of production by privatizing state-firms and withdrawing from strong control by deregulating widely. Economic decisions once made by the state are increasingly left to autonomous, privately owned firms. Even if private corporate governance characteristics continue to differ, the most general of economic contrasts – private vs. government direction – is fading.

Global economic integration has been a key factor in the salience of corporate governance questions. Once confined to local economies, differently governed firms now compete with one another, as multilateral trade agreements and regional economic blocks such as the European Union have internationalized product markets, capital markets, managerial markets, and, to a lesser extent, labor markets.

Globalization affects the corporate governance reform agenda in two ways. First, it heightens anxiety over whether particular corporate governance systems confer competitive economic advantage. As trade barriers erode, the locally protected product marketplace disappears. A country's firms' performance is more easily measured against global standards. Poor performance shows up more quickly when a competitor takes away market share, or innovates quickly.

National decisionmakers must consider whether to protect locally favored corporate governance regimes if they regard the local regime as weakening local firms in product markets or capital markets. So, the Americans debated in the 1980s whether bank-centered systems in Japan and Germany better monitored management and better encouraged long-term investment than the home-grown variety. Today, Europe wonders whether it will lag in product markets if it does not get active securities markets. International development institutions believe that corporate governance affects the rate and sustainability of developing country growth. A famous case is the International Monetary Fund's (IMF) criticism of the governance of Korean conglomerates, the *chaebol*, as allegedly producing unsustainable borrowing patterns that helped ignite the East Asian financial crisis of 1998. Concern about comparative economic performance induces concern about corporate governance.

Globalization's second effect comes from capital markets' pressure on corporate governance. First, firms have new reasons to turn to public capital markets. High tech firms following the US model want the ready availability of an initial public offering for the venture capitalist to exit and for the firm to raise funds. Firms expanding into global markets often prefer to use stock, rather than cash, as acquisition currency. If they want American investors to buy and hold that stock, they are pressed to adopt corporate governance measures that those investors feel comfortable with. Despite a continuing bias in favor of home-country investing, the internationalization of capital markets has led to more cross-border investing. New stockholders enter, and they aren't always part of any local corporate governance consensus. They prefer a corporate governance regime they understand and often believe that reform will increase the value of their stock. Similarly, even local investors may make demands that upset a prior local consensus. The internationalization of capital markets means that investment flows may move against firms perceived to have suboptimal governance and thus to the disadvantage of the countries in which those firms are based.

An independent factor in the corporate governance debate is the wave of privatizations of large state-owned enterprises in the infrastructure, natural resource, and manufacturing areas. This has often been accompanied by deregulation. Corporate governance reformers have sought accountability from large economic actors when privatization and deregulation have devolved important decisionmaking authority away from governments and into private firms. Often, political accountability and economic efficiency point in different directions. For example, in privatizing former state-owned enterprises, the state wants to maximize the price it gets from selling the firm, but it also wants to preserve political influence, often to control employment and service. The two do not always match.

Thus there are two different audiences for the corporate governance debate: one, the national political elites concerned about accountability and national economic performance; the other, the corporate elites concerned about the success of their own firm and their stakes in that firm. The interests of the two elites are not necessarily the same; indeed, corporate elites may be divided, depending on the economic stakes at risk. The old players might be fond of the incumbent corporate governance system; new entrants might more readily see the virtues of change.

* * *

Reforming corporate governance often requires changing laws (and not just the basic rules of corporate law, but also labor law, financial regulatory law, and tax law). Changing law ordinarily requires a political consensus, making agreement among political and corporate elites necessary. Other reforms can move forward independently through internal governance decisions. Corporate governance plays out on several levels, and some levels could converge while others persist, with some levels requiring national change and others able to move forward firm by firm, from the ground up. Keeping these different levels of institutions conceptually separate is crucial to understanding what is at stake. For example, consider two key corporate governance institutions: the share-ownership structure (whether ownership is concentrated or diffuse) on the one hand, the role of the board of directors on the other in say, monitoring managers. One may persist, while the other moves.

Consider further the interaction between these two elements: the board's role may be conditioned by the share-ownership structure. Most practitioner attention has focused on the role of the board and is manifested in a proliferation of best practice codes and other corporate governance guidelines. We might see considerable pressure for tighter review of management actions in publicly owned firms, increased accountability, and even increased managerial turnover. So where public firms predominate, there might be practical convergence, with different means (takeovers, charged-up boards, bank pressure) doing the job. True, there is bound to be residual divergence at the microstructure level, but it is plausible to imagine converging corporate governance standards for those firms that are fully public.

At the same time, though, ownership structures might move more slowly. Moreover, the best governance regime for "insider" systems associated with monitoring by blockholders differs from the best regime for monitoring by and for dispersed shareholders. So if differing ownership structures persist, then board-type convergence will lag as well.

* * *

The chapters in this volume address whether the forces of convergence will triumph, the mechanisms by which convergence might emerge, and the forces that induce systems to persist. Several assess the political economy that underlies both the current diversity in national regimes of corporate governance and the prospects for convergence. "Politics" is evaluated in several dimensions: first, the grand compromises in particular societies over the ends and mechanisms of corporate governance, second, the positional interests and private gains created by the extant system that may affect the possibilities for change, and third, a nation's geopolitical commitments, meaning the extent to which it is committed to the project of transnational economic and political integration.

Could convergence emerge even if governments and entrenched corporate elites oppose it? Several chapters consider how it could. First, fundamental product market and capital market pressures arising from globalization may force convergence of local regimes towards the dominant international model; to do otherwise, it's supposed, would lead to the economic decline of dissenting countries and firms. Second, individual firms may opt out of an inefficient local governance regime or opt into higher-quality foreign regimes, for example, by listing on stock exchanges that impose more exacting disclosure and other governance standards. This presumably too promotes convergence on the international model (unless opting in and out go in differing directions). Third, supranational institutions may promote convergence, either through unleashing regulatory competition or promoting harmonization. In the European Union, for example, the 1999 *Centros* decision[1] and the November 2002 *Überseering* decision[2] of the European Court of Justice call in question the "real seat rule" that subjects a corporation to the corporate law of the state where it has its "center of gravity." If pursued, this could lead to regulatory competition that in the United States led to substantial convergence on Delaware corporate law. And the European Union has also promoted convergence through efforts to "harmonize" the laws of member states, or to at least establish minimum standards, although such efforts in corporate law have not been notably successful. But because harmonization entails a political process, the "convergence" that it produces could vary from competitive convergence. Indeed, politically driven harmonization might be aimed to induce some nations to converge on an alternative to an emerging model.

Could differing corporate governance systems persist, even if competitive pressures were high? Several chapters suggest that no one system of corporate governance has yet been shown to be a sure competitive winner. Elites, both corporate and political, continue to disagree, say, on

---

[1] *Centros* v. *Erhvervs-OG Selskabsstyrelsen*, C-212/97, [1999], ECR 1–1459.
[2] *In re Überseering*, C-208/00, [2002], ECR – (Nov. 5, 2002).

whether a free-flowing market in corporate takeovers improves well-being or not. As long as competitive superiority is uncertain, structures once built have, some argue, tended to persist. Moreover, differing economic tasks may yield differing corporate governance structures, with the differences persisting even when the tasks change. Several chapters suggest how these mechanisms of persistence have been in play thus far.

* * *

Another theme we see is of "functional" vs. "formal" convergence. Different systems may obtain functionally equivalent results though the legal rules formally diverge. At the most basic level, all successful economic systems have functional similarities. For example, every system holds managers accountable for their performance in some way, to some degree. Some governance features are acquired due to regulation, others due to private adoption. Functional convergence focuses on adaptability: when it's strongly in play, different regimes, despite formal differences, can cobble together existing institutions to fulfill new demands.

A claim on behalf of functional convergence is in tension with another theme explored in the chapters, the theme of "complementarity": that some key corporate institutions are built on one another and take enough of their value from their interaction such that changing one without changing the others is hard. When complementarity is very high, convergence is harder, because too many institutions have to change in a coordinated way. Even functional convergence might drag, when even incremental, small adaptations undermine an effective integration of institutional components. A private player considering the incremental change would reject it, if the net costs due to complementarities are high enough.

* * *

The corporate governance and financial reporting problems revealed by the failures at several major US firm over late 2001–2, including Enron, WorldCom, Tyco, and Adelphia, shed new light on the convergence debate. First, the scandals emerged just at the moment when many thought that the US model was about to claim the prize as the "best in show." Systems that seem dominant, the US in the 1990s, Japan in the 1980s, recurrently prove vulnerable, and this vulnerability seems to emerge before other systems converge.

Second, the "Enron problems" powerfully illustrate the importance of institutional complementarities. In a regime in which managers receive stock-based compensation, a number of institutions seem particularly important, for example: strenuously independent accountants, robust secondary stock markets, adequately funded public securities regulators, and credible third party evaluators, such as securities analysts and credit analysts. We are made to realize that "corporate governance" consists not simply of elements but of systems. This realization – as parties come to understand the scope of the required institutional change – may in some cases speed up convergence, whether formal or functional; in other cases, it may slow it down. Transplanting some of the formal elements without regard for the institutional complements may lead to serious problems later, and these problems may impede, or reverse, convergence.

Third, the US regulatory reaction to the Enron problems may, independently, affect convergence. Congressional enactment ("Sarbanes-Oxley"), SEC (Securities and Exchange Commission) regulations, and new New York Stock Exchange listing requirements create many new mandatory elements of US corporate law, in board structure and responsibility, in financial reporting and disclosure, in obligations of accountants and lawyers. Most of these requirements will, as of now, apply to foreign corporations who choose to list on US exchanges. If foreign issuers continue to believe that this way of accessing US capital markets is important, or wish to "bond" themselves to this particular high-quality governance regime, then ironically the upshot of Enron might be greater convergence on the US model than otherwise. On the other hand, many foreign firms may well regard these intrusions as inconvenient and dysfunctional. Their aversion may well be supported by national regulators, possibly resentful of what might be seen as US overreaching. Thus some foreign issuers may delist from US exchanges and others might change their intentions in that regard. US capital can be tapped from foreign markets and the heightened requirements might enhance the importance of London, say, as a trading center, and the importance of other exchanges' listing requirements. If so, then Enron may lead away from convergence.

Thus as the chapters demonstrate, the questions about convergence of corporate governance have deep economic and political roots. The Enron fallout illuminates both what is at stake and the complexity of the question.

Systemic convergence: Henry Hansmann and Reinier Kraakman's "End of corporate history"

In "The end of history for corporate law," Henry Hansmann and Reinier Kraakman articulate the "strong" convergence position. They boldly argue not only that corporate convergence on a shareholder-oriented model is both desirable and inevitable, but that corporate governance has *already largely converged to that kind of model*. This convergence is ideologically driven: a consensus has emerged that corporate law "should principally strive to increase long-term shareholder value"; and this "normative convergence" is inducing "practices of corporate governance and in corporate law" to converge toward a "shareholder-oriented model," one that is today best exemplified by the large Anglo-American public firm. All around the world, they claim, there is now "a widespread normative consensus that corporate managers should act exclusively in the economic interests of shareholders." Similar rules of corporate law and practice are, due to the power of the ideology of shareholder primacy, emerging everywhere and will in short-order dominate, if they haven't already.

Moreover, the residue of nonshareholder-oriented institutions, already minimal, is shrinking and ought to shrink further: even a society that wants its private economic institutions "to serve the interests of society as a whole" should and will, if they have not done so already, do so through an ancillary set of regulatory institutions in labor, the environment, and the like, rather than vary the "standard" model of shareholder governance. (Rhetorically, they call the pure shareholder model the "standard" model, making variations nonstandard.)

Product market competition and ideology drive their three-stage argument, in which the shareholder model defeats all of its rivals. In summary: first, Hansmann and Kraakman argue that alternatives organized on different principles are not viable competitively (or, as we would formulate it, it is only the historical lack of product market competition that has enabled the "nonstandard" models to have survived thus far). Second, they argue that the competitive pressures faced by firms around the world are cracking and then eliminating the viability of the alternative models. And, third, they argue that the shareholder model creates and sustains a supportive ideological and political consensus in its favor.

Hansmann and Kraakman set up three rivals that competed with the victorious shareholder model: the managerial-oriented model, the labor-oriented model, and the state-oriented model. Each defeated rival has been based on the idea that a viable firm could seriously attend to objectives other than shareholder value. The "manager-oriented" model, associated with the United States in the 1950s and 1960s, was based on the view that "professional corporate managers could serve as disinterested technocratic fiduciaries who would guide business corporations to perform in ways that would serve the general public interest." They claim that this model of social benevolence collapses into self-serving managerialism, in which managers end up serving their own interests with significant costs from resource misallocation. These costs imperil the competitiveness of the model and thus account for its replacement by the shareholder-driven model in the United States.

The "labor-oriented" model, exemplified most explicitly by German codetermination but manifested in other nations, has governance structures amplifying labor's voice. Hansmann and Kraakman argue that such mechanisms are likely to be inefficient and disruptive because of the heterogeneity of interests among employees themselves and between employees and shareholders. Hence, such firms will lose out in competitive product markets. Contractual or labor regulatory solutions are superior means of labor influence, because they avoid a division of authority and interests within the firm.

The "state-oriented" model, associated particularly with France and Japan, entails a large state role in corporate affairs, either through ownership or close bureaucratic engagement with the firm's managers, to guide private enterprise in the political elite's view of the public interest. Hansmann and Kraakman argue that the turn away from socialism and the recent poor performance of economies organized on corporatist lines have discredited this model.

Thus the first stage of the convergence argument is: rival models to shareholder primacy are inefficient and would lose out in competition.

The second stage of the Hansmann and Kraakman argument is their case for competitive convergence to the superior shareholder model. Superior models do not always win out. What makes this one a winner? What is inducing firms to converge to the superior organizational form is the increasing internationalization of product and financial markets, and firms' increasing need to get "access to capital at lower cost (including conspicuously, start-up capital), [to] ... develop ... new product markets, [and the] stronger incentives to reorganize along lines that are manageri-ally coherent." Even if older firms organized on the other models persist, the new shareholder-oriented firms are growing more rapidly, especially in important product markets in which access to capital is important. Eventually they will come to dominate, if they haven't already.

The third stage of the argument, perhaps their boldest, is the claim that convergence on the shareholder model will be sustained by a parallel political convergence. A public shareholder class is, or will, emerge and counteract interest groups that might oppose the shareholder model.

The new shareholder political class will be able to beat back employees, managers, and state bureaucrats who promote, or seek to preserve, the old "managerial-oriented," "labor-oriented," and "state-oriented" models. The new class will also neutralize potential resistance from controlling, big block shareholders of the kind that have dominated in several European countries. This powerful new interest group will arise because of the diffusion of equity ownership – "we are all shareholders now" – and because, as institutions such as pension funds and mutual funds strengthen economically, their political clout will increase as well.

They might point to the recent Europe-wide report on takeovers, which in endorsing a takeover regime of shareholder choice comes very close to embracing shareholder primacy in a way that is much less managerial-, state-, or labor-oriented than the incumbent regimes in Europe.[3] The "Winter Report" fits their model of ideological convergence on a shareholder-model, an ideology that could then drive law, which in turn could drive corporate structures, practices, and governance. Since the votes so far have defeated convergence by harmonization on takeovers, however, there's still some way to go for events to catch up to the convergence theory here.

Hansmann and Kraakman are convergence optimists. Perhaps their most optimistic claim is that societies can converge on the shareholder model for its efficiency properties while maintaining very diverse conceptions of the good society. On their view, Germany, for example, might continue to protect incumbent labor interests, but this regime could and will be implemented, for competitive efficiency's sake, through "labor law" (anti-layoff rules, strong collective bargaining endowments, etc.), rather than through corporate governance and codetermination. That is, incumbent labor interests could continue to have great influence, but they would exercise that influence not through corporate law and corporate governance, but through labor law and labor contracts.

Similarly, a country may desire strong environmental amenities, but this regime could and will be implemented through "environmental law" (emission limits, liability for hazards created, etc.), rather than by, say, putting a Green on the board.

This might be a soft spot in their analysis: if regulatory regimes persist and interest group pressures continue, the impact on the firm could be

---

[3] Report of the High Level Group of Company Law Experts on Issues Related to Takeover Bids, Jan. 10, 2002 (the so-called "Winter Report," after its chair).

roughly the same whether the effects on the firm are "external" through regulation and contracting or "internal" via governance. It's also possible that if every nation has some of these features, then all firms will bear some of these costs on behalf of the local consensus, leaving them all competitive. (Just as all firms must pay their inputs, all firms must pay for some of this local ideology or interest group pressure.) If the costs are about the same, variety might persist (more Green in one country, more labor-oriented in another). And from here, the powerful impulse to corporate governance convergence might weaken: if the firm is bearing this cost, it might make little difference in product market success (the principal convergence driver) whether the cost comes through "external" regulation and contracting or through "internal" corporate governance.

Hansmann and Kraakman are also optimists in that they assume that favorable economic conditions will continue for the substantial period of time necessary to entrench the shareholder model. Firms governed by the shareholder model tend to respond rapidly to economic change because the expected future cash flow changes will immediately be impounded in stock prices. As they put it, this may lead to "more rapid abandonment of inefficient investment." The shareholder-oriented firm will strive to shift the incidence of these adjustment costs away from shareholders. This is, of course, a change from the view that managers should understand that the firm's employment practices are part of the social safety net, a view common in several nations. Implementing this sea change, which invariably shifts some economic risk to individuals, is much easier in circumstances of low unemployment than otherwise.

They do, though, hedge their bets – and temper their optimism – by adding the possibility of inefficient convergence toward a managerialist model. They consider this possibility to be real, but that the managerial tilt would be slight. That does, though, open up the possibility of diversity not convergence, as different nations and different firms have differing degrees and modes of a managerial model, especially if the "slight . . . tilt" overall turned out to be pronounced in one or another nation, here and there. But, after conceding that a persisting slight managerial tilt is a possibility, Hansmann and Kraakman draw back and conclude that "[t]he triumph of the shareholder-oriented model of the corporation over its principal competitors is now assured." The shareholder model is more effective in competition than any of the others, and increasing product market competition throughout the world is thus driving out the old models. Or has already done so.

Systemic persistence: Lucian Bebchuk and Mark Roe's "path dependence"

In "A theory of path dependence in corporate ownership and governance," Lucian Bebchuk and Mark Roe are skeptical that corporate governance and ownership structures have converged thus far, and they argue that structural imperatives help to explain why differences have persisted thus far, despite convergence in many economic areas.

Path dependence explains persistence. Structures, once built long ago, can persist even if they would not be built today. Keeping them may be efficient in a basic economic sense: the costs of tearing down and rebuilding could exceed the value of the new improved model. And keeping them may result from rent-seeking inside the firm and inside the polity. These two forces for persistence have meant that, while some structures converge, some other older structures persist, some change slowly in some dimensions, and a few change not at all.

Two sorts of path dependence, "structure-driven" and "rule-driven," slow down corporate change. Structure-driven path dependence explains why different stock ownership patterns may persist, even if legal rules converged. Rule-driven path dependence explains why, given the persistent differences in ownership structure, legal rules will not converge. Each – structure-driven persistence and rule-driven persistence – has an efficiency explanation and a rent-seeking explanation, yielding us four "nodes" to think about corporate persistence.

Efficiency-based, structure-driven persistence is best understood by thinking about complements. A particular governance structure (close ownership, diffuse ownership with managerial control, or heavy labor influence) induces complementary institutions to emerge (or strengthen), institutions that reduce the costs of the particular system or that enhance its benefits. So, diffuse ownership yields managerial agency costs as a problem, but it is associated with institutions like independent directors and transparent accounting, which mitigate those costs. Labor influence might lead to the emergence of firms whose productivity is enhanced by labor involvement and the disappearance of firms that labor involvement would hurt.

Where these complements were strong, new firms were thereby encouraged to adopt the dominant ownership structure. As more firms joined in, the cost of following the dominant pattern fell and the costs of deviation rose, because of scale economies and network externalities. Thus in a mature system with a well-established ownership structure supported by complementary institutions, firms with a differing ownership structure faced higher costs and were disfavored. Existing structures, tied to their complementary institutions, sustained path dependency, pulling in more firms of the dominant type and fewer of the other types. Junking existing institutions is often expensive. So the calculus of converting to a new institution has at least two components: first, the new institution must be more efficient. Second, it must be so much more efficient that the gains would *also* cover the cost of junking existing institutions (or of creating new ones, or of living without the complementary supports already there in the system). Path dependency of this sort – an efficient persistence of extant forms – has thus far led some important divergent ownership structures to persist, and may continue to do so.

Bebchuk and Roe also argue that structures may persist due to rent-seeking. When two systems are equally efficient, rent-seeking can induce the existing one, from which incumbents profit, to persist. But they go further, arguing that rent-seeking can induce persistence even if it is (moderately) efficient otherwise to change.

Their rent-seeking argument comes in two forms, one transactional and the other for rule-making. If controllers (such as managers in the US, blockholders in Europe, or labor interests in one nation or another) get private advantages from control and if the advantaged controller must initiate (or approve) a transaction to change corporate governance, they must be compensated for the loss of private benefits. As long as the controller's gains from an ownership transformation are not immediately large enough to make it worthwhile for the controller to give up those private benefits, the losing controller would resist change. The controller would not consent to a transaction that created a bigger pie unless it received at least as much pie as its bigger slice of a smaller pie. This places a significant barrier to the transformation from concentrated to diffuse ownership. The catalyzing entrepreneur must find adequate compensation for both the existing controllers and itself, while moving to a form that, to remain stable, must significantly constrain private benefits. Deals might overcome the controller's resistance, but deals are sometimes expensive or not attained. Thus the transformation must generate very large gains indeed.

Bebchuk and Roe caveat their account of structure-driven path dependency by noting that "rent-destroying" rule changes that eliminate the private benefits of control could alter the controller's payoff from a transformation to diffuse ownership. Their idea of "rule-driven" path dependence explains why such rules changes frequently fail. Their main argument on this score is political. The initial rules and corporate structures, whatever they are, have had distributional effects that affect the resources of groups in the political process in a way that favors the status quo. Moreover, the initial rules and structures create interest group support for the status quo. For example, diffuse ownership creates a powerful professional management lobby against hostile takeovers. This lobby as much as any efficiency consideration could account for the persistence of diffuse ownership in the United States.

Moreover, Bebchuk and Roe are less certain whether a consensus has yet emerged on the value of a shareholder-oriented system. Although they seem to share the view (with Hansmann and Kraakman) that such a system is economically appealing, its purported advantages are not so clear that national elites, both corporate and political, thus far feel compelled to adopt it.

Bebchuk and Roe's argument for persistence of important governance differences obviously contrasts sharply with Hansmann and Kraakman's claims. True, in some dimensions the two chapters operate at differing levels of generality. Hansmann and Kraakman are arguing that a shareholder-oriented model is emerging around the world. Bebchuk and Roe could be seen as arguing that even if a shareholder-oriented model is emerging, it is not so powerfully encompassing: some nations have continued to have blockholders (as their means of shareholder-orientation) and others have diffuse ownership (with concomitant institutions that support dispersed shareholding).

Bebchuk and Roe concede that extremely high efficiency gains can overcome the path-dependence, persistence mechanisms that they identify. And it is on this point that one might question whether they are satisfactorily critiquing the convergence claim. Once they have so conceded, they must simultaneously assert, to make their path-dependence mechanisms important, that some important corporate governance variation in the western nations has only moderate efficiency implications, or that elites who must engineer a change perceive them as having only moderate efficient implications, and that these sufficiently moderate efficiency properties (or perceptions) allow their "weak" (or at least "medium-strength") forces of path dependence to induce, and have induced, and may continue to induce, preexisting structures to persist.

Players can often block rule changes that would facilitate convergence. Recently, the European Parliament addressed a decade-long project for a Europe-wide takeover law, one that would make takeovers easier. Although considered a "done deal" by many, the Parliament – apparently under pressure and negative votes from German incumbent managerial and labor groups – rejected the initiative. This is one of the sticky, path-dependent processes that Bebchuk and Roe have in mind: not that incumbents can and will successfully resist all transactional and legal transformation, but that they can resist many, so that convergence has been much slower than efficiency considerations alone would have dictated. Path dependence has thus far stymied full convergence, and may continue to play an important role in corporate history.

Systemic complementarities: Schmidt and Spindler's "complementarity"

Reinhard H. Schmidt and Gerald Spindler explain in "Path dependence and complementarity in corporate governance" why divergence in corporate governance systems should rationally persist, by developing and deepening the concept of complementarity. Their chapter analyzes complementary mechanisms that can in theory induce persistence, even suboptimal persistence.

Their analysis sharpens the path dependence story with "switching costs" and "local maximization" (at the expense of overall maximization). If switching costs are high and local maximization is the dominating mode of maximization, then starting points may radically affect ending points.

Where switching costs are positive, rational economic decisionmaking can make even an otherwise suboptimal result persist. To make their point concrete, imagine land development prior to the invention of the elevator, in which half a particular parcel is devoted to commercial use, the other half to residential use. Elevators then make high-rise development optimal. It is easy to imagine that expected additional profits will exceed the switching costs for commercial developers (meaning that buildings will be torn down and replaced), but not for residential developers. Commercial leases turn over easily, so the commercial developer does not have to pay many tenants to leave; commercial tenants may have a taste for high offices, which permits premium rents. Residential leases turn over slowly (perhaps because of explicit or implicit legal protection), and so exit fees will be substantial; tenants may be unwilling to pay much of a height premium. So if developers were starting with an empty parcel, they would go for the high-rise development that is efficient with the new elevator-based technology. Zoning boards, perhaps controlled by the incumbent residents, might be reluctant even to approve height changes.

Switching costs produce path dependency, and low-rise development for the residences rationally persists.

Their second analytic source of path dependency is more complex. They focus not on a central decisionmaker calculating overall welfare for his or her society, but on discrete social actors each trying to maximize their own welfare. (Or one could imagine a centralized decisionmaker with a short horizon – of say the next general election.)

An exogenous shock threatens all firms in the economy. Each firm reacts by pursuing a strategy that "offers the best *immediate* prospect." The pressure to act immediately means that decisions will be taken with imperfect foresight, or local myopia, and the resulting local optimum will be the global optimum only by accident. In other words, path dependency can also result from imperfectly rational processes that are quite common in situations of institutional stress. For example, a bank-based financing system might be less efficient than, say, a stockholder-based system. Suppose then a global economic shock hits everyone. The stockholder-based firms strengthen their stockholder institutions, with, say, better boards of directors. Firms in the bank-based system, rather than changing overall, deepen their bank-based structure: banks further professionalize their involvement with the firm, making the bank-dominated firms stronger. One might be better than the other, but crisis could *strengthen*, not weaken, each, the better one and the weaker one. The tree, once bent. . . .

(This second mechanism – myopic reaction to an immediate crisis – could be mistakenly seen as a pure "switching cost." Posit that bank-based corporate governance has become less efficient than shareholder-based diffuse ownership. A pure switching cost explanation for bank-based persistence would be that the costs of switching are too high. Bank-based governance is $1000 less efficient, but it costs $2000 to switch. The second mechanism, though, analyzes a situation in which long-run switching is efficient. Bank-based systems are $1000 less efficient, and since it costs $800 to switch, the system is getting ready to switch. But before it starts switching, there's a shock to the system, threatening its survival. The actors then decide what to do, not based on long-term efficiency but on immediate survival. They must do what's necessary to survive until tomorrow. They will "die" if they don't invest $500 in fixing up their bank-based system *tonight*. To survive until tomorrow they *strengthen* the old system rather than change it. And then tomorrow, *after* the old system has been strengthened, the long-run balance of switching costs versus efficiency costs has changed, because the old system has been made more viable. After the short-run survival strategy is implemented, then, tomorrow, the bank-based system has efficiency costs of only $500 after the overnight investment in bank survival, and with switching costs still at $800, it's no longer efficient to switch.)

Schmidt and Spindler enrich the understanding of "complementarity." "Elements of a system are complementary (to each other) if they fit together," i.e., mutually increase their "benefit" in terms of whatever the objective function or the standard for evaluating the system may be, and/or mutually reduce their disadvantages or "costs." A system is "consistent" if all the elements are complements (or at least not anti-complements). A system that is inferior from a global perspective may nonetheless be a local optimum, in the sense that piecemeal change of particular elements may reduce complementarity. When a piece changes, the system's immediate efficiency may decrease, because the pieces no longer fit nicely, i.e., no longer are complements. Such an "inconsistent" system, with wrecked complements, could be worse than the one it replaced. And, of course, thoroughgoing change of multiple institutions simultaneously is very difficult. (Schmidt and Spindler's arguments are directed toward corporate governance institutions. But the reader could take more than that from their analysis, as it's applicable to understanding change and persistence in any structure in which complements are important.)

Schmidt and Spindler describe two complementary systems: the "outsider" Anglo-American corporate governance system, which relies on the corporate control market to monitor manager behavior (dispersed shareholder and takeovers are complements), and the "insider" German system, which relies on internal mechanisms reflected in the supervisory board. The insider system contemplates monitoring through the negotiation among stakeholder groups represented on the supervisory board and contemplates a rich set of implicit contracts among the stakeholders. The outsider system contemplates a monitoring through control markets that hold managers to account to maximize "shareholder value," assuming that contracting and markets protect the other interests. So, if we focused on the stakeholders, we would say that the German system protects stakeholders through the board forum, while the American system protects them through contracting.

Schmidt and Spindler's point here is that introducing elements of the outsider system may reduce the value of the insider system. "A 'middle-of-the-road' model of corporate governance is not likely to be viable and can, therefore, not be recommended from an economic perspective."

So, if we unpack this a bit, the German complementary model cannot readily move to the American model in steps: if the German model opened itself up to hostile takeovers and a shareholder-oriented board, then the German system's stakeholders would be "naked" without either the labor-influenced board forum (the German complement thus far) or the contractual and labor market protection (the American protection).[4]

Opening up German firms to hostile takeover threats (and, by implication, the included elements that make managers more directly accountable to public shareholders, such as greater disclosure) would impair the implicit contracts with stakeholders. If root and branch overall change is not possible, differences in corporate governance systems would persist, and that persistence would be rational.

Schmidt and Spindler also contemplate a "dark side" to convergence: inefficient convergence. The German-style insider model is more vulnerable to destabilization than the American model, "[b]ecause of its greater reliance on mutually consistent and stable expectations, trust and implicit contracts." Thus a period of "global competition and regulatory changes of all kinds and other corporate governance-related innovations from various sources," will disrupt the settled expectations that make insider systems function so well. Reformers might begin to adopt piecemeal changes that reduce their value. This could lead to a "crisis" in which the parties realize that any *consistent* system dominates a hodgepodge, and settle on the inferior but less fragile Anglo-American model. Thus, convergence optimists posit a single road to corporate governance efficiency, with competitive forces pushing firms everywhere toward that model. But Schmidt and Spindler say that optimism could be unwarranted: corporate governance systems might converge on a regime that *reduces* total social welfare.

Here we want to fight the hypothetical. Schmidt and Spindler appear to contemplate a world economy that creates periodic disruptive moments followed by relatively extended periods of stability; the momentary disruptions lead to the local optimum of outsider systems rather than the global (in the evolutionary sense) optimum of insider systems. But if the consequence of global economic integration is competitive pressure whose effects are better mediated through markets than through firms, even if only during brief but deep crises, that suggests convergence

---

[4] That is, American labor could be seen as having a market to rely upon – one can quit, cross the street and get another job. The German labor market is, we assume here, less fluid, but labor gets a voice inside the firm's supervisory board.

would be beneficial. If economic globalization both adds to social welfare (superior products at better prices) and in fact disrupts insider systems, then insider systems would no longer be superior. Perhaps if the systems do eventually converge, it would be because overall a system without deep complements and strong implicit contracts can absorb the disruptions and regain its balance more easily than one that doesn't have such deep implicit contracts.

Thus, overall Schmidt and Spindler give pause to the convergence optimism story, primarily by analyzing corporate complementarity in a sustained way. As long as complements are deep and strong, and as long as one could not change one institution without changing another, change can be harder than a simple smooth evolution to a standardized efficiency.

Systemic movement: Gilson's formal persistence and "functional convergence"

In "Globalizing corporate governance: convergence of form or function," Ronald Gilson argues for the possible emergence of a worldwide corporate governance system that is relatively uniform in functional terms, despite persisting formal differences. Selection pressures should lead to adaptive evolution of formally different systems towards functional equivalence. He explores various means by which functional convergence can occur, including private contracting and piggy-backing on the law of other jurisdictions. Functional differences can persist because of the difficulty in creating institutional complements.

Gilson starts with the recent empirical demonstration that the tenure of senior management in the US, Japan, and Germany, "is equally sensitive to poor performance, whether measured by stock market returns or accounting earnings," despite the important formal distinctions between systems of bank and other blockholder-centered finance and stock markets. This similarity in the rate of managerial turnover despite ownership differences is functional convergence of one feature of corporate governance. Selection pressure forces equivalent outcomes in one dimension – turnover – even where interest group pressure and complementarities mean that convergence in another dimension (i.e., ownership concentration) would be impossible and perhaps inefficient. Thus, there is some convergence, and some persistence, simultaneously.

Not every function can functionally converge, Gilson says. Venture capital is one such area, because bank-centered systems cannot, he argues, replicate the institutions that facilitate venture capital. Venture capital firms can, via a potential sale of stock to the public, credibly commit to an entrepreneur that the venture capitalist will return control to him or her if the business succeeds: the venture capitalist sells its stock in the successful firm out to a dispersed market and the entrepreneur, retaining a block of stock, gets control back. But a bank-centered system cannot do this because the bank's only exit strategy is to sell the entrepreneur's company to another company (because the stock market institutions are not strong enough and deep enough). As such, the entrepreneur could not readily get control back. And, if less likely to get control back, the entrepreneur is less willing to invite in the bank in the first place. In this dynamic, the banks cannot functionally substitute for a stock market in promoting venture capital, and complementarity frictions mean that the entire system is unlikely to change just to promote venture capital. Banks might functionally substitute for, say, takeovers or independent boards in inducing needed managerial turnover, but cannot substitute for stock markets in inducing venture capital investments.

Gilson goes on with a rich array of instances where functional convergence can and cannot go forward, how cross-listing facilitates functional convergence but some European nations' "real seat" doctrine – potentially undermined by recent European judicial developments – stymies it.

Government actors: Gordon's nation-state "wedge"

In "The international relations wedge in the corporate convergence debate" Jeffrey Gordon argues that the conventional efficiency and political arguments over convergence do not take account of the international relations interests of states. He contends that pursuit of (or resistance to) "transnational economic and political integration" may significantly affect the form and rate of corporate convergence. In particular, shareholder capitalism is particularly well suited for the transnational project because it most strongly checks the tendency toward nationalist economic decisionmaking. This is because shareholder capitalism reduces the state's role in economic decisionmaking, focuses decisions in a firm-specific way and looks to a verifiable transnational measure of success (stock prices), and, through the contestability of control, penalizes economic nationalism.

The contestability of control is particularly important. Transnational integration requires cross-border mergers not simply to achieve scale economies but to build businesses that are the conduits for the free flow of capital, goods, services, people, and a "transnational attitude."

Yet states may be legitimately concerned that "investment and divestment decisions may be influenced by the economic nationalism of the state in which the acquirer is organized." What can hold this economic nationalism in check is the vulnerability of the acquirer to takeover. If the acquirer exhibits significant home-country bias that reduces shareholder value, then, under a well-developed system of shareholder capitalism, this opens up an opportunity for a control entrepreneur. Thus states that highly value the transnational project may pursue corporate convergence on the shareholder capitalism model, including promotion of diffuse share ownership, despite other cross-cutting efficiency or political concerns.

Gordon illustrates the importance of the international relations "wedge" with two thickly told examples drawn from Germany. The first is the 1996 privatization of Deutsche Telekom, the German telephone company. This was triggered by the decision of the European Union to liberalize the European telecommunications market by 1998. Once the privatization decision was taken, the government heavily promoted shareholder capitalism to make the huge public offering a success. This in turn led to legal reforms to improve the governance of public firms and helped foster other institutions, such as the Neuer Markt, a venue for the hitherto rare German initial public offering. In short, the push to shareholder capitalism did not arise merely from a view of its comparative efficiency, but was stimulated by an element of the project of European union.

A second example, which shows how the transnational concern can retard corporate convergence, is Germany's role in the defeat in 2001 of the proposed 13th Company Directive on takeovers and the subsequent adoption of a German Takeover Code with substantial target protection. Throughout the 1990s Germany had actively supported a "board neutrality" provision in the 13th Directive but became increasingly concerned that its openness to cross-border mergers (reflected by Vodafone's successful hostile bid for Mannesmann in 1999) was not matched by its European Union (EU) partners. For example, important EU states retained "golden shares" in newly privatized enterprises that permitted government veto of hostile bids while these very firms became active acquirers. Other states' corporate law also retained protective provisions that would impede hostile bids. In addition to domestic managerialist and union pressures, the German response was also influenced by the transnational project. First, the absence of a "level playing field" in the EU takeover market gave rise to concerns of economic nationalism, a serious problem. But second, Germany's actions can also be understood as an act of "aggressive reciprocity" in a trade negotiation whose ultimate objective is to *lower* takeover barriers. Imposing costs is a way of bringing parties back to the table with the hope of obtaining a cooperative response, but the strategy can fail, leading to more takeover protection, more economic nationalism, and less convergence.

Gordon buttresses his case with reference to the subsequent "Report of High Level Experts," produced in an effort to resuscitate the 13th Directive. European integrationists came to realize that some of the ratification difficulties of the 13th Directive arose from the noncontestability of control in many ostensibly public European firms. They proposed a remarkable set of reforms that would push European capitalism in the direction of diffuse share-ownership. Finally, Gordon notes, some states may actively avoid convergence on the shareholder capitalism model precisely because they want to avoid transnational integration, despite the efficiency loss.

Gordon's argument can be framed in the more explicit public choice approach of Bebchuk and Roe. Gordon argues for a distinctive set of state interests, or at least interests of a particular political elite, that affect corporate governance. Consider the possibility that political elites, even political elites who think an open shareholder-primacy model works best, fear it would diminish the model they favor politically. That is, Bebchuk and Roe argue that sometimes a better model would be too costly to reach if local institutions support an alternative. And sometimes even public-regarding politicians are constrained by local interest groups that do better in the existing system than in a more efficient alternative. But, Gordon shows, *even* if the change was justified on economic grounds, and *even* if the local interest groups lacked the muscle to block local change, then political elites who otherwise would have wanted to get to the new convergent system, might still decline to do so if change would diminish their local authority.

Moreover, the political elites might even conclude that they (or their nation) would be even better off if everyone (or at least their principal trading partners) also moved in that direction. But they might condition their own willingness to move on other nations simultaneously moving. (For example, "we'll ease restrictions on cross-border hostile takeovers, if you do.") But to start this kind of negotiation risks tit-for-tat results, with nations going in different directions, at different speeds. The converse can also play out: state actors making international deals could use corporate governance symmetry and convergence as a bargaining chip for something else. (For example, "We'll drop takeover barriers, in return for your dropping trade barriers to this product.") The process Gordon describes could encompass the interest groups, but override them: the domestic industry wants easy exports; the corporate players want continuance. Political actors could decide that there are more votes (or public-regarding actors could conclude that there is more national well-being) in favoring the first and trading away the interests of the second (or vice versa).

Government actors: Milhaupt's weak and strong "property rights"

In "Property rights in firms" Curtis Milhaupt proposes that differences in "national property rights institutions account for the diversity in corporate governance systems." By property rights, he means "the rules (legal, political, or social) by which control over assets is allocated and enforced." Because of the large role of government in the "allocation and enforcement of control rights," these property rights will evolve principally through political bargaining. Because of the stickiness of political institutions, Milhaupt comes to similar conclusions about the likely persistence of local governance institutions as Bebchuk and Roe.

Milhaupt begins with the observation that different national polities differ in the degree to which they retain authority over the firm. In some nations the political players have very limited control rights over private property; in other polities politicians and bureaucrats have strong control rights over firms. When the degree of rights retention differs, the nature of corporate governance differs. Similarly, property rights regimes differ in the extent to which *legal* enforcement of property rights is available, as opposed, for example, to social enforcement mechanisms, or minimal enforcement. These elements, Milhaupt argues, explain a great deal of the corporate governance diversity around the world.

For example, in less secure property rights environments there will be smaller firms, more family ownership, less dispersed ownership. Where governments retain control rights over firms, private economic agents will make investments in "political capital" to obtain desired objectives. Such increasingly large political capital investments over time will make the firm more sclerotic, because shifting direction would lead to the loss of these large investments. Thus even where economic forces are powerful, "we should expect convergence to occur only where institutional inertia grounded in politics can be overcome." Thus convergence will be "weak, limited and episodic."

Milhaupt develops this story with three country examples, the US, Japan, and South Korea. He argues that property rights differences account for the pattern. For example, economic freedom (as measured by standard indices) is much higher in the US, next in Japan, and then Korea. There is a similar ranking on the corruption scale, with a significant gap between the US and Japan on the one hand, Korea on the other. This means that the US has the most secure property rights regime and Korea the least secure. Government control or influence over firms is much higher in Japan and Korea than in the US. He discusses the different levels of political contracting in the three systems. The differential pattern of property rights accounts for the corporate governance differences across the three countries. The protection of property rights makes possible the external governance and the market orientation of US firms. On the other hand, the South Korean government regulates firms and allocates credit, leading to firms that are family-oriented and politically governed.

As he assesses the self-reinforcing character of the property rights systems, his convergence-skepticism becomes clear. Differences in political power will persist across nations and across groups. "Managers, labor, and institutional investors are not similarly organized and do not exert identical influence on the political process across countries," Milhaupt notes. And as long as these differences meet differing levels of governmental influence, corporate governance systems will continue to diverge.

Government actors: Roe's "social democracy"

In "Modern politics and ownership separation" Mark Roe argues that political differences can induce, and have induced, ownership differences. For basic elements of corporate governance to converge, the marked differences in political orientation among the world's richest nations must narrow.

Roe so argues by linking the firm's microstructure to politics. That is, tying senior managers tightly to shareholders has been central to American corporate governance. The large public firm works with concomitant supporting norms and institutions of shareholder-wealth maximization. But in other economically advanced nations such shareholder wealth maximization norms have been weaker, or even denigrated, and there have been fewer, or weaker, institutions that would support shareholder wealth maximization.

Social democracies press managers to stabilize employment, to forgo some profit-maximizing risks with the firm, and to use up capital in place rather than to downsize when markets no longer are aligned with the firm's production capabilities. How managers use their discretion is crucial to stockholders, and social democratic pressures induce managers to act in ways that do not strictly and directly maximize shareholder wealth. Labor markets outside of the United States, and especially in continental Europe and Japan, have historically tended to be protected, and the means that aligned managers with diffuse stockholders in the United States – incentive compensation, transparent accounting, hostile takeovers, and strong shareholder-wealth maximization norms – have there been weaker and sometimes denigrated.

These labor market regularities and shareholder differences affected the ownership structure of business organizations. In reaction to the institutions that do not strongly support shareholders and to differing roles for labor, large-block shareholding has been more common there than it has been in the United States, serving to control managers more in shareholder interests. Roe lines up the world's richest nations on a left–right continuum and then lines them up on a closely owned to diffusely owned continuum, to show the two correlating. He speculates on the origins of these social and political differences: a craving for stability, a differing sense of fairness, a differing historical settlement of social and political conflict. The effects of these differences on total social welfare are ambiguous; social democracies may enhance total social welfare, but, if so, with fewer public firms than less socially responsive nations.

Only as these political differences begin to narrow, as they have been in recent years, does it become plausible to debate the mechanisms of convergence and whether some important underlying corporate institutions will tend to persist anyway. Prior to political change, he argues, convergence at the level of widespread ownership diffusion was unlikely.

Specific institutions: Charny's diversity of norms

In "The politics of corporate convergence," David Charny begins with the premise that although there could well be "a single set of the most efficient rules, or 'best practices' for corporate legal regulation, at least when viewed from the perspective of minimizing the cost of capital invested in the enterprise," he nevertheless sees no "short run tendency towards convergence." Politics and norms induce divergences to persist. Complementary social institutions – complementary to the economic and legal foundations needed for convergence – make change sticky. Legal rules are embedded within and take their meaning from nonlegal interactions and nonlegal modes of cooperation. Since these nonlegal modes differ, convergence will be hard. Even if legal rules (and their enforcement) converged, there'd be a steady proliferation of local exceptions to any "standard" set of legal rules.

Charny's political conception of nonconvergence distinguishes the grand political compromises of a society – for example, a corporatist style of governance to facilitate cooperation and coordination of affected groups – from the political interests of clear insiders, such as entrepreneurs and capital suppliers. Insiders will pursue their interests in the legislature and other rule-making forums in ways that may maximize their own gain, not necessarily the social surplus.

He focuses on the particular importance of nonlegal sanctions – social and commercial norms that "supplement or trump the commands of formal legal rules or explicit contracts." Societies will vary in the content of these nonlegal sanctions and thus the cash value of identical legal rules will vary as well. Thus, even if selection pressures are not blocked by politics, legal rules will adapt to these important local institutions of nonlegal enforcement in a way that predicts for divergence in the set of legal rules. Of course this nonconvergence could also be perverse: local norms might not promote efficiency and their revision (including revision away from efficiency) may depend, like positive law, on the local political economy.

If convergence were to occur, it would come from transformative actions of well-organized supranational or global interest groups, such as the EU, the IMF or World Bank, organizations that presumably could force adaptation to a single set of practices, and that could presumably alter local norms.

Specific institutions: Sabel's universalism on one level, diversity on another

In "Ungoverned production: an American view of the novel universalism of Japanese production methods and their awkward fit with current forms of corporate governance," Charles Sabel attacks the problem of convergence and persistence this way: one could contrast stakeholder and shareholder models, try to determine which one produces better, and posit that systems will converge. But, Sabel argues, governance can, and does, operate on an entirely different level, the governance of production, on the shop-floor and throughout the enterprise. For competitive success in today's world, collaborative innovation is essential, and each differing corporate governance system provides the means to achieve it. So stakeholder-oriented and shareholder-oriented systems can (and will) persist, but each will (and must, and can) find ways to implement collaborative innovation.

Sabel illustrates with the evolution of teams. Japanese teamwork and collaboration became famous and envied, with American critics arguing that the team benefits could not be had (easily? at all?) without changes in the firm's ownership or its orientation toward shareholders or its interaction with labor markets.

Thus Japanese-style lean production was once the envy of American managerial critics, and wholesale reconstruction of American boards and owners was recommended. That board reconstruction didn't happen: shareholding remained diffuse, boards stayed oriented toward shareholders. But, Sabel tells us, American firms nevertheless succeeded in implementing the collaborative innovation of our time, lean production. Corporate governance differences "at the top" persisted, while governance on the shop-floor converged.

Specific institutions: Hertig's enforcement differences

In "Convergence of substantive law and convergence of enforcement: a comparison," Gérard Hertig warns that one shouldn't limit attention to substantive law. Convergence might occur at that level – say, simply statements of duties to shareholders, similar mechanisms to bring suit, and so on. But differences could persist at a level more mundane than that of the interests of government players (Gordon), property rights in firms (Milhaupt), or politics (Roe). Differing systems have differing degrees and types of enforcement. And as long as the quality of enforcement continues to differ, corporate institutions that depend on enforcement will continue to differ. Moreover, the quality and type of enforcement might continue to differ not across-the-board but among corporate law institutions. So fiduciary duties might be better enforced in one jurisdiction, while insider trading rules bite more effectively in another. These differences will affect corporate governance in diverse ways.

Specific institutions: Ramseyer's *keiretsu* foundations

In "Cross-shareholding in the Japanese *keiretsu*," Mark Ramseyer examines the Japanese *keiretsu*, usually seen as one of the world's unique corporate governance forms. But, he argues, while the form differs, perhaps radically, from that prevailing in many other nations, the substantive differences have been greatly exaggerated. First off, Ramseyer argues that the *keiretsu* qualities have been overemphasized in the American literature: cross-holdings aren't all that high; those that exist are close reciprocal pairings of a single supplier with a single customer (not groups); and financial institutions (not industrial firms) are the principal owners.

Thus the explanation for *keiretsu*, he argues, should lie principally in the financial institutions' investments. True, there are some reciprocal supplier–customer investments, investments that one tends not to see in the United States, but that difference is because the same problem (governing ongoing relational contracts) is dealt with in the United States via vertical integration. Same problem, similar (but different) solution. Not the stuff of dramatic contrast.

So then the remaining significant distinguishing characteristic is the Japanese financial firms' heavy stock investments. American banks and other financial institutions have been barred from similar investments, so it's no mystery why we don't see them as stockholding players. But then Ramseyer departs from conventional wisdom about the stock investments (as either supporting the banks' loans, as protecting the investing firm's managers, or as providing a weak and contingent voice in the industrial firm's corporate governance) with a new theory: some, maybe most of the stock investments are not governance-oriented, but simple, quasi-passive investments, made when the bank has good and positive information about the subject company.

When the bank makes that loan it understands the company to which it's lending. It lends to the good companies, not to the bad ones. And once it knows the company is a good one, it makes (private) sense for it to buy that company's stock as well. The investments then are intended to be not governance devices, but something akin to inside trades (albeit purchases that aren't flipped quickly, but held for the long term). Since the banks' level of ownership changes over time, Ramseyer has a testable proposition, which he tests. Banks tend to increase their holdings during years when the stock price is rising. Special information seems to be the explanation, not corporate governance.

Summing up

The chapters trace out forces inducing convergence and forces inducing persistence in corporate governance systems. A fundamental force is efficiency. If there is one efficient corporate governance mechanism, competitive pressures push firms around the world toward that structure. But persistence advocates see, on this level, the potential for several roads to efficiency, allowing diverse corporate governance structures to persist. Moreover, complementarities between corporate governance and a society's other institutions might (a) determine different efficient systems, and (b) make even otherwise inefficient systems (if not too inefficient) persist. The major complementarities are the fits between corporate governance and financial services, product markets, political institutions, and labor institutions.

One can with these complementarities in mind imagine a general analytic framework: if complementarities are weakening, so that corporate governance evolves unconstrained, then we will find out whether one system is sufficiently more efficient than the others that it will dominate. But if complementarities strengthen (or remain strong), then the "dominating" institution (financial services, product markets, politics, or labor institutions and markets) can affect, conceivably determine, the best fitting corporate governance system, and that system will differ depending on which local complement dominates. Many of the chapters fall into one side or the other of this analysis.

But two other mechanisms could be in play that remain underexamined: what if there are several, equally efficient corporate governance mechanisms, or, better, several varieties of corporate governance, each attuned to differing tasks? But now assume a different role for complementarities: complementarities strengthen (or remain strong), but the corporate governance complements (financial services, political institutions, or labor markets) all converge because of their own economic logic. If so (strong complementarity and powerfully converging complements), then the converging complements would tend to force a corporate governance convergence as well. But in this scenario it's not due to the logic of a single efficient corporate governance system – there could be many – but to the logic of a single efficient set of complements.

For example, insider governance systems gain strength from the complementarity of bank monitoring. But assume that the worldwide competition among financial institutions forces banks to move away from relationship banking towards "transactional banking." In other words, the competitive forces in the market for financial services leads that industry towards convergence on a model which is inconsistent with the provision of high-level corporate monitoring. The bank now becomes unwilling to provide the relationship that was the source of the complementarity and corporate governance must adjust accordingly.

That is, much of the general debate about corporate governance starts with the possibility of change on the corporate side and then asks whether other institutions will adapt, a demand-side approach to complementari-ties. But it is also possible that the surrounding institutions may be the first to change, shifting the supply of complements, thereby forcing corporate governance change as a result, a supply-side approach.

The government's role in fostering (or thwarting) convergence may be in creating (or hampering) institutions that create new sorts of comple-mentarities necessary for an efficient convergence path. So one way to understand the development of deeper, more liquid, better-regulated stock markets is that this sort of activity creates new institutional comple-ments. If firms want to migrate from established insider patterns (or are forced to because the corresponding institutions withdraw from that role) the establishment of alternative institutions offers a new set of comple-mentarities.

One could imagine the converse as well: competition intensifies on different organizational levels than that which attracts the attention of corporate governance inquiry. We could imagine circumstances in which each system – consider here, say, the contrast between the dominant owner and the diffuse structure – is capable of adapting itself readily to accom-modate these heightened fields of competition. Competition is intense in these other dimensions, but each differing corporate governance system adapts and prospers, partly because it – conventional corporate gover-nance – would have become relatively less important as compared with the other institutions of competition and production.

This offers a glimmer toward a "unified field theory" of convergence or persistence. All governance systems depend upon the complemen-tarities of the institutional surround. Existing complementarities can be destroyed (or strengthened or altered) by changes anywhere in the network of relationships. These changes can come in response to market forces or government action. The changes can come on the "demand side," as corporations in response to competitive pressure seek new gover-nance arrangements, or on the "supply side," as complementary institu-tions evolve. Moreover, governments and private parties can intervene to create new institutions with a new menu of complementarities or, by constraining institutions, to shape the evolutionary path.

PART I

Systemic issues

1

The end of history for corporate law[*]

HENRY HANSMANN & REINIER KRAAKMAN

I. Introduction

Recent scholarship has emphasized institutional differences in governance, share ownership, capital markets, and business culture among European, American, and Japanese companies.[1] Despite this apparent divergence, however, the basic law of corporate governance – indeed, most of corporate law – has achieved a high degree of uniformity across these jurisdictions, and continuing convergence toward a single standard model is likely. The core legal features of the corporate form were already well established in advanced jurisdictions one hundred years ago, at the turn of the twentieth century. Although there remained considerable room for variation in governance practices and in the fine structure of corporate law throughout the twentieth century, the pressures for further convergence are now rapidly growing. Chief among these pressures is the recent dominance of a shareholder-centered ideology of corporate law among the business, government, and legal elites in key commercial jurisdictions. There is no longer any serious competitor to the view that corporate law should principally strive to increase long-term shareholder value. This emergent consensus has already profoundly affected corporate governance practices throughout the world. It is only a

[*] Earlier drafts of this chapter were presented at conferences entitled "Are Corporate Governance Systems Converging?" held at Columbia Law School, December 5, 1997, and "Convergence and Diversity in Corporate Governance Regimes and Capital Markets," sponsored by Tilburg University in Eindhoven, The Netherlands, November 4–5, 1999. We both wish to thank the New York University School of Law and its Dean, John Sexton, for generous support in this project while both authors were visiting professors.
[1] See, e.g., Mark Roe, "Some Differences in Company Structure in Germany, Japan, and the United States," 102 *Yale L. J.* 1927 (1993); Ronald J. Gilson & Mark J. Roe, "Understanding the Japanese *Keiretsu*: Overlaps between Company Governance and Industrial Organization," 102 *Yale L. J.* 871 (1993); Bernard S. Black & John C. Coffee, "Hail Britannia? Institutional Investor Behavior under Limited Regulation," 92 *Mich. L. Rev.* 1997 (1994).

matter of time before its influence is felt in the reform of corporate law as well.

II.   Convergence past: the rise of the corporate form

We must begin with the recognition that the law of business corporations had already achieved a remarkable degree of worldwide convergence at the end of the nineteenth century. By that time, large-scale business enterprise in every major commercial jurisdiction had come to be organized in the corporate form, and the core functional features of that form were essentially identical across these jurisdictions. Those features, which continue to characterize the corporate form today, are: (1) full legal personality, including well-defined authority to bind the firm to contracts and to bond those contracts with assets that are the property of the firm as distinct from the firm's owners;[2] (2) limited liability for owners and managers; (3) shared ownership by investors of capital; (4) delegated management under a board structure; and (5) transferable shares.

These core characteristics, both individually and in combination, offer important efficiencies in organizing the large firms with multiple owners that have come to dominate developed market economies. We explore those efficiencies in detail elsewhere.[3] What is important to note here is that, while those characteristics and their associated efficiencies are now commonly taken for granted, prior to the beginning of the nineteenth century there existed only a handful of specially chartered companies that combined all five of these characteristics. The joint stock company with tradeable shares was not made generally available for business activities in England until 1844, and limited liability was not added to the form until 1855.[4] While some American states developed the form for general use a few years earlier, all general business corporation statutes appear to date from well after 1800. By around 1900, however, every major commercial jurisdiction appears to have provided for at least one standard-form legal entity with the five characteristics listed above as the default rules, and this has remained the case ever since.

---

[2] See Henry Hansmann & Reinier Kraakman, *The Essential Role of Organizational Law*, 100 Yale L. J. 387 (2000).

[3] Henry Hansmann & Reinier Kraakman, "What is Corporate Law?," in R. Kraakman et al., *The Anatomy of Corporate Law: A Comparative and Functional Approach* (forthcoming, 2004); Henry Hansmann, *The Ownership of Enterprise* (1996).

[4] Phillip Blumberg, *The Law of Corporate Groups: Substantive Law*, pp. 9–20 (1988).

Thus there was already strong and rapid convergence a century ago regarding the basic elements of the law of business corporations. It is, in general, only in the more detailed structure of corporate law that jurisdictions have varied significantly since then.

The five basic characteristics of the corporate form provide, by their nature, for a firm that is strongly responsive to shareholder interests. They do not, however, necessarily dictate how the interests of other participants in the firm – such as employees, creditors, other suppliers, customers, or society at large – will be accommodated. Nor do they dictate the way in which conflicts of interest among shareholders themselves – and particularly between controlling and noncontrolling shareholders – will be resolved. Throughout most of the twentieth century there has been debate over these issues, and experimentation with alternative approaches to them.

Recent years, however, have brought strong evidence of a growing consensus on these issues among the academic, business, and governmental elites in leading jurisdictions. The principal elements of this consensus are that ultimate control over the corporation should be in the hands of the shareholder class; that the managers of the corporation should be charged with the obligation to manage the corporation in the interests of its shareholders; that other corporate constituencies, such as creditors, employees, suppliers, and customers should have their interests protected by contractual and regulatory means rather than through participation in corporate governance; that noncontrolling shareholders should receive strong protection from exploitation at the hands of controlling shareholders; and that the principal measure of the interests of the publicly traded corporation's shareholders is the market value of their shares in the firm. For simplicity, we shall refer to the view of the corporation that comprises these elements as the "standard shareholder-oriented model" of the corporate form (or, for brevity, simply "the standard model"). To the extent that corporate law bears on the implementation of this standard model – as to an important degree it does – this consensus on the appropriate conduct of corporate affairs is also a consensus as to the appropriate content of corporate law, and is likely to have profound effects on the structure of that law.

Thus, just as there was rapid crystallization of the core features of the corporate form in the late nineteenth century, at the beginning of the twenty-first century we are witnessing rapid convergence on the standard shareholder-oriented model as a normative view of corporate structure and governance, and we should expect this normative convergence to produce substantial convergence as well in the practices of corporate governance and in corporate law.

There are three principal factors driving consensus on the standard model: the failure of alternative models; the competitive pressures of global commerce; and the shift of interest group influence in favor of an emerging shareholder class. We consider these developments here in sequence.

III.   The failure of alternative models

Debate and experimentation concerning the basic structure of corporate law during the twentieth century centered on the ways in which that law should accommodate the interests of nonshareholder constituencies. In this regard, three principal alternatives to a shareholder-oriented model were the traditional foci of attention. We term these the manager-oriented, the labor-oriented, and the state-oriented models of corporate law. Although each of these three alternative models has – at various points and in various jurisdictions – achieved some success both in practice and in received opinion, all three have ultimately lost much of their normative appeal.

Recent academic literature has focused on the "stakeholder" model of the corporation as the principal alternative to the shareholder-oriented model. The stakeholder model, however, is essentially just a combination of elements found in the older manager-oriented and labor-oriented models. Consequently, the same forces that have been discrediting the latter models are also undermining the stakeholder model as a viable alternative to the shareholder-oriented model.

A.   The manager-oriented model

In the US there existed an important strain of normative thought from the 1930s through the 1960s that extolled the virtues of granting substantial discretion to the managers of large business corporations. Merrick Dodd and John Kenneth Galbraith, for example, were conspicuously identified with this position, and Adolph Berle came to it late in life.[5] At the core of

---

[5] Dodd and Berle conducted a classic debate on the subject in the 1930s, in which Dodd pressed the social responsibility of corporate managers while Berle championed shareholder interests. Adolph A. Berle, "Corporate Powers as Powers in Trust," 44 *Harvard Law Review* 1049 (1931); E. Merrick Dodd, "For Whom are Corporate Managers Trustees?" 45 *Harvard Law Review* 1145 (1932); Adolph Berle, "For Whom Corporate Managers are Trustees: A

this view was the belief that professional corporate managers could serve as disinterested technocratic fiduciaries who would guide business corporations to perform in ways that would serve the general public interest. The corporate social responsibility literature of the 1950s can be seen as an embodiment of these views.[6]

The normative appeal of this view arguably provided part of the rationale for the various legal developments in US law in the 1950s and 1960s that tended to reinforce the discretionary authority of corporate managers, such as the proxy rules promulgated by the Securities Exchange Commission (SEC) and the Williams Act. The collapse of the conglomerate movement in the 1970s and 1980s, however, largely destroyed the normative appeal of the managerialist model. It is now the conventional wisdom that, when managers are given great discretion over corporate investment policies, they mostly end up serving themselves, however well-intentioned they may be. While managerial firms may be in some ways more efficiently responsive to nonshareholder interests than are firms that are more dedicated to serving their shareholders, the price paid in inefficiency of operations and excessive investment in low-value projects is now considered too dear.

B.   The labor-oriented model

Large-scale enterprise clearly presents problems of labor contracting. Simple contracts, and the basic doctrines of contract law, are inadequate in themselves to govern the long-term relationships between workers and the firms that employ them – relationships that may be afflicted by, among other things, substantial transaction-specific investments and asymmetries of information.

Collective bargaining via organized unions has been one approach to those problems – an approach that lies outside corporate law, since it is not dependent on the organizational structure of the firms with which the employees bargain. Another approach has been to involve employees

Note," 45 *Harvard Law Review* 1365 (1932). By the 1950s, Berle seemed to have come around to Dodd's celebration of managerial discretion as a positive virtue that permits managers to act in the interests of society as a whole. See Adolph A. Berle, *Power without Property: A New Development in American Political Economy*, pp. 107–10 (1959). John Kenneth Galbraith takes a similar position in *The New Industrial State* (1967).

[6] See, e.g., Galbraith, *The New Industrial State*, and Berle, *Power without Property*, above. For an important collection of essays arguing both sides of the question of managerial responsibility to the broader interests of society, see Edward Mason, ed., *The Corporation in Modern Society* (1959).

directly in corporate governance by, for example, providing for employee representation on the firm's board of directors. Although serious attention was given to employee participation in corporate governance in Germany as early as the Weimar Republic, unionism was the dominant approach everywhere until World War II. Then, after the War, serious experimentation with employee participation in corporate governance began in Europe. The results of this experimentation are most conspicuous in Germany where, under legislation initially adopted for the coal and steel industry in 1951 and extended by stages to the rest of German industry between 1952 and 1976, employees are entitled to elect half of the members of the (upper-tier) board of directors in all large German firms. While this German form of "codetermination" has been the most far-reaching experiment, a number of other European countries have also experimented with employee participation in more modest ways, giving employees some form of mandatory minority representation on the boards of large corporations.

Enthusiasm for employee participation crested in the 1970s with the radical expansion of codetermination in Germany and the drafting of the European Community's proposed Fifth Directive on Company Law,[7] under which German-style codetermination would be extended throughout Europe. Employee participation also attracted considerable attention in the US during that period, as adversarial unionism began to lose its appeal as a means of dealing with problems of labor contracting and, in fact, began to disappear from the industrial scene.

Since then, worker participation in corporate governance has steadily lost power as a normative ideal. Despite repeated watering-down, Europe's Fifth Directive has never become law, and it now seems highly unlikely that German-style codetermination will ever be adopted elsewhere. The growing view today is that meaningful direct worker voting participation in corporate affairs tends to produce inefficient decisions, paralysis, or weak boards, and that these costs are likely to exceed any potential benefits that worker participation might bring. The problem, at root, seems to be one of governance. While direct employee participation in corporate decisionmaking may mitigate some of the inefficiencies that can beset labor contracting, the workforce in typical firms is too heterogeneous in its interests to make an effective governing body – and the problems are magnified greatly when employees must share governance with investors, as in codetermined firms. In general, contractual devices, whatever their

---

[7] Proposal for a Fifth Company Law Directive, 1983 OJ (C240)2.

weaknesses, are (when supplemented by appropriate labor market regulation) evidently superior to voting and other collective choice mechanisms in resolving conflicts of interest among and between a corporation's
investors and employees.[8]

Today, even inside Germany, few commentators argue for codetermination as a general model for corporate law in other jurisdictions. Rather,
codetermination now tends to be defended in Germany as, at most, a
workable adaptation to local interests and circumstances or, even more
modestly, as an experiment of questionable value that would now be
politically difficult to undo.[9]

C. The state-oriented model

Both before and after World War II, there was widespread support for a
corporatist system in which the government would play a strong direct
role in the affairs of large business firms to provide some assurance that
private enterprise would serve the public interest. Technocratic governmental bureaucrats, the theory went, would help to avoid the deficiencies of the market through the direct exercise of influence in corporate
affairs. This approach was most extensively realized in post-war France
and Japan. In the United States, though there was little actual experimentation with this approach outside of the defense industries, the model
attracted considerable intellectual attention. Perhaps the most influential
exposition of the state-oriented model in the Anglo-American world was
Andrew Shonfield's book *Modern Capitalism* (1967), with its admiring
description of French- and Japanese-style "indicative planning."[10] The
strong performance of the Japanese economy, and subsequently of other

---

[8] Henry Hansmann, note 2 above, 89–119; Henry Hansmann, "Worker Participation
and Corporate Governance," 43 *University of Toronto Law Journal* 589–606 (1993);
Henry Hansmann, "Probleme von Kollektiventscheidungen und Theorie der Firma –
Folgerungen für die Arbeitnehmermitbestimmung," in Claus Ott & Hans-Bernd Schäfer,
eds., *Ökonomische Analyse des Unternehmensrechts*, pp. 287–305 (1993). On the weaknesses of German boards, see, e.g., Mark Roe, "German Securities Markets and German
Codetermination," 98 *Columbia Business Law Review* 167 (1998).

[9] Some commentators, of course, continue to see codetermination as a core element of a
unique Northern European form of corporate governance. See, e.g., Michel Albert, *Capitalism vs. Capitalism* (1993) (asserting the superiority of the "Rhine Model" of capitalism
over the "Anglo-Saxon Model"). Even Albert concedes (pp. 169–90), however, the growing
ideological power of shareholder-oriented corporate governance.

[10] Andrew Shonfield, *Modern Capitalism: The Changing Balance of Public and Private Power*
(1967).

state-guided Asian economies, lent substantial credibility to this model even through the 1980s.

The principal instruments of state control over corporate affairs in corporatist economies have generally lain outside of corporate law. They include, for example, substantial discretion in the hands of government bureaucrats over the allocation of credit, foreign exchange, licenses, and exemptions from anticompetition rules. Nevertheless, corporate law also played a role by, for example, weakening shareholder control over corporate managers (to reduce pressures on managers that might operate counter to the preferences of the state) and employing state-administered criminal sanctions rather than shareholder-controlled civil lawsuits as the principal sanction for managerial malfeasance (to give the state strong authority over managers that could be used at the government's discretion).

But the state-oriented model, too, has now lost most of its attraction. One reason is the move away from state socialism in general as a popular intellectual and political model. Important landmarks on this path include the rise of Thatcherism in England in the 1970s, Mitterand's abandonment of state ownership in France in the 1980s, and the sudden collapse of communism nearly everywhere in the 1990s. The relatively poor performance of the Japanese corporate sector after 1989, together with the more recent collapse of other Asian economies that were organized on state corporatist lines, has now discredited this model even further. Today, few would argue that giving the state a strong direct hand in corporate affairs has much normative appeal.

D.   Stakeholder models

Over the past decade, the literature on corporate governance and corporate law has sometimes advocated "stakeholder" models as a normatively attractive alternative to a strongly shareholder-oriented view of the corporation. The stakeholders involved may be employees, creditors, customers, merchants in a firm's local community, or even broader interest groups such as beneficiaries of a well-preserved environment. The stakeholders, it is argued, will be subject to opportunistic exploitation by the firm and its shareholders if corporate managers are accountable only to the firm's shareholders; corporate law must therefore assure that managers are responsive to stakeholder interests as well.

While stakeholder models start with a common problem, they posit two different kinds of solutions. One group of stakeholder models looks to what we term a "fiduciary" model of the corporation, in which the board of directors functions as a neutral coordinator of the contributions and returns of all stakeholders in the firm. Under this model, stakeholders other than investors are not given direct representation on the corporate board. Rather, these other stakeholders are to be protected by relaxing the board's duty or incentive to represent only the interests of shareholders, thus giving the board greater discretion to look after other stakeholders' interests.

The fiduciary model finds its most explicit recognition in US law in the form of constituency statutes that permit boards to consider the interests of constituencies other than shareholders in mounting takeover defenses. Margaret Blair and Lynn Stout, sophisticated American advocates of the fiduciary model, also claim to find support for this normative model in other, broader aspects of US corporate law.[11] In the UK, the fiduciary model is a key element in the ongoing debate over the duties of corporate directors.[12]

The second group of stakeholder models substitutes direct stakeholder representatives for fiduciary directors. In this "representative" model of the corporation, two or more stakeholder constituencies appoint representatives to the board of directors, who then elaborate policies that maximize the joint welfare of all stakeholders, subject to the bargaining leverage that each group brings to the boardroom table. In this case the board functions ideally as a kind of collective fiduciary, even though its individual members remain partisan representatives. The board of directors (or supervisory board) then becomes an unmediated "coalition of stakeholder groups" and functions as "an arena for cooperation with respect to the function of monitoring the management" as well as an arena for resolving "conflicts with respect to the specific interests of different stakeholder groups."[13]

Neither the fiduciary nor the representative stakeholder models, however, constitute at bottom a new approach to the corporation. Rather,

---

[11] Margaret M. Blair & Lynn A. Stout, "A Team Production Theory of Corporate Law," 85 Va. L. Rev. 247 (1999).

[12] Company Law Reform Steering Group, "Modern Company Law for a Competitive Environment: The Strategic Framework," pp. 39–46 (March 1999) (setting forth the alternatives of maintaining the existing directorial duty of following enlightened shareholder interest or reformulating a "pluralist" duty to all major stakeholders in order to encourage firm-specific investment).

[13] Reinhard H. Smith & Gerald Spindler, "Path Dependence, Corporate Governance and Complementarity: A Comment on Bebchuk and Roe," Johann Wolfgang Goethe-Universitat Working Paper Series in Finance and Accounting no. 27 (1999), at 14.

despite the new rhetoric with which the stakeholder models are presented, and the more explicit economic theorizing that sometimes accompanies them, they are at heart just variants on the older manager-oriented and labor-oriented models. Stakeholder models of the fiduciary type are in effect just reformulations of the manager-oriented model, and suffer the same weaknesses. While untethered managers may better serve the interests of some classes of stakeholders, such as a firm's existing employees and creditors, the managers' own interests will often come to have disproportionate salience in their decisionmaking, with costs to some interest groups – such as shareholders, customers, and potential *new* employees and creditors – that outweigh any gains to the stakeholders who are benefited. Moreover, the courts are evidently incapable of formulating and enforcing fiduciary duties of sufficient refinement to assure that managers behave more efficiently and fairly.

Stakeholder models of the representative type, in turn, closely resemble yesterday's labor-oriented model – though generalized to extend to other stakeholders as well – and are again subject to the same weaknesses. The mandatory inclusion of any set of stakeholder representatives on the board is likely to impair corporate decisionmaking processes with costly consequences that outweigh any gains to the groups that obtain representation.

IV.   The shareholder-oriented (or "standard") model

With the abandonment of a privileged role for managers, employees, or the state in corporate affairs, we are left today with a widespread normative consensus that shareholders alone are the parties to whom corporate managers should be accountable.

A.   In whose interest?

This is not to say that there is agreement that corporations should be run in the interests of shareholders alone, much less that the law should sanction that result. All thoughtful people believe that corporate enterprise should be organized and operated to serve the interests of society as a whole, and that the interests of shareholders deserve no greater weight in this social calculus than do the interests of any other members of society. The point is simply that now, as a consequence of both logic and experience, there is convergence on a consensus that the best means to this end – the pursuit of aggregate social welfare – is to make corporate managers strongly accountable to shareholder interests, and (at least in direct terms) only to those interests. It follows that even the extreme proponents of the so-called "concession theory" of the corporation can embrace the primacy of shareholder interests in good conscience.[14]

Of course, asserting the primacy of shareholder interests in corporate law does not imply that the interests of corporate stakeholders must or should go unprotected. It merely indicates that the most efficacious legal mechanisms for protecting the interests of nonshareholder constituencies – or at least all constituencies other than creditors – lie outside of corporate law. For workers, this includes the law of labor contracting, pension law, health and safety law, and antidiscrimination law. For consumers, it includes product safety regulation, warranty law, tort law governing product liability, antitrust law, and mandatory disclosure of product contents and characteristics. For the public at large, it includes environmental law and the law of nuisance and mass torts.

Creditors, to be sure, are to some degree an exception. There remains general agreement that corporate law should directly regulate some aspects of the relationship between a business corporation and its creditors. Conspicuous examples include rules governing veil-piercing and limits on the distribution of dividends in the presence of inadequate capital. The reason for these rules, however, is that there are unique problems of creditor contracting that are integral to the corporate form, owing principally to the presence of limited liability as a structural characteristic of that form. These types of rules, however, are modest in scope. They do not – outside of bankruptcy – involve creditors in corporate governance, but rather are confined to limiting shareholders' ability to use the characteristics of the corporate form opportunistically to exploit creditors.

---

[14] In a hoary debate that cross-cuts jurisdictional boundaries, proponents of the view that corporations exist by virtue of a state "concession" or privilege have also been associated with the view that corporations ought to be governed in the interests of society – or all corporate constituencies – rather than in the private interest of shareholders alone. See, e.g., Dodd, note 5 above, at 1148–50; Paul G. Mahoney, "Contract or Concession? A Historical Perspective on Business Corporations," Working Paper, University of Virginia School of Law (1999). Conversely, proponents of the view that the corporation is at bottom a contract among investors have tended to advance the primacy of shareholder interests in corporate governance.

In our view the traditional debate between concession and contract theorists is simply confused. On the one hand, corporations – whether "concessions" or contracts – should be regulated when it is the public interest to do so. On the other hand, the standard model is, in effect, an assertion that social welfare is best served by encouraging corporate managers to pursue shareholder interests.

B.   Which shareholders?

The shareholder-oriented model does more than assert the primacy of shareholder interests, however. It asserts the interests of *all* shareholders, including minority shareholders. More particularly, it is a central tenet in the standard model that minority or noncontrolling shareholders should receive strong protection from exploitation at the hands of controlling shareholders. In publicly traded firms, this means that all shareholders should be assured an essentially equal claim on corporate earnings and assets.

There are two conspicuous reasons for this approach, both of which are rooted in efficiency concerns. One reason is that, absent credible protection for noncontrolling shareholders, business corporations will have difficulty raising capital from the equity markets. The second reason is that the devices by which controlling shareholders divert to themselves a disproportionate share of corporate benefits commonly involve inefficient investment choices and management policies.

C.   The import of ownership structure

It is sometimes said that the shareholder-oriented model of corporate law is well suited only to those jurisdictions, such as the US and the UK, in which one finds large numbers of firms with widely dispersed share-ownership. A different model is appropriate, it is said, for those jurisdictions, such as the nations of continental Europe, in which ownership is more concentrated.

This view is unconvincing, however. Closely held corporations, like publicly held corporations, operate most efficiently when the law helps assure that managers are primarily responsive to shareholder interests, and helps assure as well that controlling shareholders do not opportunistically exploit noncontrolling shareholders. The shareholder primacy model does not logically privilege any particular ownership structure. Indeed, both concentrated and dispersed shareholdings have been celebrated, at different times and by different commentators, for their ability to advance shareholder interests in the face of serious agency problems. Equally important, every jurisdiction includes a range of corporate ownership structures. While both the US and UK have many large firms with dispersed ownership, both countries also contain a far larger number of corporations that are closely held. Similarly, every major continental European jurisdiction has at least a handful of firms with dispersed ownership, and the number of such firms is evidently growing. It follows that every jurisdiction must have a system of corporate law that is adequate to handle the full range of ownership structures.

V. Competitive pressures toward convergence

The shareholder-oriented model has emerged as the normative consensus, not just because of the failure of the alternatives, but because important economic forces have made the virtues of that model increasingly salient. There are, broadly speaking, three ways in which a model of corporate governance can come to be recognized as superior: by force of *logic*, by force of *example*, and by force of *competition*. The emerging consensus in favor of the standard model has, in recent years, been driven with increasing intensity by each of these forces. We examine them here in turn.

A. The force of logic

An important source of the success of the standard model is that, in recent years, scholars and other commentators in law, economics, and business have developed persuasive reasons to believe that this model offers greater efficiencies than the principal alternatives.

One of these reasons is that, in most circumstances, the interests of equity investors in the firm – the firm's residual claimants – cannot be adequately protected by contract. Rather, to protect their interests, they must be given the right to control the firm. A second reason is that, if the control rights granted to the firm's equityholders are exclusive and strong, they will have powerful incentives to maximize the value of the firm. And a third reason is that the interests of participants in the firm other than shareholders can generally be adequately protected by contract and regulation, so that maximization of the firm's value by its shareholders complements the interests of those other participants rather than competing with them.

This reasoning is today reflected in much of the current literature on corporate finance and the economics of the firm – a literature that is becoming increasingly international. The consequence is to highlight the economic case for the shareholder-oriented model of governance. In addition, the persuasive power of the standard model has been amplified through its acceptance by a worldwide network of corporate intermediaries, including international law firms, the big five accounting firms, and the principal investment banks and consulting firms – a network whose rapidly expanding scale and scope today gives it exceptional influence in diffusing the standard model of shareholder-centered corporate governance.

B.   The force of example

The second source of the success of the standard model of corporate governance is the economic performance of jurisdictions in which it predominates. A simple comparison across countries adhering to different models – at least in very recent years – lends credence to the view that adherence to the standard model promotes better economic outcomes. The developed common law jurisdictions have performed well in comparison to the principal East Asian and continental European countries, which are less in alignment with the standard model. The principal examples include, of course, the strong performance of the American economy in comparison with the weaker economic performance of the German, Japanese, and French economies.

One might, to be sure, object that the success of the shareholder-oriented model is quite recent and will perhaps prove to be ephemeral, and that the apparent normative consensus based on that success will be ephemeral as well. After all, only fifteen years ago many thought that Japanese and German firms, which were clearly not organized on the shareholder-oriented model, were winning the competition, and that this was because they had adopted a superior form of corporate governance.[15] But this is probably a mistaken interpretation of the nature of the economic competition in recent decades, and is surely at odds with today's prevailing opinion. The competition of the 1960s, 70s, and early 80s was in fact among Japanese state-oriented corporations, German labor-oriented corporations, and American manager-oriented corporations. It was not until the late 1980s that one could speak of widespread international competition from shareholder-oriented firms.

C.   The force of competition

The increasing internationalization of both product and financial markets has brought individual firms from jurisdictions adhering to different

---

[15] To be fair, however, American commentators tended to praise corporate governance in Germany and Japan in the name of the shareholder model. Thus it was the purported ability of German banks to monitor managers and correctly value long-term business projects that caught the eye of American commentators after the 1970s, not codetermination and the labor-oriented model of the firm. See, e.g., Michael T. Jacobs, *Short-Term America: The Causes and Cures of our Business Myopia* (1991).

models in direct competition. It is now widely thought that in these more direct encounters, too, firms organized under the shareholder-oriented model have had the upper hand.[16]

Firms organized and operated according to the standard model can be expected to have important competitive advantages over firms adhering more closely to other models. These advantages include access to equity capital at lower cost (including, conspicuously, start-up capital), more aggressive development of new product markets,[17] stronger incentives to reorganize along lines that are managerially coherent, and more rapid abandonment of inefficient investments.

These competitive advantages do not always imply that firms governed by the standard model will displace those governed by an alternative model in the course of firm-to-firm competition, for two reasons. First, firms operating under the standard model may be no more efficient than other firms in many respects. For example, state-oriented Japanese and Korean companies have demonstrated great efficiency in the management and expansion of standardized production processes, while German and Dutch firms such as Daimler Benz and Philips (operating under labor- and management-oriented respectively) have been widely recognized for engineering prowess and technical innovation.

Second, even when firms governed by the standard model are clearly more efficient than their nonstandard competitors, the cost-conscious standard-model firms may be forced to abandon particular markets for precisely that reason. Less efficient firms organized under alternative models may overinvest in capacity or accept abnormally low returns on their investments in general, and thereby come to dominate a product market by underpricing their profit-maximizing competitors.

But if the competitive advantages of standard-model firms do not necessarily force the displacement of nonstandard firms in established markets, these standard-model firms are likely to achieve a

---

[16] Indirect evidence to this effect comes from international surveys such as a recent international survey of top managers conducted by the *Financial Times* to determine the world's most respected companies. Four of the top five most respected companies were American, and hence operated under the shareholder model (the fifth was Daimler-Chrysler, which is "almost" American for these purposes). Similarly, twenty-nine of the top forty firms were either American or British. See "World's Most Respected Companies," *Financial Times* website (December 17, 1999).

[17] See, e.g., Roman Frydman, Marek Hessel, & Andrzej Rapacyznski, "Why Ownership Matters? Entrepreneurship and the Restructuring of Enterprises in Central Europe," Working Paper, April 1988: firms privatized to outside owners proved superior to state firms and firms privatized to workers or previous managers in new market development.

disproportionate share among start-up firms, in new product markets, and in industries that are in the process of rapid change.[18]

The ability of standard-model firms to expand rapidly in growth industries is magnified, moreover, by access to institutional investors and the international equity markets, which understandably prefer shareholder-oriented governance and are influential advocates of the standard model. Over time, then, the standard model is likely to win the competitive struggle on the margins, confining other governance models to older firms and mature product markets. As the pace of technological change continues to quicken, this competitive advantage should continue to increase.

VI.   The rise of the shareholder class

In tandem with the competitive forces just described, a final source of ideological convergence on the standard model is a fundamental realignment of interest group structures in developed economies. At the center of this realignment is the emergence of a public shareholder class as a broad and powerful interest group in both corporate and political affairs across jurisdictions.

There are two elements to this realignment. The first is the rapid expansion of the ownership of equity securities within broad segments of society, creating a coherent interest group that presents an increasingly strong countervailing force to the organized interests of managers, employees, and the state. The second is the shift in power, within this expanding shareholder class, in favor of the interests of minority and noncontrolling shareholders over those of inside or controlling shareholders.

A.   The diffusion of equity ownership

Stock ownership is becoming more pervasive everywhere.[19] No longer is it confined to a very small group of wealthy citizens.

---

[18] In this regard it should be noted that small- and medium-sized firms in every jurisdiction are organized under legal regimes consistent with the standard model. Thus, shareholders – and shareholders alone – select the members of supervisory board in the vast majority of (smaller) German and Dutch firms. These jurisdictions impose alternative labor-or manager-oriented regimes only on a minority of comparatively large firms.

[19] Stock market capitalization as a percentage of GDP has risen dramatically in virtually every major jurisdiction over the past twenty years. In most European countries, the increase has been by a factor of three or four. "School Brief: Stocks in Trade," *The Economist*, November 13, 1999, at 85–86.

In the United States, this diffusion of share-ownership has been underway since the beginning of the twentieth century. It has accelerated substantially in recent years, however. Since World War II, an ever-increasing number of American workers have had their savings invested in corporate equities through pension funds. Over the same period, the mutual fund industry has also expanded rapidly, becoming the repository of an ever-increasing share of nonpension savings for the population at large.[20] Similarly, in Europe and Japan, and to some extent elsewhere, we have begun to see parallel developments, as markets for equity securities have become more developed.[21]

The growing wealth of developed societies is a major factor underlying these changes. Even blue-collar workers now often have sufficient personal savings to justify investment in equity securities. No longer do labor and capital constitute clearly distinct interest groups in society. Workers, through share-ownership, are coming increasingly to share the economic interests of other equityholders. Indeed, in the United States, union pension funds are today quite active in pressing the view that companies must be managed in the best interests of their shareholders.[22]

B.   The shift in balance toward public shareholders

As the example of the activist union pension funds suggests, diffusion of share-ownership is only one aspect of the rise of the shareholder class. Another aspect is the new prominence of substantial institutions that have interests coincident with those of public shareholders and that are prepared to articulate and defend those interests. Institutional investors, such as pension funds and mutual funds – which are particularly prominent in the US, though now rapidly growing elsewhere as well – are the

[20] Carolyn Kay Brancato et al., "Institutional Investor Concentration of Economic Power and Voting Authority in U.S. Publicly Held Corporations," Sept. 12, 1991, unpublished study.

[21] Latin America offers a telling example. In 1981, Chile became the first country in the region to set up a system of private pension funds. By 1995, Argentina, Colombia, and Peru had done the same. By 1996, a total of $108 billion was under management in Latin American pension funds, which by then had come to play an important role in the development of the local equity markets. It was estimated, in 1997, that total assets would grow to $200 billion by 2000, and to $600 billion by 2011. "Save Amigo Save," The Economist, December 9, 1995, at S15; "A Private Affair," Latin Finance, December 1998, at 6; Stephen Fidler, "Chile's Crusader for the Cause," Financial Times, March 14, 1997.

[22] See Stewart J. Schwarn & Randall S. Thomas, "Realigning Corporate Governance: Shareholder Activism by Labor Unions," in S. Estreicher, ed., Employee Representation in the Emerging Workplace: Alternatives/Supplements to Collective Bargaining (1998).

most conspicuous examples of these institutions. Associations of minority investors in European countries provide another example. These institutions not only give effective voice to shareholder interest, but promote in particular the interests of dispersed public shareholders rather than those of controlling shareholders or corporate insiders. The result is that ownership of equity among the public at large, while broader than ever, is at the same time gaining more effective voice in corporate affairs.

Moreover, the new activist shareholder-oriented institutions are today acting increasingly on an international scale. As a consequence, their influence now reaches well beyond their home jurisdictions.[23] We now have not only a common ideology supporting shareholder-oriented corporate law, but also an organized interest group to press that ideology – and an interest group that is broad, diverse, and increasingly international in its membership.

In the US, the principal effect of the expansion and empowerment of the shareholder class has been to shift interest group power to shareholders from managers. In Europe and Japan, the more important effect has been to shift power from workers and the state and, increasingly, from dominant shareholders.[24]

VII.   Convergence of governance practices

Thus far we have attempted to explain the sources of *ideological* convergence on the standard model of corporate governance. Our principal argument is on this normative level: we make the claim that no important competitors to the standard model of corporate governance remain persuasive today. This claim is consistent with significant differences among jurisdictions in corporate practice and law over the short run: ideological convergence does not necessarily mean rapid convergence in practice. There are many potential obstacles to rapid institutional convergence,

---

[23] See, e.g., Greg Steinmetz & Michael R. Sesit, "Rising US Investment in European Equities Galvanizes Old World," *Wall Street Journal*, Aug. 4, 1999, at A1 and A8: US investors sparking important governance changes in large European companies.

[24] Of particular interest are signs of change in the cross-ownership networks among major German and Japanese firms. New legislation proposed by the German government would eliminate the heavy (up to 60 percent) capital gains taxes on corporate sales of stock, which is expected to result in widespread dissolution of block holdings. Haig Simonian, "Germany to Abolish Tax of Disposal of Cross-Holdings," *Financial Times*, Dec. 24, 1999, at 1. In Japan *keiretsu* structures are beginning to unwind as a result of bank mergers and competitive pressure to seek higher returns on capital. Paul Abrahams & Gillian Tett, "The Circle is Broken," *Financial Times*, Nov. 9, 1999, at 18.

even when there is general consensus on what constitutes best practice. Nevertheless, we believe that the developing ideological consensus on the standard model will have important implications for the convergence of practice and law over the long run.

We expect that the reform of corporate governance practices will generally precede the reform of corporate law, for the simple reason that governance practice is largely a matter of private ordering that does not require legislative action. Recent developments in most developed jurisdictions – and in many developing ones – bear out this prediction.

Under the influence of the ideological and interest group changes discussed above, corporate governance reform has already become the watchword not only in North America but also in Europe and Japan. Corporate actors are themselves implementing structural changes to bring their firms closer to the standard model. In the US, these changes include appointment of larger numbers of independent directors to boards of directors, reduction in overall board size, development of powerful board committees dominated by outsiders (such as audit committees, compensation committees, and nominating committees), closer links between management compensation and the value of the firm's equity securities, and strong communication between board members and institutional shareholders. In Europe and Japan, many of the same changes are taking place, though with a lag. Examples range from the OECD's (Organization for Economic Cooperation and Development) promulgation of new principles of corporate governance, to recent decisions by Japanese companies to reduce board sizes and include nonexecutive directors (NEDs) (following the lead of Sony), to the rapid diffusion of stock option compensation plans for top managers in the UK and in the principal commercial jurisdictions of continental Europe.

VIII. Legal convergence

Not surprisingly, convergence in the fine structure of corporate law proceeds more slowly than convergence in governance practices. Legal change requires legislative action. Nevertheless, we expect shareholder pressure (and the power of shareholder-oriented ideology) to force gradual legal changes, largely but not entirely in the direction of Anglo-American corporate and securities law. There are already important indications of evolutionary convergence in the realms of board structure, securities regulation and accounting methodologies, and even the regulation of takeovers.

A.   Board structure

With respect to board structure, convergence has been in the direction of a legal regime that strongly favors a single-tier board that is relatively small and has a substantial complement of outside directors, but contains insiders as well. Mandatory two-tier board structures seem a thing of the past; the weaker and less responsive boards that they promote are justified principally as a complement to worker codetermination, and thus share – indeed, constitute one of – the weaknesses of the latter institution. The declining fortunes of the two-tier board are reflected in the evolution of the European Union's Proposed Regulation on the Statute for a European Company. When originally drafted in 1970, that Regulation called for a mandatory two-tier board. In 1991, however, the Proposed Regulation was amended to permit member states to prescribe either a two-tier or a single-tier system. Meanwhile, on the practical side, France, which made provision for an optional two-tier board when the concept was more in vogue, has seen few of its corporations adopt the device.

At the same time, jurisdictions that traditionally favored the opposite extreme of insider-dominated, single-tier boards have come to accept a significant complement of outside directors. In the US, independent directors have long been mandated by the New York Stock Exchange listing rules to serve on the important audit committees of listed firms, while more recently state law doctrine has created a strong role for outside directors in approving transactions where interests might be conflicted. In Japan, a similar evolution may be foreshadowed by the recent movement among Japanese companies, mentioned above, toward smaller boards and independent directors, and by the recent publication of a code of corporate governance principles advocating these reforms by a committee of leading Japanese managers.[25] The result is convergence from both ends toward the middle: while two-tier boards themselves seem to be on the way out, countries with single-tier board structures are incorporating, in their regimes, one of the strengths of the typical two-tier board regime, namely the substantial role it gives to independent (outside) directors.

B.   Disclosure and capital market regulation

Regulation of routine disclosure to shareholders, intended to aid in policing corporate managers, is also converging conspicuously. Without

---

[25] "Corporate Governance Principles: Final Report," Corporate Governance Committee of the Corporate Governance Forum of Japan, May 26, 1998.

seeking to examine this complex field in detail here, we note that major jurisdictions outside of the US are reinforcing their disclosure systems, while the US has been retreating from some of the more inexplicably burdensome of its federal regulations, such as the highly restrictive proxy solicitation rules that until recently crippled communication among American institutional investors. Indeed, the subject matter of mandatory disclosure for public companies is startlingly similar across the major commercial jurisdictions today.[26]

Similarly, uniform accounting standards are rapidly crystallizing out of the babel of national rules and practices into two well-defined sets of international standards: the GAAP (generally accepted accounting principles) accounting rules administered by the Financial Auditing Standards Board in the US, and the International Accounting Standards (IAS) administered by the International Accounting Standards Committee in London. While important differences remain between the competing sets of international standards, these differences are far smaller than the variations among the national accounting methodologies that preceded GAAP and the new International Standards. The two international standards, moreover, are likely to converge further, if only because of the economic savings that would result from a single set of global accounting standards.[27]

C.   Shareholder suits

Shareholder-initiated suits against directors and managers are now being accommodated in countries that had previously rendered them ineffective. Germany has recently reduced the ownership threshold qualifying shareholders to demand legal action against managing directors (to be brought by the supervisory board or special company representative) from a 10 percent equity stake to the lesser of a 5 percent stake or a 1 million DM

---

[26] This can be seen, for example, by comparing the EU's Listing Particulars Directive with the SEC's Form S-1 for the registration of securities under the 1933 Act. If US disclosure requirements remain more aggressive, it must be remembered that the EU Directives establish minimal requirements that member states can and do supplement. See John C. Coffee, "The Future as History: The Prospects for Global Convergence in Corporate Governance and its Implications," 93 *Nw. U. L. Rev.* 641 (1999). See generally Amir N. Licht, "International Diversity in Securities Regulation: Roadblocks on the Way to Convergence," 20 *Cardozo Law Review* 227 (1998), discussing convergence in disclosure rules, accounting standards, and corporate governance.

[27] See, e.g., Elizabeth MacDonald, "US Accounting Board Faults Global Rules," *Wall Street Journal*, Oct. 18, 1999, at 1.

stake when there is suspicion of dishonesty or illegality.[28] Japan has altered its rules on attorneys' fees to create meaningful incentives for litigation. At the same time, US law is moving toward the center from the other direction by beginning to rein in the country's strong incentives for potentially opportunistic litigation. At the federal level, there are recently strengthened pleading requirements upon initiation of shareholder actions, new safe harbors for forward-looking company projections, and recent provision for lead shareholders to take control in class actions. State law rules, meanwhile, are making it easier for a corporation to get a shareholders' suit dismissed.

D.   Takeovers

Finally, regulation of takeovers also seems headed for convergence. As it is, current differences in takeover regulation are more apparent than real. Hostile takeovers are rare outside the Anglo-American jurisdictions, principally owing to the more concentrated patterns of shareholdings outside those jurisdictions. As shareholding patterns become more homogeneous (as we expect they will), and as corporate culture everywhere becomes more accommodating of takeovers (as it seems destined to), takeovers will presumably become much more common in Europe, Japan, and elsewhere.[29]

Moreover, where operative legal constraints on takeovers in fact differ, they show signs of convergence. In particular, for several decades the US has been increasing its regulation of takeovers, placing additional constraints both on the ability of acquirers to act opportunistically and on the ability of incumbent managers to entrench themselves or engage in self-dealing. With the widespread diffusion of the "poison pill" defense, and the accompanying limits that courts have placed on the use of that defense, partial hostile tender offers of a coercive character are a thing of the past – a result similar to that which European jurisdictions have

---

[28] Theodor Baums, "Corporate Governance in Germany: System and Current Developments," Working Paper, University of Osnabruck, 1999.

[29] Already Europe has seen a remarkable wave of takeovers in 1999, culminating in what may be the largest hostile takeover attempt in history: Vodaphone's effort to acquire Mannesmann. In addition, many established jurisdictions are adopting rules to regulate tender offers that bear a family resemblance to the Williams Act or to the rules of the London City Code. See, e.g., Brazil's tender offer regulations, Securities Commission Ruling 69, Sept. 8, 1987, Arts. 1–4; and Italy's recently adopted reform of takeover regulation, Legislative Decree 58 of February 24, 1999 (the so-called "Draghi Reform").

accomplished with a "mandatory bid rule" requiring acquirers of control to purchase all shares in their target companies at a single price.

To be sure, jurisdictions diverge in other aspects of takeover law, where the points of convergence are still uncertain. For example, American directors enjoy far more latitude to defend against hostile takeovers than do directors in most European jurisdictions. Under current Delaware law, incumbent boards have authority to resist hostile offers although they remain vulnerable to bids that are tied to proxy fights at shareholders' meetings. As the incidence of hostile takeovers increases in Europe, then, European jurisdictions may incline toward Delaware by permitting additional defensive tactics. Alternatively, given the dangers of managerial entrenchment, Delaware may move toward European norms by limiting defensive tactics more severely. While we cannot predict where the equilibrium point will lie, it is a reasonable conjecture that the law on both sides of the Atlantic will ultimately converge on a single regime.

E. Judicial discretion

There remains one very general aspect of corporate law on which one might feel that convergence will be slow to come: the degree of judicial discretion in resolving disputes among corporate actors *ex post*. Such discretion has long been much more conspicuous in the common law jurisdictions, and particularly in the US, than in the civil law jurisdictions.

But, even here, there is good reason to believe that there will be strong convergence across systems over time. Civil law jurisdictions, whether in the form of court decisionmaking or arbitration, seem to be moving toward a more discretionary model. At the same time, there are signs that the US is moving away from the more extreme forms of unpredictable *ex post* decisionmaking that have sometimes been characteristic of, say, the Delaware courts. US securities law is civilian in spirit and elaborated by detailed rules promulgated by the SEC. And the Corporate Governance Project of the American Law Institute offers a code-like systematization of substantive state corporate law, including even the notoriously vague and open-ended US case law that articulates the fiduciary duties of loyalty and care.

IX. Potential obstacles to convergence

To be sure, important interests are threatened by movement toward the standard model, and those interests can be expected to serve as a brake on change. We doubt, however, that such interests will be able to stave off for long the reforms called for by the growing ideological consensus focused on the standard model.

To take one example, consider the argument, prominently made by Lucian Bebchuk and Mark Roe,[30] that the private value extracted by corporate controllers (controlling shareholders or powerful managers) will long serve as a barrier to the evolution of efficient ownership structures, governance practices, and corporate law.

The essential structure of the Bebchuk and Roe argument is as follows: In jurisdictions lacking strong protection for minority shareholders, controlling shareholders divert to themselves a disproportionate share of corporate cash flows. The controlling shareholders thus have an incentive to avoid any change in their firm's ownership or governance, or in the regulation to which their firm is subject, that would force them to share the corporation's earnings more equitably. Moreover, these corporate insiders have the power, in many jurisdictions, to prevent such changes. Their position as controlling shareholders permits them to block changes in the firm's ownership structure merely by refusing to sell their shares. Their position also permits them to block changes in governance by selecting the firm's directors. And, in those societies in which – as in most of Europe – closely controlled firms dominate the economy, the wealth and collective political weight of controlling shareholders permits them to block legal reforms that would compromise their disproportionate private returns.

But this pessimistic view seems unwarranted. If, as the developing consensus view holds, the standard shareholder-oriented governance model maximizes corporate value, controlling shareholders who are motivated chiefly by economic considerations may not wish to retain control of their firms. And, even if nonmonetary considerations lead insiders to retain control, the economic significance of firms dominated by these insiders is likely to diminish over time both in their own jurisdictions and in the world market.

A.   Transactions to capture surplus

First, consider the case of controlling shareholders ("controllers") who wish to maximize their financial returns. Suppose that the prevailing legal regime permits controlling shareholders to extract large private benefits

[30] Lucian Bebchuk & Mark Roe, "A Theory of Path Dependence in Corporate Ownership and Governance," 52 *Stanford Law Review* 127 (1999).

from which public shareholders are excluded. Predictably these controllers will sell their shares only if they receive a premium price that captures the value of their private benefits, and they will reject any corporate governance reform that reduces the value of those returns. That such controllers will prefer to increase their own returns over increasing returns to the corporation does not imply, however, that they will reject governance institutions or ownership structures that maximize firm value. Bebchuk and Roe are too quick to conclude that controllers cannot themselves profit by facilitating efficient governance.

Controllers who extract large private benefits from public companies are likely to indulge in two forms of inefficient management. First, they may select investment projects that maximize their own private returns over returns to the firm. For example, a controller might select a less profitable investment project over a more profitable one precisely because it offers opportunities for lucrative self-dealing. Second, controllers are likely to have a preference for retaining and reinvesting earnings over distributing them, even when it is inefficient to do so. The reason is that formal corporate distributions must be shared with minority shareholders, while earnings reinvested in the firm remain available for subsequent conversion into private benefits – for example, through self-dealing transactions. A controller's incentive to engage in both forms of inefficient behavior increases rapidly, moreover, if – as has been common in Europe – she employs devices such as stock pyramids, corporate cross-holdings, and dual-class stock to maintain a lock on voting control while reducing her proportionate equity stake.[31]

Where law enforcement is effective, however, inefficient behavior itself creates strong financial incentives to pursue more efficient ownership and governance structures. When share prices are sufficiently depressed, anyone – including controllers themselves – can generate net gains by introducing more efficient governance structures. It follows that controllers who can capture most or all of the value of these efficiency gains stand to profit privately even more than they profit by extracting non pro rata benefits from poorly governed firms. Controllers can capture these efficiency gains, moreover, in at least two ways: (1) by selling out at a premium price reflecting potential efficiency gains to a buyer or group of buyers who is willing and able to operate under nonexploitative governance rules; or (2) by buying up minority shares (at depressed

---

[31] See Lucian Bebchuk, Reinier Kraakman, & George Triantis, "Stock Pyramids, Cross-Ownership, and Dual Class Equity: The Creation and Agency Costs of Separating Control from Cash Flow Rights," NBER Working Paper no. 6951 (1999).

prices), and either managing their firms as sole owners, or reselling their entire firms to buyers with efficient ownership structures.

For controllers to extract these efficiency gains, however, efficient restructuring must be legally possible: that is, the legal regime must offer means by which restructured firms can commit to good governance practices. This can be done in several ways without threatening the private returns of controllers who have not yet undertaken to restructure. One solution is an optional corporate and securities law regime that is dedicated – or at least more dedicated – to protecting minority shareholders than the prevailing regime. For example, firms can be permitted to list their shares on foreign exchanges with more rigorous shareholder-protection rules. Another solution is simply to enforce shareholder-protective provisions written into a restructured firm's articles of incorporation.

It follows that even financially self-interested controllers have an incentive to promote the creation of legal regimes in which firms at least have a *choice* of forming along efficient lines – which, as we have argued, today means along shareholder-oriented lines. And, once such an (optional) efficient regime has been established, and many of the existing exploitative firms have taken advantage of the regime to profit from an efficient restructuring, there should be a serious reduction in the size of the interest group that wishes even to maintain as an option the old regime's accommodation of firms that are exploitative toward noncontrolling shareholders.

Bebchuk and Roe appear to assume that such developments will not occur because the law will inhibit controlling shareholders from seeking efficient restructuring by forcing them to share any gains from the restructuring equitably with noncontrolling shareholders. But it is more plausible to suppose that the law will allow controlling shareholders to claim the gains associated with an efficient restructuring – by means of techniques such as freeze-out mergers and coercive tender offers – in jurisdictions where controllers are able to extract large private benefits from ordinary corporate operations.

In short, if current controlling shareholders are interested just in maximizing their financial returns, we can expect substantial pressure toward the adoption of efficient law.

B.   Controllers who wish to build empires

Controlling shareholders do not always, however, wish to maximize their financial returns. Rather – and we suspect this is often true in Europe – they may also seek nonpecuniary returns.

For example, a controlling shareholder may wish simply to be on top of the largest corporate empire possible, and therefore be prepared to over-invest in building market share by selling at a price too low to maximize returns while reinvesting all available returns in expanded capacity and R & D. Alternatively, a controller may be willing to accept a low financial return in order to indulge a taste for a wide range of other costly prac-tices, from putting incompetent family members in positions of responsi-bility to preserving quasi-feudal relations with employees and their local communities. Such practices may even be efficient, if the controller values his nonpecuniary returns more than he would the monetary returns that are given up. But, where the controller shares ownership with noncon-trolling shareholders who do not value the nonpecuniary returns, there is the risk that the controlling shareholder will exploit the noncontrolling shareholders by refusing to distribute the firm's earnings and instead rein-vesting those earnings in low-return projects that are valued principally by the controller. (This can, of course, happen only where the controllers have been able to mislead the noncontrolling shareholders somehow. If the latter shareholders purchased their shares knowing that they would not have control, and that the controllers would divert a share of returns to themselves through inefficient investments, then they presumably paid a price for the shares that was discounted to reflect this diversion, leaving the noncontrolling shareholders with a market rate of return on their investment.)

Efficiency-enhancing control transactions of the type described above may have little to offer controlling shareholders of this type, since the restructuring may require that they give up control of the firm, and hence give up not only the nonpecuniary returns they were purchasing for them-selves with the noncontrolling shareholder's money, but also the nonpe-cuniary returns they were purchasing with their own share of the firm's invested capital. Thus, controlling shareholders who value nonpecuniary gains will have less incentive than purely financially motivated controllers to favor efficient corporate legal structures.

Moreover, inefficient firms with such controllers may survive quite nicely in competitive markets, and in fact expand, despite their inef-ficiencies. For example, if the controllers place value only on the size of the firm they control, they will continue to reinvest in expansion so long as the return offered simply exceeds zero, with the result that they can and will take market share from competing firms that are managed much more efficiently but must pay their shareholders a market rate of return.

Jurisdictions with large numbers of firms dominated by controllers with nonpecuniary motivations will, therefore, feel relatively less pressure than other jurisdictions to adopt standard-model corporate law. Yet even in those jurisdictions – which may include much of Western Europe today – the pressure for moving toward the standard model is likely to grow irresistibly strong in the relatively near future. We briefly explore here several reasons for this.

C.   The insiders' political clout will be insufficient to protect them

To begin with, the low profitability of firms that pursue nonpecuniary returns is likely to select against their owners as controllers of industry. As long as the owners of these firms subsidize low-productivity practices, they become progressively poorer relative to investors in new businesses and owners of established firms who seek either to enhance shareholder value or to sell out to others who will, with the result that economic and political influence will shift to the latter.

Furthermore, the success of firms following shareholder-oriented governance practices is likely to undermine political support for alternative models of corporate governance for two reasons. One reason is that – as we have suggested above – the rise of a shareholder class with growing wealth creates an interest group to press for reforming corporate governance to encourage value-enhancing practices and restrain controlling shareholders from extracting private benefits. Companies, whether domestic or foreign, that attract public shareholders and pension funds by promising a better bottom line also create natural enthusiasts for law reform and the standard model.

The second reason for a decline in the appeal of alternative styles of corporate governance is the broader phenomenon of ideological convergence on the standard model. Where previous ideologies may have celebrated the *noblesse oblige* of quasi-feudal family firms or the industrial prowess of huge conglomerates ruled by insiders, the increasing salience of the standard model makes empire building and domination suspect, and the extraction of private value at the expense of minority shareholders illegitimate, in everyone's eyes. Costly governance practices therefore become increasingly hard to sustain politically. Viewed through the lens of the new ideology, the old practices are not only inefficient but also unjust, since they deprive ordinary citizens, including pensioners and small investors, of a fair return on their investments. As civil society grows more democratic, the privileged returns of controlling shareholders, leading families, and entrenched managers become increasingly suspect.

Indeed, we expect that the social values that make it so prestigious for families to control corporate empires in many countries will change importantly in the years to come. The essentially feudal norms we now see in many patterns of industrial ownership will be displaced by social values that place greater weight on social egalitarianism and individual entrepreneurship, with the result that there is an ever-dwindling group of firms dominated by controllers who place great weight on the nonpecuniary returns from presiding personally over a corporate fiefdom.

D. The insiders who preserve their firms and legal protections will become increasingly irrelevant

Finally, even if dominant corporate controllers successfully block reform for some period of time in any given jurisdiction, they are likely to become increasingly irrelevant in the domestic economy, the world economy, or both.

At home, as we have already noted, the terms on which public equity capital becomes available to finance new firms and new product markets are likely to be dominated by the standard model. Venture capital investments and initial public offerings are unlikely to occur if minority investors are not offered significant protection. This protection can be provided without disturbing the older established firms by establishing separate standard-model institutions that apply only to new firms. An example of this is the *Neuer Markt* in the Frankfurt Stock Exchange, which provides the additional protection of enhanced disclosure and GAAP accounting standards for investors in start-up companies in search of equity capital, while leaving the less rigorous older rules in place for already-established firms.

Moreover, to the extent that domestic law or domestic firms fail to provide adequate protections for public shareholders, other jurisdictions can supply the protection of the standard model. Investment capital can flow to other countries and to foreign firms that do business in the home jurisdiction. Alternatively, domestic companies may be able to reincorporate in foreign jurisdictions or bind themselves to comply with the shareholder protections offered by foreign law by listing on a foreign exchange (as some Israeli firms now do by listing on NASDAQ).[32]

Through devices such as these that effectively permit new firms to adopt a model that differs from that applicable to old firms, the national law and

---

[32] See, e.g., John C. Coffee, note 26 above; Edward Rock, "Mandatory Disclosure as Credible Commitment: Going Public, Opting in, Opting out, and Globalization," Working Paper, September 1998.

governance practices that protect controlling insiders in established firms can be maintained without crippling the national economy. The result is to partition off, and grandfather in, the older family-controlled or manager-dominated firms, whose costly governance practices will make them increasingly irrelevant to economic activity even within their local jurisdiction.

X.   Weak forces for convergence

We have spoken here of a number of forces pressing toward international convergence on a relatively uniform standard model of corporate law. Those forces include the internal logic of efficiency, competition, interest group pressure, imitation, and the need for compatibility. We have largely ignored two other potential forces that might also press toward convergence: explicit efforts at cross-border harmonization, and competition between jurisdictions for corporate charters.

A.   Harmonization

The European Union has been the locus of the most intense efforts to date at self-conscious harmonization of corporate law across jurisdictions. That process has, however, proven a relatively weak force for convergence; where there exists substantial divergence in corporate law across member states, efforts at harmonization have generally borne little fruit. Moreover, harmonization proposals have often been characterized by an effort to impose throughout the EU various forms of regulation whose efficiency is questionable, with the result that harmonization sometimes seems more an effort to avoid the standard model than to further it.

For these reasons, the other pressures toward convergence described above are likely to be much more important forces for convergence than are explicit efforts at harmonization. At most, we expect that, once the consensus for adoption of the standard model has become sufficiently strong, harmonization may serve as a convenient pretext for overriding the objections of entrenched national interest groups that resist reform of corporate law within individual states.

B.   Competition for charters

The US experience suggests that cross-border competition for corporate charters can be a powerful force for convergence in corporate law, and in particular for convergence on an efficient model.[33] It seems quite plausible, however, that the choice of law rules necessary for this form of competition will not be adopted in most jurisdictions until substantial convergence has already taken place. We expect that the most important steps toward convergence can and will be taken with relative rapidity before explicit cross-border competition for charters is permitted in most of the world, and that the latter process will ultimately be used, at most, as a means of working out the fine details of convergence and of ongoing minor experimentation and adjustment thereafter.

XI. Limits on convergence

Not all divergence among corporate law regimes reflects inefficiency. Efficient divergence can arise either through adaptation to local social structures or through fortuity. Neither logic nor competition are likely to create strong pressure for this form of divergence to disappear, Consequently, it could survive for a considerable period of time. Still – though the rate of change may be slower – there is good reason to believe that even the extent of efficient divergence, like the extent of inefficient divergence, will continue to decrease relatively quickly.

A. Differences in institutional context

Sometimes jurisdictions choose alternative forms of corporate law because those alternatives complement other national differences in, for example, forms of shareholdings, means for enforcing the law, or related bodies of law such as bankruptcy. A case in point is the new Russian corporation statute, which deviates self-consciously from the type of statute that the standard model would call for in more developed economies. To take just one example, the Russian statute imposes cumulative voting on all corporations as a mandatory rule, in strong contrast with the corporate law of most developed countries. The reason for this approach was largely to assure some degree of shareholder influence and access to information in the context of the peculiar pattern of shareholdings that has become commonplace in Russia as a result of that country's unique process of mass privatization.[34]

---

[33] See generally Roberta Romano, *The Genius of American Corporate Law* (1993).

[34] Following Russian voucher privatization in 1993, managers and other employees typically held a majority of shares in large companies. Publicly held shares were mostly widely

Nevertheless, the efficient degree of divergence in corporate law appears much smaller than the divergence in the other institutions in which corporate activity is embedded. For example, efficient divergence in creditor protection devices is probably much narrower than observed differences in the sources and structure of corporate credit. Similarly, the efficient array of mechanisms for protecting shareholders from managerial opportunism appears much narrower than the observed variety across jurisdictions in patterns of shareholdings.

Moreover, the economic institutions and legal structures in which corporate law must operate are themselves becoming more uniform across jurisdictions. This is conspicuously true, for example, of patterns of shareholdings. All countries are beginning to face, or need to face, the same varied types of shareholders, from controlling blockholders to mutual funds to highly dispersed individual shareholders. Some of this is driven by the converging forces of internal economic development. Thus, privatization of enterprise, increases in personal wealth, and the need for start-up finance (which is aided by a public market that offers an exit for the initial private investors) all promote an increasing incidence of small shareholdings and a consequent need for strong protection for minority shareholders. The globalization of capital markets presses to the same end. Hence Russia, to return to our earlier example, will presumably evolve over time toward the patterns of shareholdings typical of developed economies, and will ultimately feel the need to conform its shareholder voting rules more closely to the rules found in those economies.

B.   Harmless mutations

In various cases we anticipate that there will be little or no efficiency difference among multiple alternative corporate law rules. In these cases, the pressures for convergence are lessened, although not entirely eliminated (since we still expect global investors to exert pressure to standardize).[35]

dispersed, but there was often at least one substantial outside shareholder with sufficient holdings to exploit a cumulative voting rule to obtain board representation. See Bernard Black & Reinier Kraakman, "A Self-Enforcing Model of Corporate Law," 109 *Harvard Law Review* 1911 (1996).

[35] Ronald Gilson refers to processes in which facially different governance structures or legal rules develop to solve the same underlying functional problem as "functional convergence." Ronald J. Gilson, Chapter 4 this volume. On the assumption that formal law and governance practices are embedded in larger institutional contexts that change only slowly, Gilson conjectures that functional convergence is likely to far outpace formal convergence. Such functional convergence, when it occurs, is what we term harmless mutation.

Accounting standards offer an example. As we noted earlier, there are currently two different accounting methodologies that have achieved prominence among developed nations: the American GAAP and the European-inspired International Accounting Standards. Because these two sets of standards evolved separately, they differ in many significant details. From the best current evidence, however, neither obviously dominates the other in terms of efficiency.

If the economies involved were entirely autarchic, both accounting standards might well survive indefinitely with no sacrifice in efficiency. The increasing globalization of the capital markets, however, imposes strong pressure not only for all countries to adopt one or the other of these regimes, but to select a single common accounting regime. Over time, then, the network efficiencies of a common standard form in global markets are likely to eliminate even this and other forms of fortuitous divergence in corporate law.

XII.   Limits on the efficiency of convergence

Having just recognized that efficiency does not always dictate convergence in corporate law, we must also recognize that the reverse can be true as well: a high degree of convergence need not always reflect efficiency. The most likely sources of such inefficient convergence, we expect, will be flaws in markets or in political institutions that are widely shared by modern economies, and that are reinforced rather than mitigated by cross-border competition.

A.   Third-party costs: corporate torts

Perhaps the most conspicuous example of inefficient convergence is the rule – already universal, with only minor variations from one jurisdiction to the next – that limits shareholder liability for corporate torts. This rule induces inefficient risk-taking and excessive levels of risky activities – inefficiencies that appear to outweigh by far any offsetting benefits, such as reduced costs of litigation or the smoother functioning of the securities markets. As we have argued elsewhere, a general rule of unlimited pro rata

In contrast to Gilson, however, we believe that formal law and governance structures are less contextual and more malleable than is often assumed, once the norm of shareholder primacy is accepted. Functional convergence – rather than straightforward imitation – is thus less necessary than Gilson supposes. We also suspect that close substitutes among alternative governance structures and legal rules are less widespread than Gilson implies.

shareholder liability for corporate torts appears to offer far greater overall efficiencies.[36]

Why, then, has there been universal convergence on an inefficient rule? The obvious answer is that neither markets nor politics work well to represent the interests of the persons who bear the direct costs of the rule, namely tort victims. Since, by definition, torts involve injuries to third parties, the parties affected by the rule – corporations and their potential tort victims – cannot contract around the rule to capture and share the gains from its alteration. At the same time, owing to the highly stochastic nature of most corporate torts, tort victims – and particularly the very large class of *potential* tort victims – do not constitute an easily organized political interest group.[37] Moreover, even if a given jurisdiction were to adopt a rule of shareholder liability for corporate torts, difficulties in enforcement would arise from the ease with which shareholdings or incorporation can today be shifted to other jurisdictions that retain the rule of limited liability.

B. Managerialism

A second example of inefficient convergence, arguably, is the considerable freedom enjoyed by managers in almost all jurisdictions to protect their prerogatives in cases when they might conflict with those of shareholders, including particularly managers' ability to defend their positions against hostile takeover attempts. Again, political and market failures seem responsible. Dispersed public shareholders, who are the persons most likely to be disadvantaged by the power of entrenched managers, face potentially serious problems of collective action in making their voice felt. And managers, whose positions make them a powerful and influential interest group everywhere, can use their political influence to keep the costs of collective action high – for example, by making it hard for a hostile acquirer to purchase an effective control block of shares from current shareholders. Corporate law might therefore converge, not precisely to the shareholder-oriented standard model that represents the ideological consensus, but rather to a variant of that model that has a slight managerialist tilt.

---

[36] See Henry Hansmann & Reinier Kraakman, "Toward Unlimited Shareholder Liability for Corporate Torts," 100 *Yale Law Journal* 1879, 1882–83 (1991).

[37] By way of contrast, in the US the largely *non*stochastic tort of environmental pollution has made an easier focus for political organizing and, as noted in the text below, has led to strong legislation that partially pierces the corporate veil for firms that pollute.

C.   How big a problem?

The problem of inefficient convergence in corporate law appears to be a relatively limited one, however. Tort victims aside, the relations among virtually all actors directly affected by the corporation are heavily contractual, which tends to give those actors a common interest in establishing efficient law. Moreover, as our earlier discussion has emphasized, shareholders, managers, workers, and voluntary creditors either have or are acquiring a powerful interest in efficient corporate law. Indeed, limited liability in tort arguably should not be considered a rule of corporate law at all, but instead should be viewed as a rule of tort law. And even limited liability in tort may come to be abandoned as large-scale tort damage becomes more common and consequently of greater political concern. We already see some movement in this direction in US environmental law, which pushes aside the corporate veil to a startling degree in particular circumstances.

XIII.   Conclusion

The triumph of the shareholder-oriented model of the corporation over its principal competitors is now assured, even if it was problematic as recently as twenty-five years ago. Logic alone did not preordain the principal elements of the standard model, including strong minority shareholder protections and corporate managers dedicated to serving the interests of shareholders above all. Rather, the standard model earned its position as the dominant model of the large corporation the hard way, by out-competing during the post-World War II period the three alternative models of corporate governance: the managerialist model, the labor-oriented model, and the state-oriented model.

If the failure of the principal alternatives has established the ideological hegemony of the standard model, however, perhaps this should not come as a complete surprise. The standard model has never been questioned for the vast majority of corporations. It dominates the law and governance of closely held corporations in every jurisdiction. Most German companies do not participate in the codetermination regime, and most Dutch companies are not regulated by the managerialist "structure" regime. Similarly, the standard model of shareholder primacy has always been the dominant legal model in the two jurisdictions where the choice of models might be expected to matter most: the US and the UK. The choice of models matters in these jurisdictions because large companies often have highly fragmented ownership structures. In continental Europe, where most large companies are controlled, the interests of controlling shareholders traditionally dominate corporate policy no matter what the prevailing ideology of the corporate form.

We predict, therefore, that as European equity markets develop, the ideological and competitive attractions of the standard model will become indisputable, even among legal academics. And as the goal of shareholder primacy becomes second nature even to politicians, convergence in most aspects of the law and practice of corporate governance is sure to follow.

2

A theory of path dependence in corporate ownership and governance

LUCIAN ARYE BEBCHUK & MARK J. ROE*

Introduction

Corporate ownership and governance differ among the world's advanced economies. Some countries' corporations are diffusely owned with managers firmly in control, other countries' corporations have concentrated ownership, and in still others, labor strongly influences the firm. During the past half-century since World War II, economies, business practices, and living standards have converged in Western Europe, the United States, and Japan. But their corporate ownership structures have remained different, and different degrees of ownership concentration and labor influence have persisted. What explains these differences? And should they be expected to persist or to disappear?

We show that there are significant sources of path dependence in a country's patterns of corporate ownership structure. Because of this path dependence, a country's pattern of ownership structures at any point in time depends partly on the patterns it had earlier. Consequently, when countries had different ownership structures at earlier points in time – because of their different circumstances at the time, or even because of historical accidents – these differences might persist at later points in time even if their economies have otherwise become quite similar.

* We benefited from the comments of Merritt Fox, Ron Harris, Marcel Kahan, Ehud Kamar, Louis Kaplow, Randy Kroszner, Benjamin Mojuye, Roberta Romano, Reinhard Schmidt, Gerald Spindler, Luigi Zingales, and workshop participants at Harvard, the University of Frankfurt, New York University, the 1997 Columbia Law School conference on convergence of systems, the 1998 meetings of the American Law and Economics Association and the Summer Institute of the National Bureau of Economic Research, and the 1999 European Symposium on Financial Markets in Gerzensee. For financial support, Lucian Bebchuk thanks the John M. Olin Center for Law, Economics, and Business at Harvard Law School and the National Science Foundation, and Mark Roe thanks the Columbia Law School Sloan Project on Corporate Governance. An earlier version of this appears in 52 *Stanford Law Review* 127 (1999).

In section I, we describe our inquiry. Why, against the background of the forces for global convergence, do the advanced economies differ so much in their corporate ownership structures? For concreteness, our analysis focuses on one important dimension of differences among countries: whether their corporations commonly do or do not have a controlling shareholder.

We distinguish in section I between two sources of path dependence. One source of path dependence – which we label *structure-driven path dependence* – concerns the direct effect of initial ownership structures on subsequent ownership structures. We show how the corporate structures that an economy has at a given point in time are influenced by the corporate structures it had earlier.

Another source of path dependence – which we label *rule-driven path dependence* – arises from the effect that initial ownership structures have on subsequent structures through their effect on the legal rules governing corporations. By corporate rules, we mean all the legal rules that govern the relationship between the corporation and its investors, stakeholders, and managers and the relationships among these players – including not only corporate law as conventionally defined but also securities law and the relevant parts of the law governing insolvency, labor relations, and financial institutions. Corporate rules themselves, we show, are path-dependent. The following two sections of the chapter analyze in turn these two main sources of path dependence.

Section II focuses on structure-driven path dependence. Here we analyze how choices of corporate ownership structure are directly influenced by the initial ownership structures that the economy had. To this end, we show how choices of ownership structure might differ in two economies that now have identical corporate rules but started with different ownership structures. We identify two reasons why prior ownership structures in an economy might affect subsequent structures – one grounded in efficiency and the other in rent-seeking. First, the efficient ownership structure for a company is often path-dependent. Due to sunk adaptive costs, network externalities, complementarities, and multiple optima, the relative efficiency of alternative ownership structures depends partly on the structures with which the company and/or other companies in its environment started.

Second, existing corporate structures might well have persistence power due to internal rent-seeking, even if they cease to be efficient. Those parties who participate in corporate control under an existing structure might have the incentive and power to impede changes that would reduce their private benefits of control even if the change would be efficient. For example, a controlling shareholder might elect not to move her firm to a diffused ownership structure because the move would reduce the controller's private benefits of control. Similarly, the managers of a company with diffused ownership, seeking to maintain their independence, might elect to prevent their firm from moving to a concentrated ownership structure even if the move would be efficient overall. And in nations in which labor unions play a role in corporate control, union leaders might seek to maintain structures that give them such power. As long as those who can block structural transformation do not bear the full costs of persistence, or do not capture the full benefits of an efficient move, inefficient structures that are already in place might persist. To be sure, all potentially efficient changes would take place in a purely Coasian world. However, as we show, the transactions feasible in our imperfectly Coasian world often would not prevent the persistence of some inefficient structures that are already in place.

Section III focuses on rule-driven path dependence. A country's legal rules at any point in time, we argue, might be heavily influenced by the ownership patterns that the country had earlier. We identify two reasons for the path dependence of rules – one grounded in efficiency and the other in interest group politics. First, even assuming that legal rules are chosen solely for efficiency reasons, the initial ownership patterns influence the relative efficiency of alternative corporate rules; the set of rules that would be efficient, we argue, might depend on the country's existing pattern of corporate structures and institutions.

Second, rule-driven path dependence might arise from interest group politics. A country's initial pattern of corporate structures influences the power that various interest groups have in the process producing corporate rules. If the initial pattern provides one group of players with relatively more wealth and power, this group would have a better chance to have corporate rules that it favors down the road. Positional advantages inside firms will be translated into positional advantages in a country's politics. And this effect on corporate rules will reinforce the initial patterns of ownership structure. For example, once a country has rules that favor professional managers and protect diffused ownership structures, these managers will have more political power and this power will in turn increase the likelihood that the country would continue to have such rules. Similarly, once a country has legal rules that enhance the private benefits to controlling shareholders and thus encourage the presence of such controllers, the controllers' political power will also increase the likelihood that the country would continue to have such rules.

To be sure, to the extent that a country has a suboptimal legal system due to interest group politics, this suboptimality might give incentives to those who set up companies to opt out of the country's legal system through appropriate charter provisions or foreign incorporation or foreign listing. In a Coasian world, such mechanisms could lead to all companies being governed by the same efficient arrangements. As we explain, however, in an imperfectly Coasian world, these mechanisms are imperfect and cannot be expected to rigorously produce such a convergence.

The focus of the analysis in sections II and III is *not* on the possibility that corporate structures and corporate rules might be *inefficient* – but rather on the possibility that those structures and rules might be *path dependent*. Our analysis of path dependence differs from an analysis of possible inefficiencies in two ways. First, corporate structures and corporate rules can be both path dependent *and* efficient at the same time because, as we show, the identity of the efficient corporate structure or corporate rule might depend on a country's original ownership patterns. Second, although another part of the analysis does concern the possibility that inefficient corporate structures or rules might arise, the focus of this part of the analysis is not on the possibility of inefficiency but on the role played by path dependence. Someone might accept that interest group politics can produce inefficient corporate rules but still expect roughly the same type of inefficient rules. For this reason, our analysis focuses not on the possibility that inefficient rules might arise but rather on showing why they would be likely to arise in different ways and to a different extent in different countries, depending on the countries' initial conditions. For example, in our analysis of interest group politics, we focus on explaining why the inefficient legal rules resulting from interest group politics might vary among countries due to the initial patterns of corporate ownership structures.

In sections II and III, we will pay close attention to the forces created by increasing globalization. In both sections, we will explain why the pressures exerted by global product and capital markets cannot be expected to fully eliminate path dependence.

While we focus on path dependence, we also discuss in section IV other reasons, not rooted in path dependence, why corporate structures might vary among countries and continue to do so over time. Path dependence focuses on reasons why countries that are otherwise similar in all other aspects of their economy might still differ in their corporate structures. However, the advanced economies might still continue to differ in some relevant aspects. Differences in the nature of firms and markets, and in opinions, culture, ideology, and political orientation might have all impeded, and might well continue to impede, convergence of corporate structures.

Path dependence, then, can play an important role in the development of corporate ownership and governance structures around the world. The sources of path dependence that we identify can explain why (despite the powerful forces pressing toward convergence in an increasingly competitive and global marketplace) the advanced economies still differ in important ways in their patterns of corporate ownership and governance. The path dependence that we identify also indicates that some important differences might persist.

I. Explaining persistent differences

In this section, we describe our inquiry, define our terms, describe the competitive forces that could be seen as whittling away structural differences, and present the problem on which we focus: why have different corporate structures persisted when so many other economic differences have not? We then identify two sources of path dependence that can help to answer this question.

A.   The focus of our inquiry

We focus on how countries differ in the structure of ownership and governance of their corporations – that is, how firms are owned and how authority is distributed among owners, the board of directors, senior managers, and employees. At present, publicly traded companies in the United States and the United Kingdom commonly have dispersed ownership, whereas publicly traded companies in other advanced economies commonly have a controlling shareholder. Indeed, while most large American companies have diffuse ownership, 85 percent of the largest German firms persist in having a large shareholder (usually family, sometimes financial) holding 25 percent or more of the firm's voting stock.[1] And while some observers believe that some "functional" corporate convergence has taken place,[2] there can be little doubt that, given the significance

---

[1] Franks & Mayer, "Ownership and Control of German Corporations," 14 *Rev. Fin. Stud.* 943 (2001) (finding in a sample of 171 German firms that single owners held 25 percent or more of voting stock in 85 percent of these companies).

[2] See, e.g., Steven N. Kaplan, "Top Executives, Turnover, and Firm Performance in Germany," 10 *J.L. Econ. & Org.* 142, 144 (1994) (finding analogous tendencies influencing turnover of board members in Japan, Germany, and the United States); Steven N. Kaplan & Bernadette

of controlling shareholders, countries that differ in their incidence of controlling shareholders have corporate structures that differ from each other substantially. These differences persist today despite the convergence of other economic institutions.

We will also look at employee involvement in firms' power structures. This is again an important dimension of current international differences. Labor is involved in the control of German corporations through codetermination, but does not have such direct, formal influence in corporations of other economies.

Our focus will be on path-dependent bases for divergence. By path-dependent bases, we mean reasons arising from the different initial conditions with which countries started. Take two countries and assume that, while different in their initial corporate structures and legal rules, the two became identical some time ago in terms of their economies, politics, types of firms, cultures, norms, and ideologies. Could differences in corporate structures still persist? They could to the extent that a country's corporate structures and rules depend, as we will argue, on the country's initial corporate structures and rules.

Given our interest in path dependence, we will focus on the corporate structures and rules prevailing in the world's advanced economies. When two countries are at sharply differing levels of economic development, there would clearly be reasons other than path dependence for their ownership patterns to differ. We focus therefore on the advanced economies because their similar stage of economic development enables us to concentrate on path dependence.

B.   The persistence of corporate differences

Globalization and the drive toward efficient structures

It might be thought that the advanced economies should by now display similar patterns of corporate structure. Companies in these countries

---

A. Minton, "Appointments of Outsiders to Japanese Boards: Determinants and Implications for Managers," 36 J. Fin. Econ. 225, 256–57 (1994) (suggesting that corporate governance in Japan plays essentially the same role as takeovers and proxy fights in the United States); Elisabeth Roman, "Une nouvelle génération s'installe à la tête du capitalisme familial italien" [A New Generation Sets up at the Head of Italian Capitalism], Le Monde, May 15, 1998, at 16 (discussing how the new generation of Italian executives are increasingly following American business models); Greg Steinmetz, "Changing Values: Satisfying Shareholders is a Hot New Concept at Some German Firms," Wall St. J., Mar. 6, 1996, available in 1996 WL-WSJ 3097228 (discussing a growing solicitude for shareholders by German executives).

face similar governance problems. All large-scale firms share some key common functions: capital must be gathered, management must be selected and disciplined, and information must be transmitted to core decisionmakers.

Organizational imperatives could demand organizational similarities. And other powerful forces, it might be argued, drive countries and firms to adopt the most efficient corporate rules and structures. Not to do so in our competitive global village runs the risk that firms and the economy will fall behind. A firm that did not adopt the best structure would be hurt either in its profits and value or in its ability to raise new capital. Countries that fail to adopt efficient rules would inflict costs on their corporations, which would then be worth less and would then be less able to raise capital; as a result, firms, factories, and businesses might suffer, or they might migrate away from the country.[3]

Another way of stating the above view is that, as efficient new technologies can spread rapidly, one might expect (by analogy) that new corporate technologies, if better, should spread rapidly. Corporate governance could be seen as a technology – similar to a manufacturing technique, an inventory management system, or an engineering economy of scale – and firms face powerful incentives to adopt the best corporate technologies possible:

> The corporation and its securities are products in financial markets *to as great an extent* as the sewing machines or other things the firm makes. Just as the founders of a firm have incentives to make the kinds of sewing machines people want to buy, they have incentives to create the kind of firm, governance structure, and securities the customers in capital markets want.[4]

The adoption of the same efficient corporate governance technologies across the advanced economies might be facilitated, on the view under consideration, by the easy flow of information about corporate technologies. Cross-border investors and multinationals bring with them

---

[3] See Frank H. Easterbrook & Daniel R. Fischel, *The Economic Structure of Corporate Law*, pp. 212–18 (1991) (arguing that competition induces convergence in state rules); Roberta S. Karmel, "Is it Time for a Federal Corporation Law?," 57 *Brook. L. Rev.* 55, 90 (1991) ("Despite these historical differences in corporate governance practice in the United Kingdom and continental countries, the laws will soon become more congruent"); cf. Harold Demsetz, "The Structure of Ownership and the Theory of the Firm," 26 *J.L. and Econ.* 375, 375–77 (1983) (arguing that there is an ineluctable pressure on corporate structures toward efficiency).
[4] Easterbrook & Fischel, note 3 above, at pp. 4–5 (emphasis added).

familiarity with foreign practices.[5] National reports regularly consider practices seen elsewhere and identify them as beneficial.[6]

Persistence

Given these pressures to whittle down corporate differences, the question arises as to why corporate ownership and governance structures have continued to differ.

To be sure, it is possible to point out movements that are reducing certain differences – e.g., the efforts to encourage wider stock ownership in Europe,[7] German banks' statements that they will sell off their stock-holdings,[8] the takeover headlines in Europe,[9] and the rising influence of American institutional investors in the United States (with the possibility that they will acquire the influence sometimes had by financial institutions in continental Europe and Japan).[10] But these stories are balanced by considerable persistence.

For example, German banks, despite their rhetoric of withdrawal from stock ownership, have thus far held on to much of their stock. In fact, during the 1990s, Germany's banks *increased* the number of influential blocks they own in the one hundred largest German firms from forty

---

[5] In the late 1990s, this cross-border investment force tended to make corporate governance converge more towards American patterns than otherwise, because the international investors most active so far in pushing corporate governance initiatives have been Americans.

[6] See generally Corporate Governance Forum of Japan, "Corporate Governance Principles: A Japanese View" (Interim Report) (1997); Competitiveness Policy Council, Reports of the Subcouncils (1993); Peter Mülbert, *Empfehlen sich gesetzliche Regelungen zur Einschränkung des Einflusses der Kreditinstitute auf Aktiengesellschaften?* [Are Rules Limiting Bank Influence Desirable?] (1996); Organization for Economic Cooperation and Development, *Business Sector Advisory Group on Corporate Governance, Institutional Modernisation for Effective and Adaptive Corporate Governance: Challenges and Responses* (1997) (seeking basic worldwide principles of corporate governance); Michael E. Porter, "Capital Disadvantage: America's Failing Capital Investment System," *Harv. Bus. Rev.*, Sept.–Oct. 1992, at 65–82.

[7] See Jeffrey N. Gordon, "Pathways to Corporate Convergence? Two Steps on the Road to Shareholder Capitalism in Germany," 5 *Colum. J. Eur. L.* 219, 220 (1999).

[8] See, e.g., Brian Coleman & Dagmar Aalund, "Deutsche Bank to Cash out of Industrial Stakes," *Wall St. J.*, Dec. 16, 1998, at A17 *m.*

[9] See, e.g., Sophie Fay & Pascale Santi, "L'Offensive de la BNP plonge le monde bancaire dans la confusion" [BNP's offensive plunges the banking world into confusion], *Le Monde*, Mar. 12, 1999, at 23.

[10] See Mark J. Roe, *Strong Managers, Weak Owners: The Political Roots of American Corporate Finance*, pp. 223–24 (1994) (hereafter Roe, *Strong Managers*).

to over fifty.[11] Thus, while German banks seem to have failed at their monitoring job in publicized cases, and while they have regularly been the target of populist sentiment, their considerable stock ownership has thus far persisted. Similarly, concentrated family ownership of Germany's largest firms persists.[12]

With respect to Japan, given the breakdown of the Japanese banking system, and the widespread recognition of the problems of Japanese corporate governance, one might have expected to observe a decline in banks' ownership of large corporate blocks in Japan. Yet, the ownership data for the largest Japanese firms indicate at most only slow movement in bank and insurer ownership in the largest firms over the past three decades.[13]

In any event, it does not matter for our purposes whether the overall variance among countries in ownership structures has been recently narrowing somewhat, remaining the same, or increasing – a question which the data is insufficient to resolve.[14] What is clear is that, notwithstanding the forces of globalization and efficiency, some key differences in corporate structures among countries have persisted. This observation raises important questions for researchers: why have such differences persisted? And will they persist in the future?

C.   Sources of path dependence

Our focus will be on the role that path dependence plays in maintaining differences in corporate structures. There are two sources of path dependence. One type of path dependence, which we will analyze in section II, is structure driven. By structure-driven path dependence, we mean the ways in which initial ownership structures in an economy directly influence subsequent ownership structures.[15] As we shall see, there are two

---

[11] Compare *Hauptgutachten der Monopolkommission, Marktöffnung umfassend verwirklichen* [To Comprehensively Implement the Opening of the Market] 187–92 (1996/1997) (over fifty 5 percent or 5 percent + financial institutional blocks in 1996), with *Hauptgutachten der Monopolkommission, Wettbewerbspolitik oder Industriepolitik* [Competition Policy or Industrial Policy], pp. 205–12 (1990/1991) (about forty 5 percent or 5 percent + institutional blocks in 1990).

[12] See Franks and Mayer, "Ownership and Control," note 1 above, at p. 25.

[13] See generally Michael S. Gibson, " 'Big Bang' Deregulation and Japanese Corporate Governance: A Survey of the Issues," Federal Reserve Int'l Fin. Discussion Paper no. 624 (1998) (concluding that reforms of financial institutions in Japan have thus far had a limited effect on corporate governance).

[14] See Roe, *Strong Managers*, at pp. 26–49.

[15] Ibid., pp. 167–97.

ways through which an economy's ownership structures might depend on its initial pattern of corporate ownership structures.

The other type of path dependence arises from corporate rules.[16] Such rules can influence corporate ownership and governance structures. Given how important corporate rules are, substantial differences in such rules among countries might be sufficient to produce substantial differences in ownership patterns. In section III we focus on rule-driven path dependence.[17] But first we focus on an equally sufficient source of path dependence: structure-driven path dependence.

II.   Structure-driven path dependence

We begin our analysis of path dependence by analyzing structure-driven path dependence. We want to begin by focusing on the "direct" effect that the corporate structures in an economy at an earlier point in time have on structures at later points. Specifically, we show how an economy's ownership structures at any time depend in part on the pattern of ownership structures that the economy had at earlier points in time.[18]

Consider two advanced economies, A and B, which have at time T_1 the same given set of legal rules and economic conditions but had earlier, at T_0, different patterns of corporate ownership structures. Suppose, concretely, that at T_0, companies in A commonly had a controlling shareholder and companies in B commonly had diffuse ownership. These structural differences at T_0 might have been due to the countries' having different legal rules earlier or initially different economic conditions. While the two countries have reached T_1 through different paths, at T_1 they have the same corporate rules and economic conditions. Would these identical rules and conditions at T_1 imply that the countries will also be the same

---

[16] See generally Lucian Arye Bebchuk, "A Rent-Protection Theory of Corporate Ownership and Control," National Bureau of Econ. Research (NBER) Working Paper no. 7203 (1999) [hereafter Bebchuk, "Rent-Protection Theory"] (analyzing how rent-protection considerations affect the choice of ownership structure at the IPO stage); Lucian Arye Bebchuk, "Rent-Protection and the Evolution of a Firm's Ownership Structure" (July 1999) (working paper) [hereinafter Bebchuk, "Rent-Protection and Evolution of Ownership Structures"] (analyzing how rent-protection considerations influence choices of ownership structure after a firm goes public).

[17] See Mark J. Roe, *Political Determinants of Corporate Governance* 159 (2003) (rule convergence necessary but not sufficient for structural convergence).

[18] See Yasu Izumikawa, "Amidst Calls for Corporate Governance Reform, Nissan Questions Role of Non-executive Directors," *IRRC Corp. Governance Bull.*, July–Sept. 1997, at 21 (noting the Japanese view that nonexecutives contribute little to corporate governance).

from T_1 on in terms of corporate structures? The answer is no. We will show next, in section II.A, how the initial pattern of ownership at T_0 might affect the identity of the efficient structure for a given company at T_1. We will then explain in section II.B how internal rent-seeking behavior might also provide existing corporate structures with some persistence power.[19]

A.   Path dependence of the efficient structure

The first reason for structure-driven path dependence is grounded in efficiency. The identity of the efficient structure for a given company at T_1 might depend on the earlier ownership patterns at T_0 and might thus differ between A and B. This difference might be due to sunk adaptive costs, complementarities, network externalities, endowment effects, or multiple optima. We briefly explain each of these reasons.

Sunk adaptive costs

Sunk costs can influence the efficient choice of a corporate ownership structure. Consider the analogous situation in which maintaining an existing factory might be efficient even if a different factory would be more efficient to build were it built from scratch: once costs are sunk in equipment with no good alternative use, continuance often is efficient. In a similar way, sunk costs can be important for determining which corporate ownership structure might be efficient at a given point. For example, in a country in which diffuse ownership was common at T_0, firms might have adapted by developing incentive compensation schemes for managers, by adding more independent directors, and by creating a debt structure that reduces agency costs.[20] Once such different adaptations take place at T_0 in countries A and B (due to their different ownership structures at

---

[19] See Roe, *Strong Managers*, at pp. 275–76.

[20] Firms develop routines that give them a competitive advantage by lowering internal transaction costs. These embedded routines make a firm well adapted to its environment, but if the environment changes radically, the firm cannot easily unlearn its routines. It withers but does not adapt, and a new firm arises with new but better-adapted routines. To the extent that this inability to unlearn embedded routines is true and applies to governance routines, adaptation is slow. See Rebecca M. Henderson & Kim B. Clark, "Architectural Innovation: The Reconfiguration of Existing Product Technologies and the Failure of Established Firms," 35 *Admin. Sci. Q.* 9, 9–10 (1990); cf. Cristiano Antonelli, "The Economics of Path-Dependence in Industrial Organization," 15 *Int'l J. Indus. Org.* 643, 644 (1997). To the extent that this potential rigidity of hardwiring is a problem, better governance will be more flexible governance.

T_0), these adaptations might make the efficient ownership structure for a given company at T_1 different in A and in B.[21]

Complementarities

Complementarities are similar to sunk adaptive costs, but they concern adaptations not by the firm whose ownership structure is under consideration but rather by other entities and institutions. Institutions, practices, and professional communities often develop in every country to facilitate the working of the nation's corporate structures. The corporate ownership structures that a country had earlier at T_0 determined what accompanying institutions, practices, and skills were developed. And these aspects of the corporate environment might in turn influence what structures would be efficient later at T_1.

Suppose that diffuse ownership structures perform better in the presence of an active takeover market and transparent accounting, and that the development of such a takeover market and transparent accounting requires investments by firms and players to acquire the needed techniques and machinery. Whether a country had such activities developing at T_0 would depend on what corporate structures it had back then at T_0. In our example, such a market might have developed in country B in which diffuse ownership was common but not in country A in which diffuse ownership was rare. This implies that, for some firms, diffuse ownership might be efficient at T_1 if they are in B but not if they are in A.

Network externalities

Network externalities may also induce persistence. The efficient ownership structure for a given company might depend on the structures that other firms in the country have. There is an advantage to using the dominant form in the economy and the one with which players are most

---

[21] For American sunk adaptive costs, see Mark J. Roe, "Chaos and Evolution in Law and Economics," 109 *Harv. L. Rev.* 641, 644–45 (1996). One foreign illustration: German firms probably adapted to codetermination by tending not to charge up their boardrooms, probably because neither managers nor shareholders were happy about enhancing labor's voice in the codetermined boardroom. (German labor must get half of the supervisory board's seats in the large firm.) They have used alternative governance structures to in-the-boardroom governance: informal meetings between the management board and shareholders who own big blocks of stock. See Katharina Pistor, "Co-determination in Germany: A Socio-political Model with Governance Externalities," in *Corporate Governance Today*, 387 (Columbia Law School/Sloan Foundation Project on Corporate Governance, 1998); Mark J. Roe, "German Securities Markets and German Codetermination," 98 *Colum. Bus. L. Rev.* 167, 168 (1998) [hereinafter Roe, "German Codetermination"]. Once the fit with codetermination was in place, the players may not have wanted to change ownership and governance.

familiar. Thus, diffuse ownership may be less costly for a firm if other firms are diffusely owned. This consideration might make it efficient for a firm to choose a controlling shareholder structure if other firms in the economy commonly have such a structure – and choose a diffuse owner-ship structure if the other firms in the economy commonly have such a structure.

Endowment effects

Endowment effects might also affect the identity of the efficient ownership structure. Players having control under an existing structure might affect their valuation of having such control, which would in turn affect the total value that alternative structures would produce.[22]

To speculate, such an endowment effect might make it harder to transform both firms governed by European-style concentrated family owners and those governed by American-style managers. European family owners, being in control, might value their control highly. Similarly, American managers, already asset rich, might highly value their posi-tion and power. In either case, asking and offer prices might differ. Given the existing control structures, the value that these two groups attach to control is higher than what they would be willing to pay for it if they did not have it. In the presence of such an endowment effect, the overall efficiency of such control structures depends on whether they existed initially.

Multiple optima

Ownership structures affect corporate governance and corporate value in many complex ways. Thus, two alternative structures could each have pros and cons compared with the other, and they could thus produce roughly equal corporate value overall. Suppose that, under the corporate rules that countries A and B have at T_1, concentrated ownership and diffuse owner-ship have largely offsetting pros and cons and thus that they are (roughly) equally efficient. Given that moving from one structure to another would involve transaction costs, maintaining the status quo might be efficient in each country. In this case, the initial pattern of corporate ownership in each of the economies can determine the subsequent pattern.

* * *

---

[22] To speculate on another possible endowment effect, it might be the case that German labor's valuation of codetermination depends on the existing conditions. That is, it might be that German labor would demand more to give up codetermination than it would be willing to pay to get it in the first place. This implies that the overall efficiency of codetermination for a given German firm depends on whether or not it already has codetermination.

Hence, sunk adaptive costs, complementarities, network externalities, endowment effects, and multiple optima might all lead the identity of the efficient ownership structure for companies at T_1 to depend on the initial structure that the company and/or other companies in the economy had at T_0. And this provides some reasons why the initial differences between countries A and B at T_0 might persist later on at T_1.

B.   Persistence of existing structures due to rent-seeking

We now turn to the rent-seeking reasons for why structures that existed at T_0 might have persistence power at T_1. Due to structural rent-seeking, structures in place might be maintained even if they are no longer efficient at T_1. Those parties that participate in control under an existing structure might have both the incentive and power to impede changes in the structure. Changing an ownership structure often requires the cooperation of those parties that control the firm. And the fact that a change in the ownership structure would be efficient would not ensure that controlling parties would always want it to occur. The controlling parties might prevent a change if it would reduce their private benefits of control so that some of the efficiency gains would be captured not by them but by others. And in such situations, structures in place might persist.[23]

Persistence of concentrated ownership

Suppose that, under the legal rules that countries A and B now have, the efficient structure for a given company Y is diffuse ownership. If company Y had diffuse ownership to begin with at T_0, then clearly it would continue to have diffuse ownership at T_1. But suppose that Y is a company in country A and, like most other companies in country A, it began with a controlling shareholder. Y might not move at T_1 to diffuse ownership. We next explain why.

The controller's roadblock. Suppose that Y has 100 shares, that at T_0 an initial owner had all of the shares, and that at T_0 she sold half of the shares to public investors and retained half of them as a control block. At

---

[23] Cf. Stacey Kole & Kenneth Lehn, "Deregulation, the Evolution of Corporate Governance Structure, and Survival," 87 *Am. Econ. Rev. Papers & Proc.* 421 (1997). Kole and Lehn show that airline deregulation called for new governance structures for the airlines. Deregulation created more managerial complexity, calling for more incentive-based managerial pay, smaller boards, and more concentrated ownership. Incumbent firms adapted slowly, although new entrants entered the market with the superior governance structure in place. Evolution was, *even after twenty years*, incomplete.

T_0, the initial owner had the incentive to choose the ownership structure that would maximize the value of the 100 shares, because at the time of decision, she owned all of the shares and internalized all of the effects of her decision. As such, we can suppose that concentrated ownership was the efficient structure at T_0 given the conditions at the time and was therefore chosen at that time.

By T_1, however, the conditions have changed so that the total value of the company's 100 shares would be higher under diffuse ownership than under concentrated ownership. Suppose that total value at T_1 to all stockholders would be $100 in a concentrated structure – consisting of $60 to the controller ($1.20 per share in the control block) and $40 to the minority shareholders ($0.80 per minority share). And suppose that the total value to stockholders would be $110 under diffuse ownership ($1.10 per share). Would the firm's controlling shareholder elect at T_1 to move to diffuse ownership?

If the initial owner went public at the later time T_1 (rather than earlier at T_0), she would have clearly chosen diffuse ownership as it would produce the highest value. By selling all the shares to dispersed investors, she would have received $110. If she were to use a concentrated structure, then she would have received only $100: $40 for the shares she would have sold to dispersed public investors and $60 for the control block that she would have retained as controller (or, equivalently, $60 from the funds she would get by selling to someone else who would be the controller). Thus, choosing diffuse ownership in an initial public offering (IPO) at T_1 would have maximized the initial owner's proceeds. Owning all 100 shares at T_1, she would have chosen that structure which would have maximized their value, and under the new legal rules in T_1, the value-maximizing structure would have been diffuse ownership, which the initial owner would have chosen. But because the company already went public at T_0, at T_1 it *already has* a concentrated ownership structure. So the question is whether the controller would move the firm toward diffuse ownership, a structure that would increase the firm's total value by $10. It turns out that this "midstream" move to diffuse ownership would not be in the controller's interest.[24]

---

[24] For an analysis of analogous efficient structural changes that will not proceed due to similar roadblocks, see Lucian Arye Bebchuk, "Efficient and Inefficient Sales of Corporate Control," 109 *Q. J. Econ.* 957 (1994) (analyzing how different legal rules governing the transfer of a controlling block might impede an efficient transfer); Mark J. Roe, "The Voting Prohibition in Bond Workouts," 97 *Yale L.J.* 232, 277 (1987) (analyzing similar obstacles for failed bond issues).

Table 2.1 *Division of firm value at T_1 under concentrated ownership*

	Shares owned	Value owned %	Value $
Controllers' block	50	60 of value	1.20 per share
Outsiders' shares	50	40 of value	.80 per share
Total of firm	100	100 of value	100
Total value			60 in controller's block + 40 in minority shares = 100

Table 2.2 *Division of firm value at T_1 under diffuse ownership*

	Shares owned	Value owned %	Value $
Controllers' block	0		
Outsiders' shares	100	100 of value	1.10 per share
Total	100	100 of value	110

Consider the most straightforward route to accomplishing the change: the controller breaking up her control block and selling the shares in her control block to dispersed shareholders. Such a transaction would not benefit the controller. The total value of the firm under diffuse ownership is $110 (or $1.10 per share); thus the controller would receive only $55 from selling her remaining 50 percent of the company's shares. That is, this sale would have provided the controller $5 *less* than the value of $60 that she would have by retaining her controlling block. Hence, she would not have benefited from breaking up her control block. To be sure, the move would raise the value of the shares that are already in the hands of public investors from $40 to $55, but this would not be a benefit that the controller would capture; the controller, of course, would not be able to raise retroactively the price at which the minority shares were sold from $40 to $55. Hence, the controller would not break up her control block at T_1, and concentrated ownership would persist *even though the move to diffuse ownership would increase total value.*

Alternatively, the move to diffuse ownership could take place at T_1 if the controller would sell all the company's assets to an entrepreneur and liquidate the company; the entrepreneur then would have the same incentives as an initial owner at T_1 and those incentives would lead the entrepreneur to take the company public with diffuse ownership. But the most the controller would be able to get from the entrepreneur under this scenario would be $110 for all the assets, and the controller would receive in the subsequent liquidation only $55. This, again, would be less than the $60 in value that maintaining the control block would provide the entrepreneur.

Under both of the considered scenarios, the controller would not benefit from the move to diffuse ownership because the move would eliminate the controller's disproportionate access to the company's value. Under the concentrated structure, the controller would capture 60 percent of the existing $100 pie, but a move to diffuse ownership would provide the controller with only 50 percent of the larger $110 pie. While the pie would grow larger, getting 50 percent of the somewhat larger pie would still be worse than getting 60 percent of the smaller pie under maintained concentrated ownership.

Thus, even though the move to diffuse ownership would increase the firm's total value by $10, the controller would not benefit from it; instead, she would lose $5. Another intuitive way to understand why the controller would not benefit from the move to the more efficient structure is that the move would confer a positive benefit on the existing dispersed shareholders. The existing dispersed shareholders would end up with $55 if the controller moved to diffuse ownership instead of $40. This $15 benefit is one that the controller would not capture and thus would not internalize in her decisionmaking. Therefore, while the move would be efficient, the controller would not be served by it, because the controller would lose her rent (the private benefits of control) and would not fully capture the efficiency gains from the move (some of which would be conferred on the existing public investors).[25]

In sum, whether or not the firm would have concentrated or diffuse ownership at T_1 depends on its initial structure at T_0. If the company were closely held at T_0 and were to go public at T_1, diffuse ownership would be chosen. Similarly, if the firm were to go public with diffuse ownership at T_0, this structure would be maintained at T_1. But if the firm went public with concentrated ownership at T_0, this concentrated ownership would be retained at T_1 and a move to diffuse ownership would not occur.

---

[25] The reason why the controller would not move to diffuse ownership is equivalent to the reason why a controller might not transfer control under an Equal Opportunity Rule even if the control transfer would be efficient. See Bebchuk, note 24 above, at 968–73.

Coasian alternatives? Might there be some other way in which the potential efficiency gain of $10 from the move to diffuse ownership could be realized? Would a gain of $10 be left on the table rather than taken? Couldn't some transaction enable the parties to share the potential $10 gain? In a purely Coasian world, the players would indeed contract to implement the move and to realize and share among them this $10 gain. But in our imperfectly Coasian world, there are impediments to the realization of this $10 gain, and not all such gains will be realized.

In a perfectly Coasian world, the move could take place through the minority shareholders' paying the controller to induce her to move to diffuse ownership. Since the minority shareholders would gain $15 from such a move, and the controller would lose only $5 from such a move, a deal could benefit both sides. The minority could pay the controller some amount between $5 and $15, say $10, in return for the controller's agreeing to move to diffuse ownership. But in our imperfectly Coasian world, collective action problems among the minority shareholders would impede such a transaction. The shareholders would find it hard if not impossible to put together the "bribe" for the controller because of a "free-rider" problem. Each shareholder would know that her nonparticipation would barely affect whether the needed amount could be raised, and thus each would have an incentive to withhold her contribution.

Alternatively, in a perfectly Coasian world, the controller could first buy the existing minority shares for $40, or for some amount between $40 and $50, and *then* move the firm to diffuse ownership and sell all of its shares for $110. As long as the payment to minority shareholders was below $50, the controller would in this way end up with more than the $60 that she would have had under concentrated ownership. But in an imperfectly Coasian world, the controller would find it difficult if not impossible to purchase the minority shares at such a price. Suppose that the controller were to make a tender offer for the minority shares at $.80 per share (or $40 in all). Such a tender offer might well fail due to a free-rider problem. Some public investors would be likely to hold out. A hold-out shareholder would see the value of her share go from $0.80 to $1.10 if the other shareholders tendered and the controller thereafter moved the firm to diffuse ownership. And if all minority shareholders were to hold out for $1.10, the controller would not be able to buy the minority shares at a price that would enable her to make any profit.

The limits of persistence: large inefficiencies. Our argument is not that the move to diffuse ownership at T_1 in the considered situation would fail no matter how large the potential efficiency gains. The move would take place if the potential efficiency gain were sufficiently large. Internal rent-seeking might enable a structure to persist only as long as its relative inefficiency is not too large.

In the situation considered above, if the move would increase total value by more than \$20 – that is, if the value under diffuse ownership would be more than \$120 at T_1 – then the controller would elect to move to diffuse ownership. Suppose that under diffuse ownership the total value of the firm at T_1 would be \$122. In this case, if the controller were to break up her control block and sell her shares to dispersed shareholders, she would receive \$61, and this would give the controller more than the \$60 that she would have had under concentrated ownership. The new pie of \$122 would thus be enough to induce structural transformation. Even though the controller would still receive only 50 percent of this new pie, the new pie would be so large that this 50 percent would have a value larger than the 60 percent of the pie that she would have had under concentrated ownership.

Our point is not that structures in place would persist due to structural rent-seeking no matter what. It is only that there is a wide range of values for which the controller's rent-seeking would block an efficient move to diffuse ownership. In our example, as long as the potential efficiency gains from a move (and thus the efficiency costs from maintaining the existing structure) are between \$0 and \$20, concentrated ownership would be maintained at T_1.

What determines the range within which concentrated ownership would persist even if it is inefficient? As the discussion of our example illustrates, the range depends on the size of the controller's private bene-fits under concentrated ownership; the larger these private benefits, the larger the range in which an existing structure will be maintained even if it ceases to be efficient.[26] As long as these private benefits are significant at T_1, this range of persistence will be significant in size.

The limits of persistence: rent-destroying rules. The persistence of concentrated ownership that might result from rent-seeking would arise only if, under the legal rules at T_1, controllers can enjoy rents in the form of some nonnegligible private benefits of control. Thus, if countries were

---

[26] Algebraically, if the fraction of the shares that are in the control block is k, the value under concentrated ownership is V, and the private benefits of control are B, then the move to diffuse ownership will not take place as long as the value under diffuse ownership does not exceed $V + [k/(1-k)]B$. This condition can be derived in a similar way to the condition in Bebchuk, note 24 above, at 971, for when controllers will block efficient control transfers under the Equal Opportunity Rule.

to adopt a legal regime eliminating such benefits altogether, this source of path dependence would be eliminated.

Suppose that, at T_1, the controller with 50 percent of the shares would capture no private benefits and thus get only $50, which is one-half of the pie under concentrated ownership. In this case, the controller would choose to move to diffuse ownership if and only if the move would increase total value. To the extent changes in rules destroy rents, they destroy the controllers' incentives to resist change. This qualification, however, would be fully relevant only under the unlikely scenario, which has not emerged yet, in which private benefits of control would not exist.

New firms. The above analysis has focused on the persistence of structures in place. What about new assets that come into the economy and are put into corporate structures? Consider an economy populated at T_1 by companies with concentrated ownership, and suppose that there are some resources owned by a sole owner at T_1, and consider the choices that the owner will make for these assets. At this stage, since the sole owner has no partners, considerations of the owner's internal rent-seeking would not affect the choice of structure. However, the considerations identified in section II.A. as to why the efficient structure might be path dependent – such as network externalities and complementarities – might affect the choice. And for reasons identified in section III, external, political rent-seeking may allow incumbents to suppress, or reduce, new entry. Whether for these reasons or for other reasons,[27] we observe that the flow of new assets and firms into the corporate sector has not thus far eliminated divergence.

Persistence of diffuse ownership

Diffuse ownership structures, once in place, might similarly persist due to internal rent-seeking by the incumbents managing such structures. Consider a company Y that, given the legal rules and conditions prevailing in countries A and B at T_1, would produce the highest total value under concentrated ownership. Nonetheless, if the company's initial structure at T_0 was one of diffuse ownership, the firm might not move to concentrated ownership at T_1.

Suppose that Y has 100 shares; that its total value to shareholders at T_1 under diffuse ownership would be $100 or $1.00 per share; that the managers would get control benefits of $3 under such diffuse ownership

---

[27] See Bebchuk, "Rent Protection and Evolution of Ownership Structures," note 16 above, at 18–21.

(from value diversions, prestige, etc.); and that under concentrated owner-ship the firm would produce a total value (to the controller and the minority shareholders combined) of $110 and a buyer is willing to pay this amount for the company in order to move it to concentrated ownership. While the move to concentrated ownership would be efficient, it might not take place.

Notwithstanding that the move to concentrated ownership would increase total value, the existing managers might prefer that it not take place because it would eliminate their private benefits of control. And as long as the managers hold less than 30 percent of the shares, their fraction of the gains from the transformation would not be enough to make up for their loss of private benefits.

The managers might be in a position to block or impede the move. They control the merger agenda and a merger cannot be initiated without their approval. They can also resist a hostile takeover bid. To be sure, if the potential gains from the move were very large, the move might still take place. But if the move would increase total value by only 10 percent, as in our example, and given the problems involved in a hostile bid, the managers might have not only the incentive but also the power to prevent the move. Thus, the desire of managers to keep the rents that they enjoy under the existing structure of diffuse ownership can provide such struc-ture with some persistence power.

Similar qualifications go with this conclusion as with the earlier conclu-sion concerning the possible persistence of concentrated ownership due to controllers' rent-seeking. If the corporate rules at T_1 provide the managers with no private benefits (a theoretical, unrealistic scenario because inde-pendence would always carry some benefits to the managers), then the managers would have no incentive to disfavor moves away from diffuse ownership. And if the legal rules at T_1 give the managers no power with respect to acquisitions, then the managers would not have any power to resist a move.

But as long as: (i) managers derive some benefits from independence, and (ii) managers have some power to resist acquisitions of control, then existing structures of diffuse ownership could have some persistence power. Thus, given that these conditions have been generally present in the past, this persistence might have played a role thus far – say, in main-taining such diffuse ownership structures in the United States – even if a move to concentrated ownership could have increased value. And when-ever these conditions will obtain in the future, this potential source of persistence and path dependence will remain relevant.

Persistence of German codetermination

Labor-preferring structures could persist for similar reasons. The most important example of a country in which labor participates in control is Germany. Germany has legal rules mandating labor participation in the board for all companies that are sufficiently large, and all such companies are thus codetermined. Our analysis suggests that dual-board structures might have some persistence power even if Germany's legal rules change to make such structures optional rather than mandatory.

Suppose that Germany changes its laws to make a dual-board structure optional rather than mandatory. Because dual-board structures are already in place, they might persist even if they are not efficient. If labor leaders (or other players) are getting private benefits from codetermination and if they have power to impede or resist changes in the existing structure,[28] they might resist a move away from codetermination. And as long as a Coasian bribe to labor leaders is illegal or transactionally costly, the move might not occur.

$$* * *$$

We have now examined three principal "pure" types of firms, one with concentrated ownership, one with managerial control, and one with mandated labor influence. Each has a tendency to persist, and this persistence power contributes to structural path dependence.

Persistence in the face of globalization

Thus, due to structural rent-seeking, structures in place could sometimes persist even if they cease to be efficient. A skeptic might question this conclusion, however, by wondering whether market forces in a global economy cannot always force controllers and managers to move to that structure that would be most efficient. But this is not the case.

Our analysis *already* took into account whatever effects might arise from product market and capital market competition. When we said that the firm's value in our examples at T_1 would be \$100 under the existing suboptimal ownership structure and \$110 following a move to a superior ownership structure, this difference of \$10 *already* incorporated all the effects on total value from all potential sources, including product and capital market competition. And we have shown that such a difference in

---

[28] We assume here that the German reform would track the standard American practice, with a firm's governance changes being initiated by the board. But even if shareholders can initiate a repeal of codetermination, the result *might* not differ if shareholders concluded that the shock to labor of throwing them off the board would lead to unrest or demoralization.

total value might be insufficient to induce parties in control to favor the move to the superior structure.

To be sure, globalization would discourage persistence of a suboptimal structure if the difference in total value between the best structure and the suboptimal one is large enough. That is, globalization would end persistence if inefficiencies are *always* so large that they would largely obliterate firms with suboptimal structure, i.e., that there would be no "mere ten percent" inefficiencies. But even with strong global capital and product market competition, not every inefficiency in structure would have such drastic consequences. Even with globalization, an existing structure could have some limited (rather than unbounded) efficiency costs (say, 10 percent of total value as in the examples we used) and thus would have some persistence power.

Product market competition. To examine the above point in more detail, let us consider why product market competition, whether domestic or global, would not always be sufficient to prevent controllers or managers from sticking to an inefficient structure.[29] While maintaining a corporate structure might involve some efficiency costs and reduce shareholder value, it would not necessarily render the company unable to compete in its product market.

While product market competition gives controllers, managers, and labor leaders valuable incentives for efficiency, it cannot always discourage them from maintaining a structure that yields them private benefits but is somewhat inefficient.[30] For one thing, a firm's choice between concentrated ownership and diffuse ownership need not affect the firm's costs or the quality of its products; rather, it might alter how the shareholders, managers, and controllers divide up the value produced by the firm. When a company's ownership structure does not affect product quality or costs, product market competition will not constrain the company's choice of ownership structure.

---

[29] Cf. Frank H. Easterbrook, "Managers' Discretion and Investors' Welfare: Theories and Evidence," 9 *Del. J. Corp. L.* 540, 557 (1984) (arguing that the product market constrains managers and controllers to choose efficient structures and arrangements).

[30] Cf. Lucian Arye Bebchuk, "Federalism and the Corporation: The Desirable Limits on State Competition in Corporate Law," 105 *Harv. L. Rev.* 1435, 1466 (1992) [hereinafter Bebchuk, "Federalism"] (analyzing why product market competition "cannot discourage managers from seeking value-decreasing rules that are significantly redistributive in their favor"); Lucian Arye Bebchuk, "Limiting Contractual Freedom in Corporate Law: The Desirable Constraints on Charter Amendments," 102 *Harv. L. Rev.* 1820, 1845–46 (1989) [hereinafter Bebchuk, "Limiting Contractual Freedom"] (discussing how product market competition cannot discourage managers from seeking value-decreasing charter amendments that are significantly redistributive in their favor).

Even if the choice of ownership structure affects the operational efficiency of a firm, product market competition often constrains the firm and its managers only weakly. Product markets are not always perfectly competitive.[31] Oligopolies can create slack, and managers and controllers can take advantage of it. Because product market competition does not threaten firms' survival in such markets even if the firms forgo some efficiencies, controllers and managers might sacrifice some potential efficiencies for the private benefits that maintaining the existing structure would yield. Some of the oligopolistic slack can be "spent" in inefficient corporate structures.[32]

Global capital markets. The world's ever-more-global capital markets provide firms, it might be argued, with incentives to adopt efficient ownership structures. If a firm maintains an inefficient structure, so the argument goes, the firm would be penalized in the capital markets and would face hurdles in raising new capital.[33] But would globalized capital providers really strike down inefficiently governed firms by refusing to finance the firms' futures?

Global capital markets cannot generally be relied on to press managers to move to the most efficient ownership structure.[34] Many established companies do not use capital markets for funds, but rather finance themselves from retained earnings. When firms do not rely on external finance, their managers and controllers will not be constrained by capital markets. Among companies that do use external finance, some use debt rather than equity, and debt markets might not often constrain a structural choice because the structural choice might have little effect on the likelihood that the company will default on its debt.

Indeed, even for firms that finance themselves by raising equity, the strength of the capital market constraint is uncertain. An inefficient ownership structure might merely mean that the company would have to issue more shares to raise a given amount of capital. This might not seriously discourage professional managers from inefficiently

---

[31] See Jean Tirole, *The Theory of Industrial Organization*, pp. 277–303 (1988) (discussing imperfect competition).

[32] See Roe, "Rents and their Corporate Consequences," 53 *Stan. L. Rev.* 1463 (2001). Roe, "The Shareholder Wealth Maximization Norm and Industrial Organization," 149 *U. Pa. L. Rev.* 2063 (2001).

[33] See Easterbrook, note 29 above, at 557.

[34] Cf. Bebchuk, "Federalism," note 30, at 1465–66 (analyzing how capital market constraints cannot generally constrain managers from seeking some inefficient state law rules that favor them); Bebchuk, "Limiting Contractual Freedom," note 30 above, at 1844–45 (analyzing how capital market constraints cannot generally discourage managers from seeking inefficient charter amendments).

maintaining a diffuse ownership structure (if they own little equity themselves). And while it might somewhat constrain controllers (who would be diluting their own holdings by issuing more shares), even they might elect to maintain the existing structure and absorb such dilution for a time when raising equity if their private benefits of control under the existing structure are large enough. When markets are uncompetitive, slack can be readily spent out of the above-market return potentially available to the firm and its managers, until the return on equity falls to the competitive rate of return.[35] Thus, while there are limits here, inefficient structures might persist in the face of globalized capital markets.

C.   Conclusion on structure-driven path dependence

The ownership structures that an economy has partly depend on the ownership structures that the economy had earlier on. Even if two nations have identical corporate rules and economic conditions at T_1, if their initial structures differed at T_0 (due to earlier differing economic conditions, for example), these differing structures at T_0 could lead to differing structures at T_1. There are two main sources for this structure-driven path dependence. First, the original structures affect which structure will be efficient for any given company: sunk adaptive costs, complementarities, network externalities, endowment effects, and multiple optima might all make the identity of the efficient ownership structure depend on earlier structures. Second, initial structures might persist because players that enjoy rents under them might have both the incentive and power to impede changes in these structures. These two sources of structure-driven path dependence help explain some key differences in ownership structures among the advanced economies that have persisted thus far. This structural path dependence might also lead to important differences among countries' corporate structures in the future.

III.   Rule-driven path dependence

Corporate rules can affect corporate governance. Thus, when two countries' corporate rules differ, this difference by itself might produce differences in their patterns of corporate ownership structures. This raises the questions of why – given that the advanced economies all have an interest in providing their companies with desirable corporate rules – their systems

---

[35] See Roe, "Rents and their Corporate Consequences," note 32 above; Roe, "Shareholder Primacy Norm," ibid.

of corporate rules have differed and whether they will continue to differ in the future.

Corporate rules, we argue, are themselves path dependent. (Recall that by corporate rules, we refer to all the rules that affect the structure of the corporation and its ownership: not just traditional state-made, in the US corporate law, but also securities law, the rules governing financial institutions and their interactions with the firm, some labor laws, and so on.) The rules that an economy has at any given point in time depend on, and reflect, the ownership and governance structures that the economy had initially. This provides another channel through which initial ownership structures can affect subsequent choices of structure: the initial structures affect future corporate rules which in turn affect future decisions on corporate structures.

Consider two economies that have similar economic conditions at T_1. As we explain below, the corporate rules that A and B have at T_1 might depend on the ownership structures that A and B had earlier at T_0. That is, if A and B had different patterns of ownership structure at T_0, their rules at T_1 might well differ as a consequence.

Differences among systems of corporate rules should be assessed not by looking at general principles but rather by examining all aspects of the corporate rules system, including elements of procedure, implementation, and enforcement, as we observe in section III.A. In sections III.B and III.C we identify and analyze two sources for the path dependence of corporate rules. We first show (in section III.B) how the preceding conditions of an economy at T_0 might affect the choice of corporate rules at T_1 even assuming that lawmaking is solely public regarding; this might result because the initial pattern of ownership might affect which legal rules would be efficient. We then show (section III.C) how path dependence might arise when lawmaking is also influenced by interest group politics. In this case, the initial pattern of ownership might influence the relative political strength of various groups of corporate players. Both of these sources of rule-driven path dependence, as we will see, can reinforce existing patterns of ownership. And they both might help explain why, even though the advanced economies have converged along many economic dimensions, their systems of corporate rules differ in many ways.

A.   Systems of corporate rules

We first should clarify what we mean by saying that two countries have different corporate rules or different systems of corporate rules. General principles of corporate law may often be the same across countries,[36] but more is at stake. Thus, all advanced countries may recognize and accept a certain fiduciary *principle*, but countries *A* and *B* might implement it radically differently.[37] Principles are important, but "the devil is in the details," and implementation counts a great deal. Two countries may be hostile to self-dealing in *principle*, but their overall legal treatment of self-dealing might differ greatly because of differences in the procedures that corporations must follow in approving a self-dealing transaction, in the nature and timing of the disclosures that the firm or the controller must make, in the efficacy of regulatory agencies like the SEC, in the incentives that public investors or plaintiffs' lawyers have to sue, in the procedures that such suits have to follow, in the standards of scrutiny that courts use, in the level of deference that courts give to the insiders' judgments, in the extent to which an effective discovery process is available, and in the ways in which evidence will be brought and considered.

What counts are all elements of a corporate legal system that bear on corporate decisions and the distribution of value: not just general principles, but also all the particular rules implementing them; not just substantive rules, but also procedural rules, judicial practices, institutional and procedural infrastructure, and regulators' enforcement capabilities. Because our concern is with the corporate rules system "in action" rather than "on the books," all these elements are quite important.

Finally, in assessing the scope of the corporate rules system, recall that by corporate rules we mean throughout all the rules that govern the relations between the corporation and all of its investors, stakeholders, and managers, as well as among these players. Thus, for the purposes of our analysis, the corporate rules system includes not only the rules of corporate law as conventionally defined but also securities law and the relevant parts of the law governing insolvency, labor relations, and financial institutions.

B. Path dependence of the efficient rules

Suppose that lawmakers in a given country are completely public regarding. Even so, rules might be path dependent because the identity of the locally efficient legal rule – the rule efficient for a given

---

[36] See Henry Hansmann & Reinier Kraakman, Chapter 1 this volume (noting that the basic formal law of corporate governance has achieved a high degree of uniformity across Europe, America, and Japan).

[37] Cf. Gérard Hertig, Chapter 10 this volume (describing variance in the quality of enforcement).

country – might depend on the rules and structures that the country had at earlier times.

Sunk costs and complementarities

Sunk costs and complementarities can induce efficient persistence. Different sets of rules might be more suitable for different types of companies. Public-regarding public officials might choose at T_1 those rules that are best taking into account the structures and rules that were in place at T_0.[38]

Existing legal rules might have an efficiency advantage because institutions and structures might have already developed to address needs and problems arising under these rules. In such a case, replacing the existing rules might make the existing institutional and professional infrastructure obsolete or ill-fitting and require new investments. Various players – managers, owners, lawyers, accountants, and so forth – might have invested in human capital and modes of operation that fit the existing corporate rules. Replacing these rules would require these players to make new investments and to adapt to the new rules. Thus, which rules might be efficient for a country at T_1 might depend on which rules it had at T_0 and what institutions and practices developed in reaction to these rules. Note that this factor would often reinforce existing rules and, in turn, existing ownership structures.

Multiple optima

The path dependence of the rules that would be efficient for a given economy might also result from multiple optima. Suppose that technologically identical firms exist at T_1 in countries A and B. Suppose that, at T_0, A's corporate rules favored concentrated ownership and A's firms commonly had concentrated ownership. And suppose that B's rules at T_0

---

[38] Why wouldn't each country adopt two separate bodies of corporate rules, one for companies with concentrated ownership and one for companies with dispersed ownership? Although different governing rules are possible, countries generally have one body of corporate rules, presumably because of the economies of scale involved in having one body of law and the problems resulting from: (1) the need to decide which body of rules to apply; and (2) players' trying to manipulate their classifications. Those familiar with the history of American corporate bankruptcy might recall the unsuccessful experience of the Chandler Act, in force in the United States from 1938 to 1978. The Chandler Act provided one set of rules for public companies (Chapter X), another for privately held firms (Chapter XI). However, in the later stages of the Act's history, public firms tried, often successfully, to use the set of rules intended for nonpublic firms. In 1978, Congress felt compelled to *abandon* the two separate systems. See Report of the Commission on Bankruptcy Laws of the United States – Part I, at 246–47 (1973).

favored diffuse ownership and its firms commonly had such a structure. Suppose that, while the types of inefficiencies prevailing in A and B might well differ, both A's rules and B's rules (and in turn A's structures and B's structures) have aggregate costs of similar magnitudes. In this case, even assuming that public officials are completely public regarding in both A and B, neither set of officials would see a reason to switch (and, given the costs that would be involved in making changes, would thus see a reason *not* to switch) to the other country's rules.

C. Path dependence of the rules that are actually chosen

Law is of course not always made by public-regarding officials uninfluenced by interest groups. Interest groups might influence the choice of legal rules, which might sometimes lead to inefficient rules being chosen or maintained. The dynamics of interest group politics depends on the existing pattern of corporate ownership. This introduces another source for the path dependence of legal rules, which we next examine.[39]

Initial conditions and the political economy of corporate rules

Legal rules are often the product of political processes, which combine public-regarding features with interest group politics. To the extent that interest groups play a role, each interest group will push for rules that favor it. Thus, the corporate rules that actually will be chosen and maintained might depend on the relative strength of the relevant interest groups.

Interest groups differ in their ability to mobilize and then exert pressure in favor of legal rules that favor them or against rules that disfavor them. The more resources and power a group has, the more influence the group will tend to have in the political process. This is the reason why interest group politics might be influenced by the existing distribution of wealth and power.[40] In particular, the existing corporate ownership structures will affect the resources (and hence political influence) that various players

---

[39] In addition, underlying political differences, see Roe, *Political Determinants*, note 17 above, provide another source of current difference. Moreover, feedback from earlier differing politics that created differing structures, which in turn support continued political differences, can be a related source of path dependence.

[40] See generally Maxim Boycko, Andrei Shleifer, & Robert Vishny, *Privatizing Russia* (1995) (discussing the effects of the initial distribution of property rights emerging out of privatization on the subsequent interest group politics); Jonathan R. Hay, Andrei Shleifer, & Robert W. Vishny, "Toward a Theory of Legal Reform," 40 *Eur. Econ. Rev.* 559 (1996) (arguing that legal rules should accommodate rather than interfere with existing business practice).

will have and thus the rules that will be chosen. Hence, corporate rules at each point in time will depend on the economy's existing corporate structures at earlier points in time.

This path dependence will often induce bodies of corporate rules to differ among countries. When a certain set of rules leads corporate control to be at the hands of one group of players, their control of existing structures will make these players more influential in subsequent interest group politics and will thus make it more likely that the country will have these or similar rules in the future. Their power within corporations will translate into power in the political process and influence on corporate rules.

Rules affecting concentrated and diffuse ownership structures

The legal rules favoring concentration or dispersion of corporate ownership affect corporate players, and these players might be influential interest groups. The power of controlling shareholders and of professional managers – and how influential they will be in corporate law politics – clearly depends on the existing ownership structures. Thus, the likelihood that rules favored by these groups will be chosen or maintained at any point in time will depend on the power that these groups have under the existing pattern of ownership structures.

Consider antitakeover rules that discourage the hostile acquisition of a company with a diffuse ownership structure. In the United States, there is an arsenal of such laws, both statutory and judge made.[41] Such rules encourage diffuse ownership and are beneficial to the professional managers of such companies. Now, a country that has had mostly diffuse ownership to begin with would have more interest group support for such rules than one without diffuse ownership to begin with. Professional managers benefit from such rules,[42] and they can use corporate resources to lobby lawmakers.[43] And professional managers are clearly a much more powerful group in a country with diffuse ownership (such as the United States) than in one with concentrated ownership (such as

---

[41] See generally Ronald Gilson, & Bernard Black, *The Law and Finance of Corporate Acquisitions* (2nd edn, 1995) (surveying the legal rules governing takeovers).

[42] Controlling shareholders are less interested in antitakeover rules, because a controlling shareholder with enough shares can stop a hostile takeover by itself, without any help from antitakeover rules.

[43] See generally C. Edwin Baker, "Realizing Self-Realization: Corporate Political Expenditures and Redish's *The Value of Free Speech*," 130 *U. Pa. L. Rev.* 646 (1982) (exploring the market forces that dictate the content of commercial speech); Victor Brudney, "Business Corporations and Stockholders' Rights under the First Amendment," 91 *Yale L.J.* 235 (1981) (discussing the First Amendment contours of corporate speech).

Germany). Thus, a country that has more companies with diffuse ownership to begin with also would be more likely to have gone down the road toward antitakeover rules – rules that might reinforce the tendency toward diffuse ownership structures.[44]

Another example of rules that are more likely to be adopted or maintained in a country with diffuse ownership are rules discouraging financial institutions from actively acquiring and using large blocks of stock.[45] Professional managers of companies with diffuse ownership favor such rules and have lobbied for them in the United States. The more powerful such managers are at any point in time, the more likely such rules will be adopted or maintained. Thus, a country that has diffuse ownership at T_0 (with or without such rules) is more likely to have such rules adopted or maintained at T_1 – and such rules will make it more likely that the initial incidence of diffuse ownership will be maintained or even increased at T_1.

Let us now turn to legal rules that are more likely to arise when ownership is concentrated and to further reinforce the prevalence of concentrated ownership. Rules that enable controllers to extract large private benefits of control are beneficial to controllers of existing publicly traded companies. In a country in which ownership is largely concentrated at T_0 (with or without such rules), controlling shareholders of existing companies will be a powerful interest group with substantial resources. The influence of this group will make it more likely that this country will have or maintain such rules at T_1.[46] And because such rules encourage the use

---

[44] For analyses of how American managers have obtained a body of takeover law that increasingly makes hostile takeovers difficult, see Lucian Arye Bebchuk & Allen Ferrell, "Federalism and Takeover Law," 99 *Colum. L. Rev.* 1168 (1999); Mark J. Roe, "Takeover Politics," in Margaret Blair, ed., *The Deal Decade*, p. 321 (1993).

[45] Such rules, which exist in the United States but not to the same extent in other advanced economies, discourage institutional ownership and thereby increase dispersed ownership. Attempts to reform many antiquated American financial rules have proved difficult and have proceeded slowly. See Roe, *Strong Managers*, note 10 above, at pp. 100, 229.

[46] Changes in corporate law generally apply to both existing and future companies. This feature tends to make existing rules persist. If it were otherwise, controlling shareholders might be indifferent to rules that would prevent *future and new* controlling shareholders from diverting value, as long as they, the incumbent controllers, were governed by the old rules that enable them to divert. See David Charny, Chapter 8 this volume. But this dichotomy would be hard to argue for convincingly, hard to enact and hard to enforce. Interest groups usually must present principled positions, then push for what they term a principled view. For a discussion of how the presence of controlling shareholders might impede corporate reforms aimed at reducing private benefits of control, see generally Bebchuk, "Rent-Protection and Evolution of Ownership Structures," note 16 above, at 25–26.

or retention of concentrated ownership,[47] the presence of such rules at T_1 will in turn help maintain or even strengthen the initial dominance of concentrated ownership.

Thus, control over corporate resources also provides political power. Those who have or share corporate control – be they controlling shareholders, professional managers, or other players – are likely to have influence because of the resources that they command. These resources will enable them to lobby, make campaign contributions, and otherwise gain political influence. These resources also provide them with visibility, access to media, high social status, and access to elite and influential groups, all of which can be helpful in influencing the corporate rules system.

The fact that those in control of corporations can push to retain or expand legal rules that favor them might move path dependence, as we have seen, in a direction reinforcing existing ownership patterns. This might occur when professional managers in diffuse ownership countries support antitakeover rules or rules discouraging financial institutions from holding blocks, and when controlling shareholders in concentrated ownership countries support rules that yield them large private benefits of control. Such an analysis might apply as well to rules establishing labor-preferring structures, such as German codetermination.[48]

Globalization and the pressure to adopt efficient rules

A possible objection to the above analysis is again one based on globalization. Increasing globalization should discourage countries from ever adopting inefficient corporate rules, so the argument goes, because the economies of those countries that do so would suffer.

Globalization, however, has not thus far had this effect, which is indeed far from surprising to us. Countries can preserve inefficient rules and can do so for long periods of time. There is in fact no mechanism that ensures that political processes will only produce and retain efficient arrangements.[49]

---

[47] See generally Bebchuk, "Rent-Protection Theory"; Bebchuk, "Rent Protection and Evolution of Ownership Structures," note 16 above.

[48] Once codetermination is in place, labor leaders have more power. And to the extent that these leaders benefit from codetermination, their greater power in the system's initial conditions will increase the chances that codetermination will persist. Employees may also have resisted changes and have had the votes to succeed. See generally Pistor, "Co-determination", note 21 above, at p. 163 (showing resistance to changing German codetermination).

[49] See Mancur Olson, *The Rise and Decline of Nations: Economic Growth, Stagflation, and Social Rigidities*, pp. 17–35 (1982) (arguing that established groups impede change).

Suppose that a country's legal rules favor an outmoded governance system. Must the rules or its constituent firms have collapsed under the threat of heightened international competition? Is it unstable? The answer is no. What counts is whether the firms produce competitive products that can be sold. The firm can compete, even with an outmoded governance structure, if it makes up for this governance disadvantage with an offsetting *international* competitive advantage. If the firm can pay for an immobile input at a lower price than firms in other countries can, it can readily survive. Or, the country might subsidize the firm (directly or via lower taxes) with higher taxes elsewhere (on an immobile element of the economy). This result, while reducing that nation's standard of living relative to others' (and accordingly, it has some limit), does not necessarily lead to economic instability. Stability depends as much on a nation's politics as it does on global competition.[50] Interest group politics can lead countries to inefficient arrangements.

Globalized capital and product markets impose costs on firms laboring under inefficient legal rules, but if a country is prepared to bear those costs, or if positionally powerful players inside the firm can make those costs be borne by outsiders, even outmoded and costly rules can persist.

Can contracts generally substitute for legal rules?

A critic might argue that, when a country chooses inefficient legal rules, corporate players will avoid them by adopting efficient arrangements through contracts. While we agree that contracting around inefficient rules can often work, it cannot generally do so. Mandatory rules often make contracting around impossible. And even when contracting around is allowed, it is often too costly to do so.[51]

True, some rules are technical, involving only two parties, and can easily be reversed by contract. If the "default" rules favor managers (or controllers) and the parties can change the corporate charter, they sometimes may do so. But three simple examples make the point that there are limits. First, one nation may induce, intentionally or not, diffuse ownership by keeping capital-gathering institutions small and barring

Countries with inefficient legal rules might not even suffer an aggregate disadvantage, if *all* countries have some inefficient rules. All countries could have inefficient legal rules, but their rules might be inefficient in different ways with the differences being partly path dependent.

[50] See Mark J. Roe, "Backlash," 98 *Colum. L. Rev.* 217, 219–21 (1998).

[51] Norms also cannot easily substitute for legal rules, for reasons similar to those that impede contracts from substituting for rules. See David Charny, "Nonlegal Sanctions in Commercial Relationships," 104 *Harv. L. Rev.* 373, 429–44 (1990); Eric A. Posner, "Law, Economics, and Inefficient Norms," 144 *U. Pa. L. Rev.* 1,697, 1,728–36 (1996).

them from actively owning large blocks of stock; those who want to contract around these rules would have to build a parallel, unregulated financial system – a costly, perhaps impossible task – and the forces that made the first system illegal will likely make the second one illegal as well.[52]

Second, consider a nation's failure to reduce the benefits that a controlling shareholder can extract from a firm. The corporate charter, or contract, could take the extraction-reducing rules that another nation has and impose them on the controlling shareholder. But adopting these rules in the corporate charter might provide limited benefits if, to be effective, the rules need the implementation system – the courts, precedents, professionals, and norms – that the other nation has. This implementation system is a "public good" as to the contracting parties and cannot be readily built by those parties to the two-way contract.

Third, for an example of mandatory rules that cannot be readily contracted around, consider our example of the German rules requiring codetermination, which mandate that half of the firm's supervisory board be labor representatives. There is no formal way to contract around this rule. A parallel structure would lack formal authority inside the firm and, if given formal authority (as was occasionally attempted in Germany in the 1970s and 1980s) would be illegal under German law.[53]

Reincorporations

Another way for corporate players to "contract around" an inefficient system of corporate rules is by reincorporating in another country. For example, a foreign firm can subject itself to US rules by reincorporating as, say, a Delaware corporation, or it can subject itself to some subset of US rules by selling shares in the United States. Reincorporation could, in theory, enable each company to remove itself from the local interest group politics (if local rules are inferior to those of some other country) and to get the rules of that other country by reincorporation.

---

[52] Cf. Roe, *Strong Managers*, note 10 above, at pp. 60–93. American financial law barred interstate banking and banks with big blocks of stock at the end of the nineteenth century. American life insurers tried to end run this bar by building an interstate insurance system, with the insurers owning big blocks of stock. But by 1906, new law barred the insurers from active ownership of large blocks of stock.

[53] German courts struck down some efforts to contract around codetermination by using subcommittees having a reduced labor representation. See Roe, "German Codetermination," note 21 above, at p. 168.

With costless reincorporation, firms could migrate to those countries with the most attractive legal rules, with a resulting pressure on countries to adopt efficient rules lest they lose all incorporations to other countries.

The possibility of reincorporation has indeed profoundly affected corporate rules in the United States. Reincorporations have led to the migration of many firms to Delaware and to the adoption by many states of rules that approximate the rules prevailing in Delaware.[54] But these migrations have been facilitated in the United States by the fact that American companies are treated similarly throughout the country irrespective of the state in which they have been incorporated. Consequently, for an American company to reincorporate from one state to another is a "pure" choice of a corporate law system and involves no other economic consequences.

This, however, is not the case in today's world for reincorporations from one country to another. Such reincorporations cannot be made simply as an instrument for choosing a different set of corporate rules because they will usually carry with them significant tax, regulatory, or other economic consequences. And as long as such impediments to reincorporation exist, reincorporations cannot replicate at a world level the effect that they have had on corporate rules in the United States.

The above discussion suggests a caveat. If the world had moved to one big federal system, then differences among countries in their corporate rules would have largely disappeared or receded. But this worldwide federal system has not emerged thus far. Steps in this direction have been tentative and infrequent. And as long as it does not emerge, the source of path dependence that we have identified in this Part will continue to operate.[55]

Moreover, even if reincorporations in another country were costless, they would enable firms and corporate players to avoid only those corporate rules that depend on the place of incorporation. But the system of corporate rules governing the relations between the corporation and its

---

[54] Academic disagreements persist regarding whether the competition among states in the US has been beneficial. Compare Bebchuk, "Federalism," note 30 above (analyzing the problems with competition among states over corporate incorporations), with Roberta Romano, *The Genius of American Corporate Law* (1993) (strongly supporting state competition). But both sides of the debate see substantial migration and standardization.

[55] The European Union's *Centros* decision moves in that direction, but only by a modest step, since it applies only to initial incorporations, not reincorporations, and may not be generally applicable. *Centros Ltd.* v. *Erhervs-og Selskabsstyrelsen* [1999] ECR Case C-212/97.

stakeholders also includes many elements which do not depend on the place of incorporation – such as the rules governing insolvency, banking, or labor contracts – and which thus cannot be avoided by reincorporation.

Public-regarding victories over interest group politics

While we have focused in this section on interest group politics, we do not assume that corporate rules are solely the product of interest group pressures. As we have shown in section III.B, corporate rules will be path dependent even assuming that lawmakers are completely public regarding. Our goal in this Part has been to show that, to the extent that interest groups play a role, and people might reasonably disagree on how substantial a role they do in fact play, this role will depend on existing ownership structures. Below we offer some remarks on how efficient corporate rules might be adopted despite interest group politics – and point out that the identity of the efficient rules that can overcome interest group pressures might still depend on existing corporate ownership structures.

The changes in legal rules that would likely induce the fiercest opposition from interest groups would be ones that directly reduce their rents. A set of rules that might be easier to pass are those that would not directly lower rents, but instead simply allow transactional changes. That is, a country may decide that instead of mandating a structure it would allow the parties to choose their own structures. Examples might include easing rules that mandate par value, that bar certain transactions such as stock buybacks, or that ban certain ownership structures. These types of rule changes are the hardest to resist in public policy terms (because it is hard to argue that having a choice is detrimental),[56] and interest groups might be less opposed to or even favor such rules because, as long as they have sufficient control, they can ensure that rent-reducing transformations take place only if they make gains that more than offset the reduction in their rents.

Some rent-reducing rules might also pass because the rent reduction is part of a larger package of legal improvements. Interest groups sometimes lose, sometimes fail to see that their ox is being gored, and sometimes are swept over in a tide of modernization. For example, a nationalist climate of self-improvement might induce political leaders to believe that the

---

[56] Even after such enabling laws are adopted, some efficient moves might not take place due to the interests of private parties in control. See the analysis in text accompanying notes 23–34 above.

financial system must be modernized. Because the type of financial system a country has can readily influence its corporate structures, corporate incumbents might lose if a country overhauls its financial system. Indeed, what convergence of legal rules there has been in Europe seems to fit this mode.

Another example is that reformers may conclude that the court system must be improved across the board to facilitate commerce. Court renovation could then as a consequence protect minority stockholders (and destroy controllers' rents) by making stockholder suits easier. Sometimes even the controllers (or the managers or the labor interests) may conclude that their lost private benefits are less than the public benefits that accrue to them with the institutional improvements.

Thus, interest group obstacles to public-regarding laws are not insurmountable. But note that whether efficient changes might be able to overcome interest group opposition, and which form they might have to take to overcome such opposition, might still depend on the relative strength of existing interest groups – and thus in turn on the existing pattern of corporate ownership.

Rules changes to facilitate structural change

Henry Hansmann and Reinier Kraakman claim that the controller's drag would be quite limited if changing the ownership or governance structure were efficient. Controlling shareholders would obtain the kind of corporate law that would enable the transition. Or managers would obtain that legislation if moving to concentrated ownership were efficient. Or labor would obtain that transitional legislation that would enable them to retain the value of their private benefits and still capture some of the efficiency gains.

While their scenario is possible, Professors Hansmann & Kraakman are too quick to posit a frictionless transition. Real-world transitions usually do not work as smoothly as they portray them.

Let's examine the transition they imagine. They begin with controlling shareholders with noticeable private benefits seeing that dispersed ownership would be more efficient. They assert that the controlling shareholders would obtain a quick freeze-out mechanism so that they could freeze out the old shareholders at their old value, then engineer ownership dispersion at a higher value.[57]

---

[57] Hansman & Kraakman, chapter 1, this volume, at p. 56.

But consider the mechanics involved. A controller owns 50 percent of the firm, but obtains 60 percent of its value. The firm is worth $100. If the firm's ownership were dispersed, it would be worth $110, but for the owner to disperse ownership directly would mean it would get only $55 for its $60 block. We argue that this structure is thus "sticky" and not easily altered unless efficiency gains are higher than $10. Let's grant Hansman & Kraakman's assumption: if the controllers could get a mechanism of a quick freeze-out put in place and liberally available, the controllers could cash the old shareholders out of the company for $40, despite that the outside shareholders own 50 percent of the company.

And let's grant that controllers could easily get the laws changed to allow such a quick and frictionless freeze-out. The freeze-out rule is then put into place. And soon thereafter the controller freezes out the minority stockholders at $40.

Then she seeks a public offering. But what price would minority stockholders pay for, say, half of the newly recapitalized firm's stock? Yes, they'd pay $55 if they could get half of the firm's cash flows in the future. But they are living in a legal regime *in which a controller can freeze them out and pay only 40 percent of the firm's value for half of the firm's stock.* Hence, the new buyers would only pay $44 for the new stock (40 percent of $110), as long as the freeze-out rule that facilitated the controller's first step at recapitalization stayed in place. (Or, they'd pay a discounted amount based on the probability and timing of any expected freeze-out. Moreover, they might pay only a bit more than $40, if they expected that the freeze-out rule would induce the controller to stay in place for a period of time, until the freeze-out occurred; and, if so, they'd expect the firm to keep its original value at $100.)

What Hansmann & Kraakman need to make this scenario work is that: (1) the controllers get a *controller*-friendly (not a shareholder-friendly) freeze-out rule in place; (2) then *all* controllers cash out all minority stockholders roughly simultaneously under a controller-friendly freeze-out rule (stragglers will be stuck in their old capital structure if they miss the boat); (3) then the freeze-out rule would be quickly changed to be minority-*stockholder*-friendly (and all necessary supporting apparatus, court decisions, banker valuation institutions, and legal precedents are put in place); and (4) the newly privately controlled firms can then go fully public at low cost without share discounts because the freeze-out rule had now become friendly to minority stockholders. Such a quick-step reversal in law is not impossible, but one wonders whether it would be easy. We are unaware of instances of such a rapid construction of a pro-controller rule, followed by its full use, and then its reversal.

Similar examples could be shown to impede managers or labor giving up authority in the firm. And, hence, corporate evolution could be, as it has been thus far, slower than other economic evolution. We are not saying that such evolution or reversal is impossible, but that it's harder than is usually contemplated, that change is sticky, and that preexisting structures have tended to remain in place due to this stickiness.

D.   Elimination of differences in rules by political fiat

In the preceding sections III.B and III.C we have shown that, in choosing legal rules, countries' choices will depend on their existing ownership structures, and the resulting choices might consequently be path dependent and vary significantly among countries. We note, in closing, a qualification: that legal rules might converge if a process of political integration leads a set of countries to agree on having an identical set of rules. That is, if lawmakers in each country are not allowed to make their own separate choices regarding corporate rules, then path dependence will disappear by political fiat.

Such a process of political integration has already been taking place in Europe. While there is no question that, when countries integrate into one political system, political fiat can produce identical rules, European officials have thus far failed in their efforts to end differences in corporate rules.[58] The difficulties that European officials have encountered can be seen as a manifestation of the strength of the forces for divergence

---

[58] The demise of the European Fifth Directive is discussed in J. J. Du Plessis and J. Dine, "The Fate of the Draft Fifth Directive on Company Law: Accommodation Instead of Harmonisation," 1997 *J. Bus. L.* 23. Similarly, the proposal for a Thirteenth Directive, which was intended to unify European takeover laws, was shelved. See Proposal for a 13th Council Directive on Company Law, Concerning Takeover and Other General Bids, *Bull. of Eur. Communities* (Mar. 1989) (presented to the Council by the European Commission on January 19, 1989). One effort has been to build a European corporate statute, with firms having the option to use the local or the EU-wide code. Thus far such efforts have failed to create strong convergence. See Erik Berglöf, "Reforming Corporate Governance: Redirecting the European Agenda," *Econ. Pol'y*, Apr. 1997, at 93, 94 ("Despite recent attempts to revive the idea, hopes for *Société Européenne* [the European company statute] currently appear dim.").

Uniformity could come via judicial decisions that undermine the "seat of business" doctrine, which has the nation of incorporation be the nation where the firm's principal business is located. A recent European judicial decision does open up the way to such movement for new incorporations. See *Centros Ltd.* v. *Erhervs-og Selskabsstyrelsen* [1999] ECR Case C-212/97. If such developments take root, change might occur.

that we have analyzed. British managers, French and Italian controlling shareholders, and German codetermined firms may each prefer a system of corporate governance that radically differs from that preferred by the others. But these players might share one common position: They might wish to preserve their positional advantage in their own firms and as such might all prefer to prevent European Union officials from imposing a common set of corporate rules.[59] A simple description is instructive:

> The [European] Commission has been promoting the concept of the European company statute *for 26 years*. Successive [EU] presidents have put it on to [sic] their agendas, only to see it founder on arguments between the member states over matters such as workers' rights.
>
> . . .
>
> What holds up agreement is that companies do not exist in isolation but are embedded in the social life of countries.[60]

In any event, regardless of how easy it is to impose identical legal rules from the center by political fiat, the analysis in this section has focused on the common case in which lawmakers in each country are free to choose the country's corporate rules. And in the common situation in which they are so free, their choices are likely to be path dependent.

E. Conclusion on rule-driven path dependence

We have shown in this section that corporate rules, which affect choices of ownership structure, are path dependent. The choice of some corporate rules depends on the existing pattern of ownership. First, public-regarding lawmakers might often find that the existing structures, and the existing institutions that have been developed to adapt to these existing structures, affect which rules would be efficient to adopt and maintain. Second, to the extent that interest group politics affects the choice of legal rules, their dynamics and consequences might again depend on the

---

[59] And countries may also become hostile to foreign structures and modes of business. French elites, for example, appear hostile to Anglo-Saxon liberalized markets and are proud of family-owned businesses that persist over generations. See Véronique Maurus, "Le Secret des Hénokiens," *Le Monde*, Mar. 18, 1998, at 12 (noting tradition of large-firm family ownership in France). American business leaders take pride in avoiding the purportedly closed structures of continental Europe.

[60] Stefan Wagstyl & Neil Buckley, "Birthpangs of a Colossus," *Financial Times*, July 12, 1996, at 17 (emphasis added). See also Klaus J. Hopt, *Company Law in the European Union: Harmonization or Subsidiarity* (Centro di studi e ricerche di diritto comparato e staniero Conference Paper no. 31, 1998) (noting the difficulty in building a European-wide corporate law).

existing ownership structures. Indeed, we have shown how this interaction between corporate ownership structures and business rules might plausibly have induced differing structures to have persisted. Thus, the two sources of path dependence of rules that we have identified can help explain why substantial differences in corporate law systems have persisted thus far.

IV.   Other bases for persistent divergence

We list in this section several other reasons for persistence of differences in corporate ownership and governance structures among the advanced economies. These reasons are not directly rooted in path dependence although they could set up the initial conditions for path dependence; rather, they concern ways in which some underlying parameters differ among these economies. We put them on the table for the sake of completeness.

A.   Differences of opinion

We have assumed that both lawmakers and corporate planners around the world can and could all identify which rules and which structures would be efficient. But lawmakers and corporate players genuinely disagree today, have genuinely disagreed in the past, and in all likelihood will continue to disagree as to which corporate rules and structures are best.

Theory and empirical knowledge often do not tell us with confidence which corporate structure or rule would be most efficient. But without theoretical or empirical confidence, corporate players and lawmakers can genuinely disagree about which structures and rules are best. Persistent differences of opinion might well have yielded, and we suspect will probably continue to yield, persistent differences in structures and rules. Indeed, it is sufficient to look at the law review or finance literature on these subjects to see how few basic corporate issues have been resolved even in the same country and culture.[61]

Now it might be argued that, even without convergence of views, natural selection might be sufficient to ensure that structures will eventually all take an efficient form. On this view, to have convergence to

---

[61] For example, after much debate in the literature, there is still substantial difference among researchers concerning the desirable regulation of corporate takeovers. See, e.g., Gilson & Black, note 41 above, pp. 730–889.

efficiency, players need *not* figure out explicitly what is optimal. Only optimal structures will survive, and natural selection will eliminate inefficient ones. People, so the argument goes, need not have understood that stores in Miami should sell swimsuits rather than furs. Stores selling the furs in Miami would have gone out of business and stores selling swimsuits would have prospered (unless there were too many of them); an equilibrium would quickly have arisen with stores selling the optimal product.

But this natural selection story, although strong for stores selling furs in Miami, might not be as compelling for national corporate structures and rules. Because the choice of ownership structure is only one of many aspects that will determine the success of a firm, natural selection by itself (without players recognizing the inefficiency) need not eliminate inefficient structures. Similarly, as long as players do not recognize the inefficiency of certain corporate rules, natural selection would not eliminate the economies that use these rules; such economies might become poorer on the margin, but would not be obliterated. Thus, natural selection by itself would not eliminate inefficient legal rules and ownership structures. The relatively worse performance of such rules and structures might lead to their replacement only if decisionmakers recognized that the rules and structures were indeed inefficient. And, as we discussed above, identifying which rules and structures are inefficient might be difficult not only for researchers but also for actual decisionmakers.

B.   Differences in firms and markets

To focus on path-dependent reasons for divergence, we have assumed that the advanced economies on which our inquiry focuses are similar in all relevant economic conditions – and, in particular, have similar firms and markets. Dropping this assumption introduces more reasons for persistent differences.

Size of economy. Some countries are smaller than others. The size of the economy influences the size distribution of its companies and the size of its capital markets. Which structure is optimal might depend on the size of a company and the size of the nation's capital markets.[62]

---

[62] Cf. William J. Baumol & Ralph E. Gomory, "Inefficient and Locally Stable Trade Equilibria under Scale Economies: Comparative Advantage Revisited," 49 *Kyklos* 509, 510–16 (1996) (analyzing the inefficient trade equilibria produced by scale economies despite market mechanisms).

What firms do. Countries might differ greatly in what their firms do and how they operate. Countries differ in their location, their natural resources, and their investments in human capital. These underlying differences, as well as benefits from specialization and network externalities, might lead to differences among countries in what their corporations do. And such differences might lead to different ownership and governance structures. Optimal corporate structures and rules might depend on the type of technologies, inputs, and workforce that a company has. Thus, if countries differ systematically in their firms and technologies, then the legal rules that would be most efficient for them might differ,[63] and the corporate ownership structures that would be most efficient would differ as well.

C. *Differences in culture, ideology, and politics*

We have viewed legal rules as a product of (i) public-regarding judgments as to which rules would produce the highest value, distorted by (ii) interest group politics. But we are not complete materialists. Culture and ideology, not only value maximization and self-interest, might influence a country's choice of corporate law.

American culture, for example, resists hierarchy and centralized authority more than, say, French culture. German citizens are proud of their national codetermination. Italian family-firm owners may get special utility from a long-standing family-controlled business, while an American family might prefer to cash out of the company earlier and run the family scion for the US Senate.

One link between political ideology and corporate ownership structures is analyzed by one of the authors elsewhere.[64] According to that analysis, countries in which social democratic ideologies are dominant may empower employees more than do countries with other types of governments, putting more pressure on managers to side with employees instead of owners. As a consequence, owners may prefer their next best means of control (to resist such pressure), and that the next best means

---

[63] This statement assumes some economies of scale for corporate rules – i.e., that it would cost more to supply a separate corporate law system for each set of companies and hence each country will develop a system to best fit its typical firms. For an example of a nation's failure to develop separate corporate law systems, see the discussion in note 38 above (discussing the American failure to bifurcate bankruptcy into public and private firms and the eventual merger of the systems).

[64] See Roe, *Political Determinants*, note 17 above.

may be concentrated ownership. As such, not only might the demand for rule changes be weak in social democracies, but the demand for differing ownership and governance structures may also persist as long as the political differences persist.

V.   Conclusion

We have developed a theory in this chapter of path dependence of corporate ownership and governance structures. We have shown how the corporate structures that an economy has at any point in time are likely to depend on those that it had at earlier times.

One type of path dependence is structure-driven. We showed how an economy's initial ownership structures directly influence subsequent choices of ownership structure. We identified two reasons for such structural path dependence – one grounded in efficiency and the other grounded in rent-seeking. First, because of sunk adaptive costs, complementarities, network externalities, endowment effects, and multiple optima, which structure is efficient depends partly on the structures with which the company and/or other companies in its environment began. Second, existing ownership structures might have persistence power, even in the face of some inefficiencies, due to internal rent-seeking. Those parties that participate in control under existing structures, as we have shown, might have an incentive and an ability to impede changes that would enhance efficiency but would reduce their private benefits of control.

The other type of path dependence is rule-driven. We showed that initial ownership structures also affect subsequent structures through affecting the corporate rules under which these subsequent structures will be chosen. We identified two reasons – one grounded in efficiency and the other in interest group politics – why a country's legal rules at any point in time might be influenced by the ownership patterns that the country had at earlier times. First, even assuming that legal rules are chosen solely for efficiency reasons, the initial ownership patterns influence which corporate rules would be efficient. Second, a country's initial pattern of corporate ownership structures influences the power that various interest groups will have in the political process that produces corporate rules. Thus, initial ownership structures that gave control to a certain group of corporate players (say, professional managers or controlling shareholders) would increase the likelihood that the country would subsequently have the rules favored by this group of players.

Our analysis sheds light on why the advanced economies differ in their patterns of corporate ownership and governance. It can explain why, notwithstanding the powerful forces of globalization and efficiency, some key differences have thus far persisted. It can also provide a basis for predicting that important differences might persist in the future. Path dependence is an important force – one that students of comparative corporate governance need to recognize – in shaping corporate governance and ownership around the world.

3

Path dependence and complementarity in corporate governance

REINHARD H. SCHMIDT & GERALD SPINDLER[*]

Introduction

Our goal is to use the concept of path dependence as developed by Bebchuk & Roe in their chapter, "A theory of path dependence in corporate ownership and governance,"[1] as a springboard for discussion of how the necessary addition of institutional "complementarity" further complicates the case for corporate governance convergence. We conclude with an example that shows how the efforts to attain convergence can produce a corporate governance regime inferior to that which it has replaced.

The substantial theoretical contribution of Bebchuk and Roe consists in their integration of four concepts: path dependence; efficiency; evolution; and convergence. In doing so, they take a considerable step beyond what Mark Roe's stimulating earlier works contained on path dependence.[2] In his 1994 book *Strong Managers, Weak Owners*, Roe had demonstrated that many institutional features observed today were shaped by idiosyncratic historical events which in hindsight seem to have been accidental in nature. The general lesson of his research is that history and politics matter, and certainly matter more than the conventional wisdom in economics and the law and economics community in America suggests. Combined with efficiency and evolution, the concept of path dependence creates a solid theoretical basis for the empirical accounts provided in Roe's book.

At the substantive level, Bebchuk and Roe derive crucial implications by applying these concepts to fundamental questions in the area of corporate governance, and they challenge the predominant view among economists as well as law and economics scholars that the corporate governance

---

[*] This chapter is based on Schmidt and Spindler (2002), which elaborates on some of the arguments and formalizes them.
[1] See also Bebchuk & Roe (1999).   [2] See Roe (1996) and Roe (1997).

systems in the major industrial countries are likely to converge at a rapid pace.

As Bebchuk and Roe admit, it may appear natural to expect that corporate governance systems will converge rather quickly since nations and firms are under pressure to adopt the most efficient corporate governance rules and structures (pp. 74–75) in order to remain internationally competitive. Yet Bebchuk and Roe state bluntly that this is not their view (p. 77), although later in their chapter, their rejection of the established view is considerably qualified by admitting that increased pressure may lead to "limits to persistence" (p. 87) of apparently inefficient institutional arrangements such as a specific national corporate governance system.

Our comment addresses both the conceptual and the substantive issues. We wish to emphasize at the outset that we completely concur with Bebchuk and Roe that path dependence certainly is an important concept as well as a fact of life and that convergence towards the "best" corporate governance system is *not* likely to happen soon. However, there are also some points of disagreement which we would like to discuss in this comment. They may not lead to a different assessment of the main propositions, but we believe that they might turn out to be important for the debate which Mark Roe has initiated. In section I, we will first discuss the conceptual underpinning of path dependence provided by Bebchuk and Roe, and then proceed to show why using the concepts underlying path dependence even systematically leads to different and possibly even more unexpected conclusions with respect to the convergence of corporate governance systems than those which Bebchuk and Roe arrive at in their chapter. We will argue that the idea of path dependence has to be supplemented by an additional theoretical concept, namely complementarity. In section II, we try to demonstrate the significance of complementarity for understanding the dynamic properties of corporate governance systems.[3]

I. Explanations for path dependence

Two slightly contradictory explanations for path dependence

In his earlier theoretical papers, Roe shows that path dependence leads to results which are at odds with simple efficiency considerations. By contrasting the outcomes of processes shaped by path dependence with

---

[3] More generally, complementarity is crucial for understanding the dynamic properties of entire legal systems and entire financial systems. For legal systems see Spindler (1993), and for financial systems see Hackethal & Schmidt (2000).

those which one would expect under the sole influence of efficiency, he refers to a conventional notion of economic efficiency which is essentially static and closely related to the standard economic concept of equilibrium. The concepts of efficiency and equilibrium underlie most discussions in economics in general and in new institutional economics in particular, and it suggests that convergence from a given institutional arrangement to the most efficient – or simply "best" – one is to be expected.

Likewise based on efficiency and equilibrium, Roe and Bebchuk and Roe add two elements to the standard economic approach, namely institutional dynamics and "realistic" assumptions like those of bounded rationality and imperfect and incomplete markets. An analysis including these elements leads to different conclusions than the standard static efficiency analysis. This fact suggests that one should take a closer look at the nature and the causes of path dependence. In the work of Roe and Bebchuk and Roe we identify elements of two different interpretations of path dependence which should, in our view, be carefully distinguished.

According to Roe, the central argument for path dependence is the following: factors determining efficient institutional arrangements change over time and cause once efficient arrangements to appear inefficient today. However, if the possible efficiency or welfare gain brought about by changing an institutional arrangement is not sufficient to compensate the costs of adjustment, "society" might *rationally* retain the seemingly inefficient institutions.[4] What we observe in reality may thus be efficient in a broader sense, namely when one accounts for what pose to be switching or adjustment costs.

Note that in Roe's account of why path dependence may occur, "society" resembles a *single* rational, efficiency-oriented decisionmaker. One is tempted to apply similar considerations to production technologies employed in a firm or energy conservation devices used in private homes, which may appear inefficient today. There is no doubt that adjustment or switching costs are real and that they "matter." We call the first account of what causes path dependence *the switching cost argument*.

Although switching costs are frequently reduced to technical facts, they are not by definition technical in nature. There is a difference between the technical and the social aspects of institutional development, and several accounts, including Roe (1996), tend to obscure this difference. In social or political processes, switching costs – and thus path dependence – can arise as a consequence of, among other things, sunk costs, entrenched

---

[4] See Roe (1996) with further references and a very instructive example on pp. 641–43.

property, and decision rights of interest groups and network externalities. Thus, whether an improvement in efficiency or welfare comes about or not depends on the details of the relevant processes.

Roe and Bebchuk and Roe offer a second explanation of path dependence that is based on recent developments in evolutionary biology.[5] The main proposition here is that evolution leads systems – or collections of "agents" striving for an improvement of their situation – only to local optima. By definition, a local optimum may be different from a global optimum. What constitutes the nearest, and seemingly most attractive, local optimum depends on the starting point at which a given biological or social system happens to be at a given point in time. This is why the development of systems is path dependent. All that is needed for the biologists' story to be convincing is the assumption of a certain degree of myopia on the part of the entities which are assumed to behave *as if* they made rational choices under external pressure to adjust. "Modern evolutionary biologists use the metaphor of natural selection leading us to the top of a local hill."[6] We therefore call this explanation of path dependence *the local hill argument.* Note that evolutionary mechanisms which may lead to path dependence can be assumed to work even in the absence of all switching costs as long as these are not defined to include all consequences of myopia.

Even though the two explanations of path dependence may not be mutually exclusive, they shed light on different facts and suggest different implications. This becomes most obvious when we look at an important corollary of path dependence. As mentioned before, there are reasons to expect that "large" inefficiency limits the persistence of institutional arrangements which are no longer up to date.[7] This amounts to saying that as long as the external pressure is not too strong, different institutional arrangements, such as different types of governance systems, may coexist side by side even though they differ with respect to the efficiency with which they fulfill *the same* function. However, when the pressure becomes too strong, path dependence does not seem to count so much any more, and only the more efficient arrangement survives.

Such a view, which is in line with established views in economics, would be consistent with the switching costs argument: the more that can be gained from undertaking certain improvements and the more that would

---

[5] See Roe (1996) and the references provided there.

[6] Roe (1996), pp. 641–43; and see also Milgrom & Roberts (1995b), pp. 238–41, in a section entitled "hill climbing".

[7] See Bebchuk & Roe (1998), p. 27, and Bebchuk & Roe (1999), p. 147.

be lost by forgoing them, the more improvements will be undertaken by rational agents, be they individuals or society acting as if it were a single individual. If more pressure leads to more adjustment and if that pressure is applied equally to different systems, it ultimately also leads to more convergence, provided that the same institutional arrangement is perceived by all agents who make the decisions under consideration to be the global optimum.

In the light of the argument taken from evolutionary biology, this view is much less plausible. Here sudden outside pressure leads, in the first place, to reactions which appear to short-sighted decision makers to offer the highest potential for solving the *acute* problem. Assume there is a firm which has various options to improve the efficiency of its operations, and that all of a sudden the intensity of competition increases; a "globalization shock" hits this firm. In order to survive, the firm needs to do something helpful, and needs to do it quickly, in order to avoid a crisis. If the reaction has to be fast *and is myopic* it may lead the firm to a local optimum, which is not a global optimum. Attempts to leave the local optimum in order to search for a global optimum may simply not be feasible if the firm does not have enough financial reserves to survive the losses which it will incur in the uncertain process of transition. Thus, the evolution of this firm will turn out to be path dependent.

If several such firms are hit by the same "globalization shock" they will all attempt to improve their situation and undertake some efficiency-enhancing measures, each one using the option which offers the best *immediate* or short-term prospect. If they are in different starting positions when the event occurs, the different firms may end up at different local optima and might be stuck there. In fact, stronger outside pressure will *decrease* the likelihood that convergence will occur, because in the presence of very strong pressure the danger that temporary deviations from a local optimum would lead to losses and the eventual failure of a firm is greater. Not more, but less outside pressure would make it easier for the individual firms to experiment and accidentally move to the global optimum and thus to converge. Convergence does not occur at all, if strong outside pressure *prevents* them from experimenting and perhaps finding the common global optimum.

We do not want to speculate on whether the switching cost argument is less useful and relevant than that of the local hill in general. In part our reservation *vis-à-vis* the explanation of path dependence as arising from the costs of making adjustments is due to the ad hoc character of the concept of switching costs. A different, and in our view more important, reason why we regard the explanation that path dependence may be due to the short-sightedness of evolution as more relevant in the case of corporate governance systems is that it yields different and more interesting implications for the central issue of the convergence of national corporate governance systems. However, in order for the local hill argument to fully develop its heuristic potential, it needs to have more structure and more substance.

Path dependence as a consequence of complementarity

Bebchuk and Roe do discuss complementarity briefly in their contribution to the present volume,[8] but it does not play a strategic role in their overall argument. In our view, their general argument that convergence may not be likely to occur soon could be strengthened considerably if complementarity were given more weight, which is why we tend to say that complementarity is still missing as an important element in Bebchuk and Roe's analysis.

Complementarity is an attribute of elements of a given system such as a corporate governance system, a financial system, the organizational or production system of a firm, or the system which constitutes the strategy of a firm.[9] Elements of a given system are called complementary (to each other) if there is the potential that they fit together well, i.e., take on values such that they mutually increase their benefit in terms of whatever the objective function or the standard for evaluating the system may be, and/or mutually reduce their disadvantages or costs. The twin concept to that of complementarity is consistency. Consistency is an attribute of the entire system which is composed of complementary elements. We call a system consistent if its elements do take on values which fit together and which thereby exploit the potential created by complementarity. By definition, not all systems with complementary elements are necessarily consistent.[10]

---

[8] See pp. 80, 96 in Chapter 2 and Bebchuk & Roe (1998). In Roe (1996) the author expresses his conviction that "each pure type (of corporate governance) may be less efficient than a hybrid that uses both . . . systems" (p. 650; our addition and omission). In a context in which complementarity plays an important role, this is not at all likely to be the case, as will be demonstrated in the next subsection.

[9] See Hackethal & Schmidt (2000), Porter (1996) and Milgrom & Roberts (1995a, 1995b).

[10] Although the concepts of complementarity and consistency are quite intuitive, as they come close to what is implied when we talk informally about something being "really a system", a formal representation may be helpful for the ensuing discussion. Such formal representations can be found in Milgrom & Roberts (1990, 1995a) and Hackethal & Schmidt (2000). Schmidt & Spindler (2002) contains a semi-formal representation.

Let us provide an illustration because it may make the relationship between complementarity and path dependence easier to understand. If the system under consideration is physical production with one output and two factors of production, then in the case of complementarity the output surface looks different from that of the standard production-theoretic model. In the three-dimensional graphical representation of the standard model of production, output can be represented as a mountain leveling off at its sides, whereas in the case of complementarity the output surface looks like a mountainous region with more than one hill and a valley between the mountains. Any substantial "improvement" in output is tantamount to walking up the mountain slope on one side. A short-sighted hiker would strive for height by climbing up that side of the valley on which she happened to be or which appeared steeper to her. This would constitute myopic behavior, which might lead her to a hilltop which is not the highest peak in the entire area. Thus, striving for *immediate* gains in height is likely to make a hiker's stroll a path-dependent one: it matters where she started and where she reaches a (local) peak.

Thus, complementarity leads directly to path dependence as a dynamic property of systems. By definition, there is no way to reach a higher peak without going down from a local peak. Therefore, striving for *immediate* gains in height is very likely to make a hiker's stroll a path-dependent one: it matters where she started to climb up and where she reaches a (local) maximum. Systems change differently from entities which are not systems, because in real life the change in a system is typically initiated by altering just one of its several elements. Assume for the moment that a given system A is perceived by some observers to be better than an alternative system B, which also suggests to some observers that the elements which make up system A are in some sense better, and that, possibly because of this, some external influence leads to the replacement of one seemingly worse element from the system B by the corresponding element from system A. If in the initial situation the two systems were consistent, then the new system resulting from the replacement of this one element is by definition inconsistent. As an inconsistent system is inferior in efficiency terms to the corresponding consistent system, the newly created system will call for measures to increase efficiency by undertaking some appropriate adjustments. One possible adjustment would consist in the replacement of the other elements of the seemingly worse system B by elements of system A such that the entire system B is ultimately replaced by the presumed better system A. The other possible adjustment is one which reflected the attempt to increase efficiency *immediately* or myopically. This can be achieved by simply restoring consistency. A fast efficiency-increasing move would consist in reversing the original move and thus in a return to the consistent system B. In certain applications, and in particular in a situation in which it would be important to quickly achieve some efficiency gain, the second form of adjustment seems more likely. This is why systems under strong pressure are likely to be trapped in a local optimum in the same way as biological evolution.

We tend to believe that systems composed of complementary elements in which consistent configurations are also local optima and multiple equilibria exist are more frequent in social life than is commonly assumed by economists and scholars from related disciplines. As we will argue in the next section, this could also be the case for corporate governance systems: it might be economically more important that the elements of a given corporate governance system fit together well, than how "good" the individual elements are perceived to be and even more than to which type of governance system a given national system belongs.

II.   Consistent corporate governance systems

Two types of consistent governance systems

Corporate governance systems are composed of complementary elements in the sense just defined. A governance system can be described by listing its elements and indicating which values these elements take on. The list of important elements includes the distribution of ownership and residual decision rights; the distribution of residual claims and shareholdings; the board structure and the composition of the supervisory board; the objective of the firm to which management is bound; the general structure of corporate law; the quality of accounting information for shareholders; the role and function of the stock market; access to capital markets; the nature of stock market regulation including insider trading regulation and takeovers; the dominant career paths in firms and the role of employees in corporate decision making. All of these elements can take on two distinct and indeed opposing values.

Evidently, not all conceivable values for these individual elements would fit together and generate a workable corporate governance system.[11] The prototypical distinction between the "outsider control system" and the "insider control system" introduced by Franks and Mayer

---

[11] For details, see Schmidt & Spindler (2002).

(1994) reflects our notion of consistent corporate governance systems. We cannot sketch here the way in which the two archetypes represent consistent configurations of complementary elements, but for detailed accounts of different corporate governance systems along this line, we refer the reader to Charkham (1994) and, for the Japanese and the German systems as they were a few years ago, to Hoshi (1998) and Schmidt (2001), respectively. These authors demonstrate not only the meaning of the concepts of complementarity and consistency but also their role in real systems. Though this view provides no basis to judge which consistent system is better, it suggests important implications for their design and their evolution.

Complementarity and the design of corporate governance systems

The normative implication of the preceding discussion is straightforward in principle, though not in practice. Given complementarity between the elements and the economic advantages of consistency, a "middle-of-the-road" model of corporate governance would not make much sense and can, therefore, not be recommended from an economic perspective. It would not necessarily improve the British corporate governance system if important elements were introduced into it which observers, regulators or legislators find useful in the German system, and vice versa. It might only lead to an inconsistent and dysfunctional mixture. In Britain, elements of an insider control system have been pushed in the 1990s, based on the findings of the Cadbury commission and on a general reappraisal of the role which institutional investors can – and, according to some observers, should – play in the governance of British companies.[12] In Germany, there have been recent legislative efforts to foster the role of capital markets and strong public pronouncements to the effect that it is time to adopt a strict shareholder value orientation as the governing principle of publicly held large German corporations. Many of these measures entail the danger that the basis on which the British system used to rest, and that which used to underpin the German system, will no longer be solid in the future.[13]

---

[12] See Charkham (1994). Charkham served as a member of the Cadbury Commission.

[13] The most visible examples which come to our minds here are the changes which have been introduced recently by the "law for improving control and transparency in the economy" and the "law to facilitate the raising of capital". This legislation is inspired by a market-oriented philosophy, which is not consistent with the model of German corporate governance, and more generally of the German financial and economic system. Hackethal,

Complementarity and the development of corporate governance systems: a lack of smooth and rapid convergence

There can be no doubt that there is at present a growing pressure on firms and nations to improve economic efficiency, among other things by introducing good corporate governance systems. Conventional wisdom in the law and economics community would have it that a vaguely described process of competition among systems leads to the result that the best system will be uniformly applied, in much the same way as competition in the market for steel will advance the best steel-making technology and ultimately lead to its universal adoption because some will adopt it whereas others who do not will be driven out of the market. But what is the best governance system? How could a possible process of change occur? Who are the relevant actors in this process, and what drives their agendas? If we wish to answer these questions, we must look at the details of the process.

It seems that reforms are easier to implement if they are undertaken step by step. However, proceeding step by step is the same as changing a given system by altering one *element* at a time in order to arrive at the (presumed) better system. By definition, complementarity implies that partial changes with respect to individual elements do not result in an improvement if the starting situation is a local optimum. In practice this could mean that a given new legal device or a nonstandard corporate governance practice is not accepted by the relevant legal and business communities. The innovation might be discontinued or abolished again or simply not adopted. Changes must therefore relate to at least a "critical mass" of elements of a corporate governance system, and this is more difficult to implement.

It seems that reforms are easier to implement if a convincing case for a new system can be made and if it is possible to encourage certain actors to become innovators adopting the new system. Certain corporations could play the role of an innovator or early adopter. However, the type of corporate governance that an individual *corporation* in a given country can use successfully strongly depends on the corporate governance system which prevails in that country, because lenders, clients, potential and current employees, and others will prefer to deal with a corporation which does not differ in a fundamental way from others with which they are

---

Schmidt, & Tyrell (2002) argue, however, that these and other recent developments in Germany are more compatible with the traditional German model than one might think.

acquainted, and courts tend to apply the rules and interpretations to which they are accustomed. Frustrating the expectations of others would create important legal and commercial risks for an innovator in the field of corporate governance.

Moreover, it is not at all clear which corporate governance system is really better. Even though corporate governance *systems* can easily be *defined* at the theoretical level, in practice it is anything but clear where the limits of a corporate governance system must be drawn and which other elements of an economic and legal system would have to change together with the core elements of a corporate governance system if the goal were to make fundamental alterations to the existing governance system. There is complementarity between the different elements of an economic, social, and legal system in which governance is embedded.

These arguments[14] suggest a dilemma: it does not appear to be likely that individual innovators and national politicians could bring about a change of corporate governance systems which would ultimately lead to a convergence to the presumed best system. Any substantive change would have to be a very comprehensive one. Thus supranational "governments" might have a role to play here. However, there is simply no supranational political authority or other entity which would have the knowledge and the power to impose, in several countries at the same time, what it might consider to be the universally best corporate governance system.[15] This leads us to the *negative* result that a simplistic story of the competition and convergence of corporate governance systems cannot be valid.

An alternative scenario: convergence towards an inefficient system

In a companion paper (Schmidt & Spindler 2002), we present an alternative account of why and how and with which economic effects convergence might come about, even though we concur with Bebchuk and Roe that a smooth and rapid convergence to the more efficient corporate governance system is unlikely to occur. The main idea is this. Let us assume that there are only two systems which countries could adopt, one being the traditional German–Japanese or insider system, and the other the Anglo-Saxon or outsider system. It is not obvious that one of them is superior in terms of its economic efficiency under *normal* and stable circumstances; and we

---

[14] For additional arguments, see Schmidt & Spindler (2002).
[15] However, see Spindler (1998) on the role which major stock exchanges might play in this context in the future.

certainly do not claim to know this either. But for the sake of making our point, let us *assume* that the insider control system is superior.

The two systems function according to different principles. More specifically, they make use of implicit contracts, mutually consistent expectations and trust to a different extent. The outsider control system is parsimonious in this respect, whereas the functioning of the insider control system requires much more in terms of mutually consistent expectations and trust.

Now let us assume that various attempts of reforming the existing corporate governance systems have been undertaken. In spite of all good intentions, their immediate effect is that of undermining consistency and thus destabilizing the existing national corporate governance systems. Let us further assume that the process of partial and inconclusive reform has reached a point in which important governance mechanisms fail to function, and that it has gone so far that there is no way of increasing or restoring economic efficiency by returning "smoothly" to the original – and consistent – systems.

Such a situation, which Roe (1996) appropriately calls a crisis, would create strong pressure from many sides to restore some kind of order *immediately* and at least on a national level. Firms and national authorities in all affected countries would search for a "workable" solution, which would have to be a consistent system as *any* consistent system is better than an inconsistent system. In this situation, a deliberate process of well-informed choices of the most efficient corporate governance system would be unlikely. Instead, the process would rather be chaotic and in all likelihood myopic, rather exhibiting the attributes of the processes assumed in evolutionary biology than those in standard economic theory.

In such a situation the criteria for determining the "winner" in the competition between corporate governance systems will be different from those which hopefully apply under normal circumstances. The system for which firms and authorities in their respective roles would probably settle would most likely not be the one with the most desirable economic consequences under *normal and stable* conditions – as such conditions do not obtain any more – but rather the one with the most attractive features in a crisis.[16] In crises, stable expectations and trust are less justified, and implicit contracts cannot be expected to be honored. Therefore, the best system would be one which relies least on these elements. Among the two prototypes of corporate governance systems, some variant of the outsider

---

[16] "What persists is what is best adapted to persist during the crisis" (Roe 1996: 663).

system would be the best choice in this situation – not because it is better under normal and stable conditions, but because it is simpler to achieve and to maintain. Thus a process of crisis-induced convergence might lead to the general adoption of that type of system which is, as we have assumed for the sake of the argument, the economically less attractive one.

Even though one might today be inclined to argue that as far as corporate governance matters are concerned, we are in an acute crisis, we do not want to make any such claim.[17] But given the importance of corporate governance and of the possible convergence, we feel that the issues raised in the preceding discussion, and in particular the question of which system would emerge as the "winner" in a crisis, is more than an intellectual exercise.

References

Bebchuk, Lucian A. & Mark J. Roe (1998), "A Theory of Path Dependence in Corporate Governance and Ownership," The Center for Law and Economic Studies, Columbia Law School, Working Paper no. 131.

(1999), "A Theory of Path Dependence in Corporate Ownership and Governance," *Stanford Law Review* 52 (1): 127–70.

Charkham, Jonathan (1994), *Keeping Good Company: A Comparison of Corporate Governance in Five Countries*, Oxford: Oxford University Press.

Franks, Julian & Colin Mayer (1994), "Corporate Control: A Comparison of Insider and Outsider Systems," Working Paper, London Business School.

Hackethal, Andreas & Reinhard H. Schmidt (2000), "Finanzsystem und Komplementarität," *Kredit und Kapital*, Supplement "Finanzmärkte im Umbruch," 53–102.

Hackethal, Andreas, Reinhard H. Schmidt, & Marcel Tyrell (2002), "Corporate Governance in Germany: Transition to a Modern Capital-Market Based System?" (forthcoming *JITE* 2003).

Hoshi, Takeo (1998), "Japanese Corporate Governance as a System," in Hopt, Klaus-J. et al., eds., *Comparative Corporate Governance: The State of the Art and Emerging Research*, Oxford: Oxford University Press, pp. 847–76.

Milgrom, Paul & John Roberts (1990) "The Economics of Modern Manufacturing: Technology, Strategy and Organization," 80 *Am. Econ. Rev.* 511.

---

[17] Note that the first version of this comment was written in 1998, after Mark Roe had presented the Bebchuk–Roe paper at a conference in Frankfurt. At that time, Enron and Worldcom were not yet household names in our home country, and hardly anybody anywhere would have expected the depth of what today appears as a crisis.

(1995a), "Complementarities and Fit: Strategy, Structure and Organizational Change in Manufacturing," *Journal of Accounting and Economics* 19: 179–208.

(1995b), "Continuous Adjustment and Fundamental Change in Business Strategy and Organization," in Siebert, Horst, ed. (1995), *Trends in Business Organization: Do Participation and Cooperation Increase Competitiveness?*, Tübingen: J.C.B. Mohr, pp. 231–58.

Porter, Michael E. (1996), "What is Strategy?" *Harvard Business Review* 74: 61–78.

Roe, Mark (1994), *Strong Managers, Weak Owners: The Political Roots of American Corporate Finance*, Princeton, NJ: Princeton University Press.

(1996), "Chaos and Evolution in Law and Economics," *Harvard Law Review* 109: 641–63.

(1997), "Path Dependence, Political Options and Governance Systems," in Klaus J. Hopt *et al.*, eds., *Comparative Corporate Governance: The State of the Art and Emerging Research*, Oxford: Oxford University Press, pp. 847–75.

Schmidt, Reinhard H. (2001): "Kontinuität und Wandel bei der Corporate Governance in Deutschland," *Zeitschrift für betriebswirtschaftliche Forschung*, Sonderheft 47–01, pp. 61–87.

Schmidt, Reinhard H. & Stefanie Grohs (2000), "Angleichung der Unternehmensverfassung in Europa: ein Forschungsprogramm," in S. Grundmann, ed., *Systembildung und Systemlücken in Kerngebieten des Europäischen Privatrechts'*, Tübingen: J.C.B. Mohr, pp. 145–88.

Schmidt, Reinhard H. & Gerald Spindler (2002): "Path Dependence, Corporate Governance and Complementarity," *International Finance* 5 (3): 311–33.

Spindler, Gerald (1993), *Recht und Konzern*, Tübingen: J.C.B. Mohr.

(1998), "Deregulierung des Aktienrechts?" *Die Aktiengesellschaft* 53: 67–74.

4

Globalizing corporate governance: convergence of form or function

RONALD J. GILSON*

Globalization has led to a remarkable resurgence in the study of comparative corporate governance. This area of scholarship had been largely the domain of taxonomists, intent on cataloguing the central characteristics of national corporate governance systems, and then classifying different systems based on the specified attributes. The result was an interesting, if perhaps somewhat dry, enterprise. We learned that national corporate governance systems differed dramatically along a number of seemingly important dimensions. Some corporate governance systems, notably those of the United States and other Anglo-Saxon countries, are built on the foundation of a stock market-centered capital market. Other systems, like those of Germany and Japan, rest on a bank-centered capital market. Some systems are characterized by large groupings of related corporations, like the Japanese *keiretsu*, Korean *chaebol*, or European holding company structures. Still others are notable for concentrated family control of large businesses, including Canada, Italy and, notably, Germany.[1] Management

* Earlier versions of this chapter were presented at the Symposium on Globalization and Law for the Twentieth Century, sponsored by Seoul National University College of Law, October 10–11, 1997, and at the Sloan Foundation/Columbia Law School Conference on Convergence in Corporate Governance, December 5, 1997. A lengthier version of this chapter has been published as Ronald J. Gilson, "Globalizing Corporate Governance: Convergence of Form and Function," 49 *Am. J. Comp. L.* 329 (2001). I am grateful for the helpful comments of Bernard Black, Jack Coffee, Ehud Kamar, Kon-Sik Kim, Hwa-Jin Kim, Mark Roe, Woong-Song Soon, and the participants at faculty workshops at Stanford and the University of Southern California Law Schools, and to Win Hwangbo for research assistance.
[1] Marco Becht & Ekkehart Böhmer, "Ownership and Voting Power in Germany," in Fabrizio Barca & Marco Becht, eds., *The Control of Corporate Europe* (2002); Julian Franks & Colin Mayer, "Ownership, Control and the Performance of German Corporations," 14 *Rev. Fin. Stud.* 943 (2001); Ekkehart Böhmer, "Who Controls German Corporations?" in Joseph A. McCahery *et al.*, eds., *Corporate Governance Regimes: Convergence and Diversity* (2002); Rafael La Porta, Florencio Lopez-de-Silanos, Andrei Shliefer, & Robert Vishny, "Corporate Ownership around the World," 54 *J. Fin.* 471 (1999).

styles also differ across national systems. In the United States and France, managerial power is concentrated, by practice in the US and with statutory support in France, in an imperial-style American chief executive officer or French présidente directeur générale.[2]

The explosive decompression of trade barriers that gave rise to global competition also had an impact on academics. We learned that the institutions of all national systems were shaped not only by efficiency, but also by history and politics. In the United States, for example, the limited role of financial institutions in corporate governance – in effect, the Berle-Means separation of ownership and control – was the artifact not just of economics, but also of populist politics operating in a federal system.[3] Similarly, lifetime employment in Japan, said to be central to Japanese corporate governance, reflected not an effort to encourage investment in worker human capital, as commonly treated in the economics literature but, rather, grew out of a post-World War II political deal intended to rationalize workforce levels and restore management control of production.[4]

Once different national governance systems were understood as more than just way stations on the road to convergence, comparative scholars began to treat institutional differences as having competitive consequences. Competition was not just between products, but also between governance systems. For example, Masahiko Aoki argued that Japanese lean production was inextricably linked to the Japanese governance system, in which main bank contingent monitoring and cross-shareholdings protected the promise of lifetime employment by shielding managers and workers from shareholder demands, but disciplined both groups in the event of poor performance.[5] Others argued that the vertical *keiretsu* structure provided an important means of mutual monitoring.[6]

[2] CCH Int'l , *French Law on Commercial Companies*, pp. 5–6 (2nd edn, 1988).

[3] Mark J. Roe, *Strong Managers, Weak Owners* (1994); Miguel Cantillo Simon, "The Rise and Fall of Bank Control in the United States," 88 *Am. Econ. Rev.* 1077, 1078–79 (1998). Some scholars have taken issue with this "political" theory. See note 22 below.

[4] Ronald J. Gilson & Mark J. Roe, "Lifetime Employment: Labor Peace and the Evolution of Japanese Corporate Governance," 99 *Col. L. Rev.* 508 (1999).

[5] See, e.g., Masahiko Aoki, "Toward an Economic Model of the Japanese Firm," 27 *J. Econ. Lit.* 1 (1990); Masahiko Aoki, "The Japanese Firm as a System of Attributes: A Survey and Research Agenda," in Masahiko Aoki & Ronald Dore, eds., *The Japanese Firm: The Sources of Competitive Strength* 11 (1994).

[6] Ronald J. Gilson & Mark J. Roe, "Understanding the Japanese Keiretsu: Overlaps between Corporate Governance and Industrial Organization," 102 *Yale L.J* 271 (1993); Eric Bergloff & Enrico Peroti, "The Governance Structure of the Japanese Financial Keiretsu," 36 *J. Fin. Econ.* 259 (1994).

Michael Porter argued that the bank-centered capital markets of Germany and Japan allowed executives to manage in the long run while US managers invested myopically out of fear that, unless catered to by a sharp focus on quarter-to-quarter earnings growth, the stock market's fickleness would be enforced by the market for corporate control.[7] At the same time, other commentators extolled the American system because its openness to external monitoring through a stock market-centered capital market allowed it to respond quickly to changes in the economic environment.[8] Finally, an important literature developed that ties the distribution of shareholdings within a country and the nature of its capital market to the quality of the country's legal and governance system.[9] Whichever side of the issue one took, the corporate governance debate came to turn on arguments about the link between particular national governance institutions and competitiveness: is this institution efficient?

From this point, it was no great leap to predictions of convergence: the force of competition would lead national systems to adopt a single efficient form. To be sure, the form on which systems would converge differed depending on which national system appeared most successful at the time of the prediction. Before the bursting of the Japanese "bubble economy," the main bank system represented the future; this array of complementary governance institutions was necessary to support lean manufacturing, the emerging standard of efficient production.[10] Not long thereafter, the Japanese bubble burst and the American economy boomed – sustained

---

[7] Michael Porter, "Capital Disadvantages: America's Failing Capital Investment System," *Harv. Bus. Rev.*, Sept.–Oct. 1992.

[8] See, e.g., Ronald J. Gilson, "The Political Ecology of Takeovers: Thoughts on Harmonizing the European Corporate Governance Environment," 61 *Fordham L. Rev.* 161 (1992); Ronald J. Gilson, "Corporate Governance and Economic Efficiency: When do Institutions Matter?," 74 *Wash. U.L.Q.* 327 (1996).

[9] See, e.g., La Porta *et al.*, note 1 above; Rafael La Porta, Florencio Lopez-de-Silanos, Andrei Shliefer, & Robert Vishny, "Legal Determinants of Outside Finance," 52 *J. Fin.* 1131 (1997); Rafael La Porta, Florencio Lopez-de-Silanos, Andrei Shliefer, & Robert Vishny, "Law and Finance," 106 *J.Pol. Econ.* 1113 (1998); Rafael La Porta, Florencio Lopez-de-Silanos, Andrei Shleifer, & Robert Vishny, "Investor Protection and Corporate Governance," 58 *J. Fin. Econ.* 3 (2000). Charles P. Himmelberg, R. Glenn Hubbard, & Insessa Love, "Investor Protection, Ownership, and the Cost of Capital," *Col. Bus. Sch. WP*, Feb. 2002 (available on SSRN), reaches similar results using different econometric techniques.

[10] A good example is a collection of articles holding out the main bank system as a model for emerging nations that came out of a World Bank financed study. See Masahiko Aoki & Hugh Patrick, eds., *The Japanese Main Bank System: Its Relevance for Developing and Transforming Economies* (1994).

growth, low unemployment and, most surprisingly, low inflation – due to its rapid response to global competition, stock market-centered capital market, and the external monitoring to which stock markets are complementary. The American system then became the apparent end point of corporate governance evolution, a consensus that appears clearly from the IMF and the World Bank's response to the 1997–1998 East Asian financial crisis. In addition to these agencies' traditional emphasis on macroeconomic matters like government deficit reduction, countries accepting financial assistance also had to commit to fundamental reform of their corporate governance system, in the direction of the American model.[11]

These predictions of governance convergence had a more serious problem than the conflict in their prophecies. National governance systems turned out to be more adaptive in function, and therefore more persistent in form, than the prophets of convergence expected. For example, it was thought that Japanese lean production, supported both by employees rendered cooperative and inventive by lifetime employment, and by close, long-term ties to suppliers, could not be matched without dramatic changes in US governance institutions. In fact, American manufacturers adopted lean production, but adapted lean production to fit their governance institutions, rather than adapting their institutions to lean

---

[11] See, e.g., Timothy Lane et al., *IMF-Supported Programs in Indonesia, Korea, and Thailand* 72–73 (Int'l Monetary Fund Occasional Paper no. 178, 1999); "Asia Pacific Talks Vow Tough Action on Economic Crisis," *N.Y. Times*, Nov. 26, 1997, at A1; William A. Bratton & Joseph A. McCahery, "Comparative Corporate Governance and the Theory of the Firm: The Case against Global Cross Reference," 38 *J. Col. J. Transnat'l L.* 213, 236, and 236n.68 (1999), catalogs European proposals of US- style corporate governance reform proposals. Ronald Dore recounts the same influence of US influence in Japan:

> What . . . all these slogans [concerning Japanese capital market reform] add up to is a general belief that (1) the principles according to which the typical neoclassical economics textbooks say the economy works are a priori correct principles, (2) those principles are best exemplified in the American economy, (3) the rightness of those principles is further confirmed by American success, and (4) Japan's present plight is not just a cyclical phenomenon and a debt-deflation hangover from the bubble; it is the natural and wholly just retribution visited on Japan for not following these principles.

Ronald Dore, "Japan's Reform Debate: Patriotic Concern or Class Interest? Or Both?," 25 *J. Japanese Stud.* 65, 66 (1999). Annelise Riles reports that "[p]opular conversation in Tokyo today" refers to the shift toward an American approach to financial market structure as a "second occupation," referring to the influx of American ideas that accompanied the post-World War II occupation of Japan. Annelise Riles, "The Transnational Appeal of Formalism: The Case of Japan's Netting Law" (Working Paper, Feb. 2000) (available on SSRN).

production. As Charles Sabel has perceptively stressed, the link between institutional form and production technology was less tight than had been assumed.[12] The American system's functional adaptivity proved to be greater than expected, leaving institutional form largely intact. Thus, the debate over convergence is not quite joined. Are we expecting a formal convergence of legal rules, as Henry Hansmann and Reinier Kraakman argue has largely been achieved,[13] or merely functional convergence that operates behind a façade of local institutions?

In this chapter I want to examine the interplay of functional adaptivity on the one hand, and institutional persistence or path dependency on the other, that will influence whether such corporate governance convergence as we observe will be formal or functional.[14] Section I maps the intersection of adaptivity and path dependency where institutional form and function collide. I then consider a range of different outcomes that may result from the encounter. Section II describes two settings, one historical and one speculative, where convergence has been or would be functional

---

[12] Charles Sabel, chapter 9, this volume; Susan Helper, John MacDuffie, & Charles Sabel, "The Boundaries of the Firm as a Design Problem," Law and Economics Center Working Paper, Columbia Law School (Feb. 1997).

[13] Henry Hansmann & Reinier Kraakman, chapter 1, this volume.

[14] For present purposes, my concern is to clarify the terms of the discussion. I am not trying to resolve the debate over the extent to which changing economic forces are sufficient to drive formally and functionally divergent systems together. On this issue, Mark Roe and Lucian Bebchuk have argued that path dependencies driven by "sunk adaptive costs, complimentarities, network externalities, endowment effects, and multiple optima" on the one hand, and by the self-interest of those who benefit from existing structures on the other, may freeze the institutions of particular countries in a noncompetitive pose, chapter 2, this volume. The self-interested fork of this argument tracks Mancur Olson's assessment that interest groups with a stake in current institutions will support policies that shrink the size of the pie if they protect the size of the groups' pieces. Mancur Olson, *The Rise and Decline of Nations* (1982). Alternatively, others lament that the relentless drive of competition has already compromised the diversity of capitalist systems that allowed the state to buffer individuals and local institutions from the forces of competition. "[A]cclerated technological change, renewed price competition and the globalization of financial markets have combined to produce a world economy in which a premium seems to be placed on speed of reaction: on rapid product change and an ability to cut costs fast . . . The destruction or devaluation of national state capacity under globalization discriminates against national economies that are socially governed by politics at the national level." Colin Crouch & Wolfgang Streek, "Introduction: The Future of Capitalist Diversity," in Colin Crouch & Wolfgang Streek, eds., *Political Economy of Modern Capitalism: Mapping Convergence and Diversity*, p. 1 (1997). As will be apparent from the balance of my discussion, I expect the outcome to be a mixed bag of formal, functional and hybrid convergence, with the particular outcome quite sensitive to local conditions.

rather than formal: removing poorly performing senior management, and disarming German codetermination. Section III takes up an example of the instrumental use of formal tools to catalyze the breakdown of path-dependent barriers to functional convergence of German cross-holding and block holding patterns. Section IV considers a setting where efforts at securing functional convergence without formal convergence have proven more difficult: the persistent relation between venture capital markets and stock market-centered capital markets. Section V takes up the potential for careful transaction design to help bridge the gap between formal and functional convergence through what I call convergence by contract. Two techniques are developed. The first provides accountability to investors through private governance mechanisms embedded in the design of the security rather than through traditional public governance mechanisms such as investor voting or capital market surveillance. The second picks up John Coffee's recent analysis of convergence through a particular contract – the stock exchange listing agreement by which a foreign issuer submits to US stock exchange governance rules and, more important, elements of US securities regulation.[15] Convergence by contract may have particular saliency in those European countries whose governance structures use techniques, like super-voting stock to preserve family control, which American institutional investors find objectionable. Finally, section VI takes up a form of convergence that operates through a hybrid of private and public ordering: the opportunity for individual companies to choose their corporate governance structure by selecting from the statutes offered by competing jurisdictions – the US race to the top/race to the bottom form of regulatory competition that may have been introduced to the European Community by the European Court of Justice (ECJ) decision in *Centros*.[16]

I. The interaction of adaptivity and path dependency

The institutional characteristics of national corporate governance institutions exhibit path dependency. Initial conditions, determined by the accident of history or the design of politics, can set an economy down a particular path. For example, the weakness of American financial

---

[15] John C. Coffee, Jr., "The Future as History: The Prospects for Global Convergence in Corporate Governance and its Implications," 93 *Nov. U.L. Rev.* 641 (1999).

[16] European Court of Justice, March 9, 1999, C. 21/297.

intermediaries, and important characteristics of Japanese corporate governance including lifetime employment and main bank relationships, find their origins not in considerations of efficiency, but in the interplay of populism and federalism in the case of the United States,[17] and in the World War II and immediate post-war experience in the case of Japan.[18] Indeed, the same outcome is possible even within a single economy. The trajectories of two high-technology industrial districts – the continued success of California's Silicon Valley and the relative decline of Massachusetts' Route 128 – owe much to the serendipitous presence of legal rules adopted in California following statehood that became important one hundred years later.[19] From those initial positions, efficiency considerations favor the addition of new institutions whose contribution to the system reflects not just their own incremental addition to output, but also the resulting increase in output of existing institutions to which the new institutions are complementary.[20] For example, barriers to financial intermediary participation in corporate governance find a complement in legal rules and institutions that protect small shareholders who, in the absence of large financial intermediaries, must provide an economy's investment.[21] Similarly, the inability to protect trade secrets embedded

---

[17] Roe, note 3 above; see also Simon, note 3 above.

[18] See, e.g., Gilson & Roe, "Lifetime Employment" *supra* note 4; Masahiko Aoki, "Unintended Fit: Organizational Evolution and Government Design of Institutions in Japan," Center for Economic Policy Research Working Paper no. 434, Stanford University (1994); Takeo Hoshi, "Cleaning-Up the Balance Sheets: Japanese Experience in the Post-war Reconstruction Period," in Masahiko Aoki & Hyung-Ki Kim, eds., *Corporate Governance in Transitional Economies: Insider Control and the Role of Banks*, p. 303 (1995); Tetsuji Okazaki, "The Japanese Firm under the Wartime Planned Economy," 7 *J. Jap. & Intn'l Econ.* 175 (1993).

[19] Ronald J. Gilson, "The Legal Infrastructure of High Technology Industrial Districts: Silicon Valley, Route 128, and Covenants Not to Compete," 74 *N.Y.U.L. Rev.* 595 (1999).

[20] This increasing return characteristic is referred to as "supermodularity." See Paul Milgrom & John Roberts, "Complementarities and Systems: Understanding Japanese Economic Organization," 9 *Estudios Economicos* 3 (1994). Milgrom and Roberts develop their analysis of how multiattribute systems develop from an initial starting point in Paul Milgrom & John Roberts, "Complementarities and Fit: Strategy, Structure and Organizational Change in Manufacturing," 19 *J. Acct'g & Econ.* 179 (1995); Paul Milgrom & John Roberts, "The Economics of Modern Manufacturing: Technology, Strategy and Organization," 80 *Am. Econ. Rev.* 511 (1990).

[21] The reader will note that this formulation finesses an important current debate between my colleagues Professors John Coffee and Mark Roe. Noting that recent empirical work by financial economists has linked the existence of strong stock markets not to US populist politics as argued by Mark Roe, but to strong legal protections for minority shareholders, Professor Coffee has put forward a "legal theory" of capital market development that he contends better fits the evidence than Professor Roe's political theory. Thus, Professor

in human capital finds a complement in a labor market characterized by extreme employee mobility.[22] Such increasing return characteristics shape the development path at each stage by favoring the selection of new institutions that increase the output of preexisting institutions, at the expense of alternatives that lack this attribute. Thus, the corporate governance system's development is driven, domino-like, by the linking of complementary institutions.[23]

In this system of institutional complementarity, institutional form is still constrained by the initial starting point, which under some circumstances may cause problems. A complementary system is difficult to change piecemeal; like leverage, complementarity has an ominous downside. When external economic changes counsel altering one institutional attribute, the change may cause the productivity of the entire system to decline dramatically because other attributes were selected to make good use of the now altered attribute.[24] The structure of the US capital market, for example, represents the efficiency-driven development of complementary institutions given the politically imposed initial condition. However, these same institutions represent a barrier to change if altered economic conditions reduce the resulting system's efficiency.

Coffee states that "[t]he most convincing explanation for this sharp disparity [between the importance of equity markets in the US and in France, Germany and Italy] is that only those legal systems that provide significant protections for minority investors can develop active equity markets . . . But once this explanation is accepted, it amounts to a rejection of the 'political theory' offered by Professor Roe and others." Coffee, note 15 above, at 644 (1999). See John C. Coffee, Jr., "Privatization and Corporate Governance: The Lessons from Securities Market Failure," 25 *J. Corp. L.* 1 (1999). Formulating the issue in terms of complementarity-driven institutional evolution allows an important role for both politics and law. The difficulty with Professor Coffee's analysis is that it treats law as exogenous. If, as Professor Roe argues, the absence of financial intermediaries was driven by politics, then the resulting increased role for securities markets and individual investors creates a demand for complementary protective law that would not be present in a system with large financial intermediaries. From this prospective, law is important, but its character – protective of minority shareholders or not – is shaped by politics, a result consistent with the reported correlation between protective legal rules and developed securities markets. Put differently, political conditions create the demand for protective law, a combination that turns out subsequently to be efficient. Cf. Gilson & Roe, "Lifetime Employment," note 3 above (lifetime employment was politically dictated but then calls forth efficient complementary institutions). For Professor Roe's analysis of Professor Coffee's criticism, see Mark J. Roe, "Political Preconditions to Separating Ownership from Control" (Working Paper, September 1999). For the empirical literature that provides the foundation of Professor Coffee's analysis, see the sources listed in note 9 above.

[22] See Gilson, "High Technology Industrial Districts," note 19 above.
[23] Milgrom & Roberts, "Complementarities and Systems," note 20 above.   [24] Ibid.

Path dependency, however, is not the only force influencing the shape of corporate governance institutions. Existing institutions are subject to powerful environmental selection mechanisms. If existing institutions cannot compete with differently organized competitors, ultimately they will not survive. Path-dependent formal characteristics of national governance institutions confront the discipline of the operative selection mechanisms that encourage functional convergence to the more efficient structure and, failing that, formal convergence as well. National institutions are thus shaped by what I have elsewhere called "corporate governance plate tectonics, in which the demands of current circumstances grind against the influence of initial conditions."[25] From this perspective, functional convergence, in which the barriers to formal institutional change are avoided, comes first. Formal convergence, which can involve ripple-like costs – including political costs – of changing complementary institutions with their own economic and political constituencies, comes as a last resort.[26]

At the outset, I should be clear about the level of generality contemplated by this typology and, in particular, the level of generality at which functional convergence can occur. Consider the proposition that effective protection of minority shareholders is necessary for a strong securities market.[27] But, as Professor Black points out, minority shareholders can be protected from controlling shareholders in two very different ways. A mandatory bid rule could require that a new controlling shareholder offer to purchase the shares of minority shareholders, as in the European Community's proposed Thirteenth Directive on Takeovers. Alternatively, strictly enforced rules against self-dealing could constrain a controlling shareholder from securing private benefits in the operation of the corporation.[28] If both the two approaches provide adequate protection, functional convergence will have occurred despite the quite different approaches, one protecting minority shareholders by assuring them an

---

[25] Gilson, "Corporate Governance and Economic Efficiency," note 8 above, at 332.

[26] Of course, convergence of any sort may fail in the face of institutions too inflexible for functional convergence and political institutions too responsive to the blocking efforts of interest groups protecting existing arrangements for formal convergence. Early twentieth-century Argentina appears to be such a failure, a then first-world country that devolved significantly beginning in the 1930s. See Mark J. Roe, "Backlash," 98 *Col. L. Rev* 217 (1998).

[27] See Bernard Black, "The Legal and Institutional Preconditions for Strong Securities Markets," 48 *U.C.L.A.L. Rev.* 781 (2001).

[28] This distinction is discussed in Ronald J. Gilson & Bernard S. Black, *The Law and Finance of Corporate Acquisitions*, pp. 1229–36 (2nd edn, 1995).

exit from their position, the other protecting them in the continuation of their position.

II. Functional but not formal convergence: replacing senior management

Recent empirical research concerning the German, Japanese, and American corporate governance systems illustrates the occurrence of functional but not formal convergence.[29] German and Japanese corporate governance is said to be long-term oriented, so that managers can ignore short-term swings in stock prices and accounting profits in choosing projects.[30] The long-term, multidimensional relationship between banks and corporations in Germany and Japan may provide the suppliers of capital better information concerning corporate performance than stock price and accounting measures.[31] In contrast, the American stock market-centered system is said to measure performance based largely on short-term oriented stock price and accounting reports, so that managers must invest in projects that provide short-term results clearly observable by one-dimensional stock market investors who have no other source of information.[32]

The institutional characteristics of all three systems – strong financial intermediaries in the German and Japanese systems and weak intermediaries in the American system – are path dependent.[33] Little formal convergence has occurred. But whether there has been functional convergence, that is, whether the formal differences any longer affect performance, is empirically testable. Any successful system must find a way to replace poorly performing senior managers. If formal institutional characteristics matter, then the monitoring of managers should be dictated by the information made available by the two systems. Because one can manage only what one can measure, the tenure of American senior managers should

---

[29] This section elaborates on Gilson, "Corporate Governance and Economic Efficiency," note 8 above.

[30] See, e.g., Porter, note 7 above.

[31] Jeremy Edwards & Klaus Fisher, *Banks, Finance and Investment in Germany*, ch. 2, sets out the argument.

[32] Jeremy C. Stein, "Takeover Threats and Managerial Myopia," 96 *J. Pol. Econ.* 61, 64–78 (1988), models such a process.

[33] On this point, Professors Roe and Coffee appear to agree. Formal institutional characteristics – for Roe, legislative barriers to the growth of financial intermediaries, and for Coffee, legal rules that protect minority shareholders – dictate the structure of capital markets. See Coffee, note 15 above, and Roe, note 3 above.

be more sensitive to short-term changes in stock price and accounting earnings than that of German and Japanese managers; only short-term results are said to be observable to US capital providers, while German and Japanese bank monitors receive sufficient information to evaluate longer-run strategies.

Empirical studies demonstrate functional but not formal convergence. Despite the striking differences in institutional form that still remain among the three governance systems, we do not observe the predicted differences among the three systems of monitoring management. Rather, we observe functional convergence. Regardless of whether the capital market is bank- or stock market-centered, the tenure of senior management in all three countries is equally sensitive to poor performance, whether measured by stock market returns or accounting earnings.[34] This functional convergence is driven by selection: a system that allows poor managers to remain in control will not succeed. We do not observe formal convergence because each system's governance institutions have sufficient flexibility to find a solution within their path-dependent limits. In the United States, stock market information and external pressure drives the solution; in Japan, main bank contingent monitoring is triggered by poor performance[35]; and in Germany, bank voting control and access to internal information through supervisory board membership,[36] are the active forces. In each case, we do not observe convergence of institutional form. Rather, each system's particular response to the problem of replacing poorly performing managers is, in evolutionary theorist Stephen J. Gould's terms, "jury-rigged from a limited set of available components"[37] supplied by the system's particular history. Functional convergence occurs at a high level of generality.

---

[34] See Steven Kaplan, "Top Executive Rewards and Firm Performance: A Comparison of Japan and the US," 102 *J. Pol. Econ.* 510 (1994); Steven Kaplan, "Top Executive Turnover and Firm Performance in Germany," 10 *J. L. Econ. & Org.* 142 (1994); Jun-Koo Kang & Anil Shivdasani, "Firm Performance, Corporate Governance, and Top Executive Turnover in Japan," 38 *J. Fin. Econ.* 29 (1995); Steven Kaplan & Bernadette Minton, "Appointments of Outsiders to Japanese Boards: Determinants and Implications for Managers," 36 *J. Fin. Econ.* 225 (1994).

[35] Masahiko Aoki, "Monitoring Characteristics of the Main Bank System: An Analytical and Developmental View," in Masahiko Aoki & Hugh Patrick, eds., *The Japanese Main Bank System: Its Relevance for Developing and Transforming Economies* (1994).

[36] See, e.g., Helmut M. Dietl, *Capital Markets and Corporate Governance in Japan, Germany, and the United States*, pp. 122–26 (1998).

[37] Stephen J. Gould, *The Panda's Thumb: More Reflections in Natural History*, p. 20 (1980). Steven Kaplan & Mark Ramseyer, "Those Japanese Firms with their Disdain for Shareholders: Another Fable for the Academy," 74 *Wash. U.L.Q.* 403 (1996), also stress the Japanese system's capacity for functional convergence.

This analysis suggests a pattern: functional convergence is likely the first response to competitive pressure because changing the form of existing institutions is costly. New institutions require new investment, and existing institutions will have developed related interest groups that render more difficult any necessary political action.

Moreover, the threat of partial change to interest groups organized around existing institutions is exacerbated by complementarity. Mancur Olson stresses that focused interest group politics motivated by protecting group welfare can block change that would be welfare-increasing for society at large, a phenomenon he argues importantly influences the relative growth rate of nations.[38] Changing the form of an institution, in order to enhance its own efficiency in response to changing economic conditions, initially may result in a reduction, not an increase, in overall system productivity. The new form may not be complementary to the other institutions that make up the system, which can result in a reduction in the performance of even those institutions whose form remains unchanged. In a system characterized by complementarity, it may be necessary to alter all remaining complementary institutions before alteration of the first will improve things.[39] The result, among other things, is to multiply the number of interest groups with rents to protect. Functional changes in existing institutions – in Gould's terms again, "a contraption not a lovely contrivance"[40] – will often be the least-cost means to respond to economic change.[41]

A second example of functional change, as opposed to more politically difficult formal change, involves the problem of reforming labor participation on the supervisory boards of large German corporations.[42] Suppose one concludes that codetermination restricts the ability of German corporations to adapt to global competition and protects existing jobholders at the expense of higher unemployment.[43]

---

[38] Olson, note 14 above.
[39] Milgrom & Roberts, "Complementarities and Systems," note 20 above.
[40] Gould, note 37 above, at p. 24.
[41] The text frames the problem in terms of blocking efficiency-inducing change. However, interest groups also can seek self-serving affirmative change. The emphasis on blocking action reflects an assumption, which I will not pause to justify here, that blocking action requires less political power than causing action to be taken, and therefore is the more pervasive problem.
[42] This discussion reflects conversations with Mats Isaksson.
[43] Katharina Pistor, "Co-determination in Germany: A Socio-political Model with Governance Externalities," in M. Blair & M. Roe, eds., *Employees and Corporate Governance* (1999), analyzes the political origins of codetermination and assesses the governance externalities inadvertently created.

Further suppose that the political barriers to formal change – legislative amendment of the relevant statute – are prohibitive at least in the short to medium run. In this setting, one can imagine a functional end run around the barriers to formal convergence, disarming rather than eliminating codetermination.

Under existing legislation, shareholder-selected supervisory members, with the aid of the tie-breaking vote cast by the chairman, command a majority of the board.[44] Thus, labor influence in the face of a shareholder-selected board majority may reflect a coalition between inside managers and labor representatives unchallenged by passive shareholder-selected board members.[45] A functional response to the problem might involve a shift in the character of the shareholder-selected supervisory board members. Should the large German banks conclude that the inflexibility created by the blocking alliance was too costly, they might respond by reinventing shareholder-selected supervisory board members so that more active shareholder members can disarm the blocking coalition.[46] To be sure, labor may respond by seeking further formal protection, but securing affirmative legislative action is likely more difficult than blocking actions that would result in formal convergence.

III.   The interaction of formal and functional convergence

In some circumstances, path dependency reinforced by formal rules presents a barrier to functional convergence. Large German banks and insurance companies hold large stakes in other publicly held German corporations and in each other.[47] [For example, Figure 4.1 shows the pattern of cross-holdings among shareholders of Daimler-Benz in 1996.]

More generally, studies report substantial blockholders in a very high percentage of German public companies.[48] Now suppose that the

---

[44] See Dietl, note 36 above, at 113; Mark J. Roe, "German Securities Markets and German Codetermination," 1998 *Col. Bus. L. Rev.* 167.

[45] Cf. John C. Coffee, "Unstable Coalitions: Corporate Governance as a Multi-player Game," 78 *Geo. L.J.*1495 (1990).

[46] Cf. Ronald J. Gilson & Reinier Kraakman, "Reinventing the Outside Director: An Agenda for Institutional Investors," 43 *Stan. L. Rev.* 863 (1991). A similar strategy relies on the use of supervisory board committees on which labor representatives do not sit. Pistor, note 43 above, surveys this strategy.

[47] See the sources cited in note 1 above.

[48] Tim Jenkinson & Alexander Ljungquist, "The Role of Hostile Stakes in German Corporate Governance," *J. Corp. Finance* 397 (2001); Michael Adams, "Cross Holdings in Germany," 155 *J. Institutional & Theo. Econ.* 80 (1999).

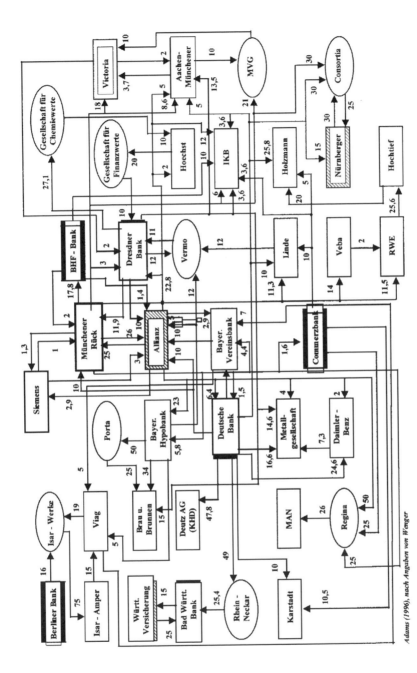

Figure 4.1 The German network of cross holdings: an example

Adams (1996), *nach Angaben von Wenger*

economic environment changes in a fashion that requires a systemic response best affected through a stock market centered capital market, rather than a bank centered capital market characterized by large block-holdings.[49] While formal corporate law creates no barriers to the holders of large blocks reducing the size of their positions, German tax law creates a substantial path dependency. Sale of these stakes are subject to a 42 percent capital gains tax (rate effective January 1, 2000) that enforces the path-dependent character of German concentrated ownership by imposing a substantial tax on a redistribution of ownership.

In December 1999, German Chancellor Gerhard Schröder proposed eliminating the capital gains tax on sales by German corporations of stock in other German corporations, with the explicit goal of eliminating barriers to dissipating concentrated cross-holdings.[50] This change in tax rules represents an interesting interaction between formal and functional convergence. The proposed tax cut – revenue neutral to the extent that the tax-induced path dependency prevented sales from ever being made – only eliminates the institutional shadow of a low basis. Determination of the most efficient distribution of shareholdings then is left largely to functional convergence, affected by the institutions' sales of their block-holdings and cross-holdings.

IV. The failure of functional convergence: venture capital and the structure of capital markets[51]

Comparisons of the United States' capital market with those of Japan and Germany focus on the different roles of banks and stock markets. The United States has a large number of comparatively small banks that for practical purposes play no role in corporate governance, and an advanced stock market that supports an active market for corporate control catalyzed by the mechanism of hostile takeovers. Japanese

---

[49] Gilson, "Political Ecology," and Gilson, "Corporate Governance and Economic Efficiency," note 8 above.

[50] Edmund Andrews, "Germany Proposes Some Tax-Free Stock Sales, Lifting Market," *N.Y. Times*, Dec. 24, 1999, at C1; Cecilie Rohwedder, "Key German Party Backs Plan to Drop Capital-Gains Tax," *Wall St. J.*, Dec. 29, 1999, at A11; Edmund Andrews, "German Stock-Sale Plan Stirs Only Limited Opposition," *N.Y. Times*, Dec. 30, 1999, at C4. While the effective date of the capital gains exclusion has been delayed by a year, the reform is reported to be going forward. Edmund Andrews, "German Stock-Sale Plan is Delayed a Year," *N.Y. Times*, Feb. 18, 2000, at C4.

[51] This section draws on Ronald Gilson & Bernard Black, "Venture Capital and the Structure of Capital Markets: Banks vs. Stock Markets," 47 *J. Fin. Econ.* 47 (1998).

and German banks are few in number, but larger in size relative to each nation's industrial firms, and are said to play an important governance role by monitoring corporate management.[52] Neither country has an active market for corporate control.

Less attention is paid to an additional systematic difference between bank- and stock market-centered capital markets: the existence of a much stronger venture capital industry in stock market-centered systems.[53] Because an active venture capital market is said to be critical to encouraging innovation, many countries have sought to replicate the United States' success. The failure of bank-centered systems to develop comparable venture capital markets demonstrates both the failure of functional convergence even at a high level of generality – banks have not been able to alter their functions in a fashion that would duplicate the stock market's role in venture capital – and the difficulty of implementing the systemic formal change necessary to the adaption of complementary systems.

In another article, Bernard Black and I have explored the link between stock markets and venture capital markets. The ability to liquidate a portfolio company investment – to "exit" – is crucial to venture capital investors. Their contribution to portfolio companies consists of both cash and noncash contributions, such as managerial services, intensive monitoring and reputation, that are linked by economies of scope. Once a portfolio company succeeds to the point that the venture capitalist's noncash contributions are of reduced value, efficiency dictates recycling those inputs so they can be invested in companies at a stage that requires them. However, the economies of scope associated with linking cash and noncash contributions dictate recycling the cash contributions at the same time. Hence the importance of exit.[54]

The particular type of exit is crucial to the entrepreneur and to the terms of the contract between the venture capitalist and the entrepreneur. When exit occurs through an initial public offering, available only in a stock market-centered capital market, the entrepreneur typically regains

---

[52] See, e.g., Aoki, "Monitoring Characteristics of the Main Bank System," note 35 above; Edwards & Fischer, note 30 above; Roe, note 3 above.

[53] Gilson & Black, note 51 above, surveys the empirical evidence on the size of national venture capital markets. See also Leslie Jeng and Phillipe Wells, "The Determinants of Venture Capital Funding: Evidence across Countries," 6 *J. Corp. Fin.* 241 (2000). Curtis Milhaupt, "The Market for Innovation in the United States and Japan: Venture Capital and the Comparative Corporate Governance Debate," 91 *Nw. L. Rev.* 865 (1997), provides an excellent account of the Japanese experience with venture capital.

[54] Gilson & Black, note 51 above, at 252–55.

the disproportionate amount of control that was shifted to the venture capitalist at the time of its investment, even if, as is typically the case, the venture capitalist does not then dispose of its entire investment. In contrast, when exit occurs by the portfolio company's sale to a third party, an exit route that *is* available in bank-centered capital markets, the entrepreneur not only forfeits the control ceded to the venture capitalist, but loses as well the elements of control he had retained. The critical impact of the opportunity to exit through an initial public offering is that, at the time of the initial investment, the parties can enter into an implicit contract that, in effect, gives the entrepreneur a call option on control exercisable on the company's success and reflected in the transaction by the release of the venture capitalist's formal levers of control on the occurrence of a public offering. Because the incentive properties of this implicit contract go to the heart of the entrepreneurial process – that is, the entrepreneur's dealings in control – its availability only in a stock market-centered capital market helps explain the absence of vigorous venture capital markets in countries with bank-centered capital markets.[55]

Bank-centered systems could respond to this competitive disadvantage through functional convergence: retain the structure of the capital market but provide funding of innovation through bank financing of start-up companies or internalization of the entrepreneurial process by large companies. If these alternative institutions yield the same functional performance as the United States's stock market-linked venture capital market, then adaption will have occurred through functional convergence without the need for more costly formal convergence.

The empirical evidence needed to assess the existence of functionally equivalent financing of innovation in bank-centered systems is not available, but anecdotal evidence supports a skeptical view. The United States has become a world leader in precisely those industries, notably biotechnology and computer-related high technology, in which venture capital markets played a central role. Moreover, large American and European pharmaceutical companies are responding to innovation in biotechnology not by direct funding of entrepreneurs, but by providing

---

[55] Ibid. at 257–64. The recent experience in the internet industry, where the make/buy decision has leaned of late toward buy, may alter this pattern. Start-ups where the goal is to provide a part of someone else's business plan by being acquired may confront a very different incentive structure. See, e.g., Scott Thrum, "Under Cisco's System Mergers Usually Work: That Defies the Odds," *Wall St. J.*, March 1, 2000, at 1 (Cisco uses acquisitions to reshape itself and plug holes in its product line; 51 acquisitions in past $6\frac{1}{2}$ years, 21 in past 12 months alone).

later-stage financing and partnering to entrepreneurial companies, mostly US-based and originally financed through venture capital.[56]

A number of European countries have recognized the apparent failure of functional convergence, and have made efforts at formal convergence, notably by starting special stock exchange segments for newer, smaller companies. The limited success to date highlights the difficulty of piecemeal change of a system made up of complementary institutions.

France and Germany first tried to create small company stock markets during the 1980s; by the 1990s these projects had been closed or marginalized.[57] Current efforts include the Alternative Investment Market of the London Stock Exchange; Euro NM, a consortium of the French Le Nouveau March, the German Neuer Markt, and the Belgian New Market; and EASDAQ, an exchange explicitly patterned after the US NASDAQ, of which the NASD, NASDAQ's operator, is a part owner. The number of recent initial public offerings, especially on the Neuer Markt, is evidence of the increasing acceptance of this institutional innovation.[58] Recognition of the importance of complementarity, however, suggests that merely creating a stock market will be insufficient to provide the institutional infrastructure necessary to support a venture capital market. Also missing are the complementary institutions that developed from the presence of stock markets in the United States: venture capital organizations, the limited partner investment vehicle, investment bankers experienced in taking early-stage companies public and, most important, a supply of entrepreneurs which the availability of venture capital financing elicits in the first place.

One approach to the complementarity-driven problem of creating multiple institutions more or less simultaneously is made available by the globalization of the capital market. As Bernard Black and I have suggested, companies with bank-centered systems can piggyback on another country's existing institutions. In particular, US venture capital institutions – NASDAQ and its institutional infrastructure, including venture capital investors, investment bankers with experience in venture

---

[56] Gilson & Black, note 51 above. Debt financing of high-technology start-up companies by banks is simply not feasible. Because of the high risk and negative cash flow characteristics of such companies, the debt instrument would have to be something like a very high yield zero coupon bond. In functional terms, the instrument would be the equivalent of equity.

[57] Sebastian Rasch. "Special Stock Market Segments for Small Company Shares in Europe: What Went Wrong?," Center for European Economic Research Discussion Paper no. 93-13 (1994).

[58] See, e.g., "Exchanges Broaden their Global Appeal," *Fin. Times*, June 11, 1999, at 6; Stewart Fleming, "The Neur Markt's Wild Ride," *Inst'l Investor*, April 1999, at 76, 77, 180.

capital-backed IPOs, and experienced lawyers and accountants – are available to European start-ups. Access to these substitute institutions can facilitate adaption during the period that local institutions develop to achieve formal convergence.[59]

V. Convergence by contract

Having examined situations where functional convergence has succeeded and, alternatively, where formal convergence appears necessary, the survey is extended by looking at a third situation that I will call convergence by contract.[60] Here I have in mind convergence in a situation where existing institutions lack the flexibility to achieve functional convergence, but where the costs, especially the political costs, of changing existing institutions make formal convergence difficult. I take up first the possibility of convergence through security design. I then consider convergence through the contract associated with a foreign company's listing its shares on a US stock exchange.

A. Convergence through security design

American investors, especially large pension funds and other institutional investors, now own substantial stakes in European publicly traded corporations. For example, the California Public Employees Retirement System ("CalPERS"), the largest US public retirement fund, holds nearly $20 billion in foreign equities, representing almost 20 percent of its total investment in equity.[61] Anglo-Saxon institutional investment of this sort translates into a significant percentage of the outstanding shares in

---

[59] Gilson & Black, note 51 above, at 271–73. Israel provides the best example of this phenomenon. According to recent estimates, more than one hundred Israeli corporations are listed on US securities exchanges, including in excess of seventy high technology companies. See Ira M. Greenstein & Lloyd Hamretz, "US–Israel Transactions Present Unique Issue," *N.Y.L.J.*, April 28, 1998, at S2; Richard Rappaport, "Beating their Swords in to IPO Shares," *Forbes ASAP*, June 1, 1998, at 93. The adaption process in Europe appears to be accelerating. While early-stage ventures received only 10.2 percent of European private equity money in 1998, investment in 1999 is said to have shifted toward early-stage financing. "Europe's Start-Up Stampede," *The Economist*, Jan. 15–21, 2000, at 63.

[60] This discussion has benefited from conversations with participants at a Swedish Corporate Governance Forum meeting, including Karl-Adam Bonnier, Raulf Gonec, Mats Isaksson, Michael Jensen, Gunnar Nord, & Robert Ohlsson.

[61] Sara Webb, "Calpers Sees New Targets Overseas," *Wall St. J.*, Oct. 20, 1997, at C1, col. 6.

particular countries: on average, 35 percent of the outstanding shares of the forty largest companies on the Paris stock exchange are held by American and British institutional investors and pension funds.[62] The figure rises to 41 percent of Dutch companies.[63]

With significant foreign investment has come demand for change in European corporate governance systems. In Netherlands, France, and Sweden, for example, substantial deviation from the Anglo-Saxon one share–one vote model can protect incumbent managers from monitoring by the capital market. Confronted with corporate governance systems that appear to lack mechanisms for external monitoring, US institutional investors have begun to urge that European companies make significant changes in their formal governance institutions to more closely resemble US-style governance. Leading the movement, CalPERS has announced a set of general principles – its six General Principles including director accountability to shareholders and a one share–one vote capital structure. The General Principles were followed with the issuance of specific standards for the United Kingdom, France, Germany, and Japan.[64]

Formal convergence of continental corporate governance to the US model can be expected to be very difficult, especially when it comes to matters of corporate control. Unequal voting regimes are designed to protect family control (and in the Netherlands foundation control); broadly weakening that control by amending the corporate statute to restrict unequal voting would face formidable political barriers. Some potential for finding a way out of the conflict between the institutional investors' demand for formal mechanisms of accountability, and the Europeans' sensitivity to relinquishing formal elements of control, arises from a kind of convergence that has taken place in the United States. The simple fact is that US institutional investors do not always demand the same formal governance structure from all entities in which they invest. Such investors, including CalPERS, happily place billions of dollars annually in entities that lack the governance mechanisms traditionally found in US public corporations. These investments go into the private equity market through the vehicle of a limited partnership in which the investors give up

---

[62] John Tagliabue, "Resisting those Ugly Americans," *N.Y. Times*, Jan. 9, 2000, Sec. 3, at 1, 10.

[63] Joel Chernoff & Patrick Farnon, "Governance Codes Vary by Market," *Pensions and Investments*, Sept. 16, 1997, at 16.

[64] These Principles may be accessed at http://www.calpers-governance.org/principles/international.

traditional governance mechanisms in return for securing the specialized services of the general partner in making investments in nonpublicly traded securities.[65]

Investors in such vehicles as venture capital limited partnerships and leveraged buyout funds are not, however, left unprotected from the familiar host of agency problems against which traditional corporate governance techniques are directed. Rather, they are protected by quite different mechanisms that are created by contract.[66] While tracing the overall governance structure of these investment vehicles is not my purpose here, examination of one feature is illustrative.

A standard private equity limited partnership has a fixed life, typically ten years, after which the partnership must be liquidated and its assets returned to investors. This fixed termination serves a number of important purposes. Most important, it balances the general partner's need for discretion in making illiquid investments characterized by enormous uncertainty, with the investors' need for a mechanism of accountability. In publicly held corporations misuse of free cash flow is policed internally by the board of directors, and externally through shareholder action either through voting or through the control market, in all cases illuminated by performance information provided through stock market prices. In private equity limited partnerships, the free cash flow problem is addressed by a requirement that the general partner distribute the proceeds of investments that become liquid, and by the requirement that the partnership terminate and the assets be returned to investors at the end of the partnership term. These features assure that the general partner will not retain indefinitely capital which it cannot invest profitably.

The need to liquidate the partnership's assets to facilitate distribution also provides an observable measure against which to weigh the general partner's performance. Prior to that point, a market measure of the value

---

[65] For example, on average pension funds supply over 40 percent of the annual commitments to US venture capital funds. See Gilson & Black, note 51 above.

[66] For an overview of the standard contract between an investor and the general partner of a venture capital limited partnership, see Gilson & Black, note 51 above; William A. Sahlman, "The Structure and Governance of Venture-Capital Organizations," 27 *J. Fin. Econ.* 473 (1990); Theodor Baums & Ronald J. Gilson, "Comparative Venture Capital Contracting: Replicating the US Template in Germany" (Working Paper, May 2000). Paul Gompers & Joshua Lerner, "The Use of Covenants: An Empirical Analysis of Venture Partnership Agreements," 39 *J. L. & Econ.* 463 (1996), provide empirical evidence of the use of covenant protection in venture capital limited partnerships. For an overview of the structure of a leveraged buyout limited partnership, see Michael Jensen, "The Eclipse of the Public Corporation," *Harv. Bus. Rev.* 61 (Sept.–Oct. 1989).

of the limited partnership's portfolio is not available because its private equity investments are not liquid.

Finally, forced liquidation operates to hold the general partner accountable for its performance. At the end of the partnership term, the investor has the opportunity to choose whether to allow the general partner to continue managing its money by choosing whether to invest in a new limited partnership formed by the general partner. The general partner then must compete with other managers for the opportunity to manage the money of investors in the liquidated partnership, with its prior performance being the central influence on the outcome.

In countries where the cost of formal convergence would be high because of family and other concentrated holdings, accountability to investors might still be achieved by use of these private equity investment techniques. While designing a security by which this could be accomplished is well beyond my ambitions here, imagine that a European company with dual-class voting in which a family controls the super-voting shares desires to raise equity capital from US institutional investors. The family, however, is unwilling unilaterally to cede its control to the public float by eliminating the dual-class structure.

An institutional investor might well be reluctant to invest when the dual-class capital structure blocks any external monitoring of the performance of the management chosen by the controlling shareholder. Suppose instead the institutional investor is offered an equity security that provides accountability by mimicking the fixed term of a private equity investment, a correspondence that makes sense because both publicly traded corporations with dual-class capital structures and private equity limited partnerships lack traditional corporate governance accountability mechanisms.

The structure of the security could take a number of forms. For example, the institutional investor could be sold low voting stock which, at the end of specified periods, would become super-voting if the company's performance did not meet a specified standard, perhaps a designated percentile among a group of peer companies. If the voting shift were triggered, family-designated management would have to compete for the opportunity to continue to manage the company. Depending on the size of the investment, actual control of the company might shift. Alternatively, the security might provide put rights that guaranteed the investor a return keyed to peer group performance; the need to raise capital to fund performance of a put-triggered redemption would have the same disciplining effect.

This short account provides not even a checklist of the provisions such a security would require, nor even a thoughtful canvas of what types of securities might be devised.[67] For now, the task is much more limited. I mean only to sketch the outlines of an intermediate contractual approach to convergence that might be appropriate when existing governance institutions lack the flexibility necessary for functional convergence and the mutability necessary for formal convergence.

B. Convergence through stock exchange listing

John Coffee has developed a second example of convergence by contract, less speculative than the arbitrage between private and public organizational forms developed in section V.A., and with the advantage of being already visible.[68] In this case, the contract is the listing agreement executed when a non-US corporation lists its securities on a US securities exchange, together with those US securities laws to which the act of listing subjects a foreign corporation.

The listing agreement itself imposes a set of governance obligations including a minimum number of independent directors, an audit committee, and an equal opportunity rule with respect to tender offers. In turn, by listing on a US stock exchange, the foreign company is obligated to register under Section 12(b) of the Securities Exchange Act of 1934, thereby voluntarily subjecting itself to a host of US securities regulations that have corporate governance implications.

For example, by listing on a US exchange a foreign company accepts the obligation under Section 13(d) of the Securities Exchange Act of 1934 to disclose holders of more than 5 percent of its outstanding stock, a significantly more stringent trigger than the 10 percent threshold required by the European Union Transparency Directive. The company also accepts the rules under Section 14(d) governing the procedural and substantive aspects of tender offers, those under Section 13(e) governing going private transactions, and those under Section 13(b) governing the making of "questionable payments." To be sure, the SEC has allowed some exemptive relief for foreign issuers when the detail of a particular requirement is

---

[67] For example, the architect of the security would have to confront management's incentive to take on too much risk in the later years of the security's term if performance is lagging. On a more mundane level, a means would be necessary to update the group of peer companies against whose performance the issuing company's would be measured.

[68] Coffee, note 15 above.

inconsistent with the law of a foreign company's home jurisdiction,[69] but the scope of governance rules adopted by the act of listing and the resulting application of the Securities Exchange Act is significant.

VI. Hybrid convergence through regulatory competition

Convergence by contract through foreign companies voluntarily listing their securities on US exchanges is made possible by a form of regulatory competition. By choosing a US listing, a foreign company selects a significant element of US governance rules in preference to those of its own jurisdiction. A similar convergence mechanism has always been available in the United States with respect to corporate law. Because in the United States a corporation's internal affairs (including especially its corporate governance) is governed by its state of incorporation without regard to its principal place of business, a US corporation can choose the state corporate law that governs its affairs by choosing its state of incorporation.[70] The aggregated choices of a majority of publicly traded US corporations have resulted in a convergence on the Delaware General Corporation Law as a *de facto* national corporate law.

Historically, convergence through regulatory competition was not available in Europe because the widespread application of the "real seat" doctrine dictated that the corporate law of the country in which the corporation's principal place of business was located governed its internal affairs regardless of the country of incorporation, a mandatory coincidence of a company's primary business location and the corporate law covering its governance.[71] At the margin, differences in corporate governance simply did not outweigh the real economic differences that grew out of a business's location, especially before the single-market initiative. As a result, Europe has supported a wide variety of corporate law regimes, ranging from the UK's Anglo-Saxon system to the German dual board and code-termined system.

On March 9, 1999, this equilibrium of diverse corporate regimes was fundamentally destabilized. In its *Centros* decision,[72] the European Court

---

[69] Coffee, note 15 above, at 688–89.
[70] Roberta Romano, *The Genius of American Corporate Law* (1993) develops the role of regulatory competition in American corporate law.
[71] See, e.g., Richard M. Buxbaum & Klaus J. Hopt, *Legal Harmonization and the Business Enterprise*, pp. 68–79, 227–28 (1988).
[72] *Centros Ltd. v. Erhverus-og Selskabsstyrelsen*, case no. C.21/297, March 9, 1999 [1999] 2 CMLR 551.

of Justice introduced regulatory competition – a hybrid between formal and functional convergence – into the European Union.

In *Centros*, Danish residents seeking to organize a corporation to do business in Denmark attempted to avoid the 200,000 Danish Crown (approximately $27,000) minimum capital requirement by organizing a UK corporation. English corporate law was attractive because it did not impose a minimum capital requirement for private corporations.[73] The newly formed UK corporation, which did not, and was never intended to do business in the UK, then applied for registration (i.e., qualification to do business in US terms) in Denmark.

The Danish Registry Office refused registration, concluding, quite accurately, that the UK incorporation was merely a means to avoid the Danish minimum capital requirement.[74] The European Court of Justice, however, relying upon the rights of establishment in Articles 52 and 58 of the Treaty, protected forum shopping for favorable corporate law by decoupling the choice of where to incorporate from the choice of where to locate the corporation's business operations:

> [T]he fact that a national of a Member State who wishes to set up a company chooses to form it in the Member State whose rules of company law seem to him the least restrictive and to set up branches in other Member States cannot, in itself, constitute an abuse of the right of establishment. The right to form a company in accordance with the law of a Member State and to set up branches in other Member States is inherent in the exercise, in a single market, of the freedom of establishment guaranteed by the Treaty.[75]

Understandably, *Centros* created "great waves of unrest on the continent."[76] But it also may have created a hybrid mechanism of convergence – formal in the sense that what is at issue is the selection of binding rules of corporate law, but functional in the sense that, as a result of the European

---

[73] Eddy Wymeersch, "Centros: A Landmark Decision in European Company Law," in T. Baums, ed., *Festschrift for Richard M. Buxbaum* (2000).

[74] That the motive of the UK incorporation was to avoid the minimum capital requirements of Danish corporate law was simply assumed by the Court. See *Centros*, §14.

[75] *Centros*, at §27. The Court's full holding is as follows: "It is contrary to Articles 52 and 58 of the EC Treaty for a Member State to refuse to register a branch of a company formed in accordance with the law of another Member State in which it has its registered office but in which it conducts no business where the branch is intended to enable the company in question to carry on its entire business in the State in which the branch is to be created, while avoiding the need to form a company there, thus evading application of the rules governing the formalities of companies which, in that State, are more restrictive as regards the paying up of a minimum share capital."

[76] Wymeersch, note 73 above.

Court of Justice's decision, European Community law may be sufficiently flexible to allow at least newly formed companies to adapt their governance structures in response to changing economic conditions.[77]

The hybrid of formal and functional convergence *Centros* makes possible can be illustrated by the choices facing a venture capitalist and a German entrepreneur seeking to make use of German engineering and scientific talent to organize a high-technology start-up company.

Formal German corporate law presents two particular problems for the standard venture capital contract used to finance early-stage high-technology businesses.[78] Central to the relationship between the investor and the entrepreneur is that, during the period prior to the investors' exit, the investor receives a level of control disproportionate to its equity ownership. In particular, representatives of the venture capitalist often will control a majority of the board of directors even if the venture capitalist puts up less than a majority of the equity. Moreover, the board, controlled or significantly influenced by the venture capitalist, can remove senior management, including the founding entrepreneur, essentially at will.[79] German corporate law – in particular codetermination and the rules governing removal of management board members – present a barrier to giving the venture capitalist the control dictated by the nature of early-stage high-technology financing.

First, fast-growing high-technology companies can reach 500 employees very quickly, thereby triggering the full codetermination requirement that one-half of the supervisory board be composed of labor representatives.[80] Since the entrepreneur can be expected to require at least some supervisory board representation, codetermination makes majority control by the venture capital investors impossible. Second, the requirement of a dual-board structure further attenuates venture capitalist control. Under German corporate law, the management board is made up of full-time company employees, who cannot be removed except for cause short of their five-year term.[81] As a result, the formal legal rule interferes

---

[77] Professor Buxbaum offers an interesting assessment of the constitutional foundation of regulatory competition in corporate law in the United States and the European Community. Richard Buxbaum, "Back to the Future? From 'Centros' to the 'Überlagerungstheoric,'" in *Festschrift für Otto Sandrock zum 70* (2000).

[78] Baums & Gilson, note 66 above, develop the differences between the environment of venture capital contracting in the US and Germany.

[79] Ibid. See Gilson & Black, note 51 above; Sahlman, note 47 above.

[80] See Dietl, note 36 above, at pp. 113–14.

[81] See Julian Frank & Colin Mayer, "Capital Markets and Corporate Control," 10 *Econ. Pol'y* 184, 206 (1990).

with central features of the control allocation critical to early-stage high-technology financing.

Centros invites German venture capitalists and entrepreneurs to select a jurisdiction whose corporate law is more favorable to venture capital contracting – say, the UK – and then register the newly formed corporation in Germany. The ability to choose a different law allows functional convergence without altering formal German corporate law by, in effect, making optional the undesirable features of German law.

To be sure, the extent to which *Centros* actually announces a regimen of regulatory competition is more complicated than to this point I have allowed. First, some European lawyers have read *Centros* narrowly, "merely referring to a case of abuse, without general significance."[82] From the perspective of an American, and therefore of an amateur at parsing the opinions of the European Court of Justice, so narrow an interpretation seems like wishful thinking. For better or worse, the Court explicitly ruled that denying branch registration to a company whose foreign incorporation has the sole purpose of "evading application of the rules governing the formation of companies" in the nation in which the company's principal place of business will be located, "is contrary to Articles 52 and 58."[83] Rather than responding to a case of abuse by a member state, the ECJ seems self-consciously to invite avoidance by those organizing businesses.[84]

Second, the effect of *Centros* may be attenuated by responsive efforts by EC member states to impose restrictions in ways that cannot be avoided by instrumental choice of where to incorporate. *Centros* quite clearly limits its application to "rules governing the formation of companies;" it does not apply to more general rules "concerning the carrying out of certain trades, professions or businesses."[85] Put differently, rules of general application, which do not depend for their application on the member state under whose laws a corporation was organized, would seem to be unaffected by *Centros*. So, for example, *Centros* would allow a newly formed UK

---

[82] Wymeersch, note 73 above, at p. 3.   [83] *Centros*, ruling paragraph.

[84] "[T]he fact that a national of a Member State who wishes to set up a company chooses to form it in a Member State whose rules of company law seem to him the least restrictive and to set up branches in other Member States cannot, in itself, constitute an abuse of the right of establishment." *Centros*, §27.

[85] *Centros* at §26. While one might argue that the phrase "rules governing the formation of companies" limits the decision to threshold issues like the minimum paid-in capital requirements, the Court elsewhere uses the broader phrase "rules of company law," which certainly would seem to extend to the decisionmaking structure mandated by a member state's company law.

corporation with a principal place of business in Germany to avoid code-termination, but would not affect the application of German legislation imposing workers' councils on all companies. Thus, the European Court of Justice has left open to EC members the strategy of replacing worker participation in decision making imposed by corporate law through the formal structure of the corporation, like codetermination and protection of management board tenure, with legislation requiring worker participation before specified actions, like plant closings, can be taken – a mandate framed as a matter of labor relations, not corporate law.[86]

At least in the high technology area, however, there is reason to doubt whether EC member states, and especially Germany, will take up the Court's suggestions for crafting a way around *Centros*. First, *Centros* shifts the burden of going forward with reform through the political system from those who favor reducing worker involvement to those who wish to preserve it. Accomplishing change is more difficult than merely having to protect the status quo.[87] Second, there is reason to believe that practical limits on the breadth of *Centros*'s application will persuade the labor

---

[86] To be sure, some commentators have taken a narrower view of *Centros*'s impact on member states' ability to regulate the internal affairs of a *Centros*-like corporation via one means or another. Some argue that the *Gebhard* exception to the right of establishment with respect to imperative requirements in the public interest, while not broad enough to encompass the Danish minimum capital requirement, may extend to social measures like codetermination. See, e.g., Werner F. Ebke, "*Centros*: Some Realities and Some Mysteries" (Working Paper, April 2000), available at Centre of European Law – Centros Papers, http://www.kcl.ac.uk/depsta/law/research/cel/centros/prog.html. Others suggest that pseudo-foreign corporation statutes may allow a member state to apply to a corporation formed under the laws of another member state certain core features of domestic corporation law when the corporation carries out its primary activities within the first state and has no substantive contact with its state of incorporation. See Vanessa Edwards, "Case Law of the European Court of Justice on Freedom of Establishment after *Centros*," 1 *Eur.Bus.Org.L.Rev.* 147, 153 (2000). This issue has been referred to the European Court of Justice in *Kamer van Koophandel en Fabriken voor Groningen* v. *Challenger Trading Company Ltd.*, Case C-410/99, in the context of the Netherlands pseudo-foreign corporation statute's application with respect to minimum capital requirements. It should be noted that, if consistent with the right of establishment, such a statute would have allowed Denmark to impose its minimum capital requirement on the UK corporation in *Centros*.

[87] An example from San Francisco, where I live, illustrates the point. For years, many residents sought to have the Embarcadero Freeway, a two-level concrete abomination that separated downtown San Francisco from the waterfront, demolished. While this group was likely a majority, a concentrated minority whose businesses the freeway benefited was successful in blocking demolition. The 1989 earthquake, operating as a mechanism of natural urban renewal, inflicted sufficient damage that the freeway had to be torn down. Thereafter, the freeway proponents were unable to muster the political influence to have it rebuilt.

movement that the game of legislative reform to avoid the decision's impact is not worth the candle.

As written, *Centros* applies only to newly formed corporations – quite literally, it affects the allocation of decisionmaking between capital and labor only at the margin. It is not far-fetched to imagine that labor, anxious to increase German penetration of the high technology industries and, hence, German employment, might not object to a reduced governance role for labor in new companies in high technology industries, especially if labor's governance role in established German industry remains unchanged.[88] Indeed, one might imagine that the European Court of Justice imposed an outcome beneficial to both management and labor that the two sides could not have accomplished on their own. Labor might have declined a political compromise that freed the new economy sector from codetermination, even if that outcome was beneficial to workers, because the compromise might signal that codetermination was negotiable in other sectors as well, a signal that would not result from a decision by the European Court of Justice.[89] From this perspective, a mutually beneficial result is possible only *because* it was externally imposed.

But what of efforts by existing large German companies to take advantage of *Centros*? Suppose an existing company sought to relieve itself of its two-tier board structure and codetermination by merging into a newly formed UK subsidiary.[90] Would *Centros* require Germany to register the new UK company, thereby extending *Centros* to any company willing to reincorporate abroad, including established German companies, and likely inciting a political response by labor if it is to retain any formal corporate governance role?

At least for now, two barriers – one based in corporate law and the other in tax law – make it unlikely that the ECJ will extend *Centros* to Germany's traditional industrial base. The corporate law barrier concerns the merger: under German corporate law, a German corporation cannot merge with a non-German corporation. The convoluted structure of the

---

[88] For an indication that German unions are becoming more flexible, see "Unions' Union," in Survey of European Business, *The Economist*, April 29–May 5, 2000, at 16.

[89] Professor Hopt makes the point nicely: "As we all know, labor codetermination in general, but particularly in the supervisory board, is a holy cow for German trade unions and any German government, not only a socialist one." Klaus J. Hopt, "Are We Heading for a European Delaware: Theses and Questions Arising from Centros" (working paper, April 2000), available at Centre of European Law – Centros Papers, http://www.kcl.ac.uk/depsta/law/research/cel/centros/prog.html.

[90] This is the typical transaction form by which US companies reincorporated in another state.

recent Daimler-Benz/Chrysler combination was necessitated to avoid just this barrier.[91] To be sure, one can readily craft an argument that legal rules which prevent the migration of companies from one member state to another also violate the Treaty's right of establishment. But that holding would require a substantial expansion of *Centros*, in practical effect from a decision allowing functional convergence at the margins of a member state's economy, to one that contemplates regulatory competition as a means of securing uniformity fully parallel to the Treaty-based harmonization through directive.[92]

Even were the ECJ to expand the reach of *Centros*, a significant tax barrier would remain. Under German tax law, shifting nation of incorporation is treated as a liquidation, thus triggering corporate level capital gains tax on the appreciation in corporate assets. For large German corporations, it is difficult to imagine that the value of the more attractive governance features of the corporate law of another EC member state would be worth the tax cost of the shift.[93]

VII. Conclusion

In this chapter, I have surveyed three kinds of corporate governance convergence: *functional convergence*, when existing governance

---

[91] Theodor Baums, "Corporate Contracting around Defective Regulations: The Daimler-Chrysler Case," 155 *J. Instit. & Theo. Econ.* 119, 122 (1999).

[92] This point is emphasized by the fact that in 1998 the European Commission prepared a draft 14th Directive that set out how shift in country of incorporation could be effected. Wymeersch, note 71 above, at p. 16. Additionally, the European Court of Justice's decision in the *Daily Mail* case, C 81/87 [1988] ERC 5483, involving the transfer of the registered office of a company from one state to another, is said to stand for the proposition "that articles 52 and 58 do not allow companies to transfer their seat." See Wymeersch, note 71 above, at p. 18. Interestingly, the Court in *Centros* does not cite *Daily Mail*.

[93] One might suppose that the European Court of Justice could extend *Centros* to prohibit imposing a tax penalty on the decision to shift nation of incorporation, but here the boundaries of the argument begin to expand exponentially. In fact, the *Daily Mail* involved a requirement that the United Kingdom taxing authority approve a transfer of jurisdiction that would eliminate a large gain on the transferring corporation's investment portfolio. The UK has since abolished the pre-transfer approval requirement, leaving only the tax treatment of transfer as a liquidation. Professor Shöng notes that "[i]f English courts and the European Court had to decide *Daily Mail* today there would be no room to discuss preliminary questions of private international law. The courts would have to address the original question whether the exit charge for an emigrating company constitutes an unjustified infringement of the freedom of establishment." Wolfgang Shöng, "The Centros Case: Tax Implications," (Working Paper, April 2000), available at Centre of European Law – Centros Papers, http://www.kcl.ac.uk/depsta/law/research/cel/centros/prog.html.

institutions are flexible enough to respond to the demands of changed circumstances without altering the institutions' formal characteristics; *formal convergence*, when an effective response requires legislative action to alter the basic structure of existing governance institutions; and *contractual convergence*, where the response takes the form of contract because existing governance institutions lack the flexibility to respond without formal change, and political barriers restrict the capacity for formal institutional change. Additionally, two forms of hybrid convergence, involving voluntary selection of different formal rules offered by other jurisdictions both within and without the European Union, were considered. The diversity of circumstances suggests that there can be no general prediction of the mode that convergence of national corporate governance institutions may take. Because the flexibility of governance and political institutions will differ not only between countries, but within individual countries based on the particular response called for by changed conditions, the most we can predict is substantial variation both across and within different national systems, what Stephen J. Gould called "a contraption not a lovely contrivance."[94]

[94] Gould, note 37 above, at p. 24.

PART II

Government players

5

The international relations wedge in the corporate convergence debate

JEFFREY N. GORDON[*]

Introduction

This chapter tries to move the corporate governance convergence debate away from the arguments over efficiency and politics towards what I will call the international relations perspective. This move has two implications. First, the pace of convergence in corporate governance is understood to depend crucially on a country's, or, perhaps more importantly, on a group of countries' commitment to a project of transnational economic and political integration. Second, this transnational project may be best advanced by the spread of diffusely held public firms on the Anglo-American model, because such ownership structures facilitate the contestability of control, which helps curb economic nationalism. So, both as a positive and normative matter, we may understand such "strong form" convergence as responding to a particular sort of political aspiration, not just efficiency grounds conventionally understood. Examples drawn from the evolution of German shareholder capitalism during the 1990s in the context of the European Union project will illustrate the argument.

The corporate convergence debate is usually presented in terms of competing efficiency and political claims. Convergence optimists assert that an economic logic will promote convergence on the most efficient form of economic organization, usually taken to be the public corporation

* I appreciate comments on earlier drafts from Mathias Baudisch, Theodor Baums, Ronald J. Gilson, Zohar Goshen, Daniel Halberstam, Ed Iacobucci, Curtis Milhaupt, Peter Mülbert, and Mark Roe and the research assistance of Sven Hodges, Wulf Kaal, David Kovel, and Virginia Tent. For financial support, I am grateful to the William L. Cary Scholarship Fund of Columbia Law School. This chapter draws on a longer work, "An International Relations Perspective on the Convergence of Corporate Governance: German Shareholder Capitalism and the European Union, 1990–2000," available on SSRN, which documents many of the factual assertions in this chapter and contains certain elaborations.

governed under rules designed to maximize shareholder value.[1] Convergence skeptics counterclaim that organizational diversity is possible, even probable, because of path-dependent development of institutional complementarities whose abandonment is likely to be inefficient.[2] The skeptics also assert that existing elites will use their political and economic advantages to block reform; the optimists counterclaim that the spread of shareholding will reshape politics. These considerations are obviously important, yet the debate thus far omits a crucial variable: national choices over strategies of corporate governance convergence (or divergence) may be based on their effects in integrating (or not) the country within transnational systems of economic and political life. These choices are usually the product of elite opinion with differing degrees of democratic ratification. In other words, convergence may proceed or be hindered irrespective of efficiency considerations at the corporate level, or even irrespective of conventional domestic politics, depending on the role that convergence plays in an explicitly state level transnational drama.

On this view shareholder capitalism, which means to reference the Anglo-American model of public ownership and strong equity markets, is particularly well-suited as the optimal convergence form not necessarily because of organizational or productive efficiencies but because of its advantages in the control of economic nationalism, the tendency to which is a major obstacle to the transnational integration project. That is, the long-term willingness of states to pursue transnational integration depends upon the control of economic nationalism because no state wants to participate in a regime of potential systematic national disadvantage. The construction of international trading regimes such as the World Trade Organization (WTO) on the basis of principles of mutuality and reciprocity bears out this point. As the transnational project becomes more elaborated, the problem of economic nationalism arises at the level of the firm. Shareholder capitalism helps police economic nationalism by reducing the role of the state in economic decisionmaking, by decentralizing such decisions to the level of the firm, and by subjecting such firm-level decisions to a neutral, transnational standard of the share price. In particular, shareholder capitalism opens up the contestability of corporate control.

Such contestability is important in relation to cross-border combinations, which are crucial to the integration project. Cross-border mergers

---

[1] See, for example, Henry Hansmann & Reinier Kraakman, Chapter 1, this volume.
[2] See, for example, Lucian Bebchuk & Mark J. Roe, Chapter 2, this volume.

can create entities of optimal size and scope for transnational enterprise. But apart from such efficiencies, cross-border mergers can build businesses that are particularly good conduits for the transnational free flow of capital, good, services, and people, and, no less, a transnational attitude. Nevertheless cross-border mergers entail special risk. The government of the state of the target's organization will be legitimately concerned that investment and divestment decisions will be influenced by economic nationalism benefiting the state of the acquirer's organization. Will the acquirer show home-country bias in either facilities location decisions or in layoffs or downsizings? Another way to put the question: will the minister insist that the new plant be located in Lyon rather than Düsseldorf?

What best protects against such potential economic nationalism is the mutual vulnerability to takeover bids by both putative acquiror and target that is the hallmark of shareholder capitalism. To see this, assume the acquirer begins to show significant home-country bias. This inefficiency in the acquirer's operations will lead to a fall off in shareholder value that would create an opportunity for a control entrepreneur, if the acquirer was also exposed to the possibility of a hostile bid. In other words, exposure of firms to the threat of hostile takeover on roughly equal footing will help constrain economic nationalism while permitting valuable cross-border merger activity. This is not to say that mutual exposure to takeovers is a complete solution to the economic nationalism problem. A government could make payments or provide subsidies to cover the costs to the firm of economic nationalism and thus protect shareholder value. But such payments might be fiscally infeasible, they could be matched by a competing government, and, of course, such payments could be forbidden by the transnational regime. Takeover vulnerability makes it harder for a government to promote economic nationalism simply by imposing the costs on shareholders.

One implication of this view is the importance of what might be called "strong form" convergence on the shareholder-capitalism model, that is, the spread of public firms with relatively diffuse ownership. The control of economic nationalism requires more than the simple privatization of former state-owned enterprise; even for firms with a long history of public ownership, concentrated ownership may conduce to economic nationalism. Some have argued that concentrated ownership should cut the other way: that governments will have less sway over the managers of private firms or public firms with concentrated ownership because shareholders in such firms are better able to police managerial behavior and can better resist government pressure. In my view, the behind-the-scenes deal-making between the government and concentrated or private owners – the national elite – in the service of economic nationalism is, over the long term, more likely to resist solution than such pressure brought against the managers of truly public firms. This is because government compensation for the cost of economic nationalism will be harder to observe and police for concentrated or private ownership firms than for public firms. For example, the government can compensate a controlling shareholder through a transaction or a concession involving an unrelated business; it would be impossible to compensate all shareholders in a public firm in the same way. Thus managers of a diffusely owned firm who accede to a costly government request will face public equity market response and will be unprotected by concentrated owners. In a regime of contestable control, this should constrain managerial behavior. Finally, the evolving international share ownership of diffusely owned public firms can, over time, make economic nationalism seem more anachronistic. In these respects, the transnational integration objective generates a case for diffuse ownership that does not necessarily follow from efficiency-based arguments for convergence. Diffusely owned firms may not be more efficient (indeed, to the contrary) but the contestability of control may more effectively restrain economic nationalism.[3]

This chapter develops these arguments through examples drawn from the evolution of German shareholder capitalism in the 1990s in the context of the EU project of transnational economic and political intergration. First I discuss two examples in which this transnational project did in fact affect the pace of convergence. Then I show how EU integrationists have understood the problem of limited contestability and are trying to fashion rules whose ultimate effect would promote migration away from concentrated ownership toward diffuse ownership structures – in other words, how the transnational project is bound up with strong form convergence.

The first example is the 1996 privatization of Deutsche Telekom, triggered by the European Union's project of building a continental telecommunications system. The Telekom privatization in turn led the German

---

[3] This is not to say that efficiency has no role to play. The presumptive motive for most cross-border mergers is to attain scale or scope efficiencies. But diffuse share ownership enters the picture not as the necessarily most efficient organizational form but as creating conditions in which economic nationalism is subdued to the point that cross-border mergers become feasible in the international relations sense.

government, eager to obtain a high price, to promote shareholder capitalism by cultural, market, and legal intervention. So here the state's commitment to a transnational project fostered convergence beyond what could have been expected solely from efficiency considerations and despite the unsettling of the local status quo.

The second example is the way the economic nationalism shown by its EU partners in the protection of state champions led Germany to pull back from ratification of the "board neutrality" position of the proposed 13th Company Law Directive on Takeovers. Instead, Germany adopted a takeover law that permits the supervisory board to approve defensive measures without a shareholder vote. This can be understood as a move of "aggressive reciprocity" in the trade negotiation sense – a raising of barriers by Germany with the goal of precipitating a negotiation that will in the end produce lower barriers and a more level playing field. This move, played out in pursuit of transnational integration, will lead away from convergence in the short run and, like many such acts, may produce a degenerate spiraling away from the cooperative outcome and, ultimately, less convergence. In both of these cases, simple economic efficiency and the standard political stories may play a subsidiary role to overarching transnational objectives.

European integrationists came to realize that some of the ratification difficulties of the 13th Directive arose from the noncontestability of control in many ostensibly public European firms. This meant that the condition of mutual vulnerability necessary for the satisfactory control of economic nationalism was absent. In a remarkable report proposing a revised 13th Directive, a group of EU company law experts called for a mechanism by which a hostile bidder could "break through" certain ownership structures or legal barriers and obtain control.[4] On first inspection, these extraordinary, awkward measures are simply substitutes for the contestability that would naturally arise from diffuse, rather than concentrated, public ownership. On further examination, they offer an evolutionary path away from patterns of concentrated ownership toward the diffuse ownership of shareholder capitalism. Yet the origins and explanation for this far-reaching convergence agenda are to be found in the transnational integration project, not in the conventional arguments about efficiency.

---

[4] *Report of the High Level Group of Company Law Experts on Issues Related to Takeover Bids*, Jan. 10, 2002.

I.   The privatization of Deutsche Telekom and the fostering of shareholder capitalism

Privatization of state-owned enterprises (SOEs) swept the world in the 1980s and 1990s.[5] The movement was stimulated by the privatization program of Thatcherite Great Britain, which was deemed a great, even surprising, economic success. Highlighted by the initial public offering of British Telecom in November 1984, the program reduced the role of SOEs in the UK economy from more than 10 percent of GDP in 1980 to virtually nothing by the mid-1990s.

Privatization moved to other industrialized countries (for example, the privatization program of France after the election of Jacques Chirac as prime minister in 1986) and to several other European countries in the 1990s, especially France (under the Socialists), Italy, and Spain.[6] Many Asian countries also began to implement privatization programs, including Japan's sale of Nippon Telegraph and Telephone in three huge public offerings in the period February 1987 to October 1988, for approximately $80 billion.

Ironically this privatization movement was not particularly important in the political economy of Germany. Most of the country's significant businesses were already privately owned.[7] For example, in 1978 the central German government owned enterprises that accounted for approximately 4 percent of total turnover, compared with France, 25 percent; Italy, 52 percent; the UK, 12.5 percent; and a European average of approximately 14 percent.[8] This was in part the result of the country's post-World War II politics, presided over by the conservative Adenauer governments, which avoided major nationalizations. Nevertheless privatizations of various state enterprises were initiated in the 1960s and the 1980s with decidedly mixed results. For example, in 1961, a 60 percent block of Volkswagen was sold to the public but stock price declines led to

---

[5] See generally William L. Megginson & Jeffry M. Netter, "From State to Market: A Survey of Empirical Studies on Privatization," 39 *J. Econ. Litt.* 321 (2001).

[6] See Tony Jackson *et al.*, "State-Run Groups Get Used to New Identity: Europe's Governments are Finding Both Political and Commercial Reasons for Turning to Privatisation," *Financial Times*, Jan. 24, 1994, at 15.

[7] This account draws from Josef Esser, "Privatisation in Germany: Symbolism in the Social Market Economy?" in David Parker, ed., *Privatisation in the European Union: Theory and Policy Perspectives*, pp. 102–04 (1998).

[8] Ibid., pp. 105–06.

a government bailout of small shareholders later in the decade.[9] A new privatization wave in the mid-1980s led to the sale of the federal government's remaining stakes in Volkswagen (although one of the *Länder*, Lower Saxony, retained 20 percent) and in the industrial conglomerate VIAG (although another *Land*, Bavaria, bought a 15 percent stake, which it sold off in the 1990s). The federal government also sold its stake in another industrial conglomerate VEBA in 1985, but contrary to its goal of obtaining wide distribution of the shares, virtually all of them were purchased by existing large holders.[10]

Thus prior privatizations in Germany, unlike the experience in the UK, were not part of general economic liberalization, much less the creation of a shareholder culture. Rather, the goal had been to "share the wealth," to create a *Volksaktien* ("people's share") in significant industrial enterprises. Even by this more modest standard, privatization had not been a great success.

Yet in the privatization of Deutsche Telekom in 1996 the parties executed what was then the largest-ever initial public offering of a European company and succeeded in placing a large amount, 40 percent of the total shares, worth approximately $5 billion, with German retail purchasers. Nearly 2 million Germans subscribed to the offering, including 400,000 who had never previously owned shares. The argument is this: the transaction was precipitated by the EU's new telecommunications regime, a product of the transnational impulse. In the name of fostering competition and controlling economic nationalism, the new regime would end the privileged monopoly position of a state-owned telecommunications carrier like Deutsche Telekom. This in turn made privatization and access to equity capital markets important to Telekom's success if not survival. In order to make the transaction itself successful, German political and business elites promoted shareholder capitalism much more vigorously than otherwise would have been the case. The Deutsche Telekom transaction became a moment of high social mobilization, in which an idea that was the province of the elites was successfully argued to the populace generally. The immediate effect was obvious: a high price for Deutsche Telekom shares. But there were immediate secondary effects as well: for example, the quick ramping up of a new stock market

---

[9] See William L. Megginson *et al.*, "The Financial and Operating Performance of Newly Privatized Firms: An International Empirical Analysis," 49 *J. Fin.* 403, 406–07 (1994).

[10] Esser, note 7 above, pp. 107–10.

aimed especially at raising equity from public shareholders for high-tech start-ups, the Neuer Markt, modeled on NASDAQ; the development of German corporate law in a public shareholder-protective direction; and the acceptance only three years later of an unprecedented hostile bid for a German public company, the Vodafone takeover of Mannesmann. These social and institutional developments are set in wet concrete. The post-2000 stock market swoon, including the fall of the "T-share" below the initial offering price, the worldwide recession, and, more recently, the financial disclosure and corporate governance problems associated with "Enron," may yet be their undoing.

Germany's response to EU telecommunications reform

Europe has been integrating economically for the past half-century, step by step.[11] Telecommunications integration began in 1987; the endpoint was full opening of national markets to competition by 1998.[12] The privatization of Deutsche Telekom came out of Germany's response to that transnational project.

As with most European countries, telecommunications in Germany was provided by a "post-telephone-telegraph" entity ("PTT") within the government that was both monopoly operator and regulator. The German PTT, the Deutsche Bundespost, has deep historical roots. Its creation was associated with the unification of the German states and the establishment of the German Empire in the 1870s. The Bundespost was founded as a government department in 1876, received an additional mandate, telephony, in 1877, and eventually came to include a financial services branch to provide credit union-type services through the post office. The Bundespost was headed by the Minister of Posts and Telecommunication, a cabinet member. Its employees were federal civil servants.

Germany's first response to the new EU telecommunications policy and directives could be described as minimalist. Although the ostensible purpose of the initial reform was to separate "sovereign" and

---

[11] See generally Paul Craig & Grainne De Burca, *EU Law: Cases, Text, Materials* (2nd edn, 1998); Joseph Weiler, "The Transformation of Europe," 100 *Yale L.J.* 2403 (1991). I describe European telecommunications reform and the German response in some detail in "An International Relations Perspective on the Convergence of Corporate Governance: German Shareholder Capitalism in the European Union: 1990–2000," available on SSRN.

[12] The important initiatory document was an EU Commission "Green Paper," "Towards a Dynamic European Economy – Green Paper on the Development of the Common Market for Telecommunications Services and Equipment," Report COM 87(290 final) (1987).

"entrepreneurial" decisionmaking and to create a Telekom entity, autonomy was limited and nothing like privatization was in prospect. The subsequent emphasis in the Maastricht Treaty (1992) on telecommunications and the ensuing Commission directives calling for complete liberalization of telecommunications markets by 1998 made it clear that this initial German reform was insufficient. The then coalition government (Christian Democrats and Free Democrats) and Deutsche Telekom management vigorously promoted privatization as the necessary next step to equip Telekom to compete in the liberalized environment: a source of new equity to overhaul its networks (and to complete the modernization of the East), flexibility to downsize and reorient its workforce, freedom to pursue cross-border alliances, and stimulus for an entrepreneurial and innovative spirit in the company. The matter was complicated by the government's desire to privatize all three functions of the Bundespost and by the opposition of the incumbent unions. Nevertheless the case for privatization in light of the EU-wide telecommunications policy proved decisive, and so on January 1, 1995, Deutsche Telekom became a private corporation subject to the general German corporate law, the Aktiengesetz, but 100 percent owned by the government. Telekom's management was entirely separate from the other two former Bundespost entities and its financial responsibility to them ended. It became subject to the general system of tax. In other words, although Deutsche Telekom was regulated as a public utility, meaning some government involvement in rate-setting and other terms of service, it was financially independent and accountable for its financial results. Of particular importance, the new reform legislation explicitly contemplated the sale of a substantial stake in the company through a public offering, so the goal was not just formal privatization but the creation of a publicly owned company.

The privatization and shareholder capitalism

So the forces flowing from EU integration were an important catalyst in the privatization of Deutsche Telekom. To be sure, state-owned telecommunications utilities were favorite candidates for privatizations throughout the world[13] and Deutsche Telekom would have faced the same competitive and capital-raising pressures that led to other such transactions. Yet the

[13] See Bernado Bortolotti *et al.*, "Sources of Performance Improvement in Privatized Firms: A Clinical Study of the Global Telecommunications Industry," WP 26.2001FEMI (April 2001), available on SSRN.

EU liberalization added to that pressure, in no small part by catalyzing privatizations of virtually every state-owned European telecommunications company. Privatization in Germany was a close case and certainly the timing owed much to the EU project.

But what is the connection between the decision to privatize Deutsche Telekom and the effort to use the transaction to promote the cause of shareholder capitalism in Germany? The privatization could have been handled in different ways. For example, in more typically German fashion, the shares could have been placed with German financial intermediaries, other institutional investors, and other industrial behemoths. The firm would have been "public" but owned and controlled through substantial blockholders, tightly bound into "Germany Inc."

There had come to be consensus among German business elites and political actors that the development of shareholder capitalism was important for Germany's economic development.[14] Germany was eager to replicate the success of Silicon Valley in spinning out technological innovation that produced highend jobs as well as investor returns. An active stock market that provided a successful entrepreneur with a lucrative exit strategy through an initial public offering seemed integral to the Silicon Valley model.[15] Yet initial public offerings (IPOs) historically were rare in Germany – only ten in all of 1994 – and the stock markets were famously illiquid[16] and volatile.[17] This stemmed in large part from public retail investor reluctance to take on the risk associated with stock purchases, especially IPOs. For example at the beginning of 1996 (the year of the Deutsche Telekom transaction), only 5 percent of Germans owned common stock, as opposed to 18 percent of the British and

---

[14] Some of this follows Jeffrey N. Gordon, "Pathways to Corporate Convergence? Two Steps on the Road to Shareholder Capitalism in Germany," 5 *Colum. J. European L.* 219 (1999).

[15] See Bernard S. Black & Ronald J. Gilson, "Venture Capital and the Structure of Capital Markets: Banks vs. Stock Markets," 47 *J. Fin. Econ.* 243, 246–52 (1998) (comparing venture capital markets in the US and Germany).

[16] In 1994, just three companies – Deutsche Bank AG, Daimler-Benz, and Siemens AG – accounted for a third of the volume in German public markets; the top six firms accounted for almost 50 percent. Peter Gumbel, "Cracking the German Market: The Hard Sell: Getting Germans to Invest in Stocks," *Wall St. J.*, Aug. 4, 1995, available at 1995 WL-WSJ 8736770. There were 810 publicly traded firms in 1994. Firms ranked 50 to 810 accounted for less than 12 percent of volume. Harmut Schmidt *et al.*, *Corporate Governance in Germany*, p. 59 (1997).

[17] See generally Stefan Prigge, "A Survey of German Corporate Governance," in Klaus Hopt *et al.*, *Comparative Corporate Governance: The State of the Art and Emerging Research*, pp. 943, 986–90 (1998).

21 percent of Americans.[18] From a balance sheet perspective, in Germany common stock holdings accounted for 6.9 percent of household assets, in Britain 9.1 percent, and in the US 18.7 percent, at the beginning of 1996.[19] Market capitalization as a percentage of GDP was 23 percent in Germany, 120 percent in Britain, and 92 percent in the US, at the beginning of 1996.[20] In general German investors preferred bonds to stocks, and markets had rewarded their conservatism: the cumulative bond returns over the ten-year period ending 1995 exceeded stock returns, 103.5 percent to 52 percent.[21]

German political and business elites had another motive in developing shareholder capitalism through the Deutsche Telekom transaction. German demographics – namely, the relative ageing of the population as the birthrate declined – was beginning to undermine the existing pension system, in which workers looked almost exclusively to the state for a generous defined benefit pension payment. Ultimately, financial solvency would require at least partial replacement of the state plan, funded from tax revenues on a "pay as you go" basis, by a private contributory plan, whose payout would depend upon its investment returns. Appropriate equity investments could deliver greater long-term returns than fixed income investments and thus make the shift more politically palatable; fostering shareholder capitalism would help investors obtain better outcomes in contributory plans.

Finally the government (and the management) had a particular reason to sell Deutsche Telekom shares to the public rather than to financial intermediaries and other institutions. As became clear as the transaction unfolded, this would maximize the sale price for the shares. Since the proceeds were flowing directly to the company, this would increase the value of the government's remaining 76 percent stake (independent of the pricing effect) and of course make more funds available for corporate purposes. This became visibly important shortly after the transaction, when the government arranged partial "sales" of its stake to an affiliated financial institution, the Kreditanstalt für Wiederaufbau (Credit Bank for

---

[18] See Silvia Ascarelli, "A Good Connection: Deutsche Telekom IPO Draws Bullish Response from Skittish Germans," *Wall St. J. Eur.*, October 9, 1996, available at 1996 WL-WSJE 10752128 (citing survey by the German Share Institute).

[19] Bank of Japan, International Department, *Comparative Economic and Financial Statistics: Japan and Other Major Countries* (2000).

[20] Author's calculation based on OECD data.

[21] Silvia Ascarelli, "Deutsche Telekom Courts Small Investors for Its IPO," *Wall St. J. Eur.*, August 22, 1996, available at 1996 WL-WSJE 10749319 (quoting Solomon Brothers' study).

Reconstruction) over three successive years, 1997–99. The sales, which amounted to a 25 percent stake in Deutsche Telekom, helped address budgetary shortfalls that were made critical by the need to satisfy the participation criteria for "economic and monetary union (EMU)," the EU common currency regime.[22]

How the deal was sold to the German public and to institutional investors

The transaction planners in the Deutsche Telekom offering followed what appears to be a two-pronged strategy to obtain a high price for the offering: work hard to enhance retail demand for the offering by the German public and take other measures that would lead institutional investors to buy in the aftermarket to bolster the price. In contrast to privatizations in countries such as Britain and France, where shares were often sold at a discount to comparable private equity offerings, the Deutsche Telekom offering was fully priced, yet that price came to be supported by the structure of demand generated by the transaction planners.

The planners knew that they had a substantial uphill battle to transform German attitudes toward stock ownership. For example, in June 1996 *Focus* magazine reported survey results that 57 percent of Germans did not want to buy Telekom shares "under any circumstances". *Focus* noted that, if anything, Germans had less appetite for equity risk than before: in the 1970s, every tenth German owned shares; in 1996, less than half that number did.[23]

There were a number of economic and purely promotional steps taken to bolster retail German demand. On the economic side, the planners used discounts, share bonuses, and a promise of a large initial dividend. On the promotional side, the planners undertook a year-long DM 85 million media campaign to make stocks generally, Telekom in particular, seem a natural, even fashionable, investment choice, among those who had traditionally looked for fixed income investments. Perhaps the high point was a nationally televised awards program on which Telekom CEO

---

[22] Indeed, the push for EMU – a paradigmatic example of transnational economic and social integration – could independently be analyzed as a force for corporate governance convergence. It is not only that governments sought budgetary relief through privatizations but also that the common currency would foster cross-border equity investment, reducing the home-country bias. See Gikas A. Hardouvelis *et al.*, "EMU and European Stock Market Integration" (WP, Sept. 2001) (available on SSRN).

[23] "Telekom-Shares: A People Agrees," *Focus Magazin*, no. 24, June 10, 1996, at 180 (Virginia Tent transl.). This was at least in part because of the unhappy experience with Volkswagen and Veba discussed previously.

Ron Sommer gave out prizes to contestants who had assembled the best-performing stock portfolios over a three month period. The "T-share" became a brand name, and people would signal one another with hands in perpendicular, a "T."

The German commercial banks also played a significant role in steering German investors into the offering. Enlisting the banks' support was important, because in many cases share purchases would be funded with money that might otherwise go into certificates of deposit or other bank products. Thus all the major German banks were members of the underwriting syndicate and the various retail purchaser incentives described above were limited to investors who purchased through an account at such a participating bank.

But the transaction planners also wanted substantial institutional participation worldwide. This would open the way for the German government's eventual secondary offerings and for the company's use of its stock as an acquisition currency. Thus the company organized a global public offering that included a leading US underwriter, Goldman, Sachs & Co., as a "global coordinator" along with local favorites Deutsche Bank and Dresdner Bank. The issue was vigorously marketed by dozens of banks in the underwriting syndicate to 3,700 institutional investors throughout the world participating in 60 road shows and presentations held in 30 cities.[24] In addition to its primary listing on the Frankfurt Stock Exchange (and several German regional exchanges), the stock was listed on the New York Stock Exchange (where it would trade as American Depository Receipts [ADRs]) and the Tokyo Stock Exchange.

* * *

The scene on Monday, November 18, the day that Deutsche Telekom opened for trading on the Frankfurt Stock Exchange, was striking. " 'The Stock Market Is Bubbling,' cheered a banner front-page headline in the mass-market *Bild*."[25] Mounted policeman kept control of the crowds that gathered outside. Deutsche Telekom had erected a corporate promotional sculpture – "71 big, flashing lighted cubes in Telekom's new official color, magenta – which incongruously covered most of the plaza in front of the stately renaissance facade of the Frankfurt Stock Exchange."[26] The day's trading (including special afterhours trading on the electronic trading system IBIS) ended at DM 32.58, up 14 percent.

---

[24] Laura Covill, "Deutsche Telekom: Telekom Rules OK," *Euromoney* (December 1996).

[25] See Mary Williams Walsh, "High Marks Frenzied Deutsche Telekom Trading Ushers in New Era," *LA Times*, Nov. 19, 1996, available at 1996 WL 12757682.

[26] Ibid.

The offering had been five times oversubscribed. This demand, led by German retail purchasers, enabled Deutsche Telekom to set a high offering price and to limit the special economic incentives for retail sales. It also led to a 20 percent increase in the overall offering, to the underwriters' exercise of their over-allotment or "greenshoe" option, and to an enlargement of a special employee allocation. The offering netted the company approximately DM 19.4 billion (US $12 billion). Ultimately German investors received a 67 percent allocation, 60 percent of which (meaning 40 percent of the entire offering) went to German retail customers, 14 percent went to the Americas, mostly the US, 8 percent for Britain, 6 percent for continental Europe, and 5 percent for Asia and the rest of the world. The original plan had called for only a 25 percent placement with the German retail public. Shareholder capitalism in Germany had received a major boost.[27]

Evidence that shareholder capitalism took deeper root following the transaction

You might ask: how can the Deutsche Telekom transaction count as much of an advance of shareholder capitalism in Germany when there are so many features that fit with the established insider governance system?

---

[27] Deutsche Telekom successfully concluded two subsequent follow-on underwritten public share offerings, one for the company, the other a secondary offering for the German government, and a merger with the US firms VoicestreamWireless and Powertel. These share issuances have substantially increased and internationalized the shareholding base (close to 3 million shareholders) and reduced the government's ownership position to 43 percent, as of year-end 2001. As of June 2002, 40 percent of the nongovernment shares (23 percent of the entire equity interest) were held by German institutions or citizens; North Americans held 29 percent of the free float, meaning 17 percent of the entire equity interest.

In the wake of the post-2000 collapse in the telecommunications sector, Telekom stock has fallen (as of July 2002) 90 percent below its March 2000 peak and, perhaps more painfully, below the initial market price. Despite some initial concerns, there has been no retail investor exodus, nothwithstanding disappointment, even bitterness. Some measure of the successful rooting of shareholder capitalism in Germany may be that anger is directed against the company rather than in a call for a government bailout, as per Volkswagen in the 1970s. Indeed, this investor anger led to the ouster of CEO Ron Sommer – albeit in a politically mediated fashion. Despite public support of Sommer as recently as May 2002, Chancellor Schröder – in the midst of the parliamentary elections campaign in which his economic stewardship was an important issue – found the need to take action. (Arguably politics had played a double role: first, in retaining an executive despite the collapse in stock price to avoid public acknowledgment of a bad business strategy; and then second, in driving the timing and messy manner of his firing.)

After all, the government remained as 76 percent owner with an under-standing that it would preserve its majority stake at least until 2000. Even after another primary offering, a secondary offering of German government stock, and a stock acquisition of a major US firm (VoiceStream Wireless), the government owned 43 percent (as of year-end 2001). The supervisory board was designated with five-year terms in 1995; virtually the entire board was recently reelected for another set of five-year terms. It takes a 75 percent shareholder vote to remove a supervisory board member, meaning the government has a veto over removal. This means that, as a practical matter, Deutsche Telekom is protected from a hostile takeover bid. Moreover, the initial public offering was sold as much on its risk-avoidance steadiness as on the risk-taking upside. As noted above, the company virtually promised a high dividend payout that would be comparable to a bond yield.

Nevertheless the Deutsche Telekom privatization was a turning point (if not necessarily an irreversible one) because it demonstrated that it was possible to raise large amounts of equity capital from German retail investors. The promotional effort succeeded in its most ambitious project: to sell to the German public the idea of stock market investing generally, not just the T-share in particular. It achieved a necessary precondition for the development of shareholder capitalism because it showed the potential benefit of institutional change: access to large amounts of capital, no strings attached. The availability of public equity capital demonstrated by the Deutsche Telekom transaction fit well with a corresponding change in the availability of public debt via the growth of public bond markets in Germany, and then, after EMU, the explosive growth of a European bond market. Insider governance lost its privileged position in the supply of outside capital.

The Deutsche Telekom transaction also changed the politics of share-holder capitalism in Germany. It added at least a million people to the German shareholder roles and, even more important, heightened the saliency of shareholder value and shareholder protection. An idea that had been the province of a certain business and academic elite was trans-formed into an element of popular understanding.[28] Moreover, the trans-action gave the German government a direct interest in public shareholder

---

[28] See, for example, "Fidelity Investments, Fidelity's Targeted International Equity Funds," *Semiannual Report* 47 (April 30, 1998) (comments of Alexandra Edzard, portfolio manager of Fidelity Germany Fund). ("The market was strong, driven by German investment in the stock market. This pro-investment sentiment reflected a sea change in German attitudes... [Previously]. The stock market was viewed with suspicion. In 1996, Deutsche Telekom...

protection. The government bore the costs of the corporate governance arrangements. The market price of the initial and subsequent offerings of Deutsche Telekom stock (including the government's secondary offerings) would reflect (with an appropriate discount rate) the public shareholder protections that would apply after the government lost its control position. Thus the government came to have a distinct budgetary interest in better protection of public shareholders.

Evidence for the impact of the Deutsche Telekom privatization on the rise of shareholder capitalism is found in a number of places: the supply side and demand side for equity capital, institutional changes that facilitate public offerings (most particularly the Neuer Markt), changes in the legal infrastructure of public shareholder protection, changes in academic opinion, and, perhaps most dramatically, the change in attitudes about hostile takeover activity, as reflected in the widespread view that the outcome of a hostile bid for the venerable German firm Mannesmann by a UK raider Vodafone was a question of shareholder choice.

1. Empirical evidence: changes in ownership patterns and market valuations

There are a number of empirical indicia of the opening to shareholder capitalism in the period following the privatization of Deutsche Telekom. One important measure is market receptivity to initial public offerings because this opens a new channel of finance that is, almost by definition, sensitive to shareholder interests. But the increased availability of this capital-raising mechanism also reflects various institutional, even legal, developments that foster and protect shareholder interests generally, and cultural changes that encourage investors to make investments through direct share ownership. In other words, a change in the potential supply of public equity capital not only enhances shareholder capitalism – extends its reach – but also indicates the spread of background conditions for its success. As Table 5.1 indicates, there has been a sharp increase in the number of IPOs in the period. Early in the decade, there were on average fifteen to twenty IPOs annually. This reflects only a limited increase over the 1970–1990 period of approximately ten IPOs annually. The number of IPOs exploded towards the end of the decade, when many high-tech start-ups went public on a newly formed German rival for NASDAQ, the Neuer Markt. As Table 5.2 illustrates, IPOs provided increasingly larger

listed shares on the Frankfurt exchange. Since then, Germans have begun to embrace a new equity culture facilitated by financial market reforms.")

Table 5.1 *Number of initial public offerings, 1990–1999*

1990–92	1993–95	1996	1997	1998	1999	Total, 1990–1999
51	39	20	35	67	168	380

Source: Christoph van der Elst, "The Equity Markets, Ownership Structures and Control: Towards an International Harmonisation?" (University of Ghent Financial Law Institute Working Paper 2000), table 7.

Table 5.2 *Equity raised by IPOs as percent of GDP, 1990–1999*

1990–92 avg	1993–95 avg.	1996	1997	1998	1999	1990–99 avg
0.10%	0.11%	0.65%	0.15%	0.20%	0.91%	0.25%

Source: Christoph van der Elst, "The Equity Markets, Ownership Structures and Control: Towards an International Harmonisation?" (University of Ghent Financial Law Institute Working Paper 2000), table 8.

infusions of equity capital over the period, not just in absolute dollar terms, but normalized for increases in GDP. As in the United States, there has been a significant fall-off in IPOs both in number and in dollar amount in light of increased investor skepticism. But Germany's first exposure to the IPO cycle is part of the conditioning of sophisticated capital markets.

Another measure is the increasing importance of equity to the portfolios of individuals, both as "stock" and "flow." This is a measure of the demand side – the willingness of individuals to acquire and hold equity assets. As Figure 5.1 shows, the value of household holdings of public equity as a percentage of total financial assets significantly increased in the post-1996 period (and at a faster rate than in the pre-1996 period). Figure 5.2, which tracks equity acquisitions as a percent of total household financial asset acquisition, reflects a surge in equity additions in the post-1996 period. Undoubtedly some of this increase came from the increase in stock market values in the period; hence the flattening of the curve in the 1999–2000 period. But nevertheless, by the end of the decade, most of the marginal gain in household wealth derived from public equity. Even if some portion of the increase derives merely from appreciation of existing equity holdings rather than new purchases, it still draws the connection between household wealth and shareholder value. This connection helps establish a political economy conducive to further developments favorable to shareholder capitalism.

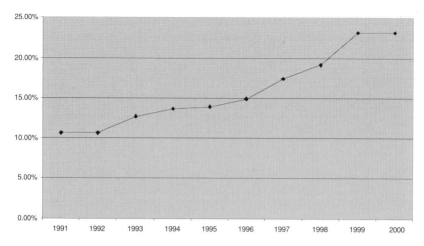

Source: Bundesbank, own calculations

Figure 5.1 Household public equity assets as percentage of total household financial assets

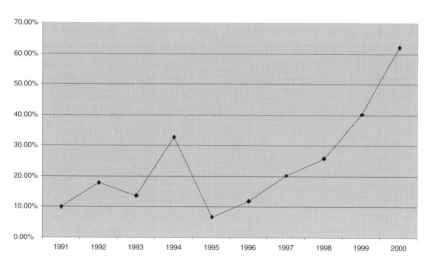

Source: Bundesbank, own calculations

Figure 5.2 Household public equity acquisitions as percentage of total household financial assets acquisitions

Table 5.3 *Shareholders in publicly traded companies (direct ownership) (in millions; as percentage of population)*

Year	1988	1992	1994	1996	1997	1998	1999	2000
No.	2229	2661	2736	2675	2767	3218	3775	5121
% pop	4.9	4.2	4.4	4.2	4.4	5.1	5.9	8

Source: DAI Factbook, April 2001.

Table 5.4 *Shareholders in stock mutual funds (in millions; as percentage of population)*

Year	1997	1998	1999	2000
No.	1751	2458	3582	6601
% pop	2.8	3.9	5.6	10.3

Source: DAI Factbook, April 2001 (time series begins in 1997).

This evidence of a strengthening of the demand for equity capital is also reflected in the significant increase in the number and percentage of shareholders in Germany (see Table 5.3). Equity mutual funds became a particularly popular way for individuals to participate in the stock market, much as in the United States. "Banks are making an effort to lure depositors away from relatively low-yielding savings vehicles and into stock mutual funds."[29] Growing from essentially negligible importance in the early 1990s, equity mutual funds became as important a vehicle for equity investment as direct stock ownership (see Table 5.4). By the end of the decade, the penetration of stock ownership including ownership of equity mutual funds increased almost fourfold over the prior level (Table 5.5).

One classic way to think of the influence of shareholder capitalism is in terms of ownership structure. Concentrated ownership is associated with insider governance system, dispersed (or "diffuse") ownership, with outsider governance systems, and often the debate about convergence comes down to a question about the persistence or not of that particular systemic difference. The best evidence suggests that there has

[29] Ibid.

Table 5.5 *Shareholders in public companies (including through employee stock ownership plans) and in mutual funds (including "mixed funds") (in millions; as percentage of population)*

Year	1997	1998	1999	2000
No.	5601	6789	8231	11828
% pop	8.9	10.7	12.9	18.5

Source: DAI Factbook, April 2001 (time series begins in 1997).

been a significant increase in the number and percentage of public firms in Germany with diffuse ownership. In 1990, approximately 10 percent of the public firms were either widely held or otherwise lacked a 25 percent "blocking" shareholder.[30] By 1999, approximately 25 percent of a larger number of public firms were diffusely held.[31] This is a significant change that would be unlikely in the absence of the development of better minority shareholder protection and in the gradual unwinding of the cross-holding inducements of the insider system.[32]

One familiar way of illustrating the increasing importance of equity to a country's political economy is the ratio of market capitalization to GDP. As might be expected this ratio significantly increases for Germany over the period, from approximately 20 percent in 1991 to 67 percent in 2000, and the sharpest part of the increase comes in the post-1996 period. As Figure 5.3 also shows, however, Germany's ratio increased at

---

[30] Tim Jenkinson & Alexander Ljungvist, "The Role of Hostile Stakes in German Corporate Governance," 7 *J. Corp. Finance* 397, 405 (2001).

[31] See Christoph van der Elst, "The Equity Markets, Ownership Structures and Control: Towards an International Harmonisation?" in K. Hopt and E. Wymeersch, eds., *Capital Markets and Company Law* (2003).

Alternative measures of the extent of diffusely owned firms are provided in Raphael La Porta *et al.*, "Corporate Ownership around the World," 54 *J. Fin.* 471 (1999). Using 1995–96 data and different definitions of "diffusely held" (presence of 20 percent blockholder or 10 percent blockholder), La Porta *et al.* find that 50 percent (35 percent) of the largest German public firms are diffusely held, but only 10 percent (10 percent) of medium-sized German firms. See La Porta *et al.*, at pp. 492–95, tables II–III.

[32] Somewhat to the contrary is ambiguous evidence that ownership concentration over the 1994–98 period, as measured by the Herfindahl index, increased in more listed German manufacturing firms than it decreased; on the other hand, the median decrease is greater than the median increase. See F. Jens Köke, "New Evidence on Ownership Structures in Germany," ZEW Discussion Paper 99-60 (June 2000) (available on SSRN). But this work also classifies 37 percent of these firms as "widely held," meaning no identifiable controlling blockholder.

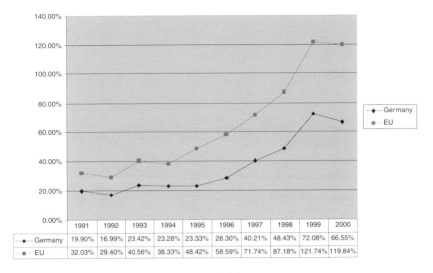

	1991	1992	1993	1994	1995	1996	1997	1998	1999	2000
Germany	19.90%	16.99%	23.42%	23.28%	23.33%	28.30%	40.21%	48.43%	72.08%	66.55%
EU	32.03%	29.40%	40.56%	38.33%	48.42%	58.59%	71.74%	87.18%	121.74%	119.84%

Source: Federation of European Stock Exchanges; own calculations

Figure 5.3 Ratio of market capitalization to GDP: Germany vs. EU (value-weighted)

approximately the same rate as for other EU countries, suggesting the presence of a common underlying phenomenon that enhanced shareholder capitalism throughout the EU.[33]

One possible objection to the significance of changes in the market capitalization/GDP ratio is that the increases in the ratio may reflect only general market factors associated with the 1990s stock market boom rather than any deeper change, such as greater use of public equity in external finance, enhanced value of minority shares because of greater shareholder protection, or more rapid growth of public firms. This caveat is at least partially addressed by Figure 5.4, which compares the market capitalization/GDP ratio of Germany and the UK. Here the UK, whose commitment to shareholder capitalism did not significantly change during the period, serves as a control against general market factors. In the early 1990s until 1996, the ratio of ratios, Germany to UK, was around 20 percent. The curve sharply kinks after 1996; as of 2000, the ratio of ratios was

---

[33] One candidate would be the privatization of SOEs, which accounted for a much larger share of the economy in many other EU countries (for example, France, Italy, Spain) and whose impact in jump-starting a shareholder culture was significant. See generally, Megginson & Netter, "From State to Market," note 5, above; Maria Boutchkova & William L. Megginson, "Privatization and the Rise of Global Capital Markets," *Financial Management*, Fall 2000 (available on SSRN).

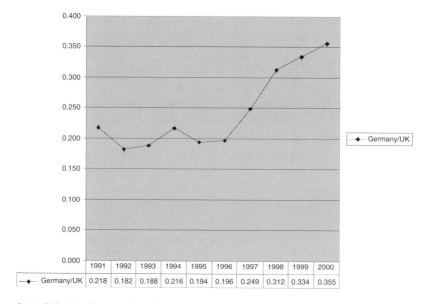

	1991	1992	1993	1994	1995	1996	1997	1998	1999	2000
Germany/UK	0.218	0.182	0.188	0.216	0.194	0.196	0.249	0.312	0.334	0.355

Source: Federation of European Stock Exchanges; own calculations

Figure 5.4 German market cap/GDP vs. UK market cap/GDP

35 percent. This suggests a significant element of convergence by Germany on the shareholder model in the period.

There are different levels at which to frame the convergence question, as the market capitalization/GDP ratio makes us aware. One question is whether the managers of an existing set of public firms are more likely to seek to maximize shareholder value in ways that predictably should lead to a higher stock price for a given underlying cash flow. That question points in the direction of convergence of governance arrangements and, perhaps even more important, ownership structures, concentrated or diffuse, that affect how a particular set of legal rules will play out in practice (and what legal rules will be chosen). But another question is the extent to which the economy is organized through public firms: whether economy activity is guided by managers who are exposed to capital market signals or not. Germany's relatively low market capitalization/GDP ratio and yet its convergence toward the UK may say less about changes at existing public firms and more about the evolution of the German economy towards a system in which much more of the activity is conducted by public firms. Germany has been famous for its *Mittelstand*, its medium-size enterprises, mostly family owned, which account for an unusually large part of its

Source: ELC International; own calculations

Figure 5.5 Sales of German public companies in top fifty as percentage of GDP

economy activity. The changing market capitalization/GDP ratio may indicate the shrinking of this sector. Even if the ownership structure of large German firms has not radically changed in the 1990s, convergence may express itself even more importantly in the increasing extent to which public firms account for economic activity – because even classic insider governance of a public firm will be more sensitive to stock market signals than a private firm. As more of the economy is exposed to such signals, it is bound to affect governance even at insider firms.

The empirical conjecture from the market capitalization/GDP ratio is borne out by directly tracing the importance of public companies to German GDP over time. We collected data on the sales of the largest 50 German companies over the 1991–2000 period, determined which of those companies were public, and then mapped a ratio of those large public company sales to GDP. (Sales and GDP are not strictly comparable, since the latter is a value-added measure.) As Figure 5.5 shows, this ratio increases sharply in the post-1996 period, from 30 percent to nearly 70 percent. A number of possibilities suggest themselves: public firms are growing faster than private firms (suggesting the value of capital market signals and pressure to firm performance) or, perhaps, public firms are acquiring private firms, using their appreciated stock as acquisition currency. But in any event, this evidence, along with other quantitative evidence, suggests significant movement toward shareholder capitalism, tied in time to the privatization of Deutsche Telekom.

2. Institutional evidence: the launch of the Neuer Markt

Perhaps the most striking evidence of institutional change following the Deutsche Telekom transaction was the founding and explosive growth of the Neuer Markt, which was established by the Deutsche Börse in 1997 as a NASDAQ-competitor in the launch of initial public offerings for high technology companies of minimal seasoning. The main "official" exchange of the Deutsche Börse was a notoriously inhospitable place for an initial public offering, because of listing rules that required several years of profits and other signs of financial soundness. In offering a home for "young growth companies" the Neuer Markt substituted disclosure and transparency for seasoning. For example, its rules required an issuing prospectus on an international standard, IAS or GAAP accounting standards, and periodic reporting, quarterly and annually, also on an international standard. In particular, this continuous reporting requirement was an innovation in Germany; issuers that listed on the "official" market (Amtlichter Handel) or the "regulated" market (Geregelter Handel) were not subject to similar requirements. There were additional Neuer Markt listing requirements, including at least a 20 percent free float, a six-month lockup period for existing shareholders, and acceptance of the voluntary Takeover Code of the Stock Exchange Commission of Experts (modeled on the UK City Code).[34]

The Neuer Markt was very successful, especially in light of prior German history. It opened for business in March 1997 and the pace of IPO activity rapidly increased:

1997 –	13
1998 –	43
1999 –	133
2000 –	139

As of 2001, more than 340 companies were listed on the Neuer Markt, 56 of them headquartered outside of Germany. Unlike the "official" market, individual investors were especially vigorous market participants, owning approximately 50 percent of the free float of listed companies.[35]

[34] See "Rules of Neuer Markt," available at http://deutsche-boerse.com/nm/index_e.htm
[35] An account of the importance of the Neuer Markt as evidence of the change in German shareholder culture in the 1990s would be incomplete without discussion of the Neuer

The impulse to create the Neuer Markt may have come from the concern about German competitiveness with Silicon Valley in creating high-technology enterprise, but the turn to shareholder capitalism to remedy the situation might not have been possible without the prior Deutsche Telekom transaction. It appeared that part of the US success had been the role of a particular entrepreneurial intermediary, the venture capitalist, who functioned best with an exit route via a stock market. But the creation and ultimate success of such a market for Germany depended on investor demand and liquidity, which in turn depended (at least on the NASDAQ model) on the participation of retail investors. Neither industrial companies nor financial institutions were likely to buy significant shares for their own account (since these start-up firms were certainly not going to be governed on the insider model). Unlike the US, Germany had no cash rich pension funds. Thus, retail demand, either through mutual funds or direct purchases, was going to be crucial, and while the Deutsche Börse worked very hard to attract foreign market participants, a high level of German participation would be essential. The Deutsche Telekom transaction proved that Germans would buy stock and, in the huge marketing push, it persuaded many Germans that equities were a legitimate part of an investment portfolio. Undoubtedly the appreciation in the DAX and

Markt's problems and the September 2002 decision of the Deutsche Börse to shut it down by year-end 2003. Instead, the Börse will create a technology segment of its main market, based on disclosure requirements similar to the Neuer Markt (though supported by a better enforcement regime) and a technology-focused index.

The Neuer Markt had come under sharp criticism not only because of the sharp decline in share values over 2000–2002 but also because of price volatility, which led to allegations of price manipulation, and cases of outright fraud in publicly issued financial reports. Characteristically for a market which gained credibility through high-quality listing standards, the interested parties initially pursued tightening the standards. Subsequent commentary focused particularly on enforcement mechanisms, in light of the importance of credibly accurate and honest disclosure in investor evaluation of unseasoned companies. The absence of an omnibus antifraud provision like Section 10b of the 1934 Securities Exchange Act and the ambiguous legal status of disclosures filed under private listing standards created an enforcement deficit. This enforcement question was addressed by enactment in 2002 of the Fourth Financial Markets Promotion Act, which gives the Börse the delegated power to put its listing requirements – including the elements of a high-quality disclosure regime – into public law Exchange Rules, with the aim of enhancing enforcement and thus investor confidence. (See "Deutsche Börse Presents New Equity Market Segmentation," posted on Deutsche Börse website, visited Oct. 3, 2002.)

More important than the demise of the Neuer Markt is the persistence and spread of its disclosure-based listing strategy, and the augmentation of private efforts to create a high-quality disclosure regime with a public enforcement backstop. These are both important elements in creating conditions for the development of public equity markets and ultimately to the spread of diffusely owned firms. See generally, Rafael La Porta et al., "What Works in Securities Laws?" NBER WP W9882 (available on SSRN).

the by-then famous appreciation of the NASDAQ index played a critical role in the successful launch of the Neuer Markt, but the prior success of the Telekom IPO was a powerful reassurance.

3. Subsequent legal changes: toward protection of shareholder rights

Following the Telekom transaction, there were a number of reforms that added to public shareholder protection and increased the exposure of public firms to capital market pressures. The most important of these changes was the 1998 Act on Control and Transparency of Enterprises (KonTraG).[36] The legislation was adopted in response to a number of high-visibility monitoring failures by supervisory boards, in particular instances of apparent negligence by "Hausbank" representatives on supervisory boards. The legislation was also designed to cut back the traditional bank influence over the proxy system of dispersed public companies and to limit various antitakeover strategies at German firms. In particular, the Act strengthened the monitoring capacity and responsibility of the supervisory board, limited the voting prerogatives of a bank that owns more than 5 percent of the shares of a particular firm, and prohibited creation of super-voting stock or caps on voting rights, which protected public shareholders by restricting the separation of voting rights from cash flow rights.

The desirability of many of these reforms had been apparent for some time. A reform package had been put forward in 1994 in response to an emerging consensus about the weakness of the governance system for public companies, underscored by dissatisfaction expressed by international institutional investors.[37] But the legislation stalled because of opposition by managers who were unhappy with the governance interventions and in particular the limits on capped voting, a favorite takeover protection.

The Telekom privatization played a significant role in its adoption in two ways. First, most obviously, the popular mobilization on behalf of shareholder capitalism associated with the Telekom transaction made "public shareholder protection" a populist cry and changed the political calculus. But second, the government could see budgetary benefits

---

[36] Gesetz zur Kontrolle und Transparenz im Unternehmensbereich, Bundesgesetzblatt I vom. 30.04.1998, 786 ff. See Theodor Baums, "Corporate Governance in Germany: System and Current Developments" (University of Osnabruck WP, 1998), available at http://www.uni-frankfurt.de/fb01/baums; Uwe Seibert, "Control and Transparency in Business (KonTraG): Corporate Law Reform in Germany," 10 *Eur. Bus. L.Rev.* 70 (1999).

[37] Lex, "German Corporate Governance," *Fin. T.*, Nov. 7, 1994, at 20.

from corporate law that better protected public shareholders and that thereby should narrow the "minority discount."[38] The government's plan to sell part of its Telekom stake to help meet budgetary criteria for EMU meant that, like many selling shareholders, it wanted to book the highest possible sale price. Public shareholder protection thus became both politically popular and fiscally prudent.

4. Changing attitudes toward hostile bids: the path to Mannesmann/Vodafone

Perhaps the most visible evidence of a shift toward shareholder capitalism in Germany in the course of the 1990s was the change in public and elite response to hostile takeover bids, away from shock, even horror, at the disruption of established relationships towards grudging acceptance of shareholder choice. This evolution was vividly illustrated by the contrasting outcomes of Pirelli's failed bid for Continental in 1991 and Vodafone's successful bid for Mannesmann in 1999. In both cases, the hostile bidder was a foreign raider; in both cases the target was embedded in the German industrial establishment. If anything, the Vodafone bid was much brasher, since the UK bidder was an upstart (founded in 1985) and the German target, founded almost 100 years earlier, exemplified German industrial prowess as well as economic adaptability. Moreover, the size of the transaction, $180 billion, and the acceptance of acquirer's stock as consideration, suggested that size didn't matter when it came to takeover protection. Thus the takeover of Mannesmann, apparently the first successful hostile tender offer for control of a German public corporation, both reflected a transformation and may hasten a further one.[39]

There were several notable elements in the Mannesmann transaction. First was the general attitude of Mannesmann's management, especially its CEO Klaus Esser. Mannesmann pursued no preclusive defensive

---

[38] For example, the "voting rights premium" for Germany – the price differential between voting and nonvoting shares – declined over the 1990–98 period (from approximately 30 percent to 20 percent). See Eric Nowak, "Recent Developments in German Capital Markets and Corporate Governance," 14 *Bank of Am. J. of Applied Corp. Fin.* 35, 37 (2001). A change in this premium is widely taken as reflecting changes in minority shareholder protection. See also Olaf Ehrhardt & Eric Nowak, "Private Benefits and Minority Shareholder Expropriation – Empirical Evidence from IPOs of German Family-Owned Firms" (WP, March 2002) (available on SSRN) (narrowing minority shareholder discount in the later 1990s).

[39] I have elsewhere described these transactions, Pirelli/Continental, Mannesmann/ Vodafone, and Krupp/Thyssen. See "An International Relations Perspective on the Convergence of Corporate Governance: German Shareholder Capitalism and the European Union, 1990–2000," available on SSRN.

measures, sought no defensive blockbuilding by industrial or financial allies, and turned down political help that might have been forthcoming. Instead, it argued the merits of its strategy against the Vodafone alternative, an argument pitched to its shareholders and the equity markets. Its capitulation came when it became clear that Mannesmann's shareholders found Vodafone's offer economically compelling.

Second was the public nature of the takeover battle, reminiscent in its media intensity to the Deutsche Telekom privatization. The dueling CEOs gave press interviews and made numerous personal appearances. The companies took out full-page ads in national and large regional newspapers to argue their case. In part the publicity was to attract the votes of public shareholders, because the stock ownership of Mannesmann was genuinely dispersed. The more important reason, however, was that the bid triggered a far-ranging debate over hostile takeovers as an appropriate mode of economic behavior. This had particular valence because only two years before (in 1997), in the wake of Krupp's hostile bid for Thyssen, 30,000 workers had taken to the streets to demonstrate against such "Wild West" tactics.[40] So Vodafone and its CEO emphasized the synergy motives for the merger: that the combination of networks would create value, that no layoffs were planned, that Düsseldorf would remain a headquarters city, that the bid was rooted in an industrial logic, not one of those objectionable US-style speculative bids. But the larger issues were always in sight: whether shareholder capitalism would become increasingly influential

---

[40] Certainly with hindsight, the defeat of Krupp's hostile bid seems like a prior regime's last stand rather than a victory. Shortly after the "defeat," the two firms entered into a "friendly" merger brokered by political leaders that entailed significant consolidation of their steel operations. The most enduring impact of the Krupp bid may have been with respect to German banks. First, the participation of Deutsche Bank and Dresdner Bank put the good-housekeeping seal on hostile deal activity, much as Goldman, Sachs' and Morgan, Stanley's advice to raiders in the 1970s reflected changing attitudes in the US financial establishment. Moreover, the antibank sentiment stirred up by the initial bid contributed to the pro-shareholder cutbacks in the banks' governance power in the 1998 KonTraG, in particular, limitations on the banks' power of proxy voting. On the labor front: although worker opposition torpedoed the hostile bid, the episode showed the breakdown in worker solidarity on which the German corporatist model of Rheinish capitalism was based. As Höpner puts it, "While IG Metall was fighting hostile takeovers as an illegitimate instrument of economic behaviour, Krupp employees were supporting the takeover attempt." See Martin Höpner, "Corporate Governance in Transition: Ten Empirical Findings on Shareholder Value and Industrial Relations," MPIfG WP 2001/5 (2001) (available on SSRN). In other words, employees were focusing on firm specific outcomes rather than "class" outcomes. This is consistent with the claim that one effect of shareholder capitalism is the decentralization of decisionmaking, with the welfare of the firm as the variable of interest.

in Germany, including but not limited to acceptance of public control contests for large German public corporations.[41]

Much had changed in the period beginning after the privatization of Deutsche Telekom, even after the failed Krupp bid. Telekom itself had raised another $11 billion in a primary offering. The Neuer Markt had taken off. Perhaps most important in practical terms, German firms had been acquirers in high-visibility takeovers: British targets, for example, Rolls Royce (VW), Rover (BMW), and Orange(Mannesmann); US targets, Bankers Trust (Deutsche Bank) and Chrysler (Daimler); even Italian targets, Omnitel, Infostrada (Mannesmann). German firms had also suffered from the nationalist policies of others, for example, Deutsche Telekom's thwarted bid for Telecom Italia. Mannesmann itself was 60 percent owned by foreigners at the time of the bid.

Thus there seemed to be no political traction in opposing the takeover bid. Indeed, Chancellor Schröder's efforts to intervene came in for harsh criticism. He was initially quoted as indicating that the market should decide: "Whoever wants to buy a British company – like Mannesmann with Orange – can't say: We're allowed, but they're not."[42] But then, in apparent response to pressure from SPD party leaders, he began tacking in opposition: "Hostile takeovers destroy an enterprise's culture. They harm the target, but also, in the medium-term, the predator itself." He played the nationalism card: "I much prefer Franco-German cooperation because it is friendly."[43] His comments ignited a storm of criticism in Germany, England, and elsewhere.

* * *

---

[41] Moreover, the German unions affected by the Vodafone bid approached the transaction with sophistication. Despite the potential loss of governance participation rights, IG Metall came to appreciate some of the economic logic of the transaction, in particular, the strategy of spinning off the "classic" divisions of Mannesmann (machine tools and auto products). In the recent past all the cash flow had been directed to Mannesmann's telecom investment; these divisions might fare better as stand-alones. Although the union leadership vigorously opposed the transaction along the way, what was more important is what they avoided: no "general strikes" at the company and no effort to raise the political stakes to a fever pitch. By the end, the labor bench of the Mannesmann supervisory board voted in favor of the transaction. See Gregory Jackson & Martin Höpner, "An Emerging Market for Corporate Control? The Mannesmann Takeover and German Corporate Governance," MPIfG WP 01/4 (2001) (available on SSRN).

[42] William Boston, "Hostile Deal Could Breach German Resistance – Mannesmann has Weapons in Vodafone Contest, but Others Hang Back," *Wall. St. J.*, Nov. 17, 1999, at A17, available at WL-WSJ 24922274.

[43] "Anglo-Saxons at the Gates," *Wall. St. J.*, Nov. 24, 1999, at A18 (editorial), available at 1999 WL-WSJ 24923243.

So in barely the space of a decade public and elite attitudes have dramatically shifted. What was seemingly unthinkable – the "loss" of a German firm to a foreign interloper – has now become part of the economic landscape. The process that began with the privatization of Deutsche Telekom has pushed Germany very far on the road towards shareholder capitalism. The ownership structure stands in the way, yet, as we shall see, the "strong force" of institutional complements that holds stakeholders in the governance nucleus is dissipating. But a seismic event like the Mannesmann takeover has aftershocks. If previously the assumption was that nationalist economic protectionism was objectionable but relatively unimportant (because the Germany financial and industrial community would organize the necessary defense), now the protectionist problem becomes critical.

II. The collapse of the 13th Directive and Germany's new stance on target defenses

A. *The origins of the 13th Directive*

The harmonization of European corporate law (or "company law") has been a difficult topic, both theoretically and practically. Although a harmonized, if not necessarily uniform, law has some obvious scale-economies in a continent-wide legal system, the process by which this harmonization occurs is problematic. American scholars particularly have argued that imposition of harmony through a political process rather than through competition is likely to produce an inefficient result that, worse, will be rigidified by the political barriers to modernization. American corporate law is a harmonized product, in significant measure because of the competitive triumph of Delaware, and highly adaptive because of these competitive forces.[44] The EU lawmaking process that would generate a uniform corporate law is, by contrast, a study in complex politics, complicated by a multitiered structure in which a law proposal must achieve acceptance by the eurocrats (the European Commission), the particular

---

[44] The purported importance of regulatory competition to US corporate law is undercut, or at the very least complicated, by the fact that a significant amount of US corporate law is determined at the federal level, most notably through SEC regulation of the disclosure and proxy process, and by forms of self-regulation under SEC guidance, most notably though stock exchange listing requirements. In the wake of the accounting scandals of 2001/2002, Congress intervened in US corporate governance in the Sarbanes-Oxley Act of 2002, which, among other things, imposed requirements on the makeup and function of boards and limited certain forms of executive compensation.

states (the Council), and then, in important cases, a popularly elected body of uncertain mandate (the Parliament). Thus some have criticized the prospect of European corporate law harmonization as susceptible to strong influence by groups not particularly interested in the efficiency of corporate law.[45] This opposition to regulatory harmonization runs up against the fact that European choice of law rules do not readily permit the jurisdictional competition that might otherwise lead to harmonization,[46] so, as a practical matter, EU-level lawmaking or fortuitous national copying are the only options.

But harmonization has also come under attack from the localists, who argue that harmonized law will threaten cherished local values. A law that settles on a dual board structure and codetermination in the boardroom is opposed by the British, but a law that settles instead on the single board model is vigorously rejected by the Germans and the Dutch.[47] The consequence of these cross-cutting claims is that the project of harmonized company law in the EU has yielded relatively little fruit. Thus far, eight company Directives have been adopted, mostly between 1968 and 1978, of relatively meager content; most of the corporate law in Europe is internal to member states.[48] A statutory framework for a new "Societas Euoropeae," a "European Company," was finally adopted in 2001, thirty

---

[45] More recently "harmonization" has been replaced as an explicit EU goal in favor of "minimum standards," which, under the principles of subsidiarity, permit some national diversity within a common framework. The generation of minimum standards presents many of the same problems of political economy as harmonization.

[46] But see *Centros* v. *Erhvervs-OG Selskabsstyrelsen*, C-212/97, [1999], ECR 1-1459 (permitting establishment in a member state of a business that uses a shell incorporation in another member state). The direct effects of *Centros* are limited, since it applies to new businesses only, rather than reincorporations of existing businesses. Moreover, reincorporation of an existing business in another EU state will often trigger significant tax liability, since it may be treated as liquidation of the business. On the other hand, a more recent ECJ case, *In re Überseering*, C-208/00, [2002], ECR 1-9919, goes further in undermining the legal seat rule, since it apparently clarifies that a German national, say, can acquire (or, presumably, establish) an English corporation and use it to conduct business activities in Germany, thereby evading various German corporate governance rules, including codetermination, Accord, *Inspire Art*, C-167/01 [2003] ECR–.

[47] See generally George Berman *et al.*, *Cases and Materials on European Union Law*, 803–05 (2nd edn, 2002).

[48] See Walter Ebke, "Company Law and the European Union: Centralized versus Decentralized Lawmaking," 31 *Int'l Law* 961 (1997); Terence L. Blackburn, "The Societas Europea, the Evolving European Corporation Statute," 61 *Fordham L. Rev.* 695 (1993). For recent developments and a general overview, see "Report of the High Level Group of Company Law Experts on a Modern Regulatory Framework for Company Law in Europe," Nov. 4, 2002, web-posted at http://europa.eu.int/comm/internal_market/en/company/company/modern/consult/report_en.pdf (visited Dec. 30, 2002).

years after the first draft.[49] The impact of this new European entity, which becomes possible as of 2004, is highly uncertain, however, since the framework provides for worker participation rights similar to the works council elements of codetermination, strongly objected to by UK firms at least.[50]

Into this gridlock comes the proposed 13th Company Law Directive on Takeovers, proposing to regulate key terms of takeover bids and the relative positions of boards and shareholders in responding to hostile bids, highly contentious issues that go to the core of corporate structure and to the shareholder capitalism debate. Remarkably, after a fifteen-year gestation period, the 13th Directive almost passed in summer 2000, defeated at the last minute by a turnabout from Germany, one of the staunchest supporters. Some version may yet be adopted.[51] Both the manner of its defeat and the effort to revive it demonstrate quite powerfully the "international relations" thesis: that convergence on the shareholder model is profoundly influenced by the pursuit (or avoidance) of economic and political integration. The 13th Directive grew out of a 1985 White Paper on completing the Internal Market.[52] The Commission presented its initial proposal to the Council and the European Parliament in January 1989, and after comments and negotiations, an amended proposal in September 1990. The amended first proposal was criticized as too detailed an intervention into member states' law. It set forth detailed bid procedures, including the content of mandatory disclosure documents to be produced for shareholders by both the acquirer and the target. It required state supervisory authorities to assure the equal treatment of shareholders and set forth the obligation of target boards to act "in the interest of all the shareholders." In many respects it followed the UK City Code in requiring the board to obtain shareholder approval before employing defense tactics and in enacting a "mandatory bid" provision that required

---

[49] Council Regulation on the Statute for a European Company (EC) No. 2157/2001(Oct. 8, 2001).

[50] Council Directive supplementing the Statute for a European Company with regard to the Involvement of Employees, 2001/86/EC (Oct. 8, 2001).

[51] See "Report of the High Level Group of Company Law Experts on Issues Related to Takeover Bids," Jan 10, 2002 (available at www.europa.eu.int/comm/internal_market/en/company/company/official/ (hereinafter "Experts Report on Takeovers"); Proposal for a Directive of the European Parliament and of the Council on Takoever Bids, COM (2002) 534 Final, 2002/0240(COD) (Oct. 2, 2002).

[52] This history draws on the Experts Report on Takeovers, at 13–17, and George Berman et al., Cases and Materials on European Union Law 804–05 (2nd edn, 2002). For a concise account, see Gabriele Apfelbacher et al., German Takeover Law: A Commentary 4 (2002). See generally Christian Kirchner & Richard W. Painter, "A European Modified Business Judgment Rule for Takeover Law," 2 Eur. Bus. Org. L. Rev. 353–400 (2000).

a party obtaining one third of a company's voting rights to make a bid for the rest at an equitable price. It contemplated recourse to the courts for enforcement, however, rather than the self-regulatory model of the City Code.

The Commission withdrew the proposal and tried again, in February 1996, in a shortened version, a "framework directive," that stated general principles and left states with much more discretion over the particulars. For example, the 1996 proposal, unlike the first one, did not set forth a specific percentage threshold for a mandatory bid. It did, however, retain the "board neutrality" position of its predecessor. After further deliberations that extended over a three-year period, in June 1999 the Internal Market Council came to a political agreement on the Directive. The final version of the board neutrality provision in Article 9 of the June 1999 Council draft, obliged member states to require that

> during the period [beginning when the offer is publicly noticed and ending when the results are announced or the bid is withdrawn] the board of the offeree company shall obtain the prior authorisation of the general meeting of the shareholders, given for this purpose, before taking any action which may result in the frustration of the bid, other than seeking alternative bids, and notably before the issuing of shares which may result in a lasting impediment for the offeror obtaining control of the offeree company.[53]

This agreement crashed on the Rock of Gibraltar. The Council agreement was made contingent on a resolution of dispute between Spain and the UK arising from the contested status of Gibraltar.[54] The dispute arose because Article 4 of the Directive specified that "Member States shall designate the authority . . . which will supervise all aspects of the bid." Spain wanted to avoid the creation of a separate authority for bids in Gibraltar. (!!) This pivotal issue of commerce found its eventual resolution almost a year later and the Council adopted a common position on June 19, 2000. But by now Germany had changed its view on the 13th Directive, especially because of the board neutrality provision which it had once

---

[53] For the Council text and the proposed amendments of the European Parliament, see European Parliament, Recommendation for Second Reading, 8129/1/200 – C5-0327/2000-1995/0341 (COD). The ultimate Council common position was put forth on June 19, 2000. Article 9 also provided that state laws could nevertheless permit a target to "increase the share capital" during the period of bid pendency if authorization for the issuance had been received no more than eighteen months prior to the initiation of the bid so long as preemptive rights were preserved.

[54] For a discussion of recent efforts to resolve the conflict, see "A Deal too Far? Britain and Spain are Talking of Joint Sovereignty. Gibraltarians are Twitchy," *Economist*, Jan. 17, 2002.

championed. Its opposition was pivotal to the ultimate rejection of the Directive by the European Parliament in July 2001.

B. Germany's new vulnerability

The world changed for corporate Germany between the June 1999 Council agreement and Parliament's vote. Vodafone had successfully concluded its hostile takeover of a famous German company, Mannesmann, after the first successful Anglo-American-style hostile tender offer in Germany. Moreover, in December 1999 the German government made the surprise revelation of its intention to propose repeal of the capital gains tax on shareholdings of corporations, which was eventually adopted in July 2000.[55] The repealer, to take effect January 1, 2002, would make possible for firms to dispose of their cross-holdings without a ruinous tax penalty (an estimated 52 percent rate on realized gains).[56] At the time the proposal was announced, these cross-holdings were valued at €250 billion, approximately 15 percent of Germany's then stock market capitalization.[57] Indeed, some have attributed the web of cross-holdings that characterized current ownership structures for many German firms and the resulting political economy principally to the lock-in effect from the high capital gains rate.[58] Regardless of the past role of the insider stakes, many financial firms obviously now wanted to dispose of their corporate holdings – invested capital on which they earned a substandard rate of return – in order to reposition themselves for competition in the global economy. Deutsche Bank, for example, had already spun off its corporate holdings into a separate subsidiary in anticipation of a sell-off or spin-off.

There had been important prior institutional changes as well: "Hausbanks" were repositioning themselves as investment banks. This seems to explain the willingness of Deutsche Bank and Dresdner Bank to finance and otherwise aid Krupp-Hoesch's hostile bid in 1997 for Thyssen, despite their seats on the Thyssen supervisory board – an event that arguably would validate hostile bids much like the 1970s decisions of US blue chip

---

[55] See generally, Mark H. Lang *et al.*, "Bringing Down the Other Berlin Wall: Germany's Repeal of the Corporate Capital Gains Tax" (Working Paper, Jan. 2001)(available on SSRN).

[56] Ibid., at 40.

[57] Benjamin W. Johnson, "German Corporate Culture in the Twenty-First Century: The Interrelation between the End of Germany, Inc. and Germany's Corporate Capital Gains Rate Reform," 11 *Minn. J. Global Trade* 69, 71 (2002).

[58] See Friedrich Kübler, "Comment: on Mark Roe, German Codetermination and German Securities Markets," 5 *Colum. J. Eur. L.* 213 (1999).

banks like Morgan Stanley and Goldman Sachs to represent raiders. More-over, the adoption in 1998 of the KonTraG eliminated capped voting, which had been such a useful defensive feature against Pirelli's bid for Continental in the early 1990s. Thus law firms rushed to staff up for what was anticipated to be a "big bang" of merger and restructuring activity in Germany beginning in 2002.

Germany had moved profoundly towards shareholder capitalism. Hostile takeover bids, even of the largest firms, were for the shareholders to resolve. This seemed to be the upshot of Vodafone/Mannesmann. The state would no longer provide an artificial barrier to the unwinding of inefficient control positions, an artificial determinant of the character of share-ownership. This was the result of the tax law change. Perhaps corpo-rate blockholders would merely reshuffle the cards among themselves in the traditional German pattern of transactions in control,[59] but after the successful hostile tender offer in Vodafone, the door was now open to genuine outsider bids, including foreign bids. Banks were giving up their supervisory board seats and whatever commitment that entailed.[60] If the banks were now pursuing investment banking and the corporate blockholders were sellers at the right price, then the complementarities that sustained concentrated ownership would disappear and a new form of ownership structure would emerge. German managers and unions were obviously concerned about these possibilities, which would disturb existing economic and political settlements. The board neutrality posi-tion of the 13th Directive now become the center of an intense lobbying effort to persuade the government to oppose the directive. A particularly effective supplicant was Ferdinand Piëch, the CEO of Volkswagen, whose supervisory board was once chaired by Chancellor Schröder. (Recall that Schröder was also once prime minister of Lower Saxony, which held a 20 percent VW stake.)

But there was a separate concern which could not be dismissed as mere self-seeking protectionism: the "level playing field" problem. At the same

[59] See Julian Franks & Colin Mayer, "Ownership and Control of German Corporations," 14 *Rev. Fin. Stud.* 943 (2001). For an assessment of the immediate effects of the tax law change, see "The Tax Man Goeth: The Abolition of Tax on Sales of Shareholdings has Already Made an Impact," *Economist*, Jan. 10, 2002 (reasons not to expect a "rush of sales," including previous ability to maneuver around tax law, long-run strategic objectives, remaining tax barriers, and decline in German stock market values).

[60] Supervisory board seats held by banks in the largest 100 corporations declined from 29 in 1996 to 17 in 1998. Deutsche Bank announced in March 2001 that it would no longer chair the supervisory board of nonfinancial corporations. See Höpner & Jackson, note 41, above.

time that the European Parliament was in its final deliberations on the 13th Directive, the EU Advocate General issued a surprising blanket rejection of several actions brought by the Commission before the European Court of Justice against "golden shares" held by member countries that protected privatized former SOEs.[61] The Commission had contended that golden shares, which give governments veto rights over recapitalizations, takeovers, and other fundamental transactions in privatized companies, violated the EU rules and treaties on competition policy and the free movement of capital. The Advocate General's opinion (which does not bind the ECJ but which is ordinarily persuasive) sustained:

- Portugal's requirement of ministerial approval for a 10 percent stock acquisition in a privatized company;
- France's requirement for ministerial approval of a stock acquisition above a certain threshold in Elf Aquitaine;
- Belgium's requirement of ministerial approval of a significant stake in the Société nationale de transport par canalisations on the test of whether it disserved Belgian national interests.

Countries like France, Italy, and Spain, had undertaken large-scale privatizations of SOEs in the 1990s and retained golden shares in some of the most substantial enterprises in the country.[62] By contrast, Germany's privatization program was relatively small (except for Deutsche Telekom) because the level of prior state ownership was much less, and, as to the privatized firms, Germany did not retain a golden share. Thus Germany faced a situation in which large acquisitive enterprises might

---

[61] *Commission v. Portuguese Republic, French Republic and Kingdom of Belgium*, C-367/98, C-483/99, C-503/99 (Opinion of Advocate General) (July 3, 2001) (available at Eurolex). See "EU Advocat General Would Allow 'Golden Shares,'" *Fin. T.*, July 3, 2001. The action was particularly a surprise because of the May 2000 decision of the European Court of Justice, *EU Commission v. Italy*, C-58/99 (May 23, 2000) (available at Eurolex), which struck down golden shares maintained by Italy in Telecom Italia and ENI. See John E. Morris with Robert Galbraith, "Trying to Kill the Golden Share," *Corporate Control Alert*, June 2000, at 7–9. On golden shares generally, see Stefan Grundmann & Florian Möslein, "Golden Shares. State Control in Privatised Companies: Comparative Law, European Law and Policy Aspects" (forthcoming Euredia 2004).

The Commission's threatened action against golden share-like antitakeover protections for Volkswagen backfired, since it led VW to intensify its lobbying against the directive. See Paul Hofheinz & Scott Miller, "EU Questions German State's VW Veto," *Wall St. J.*, May 11, 2001, at A12; Edmund Andrews, "Europeans Open Door for Hostile Takeovers," *N.Y. Times*, June 7, 2001.

[62] A large percentage of share issuance in the EU is a consequence of privatization of SOE's, in which governments often retain a significant ownership stake. See Steve Jones *et al.*, "Share Issue Privatizations as Financial Means to Political and Economic Ends," 53 *J. Fin. Econ.* 217 (1999).

pursue hostile cross-border acquisitions of German firms, secure in the knowledge that they were shielded from countermeasures by the golden shares.[63] Moreover, on occasion state-owned firms, totally protected from a takeover bid, had pursued acquisitions. The implications were very serious. Obviously cross-border mergers were important to the integration of the European economy and ultimately its political economy. The single market called out for firms large enough to achieve appropriate scale economies. It was forseeable that this might entail consolidating facilities or divestments or downsizings, which might mean that a given firm would direct resources to one particular country, and away from another, despite the origins of the constituent firms. The risk to the project of economic and political integration is economic nationalism, mercantilism redux in the making of those resource allocation decisions. Economic geography matters. It would quickly become intolerable if French acquirers (for example) of German targets began to shift facilities and resources to French venues in response to explicit or implicit direction of the French government, to bolster French jobs at the expense of German jobs. Yet this was the threat of the golden shares.

One important protection against nationalist behavior is mutual vulnerability in the market for corporate control. In such a world, an inefficient diversion of resources to France would be punished in the capital market – which cares about cash flow, not favor curried with the minister – and would send a signal to a control entrepreneur. The behavior of management would be appropriately constrained. But this feedback system would be at serious risk in the case of a firm in which France retained a golden share. In other words, a golden share interferes with the mutual vulnerability that assures the credibility of the nonnational basis for resource allocation.

The point is more general. Golden shares exemplify the more general problem of national law (voting caps, for instance) that protects the control position of national elites who will be susceptible to entreaties and expectations about favoritism on national grounds. Even if the French government is not a shareholder it may be tempted to exert nationalist pressure on controlling shareholders or perhaps intercede with managers in the diffusely held firm. It's the mutual vulnerability to the control market that checks those tendencies. Thus local takeover protection,

---

[63] In some of these cases, states had exercised golden share provisions to protect newly privatized companies. The Commission nevertheless had pursued an aggressive agenda against all golden shares. See Victorya Hong, "Golden Era Over for Golden Shares?," *The Daily Deal*, April 5, 2001.

which is hardly limited to golden shares, may encourage and sustain the economic nationalism that disrupts economic and political integration.

The "level playing field" objection, then, was the special concern that now drove German resistance to the 13th Directive, which it had strongly advocated over the prior decade.[64] In other words, the standard story of private rent-seeking by managers and union does not do justice to the other compelling issue at stake: the prospects for economic and political integration.

C. *The final act in the the European Parliament*

The Council had come up with an agreed position in December 2000. In spring 2001 the Parliament took a different tack, proposing twenty amendments, adding, for example, a right of employees to receive information and to be consulted about a bid and a board's right to resist a hostile offer. As part of the EU's codecision procedures, the Commission and the Parliament entered a conciliation process in which an agreement was hammered out that gave the employees certain information rights and that crucially preserved the right of prior shareholder approval for target board defensive measures. The Conciliation Commitment drafted a joint text on June 6, 2001.[65] Indeed, the Geman government was nominally on board on this final draft (although it later allegedly rallied its MEPs to vote against) because of a compromise that permitted a five-year postponement of the effective date of Article 9's board neutrality provsions.[66] The Advocate General's opinions in favor of golden shares came down on July 2. Parliament took up the measure almost immediately thereafter. It failed on a tie vote, 273–273, on July 4, 2001.

D. *Germany's new takeover law*

Even before the final vote on the 13th Directive, Germany moved to adopt a law regulating takeovers. It had previously operated without one, relying instead on a voluntary Takeover Code (*Übernahmenkodex*) adopted in

---

[64] See Paul Meller, "Europe Plan on Mergers Hits a Snag; Germany Switches on Crucial Element," *N.Y. Times*, May 3, 2001, at D1.

[65] 1995/0341 (COD), C5-0221/2001; PE-CONS 3629/1/0, Rev 1, DRS 27, CODEC 493 (June 19, 2001).

[66] See Paul Hofheinz, "Europe Gives Muted Applause to Mergers Bill," *Wall St. J.*, June 7, 2001, at A18; Deborah Hargreaves, "Germans Seek to Kill off EU Takeover Directive," *Fin. T.*, July 2, 2001.

1995 based on the English City Code. As of 1997 approximately 80 percent of the DAX 30 companies but only 60 percent of the MDAX companies had agreed to comply.[67] Foreign offerors, however, rarely tied themselves to the Code and there was no enforcement machinery.[68] The Mannesmann transaction and the prospect of bids stimulated by the unwinding of block-holdings after the tax law change put takeover legislation on the agenda.

In many respects the proposed legislation tracked the 13th Directive in its then current form, adding additional protection for workers, and, more controversially, limiting the right to make exchange offers to acquirers that listed on a European exchange.[69] The May 2000 draft also contained the provision that Germany was then pushing for in the Directive, namely, permission for pre-bid shareholder authorization of defensive measures.

In draft legislation as of October 2001, the exception to board neutrality was relatively narrow. In addition to actions that a "prudent and diligent manager" would otherwise take, or a search for a competing bid (a "white knight"), management could employ only those defensive measures for which it had obtained shareholder approval *prior* to the announcement of the bid, and only to the extent that the measures had been authorized by a vote of at least 75 percent of the share capital. The authorization period was limited to eighteen months.[70] In a draft of November 8, 2001,

---

[67] See Karl-Herman Baumann, "Takeovers in Germany and EU Regulation Experience and Practice," in Klaus Hopt *et al.*, *Comparative Corporate Governance: The State of the Art and Emerging Research*, pp. 659–65 (1998). For an account that includes adoption of the new law, see Gabriele Apfelbacher *et al.*, *German Takeover Law: A Commentary*, pp. 1–7 (2002).

[68] Ralf Thaeter & Keith Frederick (Gleiss Lutz Hootz Hirsch), The German "Securities Acquisition & Takeover Act" (firm memo, undated mss, Dec. 2001). See generally Christian Kirchner & Richard W. Painter, "Takeover Defenses under Delaware Law, the Proposed Thirteenth EU Directive and the Proposed German Takeover Law: Comparison and Recommendations for Reform," 50 *American Journal of Comparative Law* 451 (2002).

[69] See Ralph Atkins, "Germans Agree on Code to Govern Takeovers," *Fin. T.*, May 18, 2000. To be sure, the Act is more than an "anti-takeover law." It regulates all aspects of public bids in Germany, and insofar as it establishes clear rules and procedures and brings some useful innovations to German corporate law such as the freeze-out merger, it may aid the making of offers for German firms, including hostile offers. Nevertheless its distinctive feature, the subject of extended debate during the legislative process, is the antitakeover element.

    The Act is formally cited as "Wertpapiererwerbs- und Übernahmegesetz" v. 20 Dezember 2001 (BGBl. I. S. 3822). A useful summary of its provisions are found in the *Int'l Fin. L. Rev.* (March 2002). A more extensive, very useful account, including a legislative history, is provided by Gabriele Apfelbacher *et al.*, *German Takeover Law: A Commentary* (2002).

[70] Draft of a Bill on the Regulation of Public Offers for the Acquisition of Securities and the Regulation of Takeovers (Wertpapiererwerbs-und Übernahmegesetz – WpÜG) (Cleary Gottlieb Steen & Hamilton transl.) (Section 33).

from the government's public finance committee, a remarkable addition to management board authority appeared: "*or actions which have been approved by the target's supervisory board.*"[71] In other words, the supervisory board is now empowered to approve target defensive measures without any shareholder approval whatsoever. Although the scope of this discretionary power is not yet clear,[72] this appears to eliminate the general shareholder veto as well as the shareholder veto over particular defensive measures. The supervisory board is well insulated from pressures that might produce independent scrutiny of the requested defensive measures on behalf of shareholder interests. Recall that half the members of the supervisory board are employee representatives and that even shareholder representatives are elected for five-year terms, removable only upon a 75 percent shareholder vote. The actions of the supervisory boards are subject to the usual German company law fiduciary duties of care and responsibility in acting in the company's best interest, but Germany does not have a robust tradition of judicial review of board action, certainly not in the quick-paced time frame of a contested bid, nor does it permit contingent-fee litigation, which has policed fiduciary duty compliance in the United States. The new legislation, effective in January 2002, may well unleash a broad range of target defensive measures in contested takeover bids in Germany.

It is notable that defensive tactics in Germany will evolve differently from the US pattern. This is because the US favorite, the "poison pill," would not be feasible under German corporate law because its discriminatory feature would violate strong mandates for preemptive rights.[73] If so, German antitakeover measures will resemble those used in the US in the 1970s and early 1980s: for example, defensive acquisitions to create competition policy problems for the acquirer, setting up a blocking position for a "white knight" through a sweetheart sale of securities; selling off assets that an acquirer might prize, the "crown jewels"; reshaping the capital structure, as through additional leverage, to make the target less desirable; creating so-called "tin parachute" agreements

---

[71] Section 33(1) (Thaeter & Frederick transl.).

[72] See generally Gabriele Apfelbacher *et al.*, *German Takeover Law: A Commentary*, pp. 281–315 (2002).

[73] This follows Jeffrey N. Gordon, "Das neue deutsche 'Anti'-Übernahmegesetz aus amerikanischer Perspektive" [An American Perspective on the New German Antitakeover Law], 12 *Die Aktiengesellschaft* (December 2002). German law requires a 75 percent vote for the limitation of preemptive rights [AktG' 186(4)] and requires an explicit written explanation before the shareholder vote. A poison pill has almost never been put to shareholder vote in the US principally on the belief that the shareholders would reject it.

that promise large bonus payments to rank-and-file employees upon a control shift; exotic tactical moves, such as the so-called "Pac-Man" defense of responding to a hostile bid with a counterbid for the putative acquirer. Unlike the pill, which can be redeemed by the board to permit a bid to proceed, these tactics are often irreversible. They reduce value; they disrupt the economic logic of the firm; they can destroy the firm in order to save it. Such self-destructive measures are now used by virtually no firm in the US, but they may be inevitable in light of other features of German corporate law.

One way to understand Germany's protectionist move in the Takeover Act is as a frustrated response to the 13th Directive's failure to promote adequate European-wide takeover regulation, in particular the failure to address the level playing field problem. The Takeover Act can be seen as a move in a trade negotiation, an example of "aggressive reciprocity." When trading partners fail to lower barriers, one response is to raise your own. This move, which imposes costs on partners as well as oneself, may stimulate a negotiation to achieve the first best cooperative outcome, a mutual lowering of barriers. In the context of cross-border mergers, the way for Germany to promote its objective of economic and political integration, and its strategy of mutual vulnerability to control transactions, is to raise its barriers. This is what added takeover protection does: in permitting new target defense measures it raises the barriers to obtaining control of German-based firms. Such a move makes hostile transactions more difficult, both entirely domestic and cross-border, and in that sense may be seen as a step away from shareholder capitalism. So in this context the desire for economic and political integration slows down the move to shareholder capitalism.

Yes, the standard rent protection and domestic interest group stories are undoubtedly a significant contributor to Germany's antitakeover move, and represent to that extent a resistance to shareholder capitalism on the Anglo-American model. But there is an important additional element that may be pivotal. The ambition for economic and political integration is shaping German attitudes to shareholder capitalism, for the most part towards convergence but here, crucially, a move away. Ultimately it may be that Germany's aggressive reciprocity evokes a cooperative response, a joint move towards easier cross-border bids. But the attainment of that first best outcome may not be possible in light of the political economy of Germany's partners. The result may be a degenerate equilibrium of increasing takeover protection and more economic nationalism. In effect, the trade negotiation may fail, leaving trade war in its wake. Member states may also understand the economic and political integration that shareholder capitalism will bring, and may resist it for precisely that reason. The point is that this divergence away from shareholder capitalism, much like the convergence in the wake of the Deutsche Telekom privatization, needs telling not just in terms of the standard stories of efficiency and politics, but as part of a country's international aspirations, its conscious effort to pursue (or avoid) a greater sense of union with its neighbors.

III.   The effort to revive the 13th Directive within a framework of mutual takeover vulnerability

The response within the European Commission to the defeat of the 13th Directive and to Germany's new takeover law bears out the claim that the transnational integration motive plays a large role in the push for shareholder capitalism. As part of the Parliamentary debate, the Commission agreed to convene a "High Level Group of Company Law Experts" to address some of the open issues, in particular, the level playing field concerns that ultimately proved fatal to the Directive. That Experts Group issued its report in January 2002.[74] The Report is a bold proclamation on behalf of European economic integration, the role that shareholder capitalism plays in its achievement, and the importance of eliminating national barriers to control transactions. It endorses eliminating "technical" elements that foster concentrated rather than diffuse ownership, such as the control prerogatives of dual-class common stock against a hostile bid, and remits to further study problems associated with "structural" elements, such as interlocking or pyramidal ownership structures.[75]

The Experts Report states:

> An important goal of the European Union is to create an integrated capital market in the Union by 2005. The regulation of takeover bids is a key element of such an integrated market.
>
> Many European companies will need to grow to an optimal scale to make effective use of the integrating internal market . . . Takeover bids are a means to achieve this for those engaged in business of both bidder and target.

---

[74] Experts Report on Takeovers, note 51, above.

[75] The distinction between "technical" and "structural" barriers to takeovers was apparently coined by Ron Gilson. See Ronald J. Gilson, "The Political Ecology of Takeovers," in Klaus Hopt & Eddie Wymeersch, *European Takeovers: Law and Practice*, p. 65 (1992).

> Takeover barriers existing in various Member States more often tend to result in control over listed companies being uncontestable . . . this is undesirable in the European context [even if done in the US], as an integrated capital market has to be built up in order for business to fully benefit from and make effective use of the integrating internal market in Europe.[76]

In order to operationalize this objective, the Experts Report calls for a new directive that reaffirms the importance of board neutrality and shareholder choice found in the prior draft of the 13th Directive. But its crucial move is to call for the overcoming of golden share and most other state-created barriers to control via a potent "breakthrough" provision that lets a holder of majority or required supermajority (but in no event more than 75 percent) of cash flow rights take over the firm. The Experts Report summarizes its conclusions in this area as follows:

> Companies will be required to disclose complete information about their capital and control structures . . . After announcement of the bid, the board of the offeree company should not be permitted to take actions frustrating a takeover bid on the basis of a general meeting authorisation given prior to the bid . . . A rule should be introduced which allows the offeror to break-through mechanisms and structures which may frustrate a bid, as defined in the articles of association and related constitutional documents, in the case of a takeover bid which achieves such a measure of success as clearly to justify this. The threshold for exercising the break-through right should not be set a percentage higher than 75 percent of the risk bearing capital of the company on the date of the completion of the bid . . . Provisions in the articles of association and other constitutional documents deviating from the principles of shareholder decisionmaking and proportionality between risk bearing capital and control shall be overridden.[77]

The key intellectual move of the Experts Report is to insist on the "proportionality between risk bearing capital and control . . . once a takeover bid has been announced." This means that all post-bid decisions, including whether to authorize particular defensive measures, should be taken in proportion to what an American would call common share ownership, not voting rights.[78] The Report wants to reject the prerogatives of shareholders who currently possess majority control rights but

---

[76] "Experts Report on Takeovers," note 51 above, pp. 18, 19, 41.   [77] Ibid. pp. 42–43.

[78] Compare, for example, the 2002 amendment of Del. Corp. Code § 212, which clarifies that "votes" rather than "shares" count for the 85 percent threshold in the antitakeover provision § 212 or the 90 percent threshold in the short-form merger provision, § 253.

minority cash flow rights to determine the outcome of a bid. To be sure, its breakthrough remedy is incomplete, since it applies only to internal governance arrangements, not to pyramid structures or, apparently, cross-holdings or shareholders' agreements, despite the recognition that such ownership structures present analytically the same proportionality problem.[79] The Experts Report seems to draw a distinction between what might be called "technical disproportionality" and "structural disproportionality." It rejects the "technical disproportionality" that arises from direct "state action" such as capped voting or super-supermajority provisions (which it would bar) or from "corporate action" such as dual-class capital structures or transfer restrictions (which it would break through). But it would not take on "structural disproportionality" that arises from ownership decisions that do not depend on such state or corporate action for their effectiveness, despite the analytic similarities. The Experts Report remits such structural problems to further Commission review. Arguably the failure to take on such problems is a major weakness in the Report's effort to create mutual takeover vulnerability.[80]

---

[79] "Experts Report on Takeovers," note 51 above, pp. 38–39.

[80] Contra Lucian Bebchuk & Oliver Hart, "A Threat to Dual-Class Shares," *Financial Times*, May 31, 2002, I do not believe that the failure to address pyramidal structures undoes the Report. To be sure, the Report would have much less immediate impact in Italy, say, where pyramids are common among public firms, than the Netherlands, which uses dual-class stock. But pyramids are not a low-cost substitute for dual-class stock in firms newly going public, as Bebchuk & Hart suggest. A pyramidal structure that would give an owner the same level of control as dual-class stock requires the creation of multiple levels of public firms; this would generate considerable resistance in markets where they are not established and could easily be controlled through listing requirements. In a stylized case where an owner wants to put up $10 in capital, absolute majority voting control of a public entity with a value of at least $100 would require a 3- or 4-level pyramid (depending on how you count), as against a single public company with dual-class stock with ten votes per super-voting share. Moreover, Bebchuk & Hart assume that fiduciary duties would remain stable in the face of a move to a form which so obviously gains its value from weak legal protection of minority shareholders. See generally Ronald J. Gilson & Jeffrey N. Gordon, "Controlling Controlling Shareholders" (forthcoming. U. *Penn. L. Rev.*, 2004) (available on SSRN).

The Experts Report is flawed in another, perhaps more basic sense, however: its breakthrough remedy would not work against golden shares, which give the government the right to limit accumulation beyond certain threshold percentages, meaning that an unwelcome bidder would never achieve the breakthrough trigger. (These accumulation barriers are transfer restrictions outside the usual stock exchange prohibitions of transfer restrictions on listed shares.) However, a few months after issuance of the Experts Report, the European Court of Justice greatly restricted the availability of golden shares to circumstances of a precisely tailored fit to particular national interests. See *Commission* v. *France*, C-483/99 (June 4, 2002); *Commission* v. *Portugal*, C-367/98 (June 4, 2002); *Commission* v. *Belgium*, C-503/99 (June 4, 2002). In particular the ECJ (which rejected the opinion of its

The Experts Report has a strained reliance on efficiency arguments that suggests the importance of transnational considerations apart from efficiency. The Report rejects what might be called "national efficiency" in favor of "transnational efficiency." That is, the Report concedes that particular ownership structures and voting arrangements that restrict takeovers might be efficient in light of national financial institutions (institutional complementarities, it might have said).[81] The Report also acknowledges theoretical arguments that firms efficiently use different ownership and control structures; it further acknowledges that at least for some states, these control mechanisms may be accurately impounded in share prices. (Indeed, the Report could have cited the evidence on differential market prices that may compensate noncontrolling shareholders for the loss of control and the fact that these differentials vary systematically across countries, suggesting that investors are sensitive to different levels of protection.[82]) Nevertheless, this level of efficiency is not good enough, a mandatory rule is required, because "most" markets are not adequate:

> These more and less developed markets must be integrated on a European level to enable the restructuring of European industry and the integration of European securities markets to proceed with reasonable efficiency and speed.[83]

In other words, control structures that impede takeovers – even if efficient on a national scale – are objectionable because they interfere with the project of transnational economic integration. This consists of two elements: first, industrial restructuring on a European scale, and second,

---

Advocate General) regarded golden shares as presumptively restricting the free movement of capital, and, to an American eye, adopted something like a "compelling state interest/less restrictive alternative" framework for evaluating them. This vigorous endorsement of the basic commerce clause-like implications of Article 73b(1) of the EC Treaty (now Article 58(1)(b)) has surely strengthened the basic appeal of the efforts of the Experts' Report to enhance the cross-border contestability of control. See generally Johannes Adolff, "Turn of the Tide? The 'Golden Share' Judgments of the European Court of Justice and the Liberalization of the European Capital Markets," 3 *Germ. L.J.* (8-1) (August 2002) (available online only at www.germanlawjournal.com).

81 "Experts Report on Takeovers," note 51 above, p. 22.

82 See, e.g., Alexander Dyck & Luigi Zingales, "Private Benefits of Control: An International Comparison," 59 *J. Finance* (forthcoming 2004)(value of control varies between 4 percent and +65 percent, with average value of +14 percent); see also Tatiana Nenova, "The Value of Corporate Control and Control Benefits: A Cross Country Analysis," 68 *J. Fin. Econ.* 325 (2002).

83 "Experts Report on Takeovers," note 51 above, p. 23. Compare, e.g., Jeffrey N. Gordon, "The Mandatory Structure of Corporate Law," 89 *Colum. L. Rev.* 1549 (1989).

the creation of European-wide capital markets. No one can really know about the comparative efficiency of those two industrial/financial set-ups, but the transnational project becomes the driver.

Indeed, the importance of the transnational project is reflected in the Experts Report's resolution of what an American might think of as a "regulatory takings" question. The holders of disproportionately voting shares would lose a prerogative of significant economic value, reflected in the differences between the value of supervoting and limited voting shares that are seen throughout the EU.[84] Presumably that price difference impounds the private benefits of control in such shares. But in general "[T]he bidder should not be required to offer compensation" after a breakthrough.[85] The reason: "The loss of these special rights would be the result of a public policy choice made by the European Union and the Member states in order to create a level playing field for takeover bids across the Union."[86] It's the creation of a transnational market that justifies this extraordinary shift in value.

So the Experts Report would foster convergence on shareholder choice in the takeover setting, based on proportional ownership of residual cash flow rights. In a sense the Experts Report can be read as proposing substitute mechanisms and rules to produce the contestability that would naturally arise from diffuse ownership. But the effect, and perhaps the ambition, of the Experts Report would go much further. Its shareholder proportionality rule for takeovers would have broad implications for ownership structure more generally, favoring evolution toward the diffuse ownership pattern of shareholder capitalism. This is because it will become more difficult for controlling shareholders to retain the private benefits of control that sustain concentrated ownership patterns. Under the proposed breakthrough rule (based on shares, not votes), any significant pricing gap between supervoting and limited voting shares creates a potential arbitrage opportunity for a control entrepreneur. In other words, private benefits are always at risk from a hostile bidder. There is a double effect favoring the growth of diffusely held firms. The breakthrough mechanism both creates conditions of greater minority shareholder protection said to be necessary for development of public equity markets with diffusely held firms and reduces incentives to create

---

[84] See sources cited in notes 38 & 82 above.

[85] "Experts Report on Takeovers," note 51 above, p. 7. The Report remits to further review the possibility of appraisal in "exceptional" cases.

[86] Ibid., pp. 5, 35.

and maintain concentrated ownership structures in the first place. In the United States, robust articulation and enforcement of fiduciary duties of controlling shareholders offer adequate minority shareholder protection; takeovers help solve the managerial agency problems associated with the diffusely held firm. In the EU, where legal protection of minority shareholders is weaker, takeovers under the breakthrough rule help solve controlling shareholder agency problems and thereby make the diffusely held firm a plausible option, perhaps even a favored option. Moreover, the relatively free market in corporate control that would result from a regime on a revised 13th Directive will also reduce managerial agency costs, in a way that may substitute for some of the corporate governance and stock option-based mechanisms that have arisen in the US to control such problems.[87]

But note that such convergence on shareholder capitalism is not necessarily efficient, at least in the national setting. Concentrated ownership offers some distinct advantages in controlling managerial agency costs; some of the private benefits may be appropriately compensatory.[88] Yet concentrated owners of less than 50 percent of the share capital may feel their appropriate returns are always at risk from a hostile bidder. Moreover, establishing the right set of financial institutional complements for shareholder capitalism may be difficult and expensive. Indeed, a particular form of corporate ownership structure may fit with a set of social institutional complements as well. This has been the source of purported efficiency advantages of the German corporatist model.[89] But the 13th Directive project bespeaks commitment beyond such potential national efficiencies to EU project of transnational of economic and political integration.

The prospects for proposal and adoption of a revised 13th Directive along the lines of the Experts Report are uncertain, perhaps diminished by the sharp decline in stock market values, the related decline in

---

[87] On the US model and some recent concerns, see Jeffrey N. Gordon, "What Enron Means for the Management and Control of the Modern Business Corporation: Some Initial Reflections," 69 *U.Chi. L. Rev.* 1233 (2002).

[88] See, e.g., Ronald J. Gilson, "Evaluating Dual Class Common Stock: The Relevance of Substitutes," 73 *U.Va.L. Rev.* 807 (1987) (offering an efficiency explanation of dual-class capital structures in an efficient IPO market).

[89] See generally Mary O'Sullivan, "The Political Economy of Corporate Governance in Germany" (Jerome Levy Institute WP No. 226) (Feb. 1998); Gregory Jackson, "Corporate Governance in Germany and Japan, Liberalization Pressures and Responses," in Kozo Yamamura and Wolfgang Streeck, eds., *End of Diversity?: Prospects for German and Japanese Capitalism* (2003).

cross-border merger activity throughout the world, and the loss in prestige of the shareholder capitalism model in light of the potential weaknesses revealed by the Enron and WorldCom financial frauds.[90] Nevertheless the Experts vision of a 13th Directive is still a powerful signal and a beacon. In substantially increasing the control contestability of corporations in the EU it would work a revolution in EU corporate governance and a revolution in much else besides.

In most respects Germany (ex the expansion of supervisory board anti-takeover authority of its recent Takeover Law) would comply with the Experts Report's directive. The principal barrier to contestability in Germany is the share ownership structure, in which large blocks (greater than 25 percent) are common – although insofar as these blocking positions are held together through shareholder agreements, they would be subject to "breakthrough." So Germany's "aggressive reciprocity" in rejecting the prior draft of the 13th Directive and its adoption of a Takeover Law with heightened takeover defenses might well have been a genuinely catalytic event.

Conclusion

The recent accounting and corporate governance embarrassments in the US may offer an interesting test of whether convergence is driven principally by efficiency reasons or by the international relations theory presented here. The US problems have somewhat damaged the prestige of the US model of shareholder capitalism and the efficacy of high-powered incentives in aligning manager and shareholder interests in the diffusely held firm. The episode has a grim parallel to the monitoring failures of the German banks in the 1980s: in both, a purported strength proves not so strong. So the efficiency-based argument on behalf of convergence in corporate governance seems less powerful, especially the argument of strong form convergence on diffuse share ownership. Yet the US scandals

[90] Indeed, In October 2002 the European Commission proposed a revised 13th Directive that would eliminate capped voting and various transfer restrictions, but, in a retreat from the Experts Report, would permit maintenance of dual-class structures. Proposal for a Directive of the European Parliament and of the Council on Takoever Bids, COM (2002) 534 Final, 2002/0240(COD) (Oct. 2, 2002). Germany apparently is threatening to oppose the new proposal because it at once threatens the so-called "Volkswagen law" that imposes a 20 percent voting cap for that firm (meaning a hostile bidder could not outvote Saxony, the German state that holds a nearly 20 percent block in Volkswagen) while not addressing other level playing field problems. Paul Hofheinz, "Germany Will Again Oppose EU Reform of Takeover Rules," *Wall St. J.*, Sept. 25, 2002, at A11.

do not undermine the importance of transnational economic and political integration in the EU and elsewhere, nor do they undercut the peculiar advantages of shareholder capitalism for those purposes. If convergence continues in the face of stock market declines, the general loss in investor confidence, and the uncertainties about the risk inherent in a US-style system, this will suggest a powerful alternative motive at work, the desire to pursue the transnational project.

6

Property rights in firms

Introduction

Property rights are where the whole debate began. Berle and Means unwittingly set the stage for modern-day comparative corporate law scholarship in 1932 with a straightforward and powerfully compelling theory rooted, as they put it, in "the traditional logic of property"[1]: to fulfill the need for vast pools of capital, firms issue shares to large numbers of dispersed shareholders; scattered ownership allows control to concentrate in the hands of managers. Corporate governance, in this universe, focuses on aligning the interests of shareholder "owners" who provide the capital and corporate managers who run the firm.

Some sixty years after this initial insight, legal scholars, beginning with Mark Roe, pointed out in equally compelling terms that the logic of Berle and Means skips a crucial step: in some economies, powerful financial intermediaries take the place of organized stock exchanges as the chief mechanism for raising capital.[2] In these economies, banks may have the information and incentives to monitor firms, and the problem around which a half-century of American corporate law theory is built fades in importance.

Explicit in this view is a powerful but narrow perspective on diversity in national corporate governance systems. On the theory that "finance

[*] This chapter was previously published in 84 *Virginia Law Review* 1145 (1998). For comments on the original article, I thank Steve Bainbridge, Mitu Gulati, Henry Hansmann, Bill Klein, Ronald Mann, Geoff Miller, Mark Ramseyer, Mark Roe, Ed Rubin, Gary Schwartz, Paul Sheard, Richard Steinberg, and Bob Thompson. I also thank participants at a Japanese Ministry of International Trade and Industry symposium and two conferences sponsored by the Sloan Corporate Governance Project at Columbia Law School for stimulating discussions of earlier drafts.

[1] Adolf A. Berle & Gardiner C. Means, *The Modern Corporation and Private Property*, pp. 333–39 (1932).

[2] See Mark J. Roe, "Some Differences in Corporate Structure in Germany, Japan, and the United States," 102 *Yale L.J.* 1927 (1993).

determines governance,"[3] prominent scholarship has focused on the way political and historical idiosyncracies have shaped the law of financial institutions and the resulting ownership structure of large corporations. Roe summarizes this diversity theory from his critique of Berle and Means: "Different political paths yielded different financial institutions, and different financial institutions yielded different corporate structures."[4]

Actually, the analytical core of a more complete explanation for governance diversity is suggested by Berle and Means' work itself. As this chapter will show, these early commentators were right to focus on property rights in fashioning a theory of corporate governance; the real oversight blinding their successors to the possibility of alternative systems lay in the hidden assumption that, when filtered through national institutions, the "logic of property" dictates universal outcomes.

This chapter makes two central claims. The first is that property rights institutions are the principal source of diversity among national corporate governance systems.[5] This diversity claim is simply that distinctive forms of industrial organization and control should be understood as a function of the national frameworks for the allocation and enforcement of property rights in which firms operate. Two important distinctions among national property rights institutions can be made for purposes of comparative corporate governance analysis: (1) the extent to which control rights over assets are allocated to politicians and bureaucrats rather than private economic agents; and (2) the degree to which control rights over assets are legally as opposed to politically or socially enforced.

If this first claim is accurate, the focus of most comparative corporate governance literature to date is too narrow. The key independent variables in corporate governance are not the legal rules governing financial intermediaries,[6] but the broader set of rules worked out among public and private actors concerning control rights over assets. Thinking about corporate control systems primarily from the perspective of financial or corporate laws may limit the ability to understand why governance

---

[3] Mark J. Roe, "Foundations of Corporate Finance: The Pacification of the Insurance Industry" 93 *Colum. L. Rev.* 639, 642 (1993).

[4] Roe, note 2 above, at 1957.

[5] By property rights institutions I mean simply the rules (legal, political, or social) by which control over assets is allocated and enforced.

[6] See e.g., Mark J. Roe, *Strong Managers, Weak Owners: The Political Roots of American Corporate Finance*, p. ix (1994) (focusing on the politics of financial rules in arguing that "American corporate structures are in considerable part the result of political decisions . . . about the organization of financial intermediaries.").

mechanisms differ across countries. Legal constraints on corporate structure and governance are often swamped by more direct political impulses and more amorphous social control mechanisms. The property rights analysis offered here is consistent with and builds on the existing literature, while providing a more complete explanation for governance diversity and a more useful tool of *comparative* analysis.

The very existence of diverse governance regimes, particularly in the face of recent historical and economic developments, raises an important question that my second claim attempts to answer: are distinctive national governance systems converging? If alternative governance structures exist in a number of successful countries, a global competition in these structures is possible, providing a natural experiment in the optimality of economic forms. In fact, such experiments are occurring in Eastern Europe and Asia. As command economies collapsed in Eastern Europe, public and private actors struggled to fill the void with the rudiments of a market economy. Since successful Western economies provide the obvious models for imitation, this competition loosely pitted the bank-oriented model of Japan and Germany against the stock market-oriented model of the UK and the United States.[7] At the same time, the Asian financial crisis altered views of the relative merits of "Asian" and "Western" styles of capitalism. No less an economic prognosticator than Federal Reserve Chairman Alan Greenspan has publicly declared the victory of Western capitalism over the Asian variety that until recently appeared so invincible.[8]

Simultaneously, the prospect of a different form of governance competition is raised by the increasing globalization of capital and product markets. Economic theory predicts that firms will be forced to adopt relatively uniform organizational structures to survive and prosper in large, specialized, and efficient global markets. Firms that continue to play by idiosyncratic domestic rules, the theory predicts, will face extinction. Thus, markets lead to the emergence of similar control mechanisms. As one commentator has put it, "the expectation that structures of production and of the economy at large in the most advanced

---

[7] See, e.g., Roy C. Smith & Ingo Walter, "Bank Industry Linkages: Models for Eastern European Economic Restructuring," New York University Salomon Center Working Paper no. S-92-48 (1992).

[8] See David E. Sanger, "Greenspan Sees Asian Crisis Moving World to Western Capitalism," *N.Y. Times*, Feb. 13, 1998, at C1 (reporting on Greenspan's view of the Asian crisis as "a very dramatic event towards a consensus of the type of market system which we have in [the United States]").

industrial countries are and should be converging is still alive and well today."[9]

The second claim advanced is that, even assuming the existence of both an optimal corporate governance system and exogenous forces that would inspire homogenizing changes in existing national patterns of industrial organization, the convergence of national corporate governance systems will be slow, sporadic, and uncertain. To explain why, the chapter again turns to property rights analysis. The implication of my first claim is that governance change requires change in property rights institutions. Institutional change, however, is sticky; even if private economic agents everywhere would respond uniformly to international economic forces, there is no reason to believe that the same is true of the politicians and bureaucrats who hold important control rights over firms in every economy. Put differently, convergence will be limited because while global financial and product markets may push managers to adopt similar organizational structures in order to remain competitive, an efficient political market supplying the same incentives to political actors everywhere does not exist.[10]

In this chapter, I offer a preliminary property-rights-based approach to diversity and convergence in corporate governance. I seek to translate the existing path dependence stories into more useful forms of institutional analysis. In the process, I enlarge the sample used for comparative study by illuminating a political and family-based model of corporate governance that is not adequately explained by the existing literature. The chapter examines corporate governance in the United States, Japan, and South Korea – a natural focus for a study of diversity and convergence in corporate governance. Improbably linked by historical circumstance, the governance systems of the three countries have been extensively cross-pollinated, yet their systems of corporate monitoring and control look very different. Stock ownership of American firms is relatively dispersed, financial intermediaries are relatively weak, and market- and law-oriented governance mechanisms prevail. Japan's pre-war *zaibatsu* conglomerates were forcibly disbanded, only to be replaced by the *keiretsu* corporate groups and main bank alliances. In South Korea, the *chaebol* – large, diversified industrial groups centered around a founding

---

[9] Suzanne Berger, "Introduction," in Suzanne Berger & Ronald Dore, eds., *National Diversity and Global Capitalism*, pp. 1, 4 (1996) [hereinafter *Diversity and Capitalism*].

[10] For similar ultimate conclusions on the convergence question reached through quite different analytical constructs, see Lucian Ayre Bebchuk & Mark J. Roe, "A Theory of Path Dependence in Corporate Ownership and Governance," 52 *Stan. L. Rev.* 127 (1999).

entrepreneur – confound American corporate governance theory with a model of family capitalism uniting ownership and control.

The chapter is organized into five sections. Section I uses insights from the new institutional economics to sketch a property rights theory of governance diversity. Sections II through IV employ the property rights approach to explain corporate governance diversity among the United States, Japan, and South Korea. Section II outlines the substantial governance differences among the three countries despite forces for convergence. Section III uses cross-country empirical data on factors such as economic freedom, corruption, and political risk, as well as stylized accounts of regulatory politics in the three countries, to create a spectrum of property rights linked to the allocation and enforcement of control rights over firms. Section IV explains the observed governance differences from a property rights perspective. Section V argues that the political economy of property rights regimes will limit the convergence of national corporate governance systems.

I.   Diversity

Why are firms in different economies organized and controlled in different ways? Property rights institutions underlie all systems of economic exchange and define governance structures everywhere. Property rights institutions, however, are not homogeneous. Differences in national property rights institutions account for the diversity in corporate governance systems.

Property rights and corporate governance

As noted in the Introduction, property rights have long been a focus of corporate governance commentators. Traditional economic analysis of property rights, however, suffers from three related flaws that diminish its usefulness as a tool of comparative analysis. The first is the omission of political and legal institutions from theories of economic growth.[11] The second is the tendency to treat property rights as a precondition for economic development that is either completely satisfied or unsatisfied in a particular community. In fact, property rights cannot simply be "put

---

[11] Tom Bethell, "The Law of the Land: Rule of Law as a Precondition of Economic Growth," *The American Spectator*, Aug. 1996, at 18. Since the original publication of this chapter in 1998, there has been an explosion of interest in legal determinants of economic growth and capital market development.

in place" as standard economic analysis assumes; rather, they develop in evolutionary processes shaped by market and social interactions as well as state coercion.[12] Third, traditional economic analysis assumes that there is an ideal, market-conforming control structure for economic activity, without paying much attention to how control structures emerge or evolve.[13]

Generalizations about property rights structures thus mask significant national variations in economic organization and control, even among highly developed countries. By exposing these assumptions and unpacking the black box of property rights, it is possible to analyze corporate governance systems as a function of the larger set of rules governing economic exchange that have evolved in different communities. Corporate governance is about control structures for firms. An effective way to analyze these control structures is to examine them in the context of property rights, which are control structures for the entire economy.

Fortunately, an analytical framework for such an undertaking already exits. In the new institutional economics, property rights are viewed simply as *control rights*[14] over physical and human assets.[15] More specifically, they are institutions (or sets of rules and enforcement attributes) that help people form reasonable expectations about control over assets.[16] These institutions consist of laws, administrative arrangements, and social norms relating to the allocation and enforcement of control rights over assets. While many of these rules are products of conscious design by the state, others arise spontaneously out of repeated private interactions.[17]

---

[12] Andrzej Rapaczynski, "The Roles of the State and the Market in Establishing Property Rights," 10 *J. Econ. Perspectives* (87): 87 (1996).

[13] Thrainn Eggertsson, "Economic Perspectives on Property Rights and the Economics of Institutions," in Paul Foss, ed., *Economic Approaches to Organizations and Institutions*, pp. 47, 48 (1995).

[14] See Sanford J. Grossman & Oliver D. Hart, "The Costs and Benefits of Ownership: A Theory of Vertical and Lateral Integration," 94 *J. Pol. Econ.* 691, 693–95 (1986).

[15] Often, control over a tangible asset carries with it the potential to control human actions. Oliver Hart & John Moore, "Property Rights and the Nature of the Firm," 98 *J. Pol. Econ.* 1119, 1121 (1990); see *also* Yoram Barzel, *Economic Analysis of Property Rights*, p. 99 (1989) (arguing that property rights analysis applies to all human behavior).

[16] Harold Demsetz, "Toward a Theory of Property Rights," 57 *Am. Econ. Rev.* 347, 347 (1967); Svetozar Pejovich, *The Economics of Property Rights: Towards a Theory of Comparative Systems*, p. 4 (1990); Gary Libecap, *Contracting for Property Rights*, p. 1 (1989).

[17] See Holger Schmeiding, "Property Rights, Institutions, and Market Reform," in Hendrikus J. Blommenstein & Bernard Steunenberg, eds., *Government and Markets: Establishing a Democratic Constitutional Order and a Market Economy in Former Socialist Countries*, pp. 159, 163 (1994).

As structures to allocate and enforce control over scarce resources, property rights institutions are a central factor in economic organization and decisionmaking. These institutions guide incentives, apportion decisionmaking authority, and determine the level of transaction costs in economic exchange. Together, they supply the structure for economic activity.

Property rights shape corporate governance in two fundamental and related ways. First, they determine what types of firms will emerge in a given environment. Like all organizations, firms arise in response to the incentives and transaction costs generated by the existing institutional framework. By creating the opportunity sets of costs and rewards in an economic system, property rights give shape to firms – determining, in effect, who the players are. For example, large public firms with dispersed shareholders are not prevalent in insecure property rights environments, because it is too costly to establish the required corporate control mechanisms. Second, the specific governance mechanisms available to firms are constrained by existing property rights institutions, which specify the legitimate forms of control in any given community. Put differently, governance technology can only be selected from the portfolio of available control mechanisms supplied by property rights institutions. To take two basic examples, stock options and shareholder derivative litigation will not serve as managerial incentives and constraints where institutional settings disfavor the use of these governance devices. Property rights institutions thus not only determine who the players are, they also supply the rules of the game.

Institutional diversity, governance diversity

From this discussion, it follows that property rights institutions are a principal source of diversity among national corporate governance systems. The organization and control of firms is shaped by the distinctive property rights environments in which they were formed.

Crucial to the understanding of governance diversity and the potential for convergence is the recognition that property rights institutions evolve largely through political bargaining.[18] Firms have incentives not only to

---

[18] Libecap, 16 above, pp. 10–11. Institutional change can also result from the evolution of informal constraints such as social norms, but this is typically a much more gradual process. Douglass C. North, "Transaction Costs, Institutions, and Economic Performance," p. 11 (International Center for Economic Growth Occasional Paper no. 30, 1992).

innovate with respect to governance technology within the confines of existing institutions, but also to try to change the institutions themselves. Since the government is a major actor in the allocation and enforcement of control rights in any system, those efforts will usually involve the political process. Thus, corporate governance change requires institutional change; institutional change, in turn, is determined principally by political contracting.

The property rights perspective just outlined is of course consistent with the view that corporate governance systems are historically and politically contingent. History matters because property rights are partly artifacts of past political and social practices. Politics matter because property rights are shaped by bargaining among competing interest groups for control rights over scarce resources. However, the perspective offered here extends the insights from prior literature by providing a broader and more useful tool of comparative analysis than the long-prevailing approach of analyzing political and historical influences on laws affecting financial intermediaries. Two simple observations indicate that, critical as they may be, insights from that approach are limited. First, political power finds expression in law only part of the time. The rest of the time, it is expressed either more directly (the exercise of raw power) or more ambiguously (the exercise of discretion). Since laws are only one of many components of an institutional structure, it is not sufficient to examine legislation exclusively to understand why corporate governance differs from one economy to another. Second, since control rights over firms are defined by much more than finance, it is not sufficient to analyze the control rights held by financial intermediaries.

A more comprehensive approach to governance diversity would focus on the different ways in which control over physical and human assets is allocated and enforced in different systems and the complementary institutions that have grown up in support of these control structures.[19] For purposes of comparative corporate governance analysis, two key variables in national property rights institutions are the extent to which control rights over assets are: (1) allocated to political versus private agents, and (2) legally as opposed to extra-legally enforced.

---

[19] The approach advocated here has parallels in the empirical work of Rafael LaPorta, Florencio Lopez-de-Silanes, Andrei Shleifer, & Robert W. Vishny. See, e.g., Rafael La Porta et al., "Law and Finance," 106 *J. Pol. Econ.* 1113 (1998); Rafael La Porta et al., "Legal Determinants of External Finance," 52 *J. Fin.* 1131 (1997) (finding that countries with weaker legal protections for investors have less developed capital markets).

Allocation between political and private actors

In all countries, the boundary between public and private enterprises is porous because political actors everywhere retain significant control rights over firms. This they accomplish either directly, through state ownership of assets, or indirectly through regulation, taxation, and subsidization of private firms. Examples of the mixed nature of all economies abound, but "privatization" in Eastern Europe provides the most dramatic illustration. Even though significant physical control rights over firms were wrested from the hands of bureaucrats and politicians in these formerly socialist countries, political agents retained substantial control rights that could be used for their own benefit.[20] As one commentator describes the situation in this context, "even after control rights are taken away, politicians can direct government resources to subsidize firms and thus continue to get their way with a firm after privatization."[21] The situation for firms in established market economies differs only by degree: political agents in such systems also use regulation and other tools to "continue to get their way with" private enterprises.

The allocation of control rights over firms in any system is thus the result of a struggle between public and private actors.[22] In some economies, however, political agents – politicians and bureaucrats – have the upper hand; in others, private economic agents – shareholders, managers and employees – have prevailed in the struggle. The allocation of control rights over firms in different countries runs along a spectrum ranging from nearly absolute political control, such as existed in the former Soviet Union, to substantial control by private economic agents in free market economies. Thus, the extent and mechanisms of political control over firms across countries is a crucial aspect of governance diversity.

Legal enforcement

A second key distinction among property rights regimes is the availability and cost of *legal* enforcement of control rights over a firm's assets. Although property rights are typically associated with legal enforcement,

---

[20] See Andrei Shleifer, "Establishing Property Rights," *World Bank Research Observer,* pp. 93, 95 (Ann. Conf. Supp. 1994); See also Andrei Shleifer & Robert W. Vishney, "Politicians and Firms," 109 *Q. J. Econ.* 995 (1994).

[21] Shleifer, note 20 above, p. 94.

[22] Indeed, this struggle is central to the emergence of property rights generally, which Douglass North describes as "the result of an on-going tension between the desires of the rulers of the state, on the one hand, and efforts of . . . [private] parties to exchange to reduce transaction costs, on the other." Douglass C. North, *Structure and Change in Economic History,* p. 18 (1981).

control rights can also be enforced physically, or by convention, custom, or the threat to terminate repeated dealings. For control rights to be legally enforced, legal enforcement must be both possible and the lowest cost alternative, *given the institutional environment* in which a firm is operating.[23] The inquiry thus entails those parts of the institutional environment that are under the control of the government (the formal legal system) as well as the parts supplied by the players themselves (social and market constraints).

Use of legal governance mechanisms obviously presumes the existence of a host of official enforcement institutions, including functional courts with adequate remedies and trained professionals, that may or may not exist in a given system. Even where this formal institutional backdrop exists, however, "going to law" may not be a viable or preferred option.[24] Not all control rights contemplate legal enforcement. Even those that do might be enforced more cheaply by other means. Corporate constituents everywhere make important governance-related investments in the form of social capital – "the component of human capital that allows members of a given society to trust one another and cooperate in the formation of new groups and associations."[25] Accumulation of social capital raises the relative cost of resort to legal mechanisms. Stated differently, trust and cooperation reduce transaction costs by allowing control rights to be allocated and enforced informally.

Thus, governance systems will differ in the extent to which control rights are legally enforced. Resort to legal enforcement will vary across systems with the development of formal legal systems, the allocation of control rights, the nature of the control rights utilized, and the magnitude of social capital investments made by economic agents.

Implications

The analytical framework described above suggests a comparative institutional approach to corporate governance and identifies several possible

---

[23] Enforcement options are obviously affected by the allocation of control in a given community.

[24] See, e.g., Stewart Macaulay, "Non-contractual Relations in Business: A Preliminary Study," 28 *Am. Soc. Rev.* 55 (1963) (supplying the classic account of the prevalence of nonlegal enforcement mechanisms in business); Eric A. Posner, "The Regulation of Groups: The Influence of Legal and Nonlegal Sanctions on Collective Action," 63 *U. Chi. L. Rev.* 133 (1996) (emphasizing the importance of nonlegal mechanisms in regulating conduct).

[25] Frances Fukuyama, "Social Capital and the Global Economy," 74 *Foreign Affairs* 89, 90 (1995).

sources of governance diversity. A number of implications can be drawn from the discussion to guide the analysis in the remainder of the chapter:

1. Property rights institutions in a particular community will determine the ownership structure and control of firms. Specifically, there will be greater family control, more small firms, and less public ownership in less secure property rights environments.[26]

2. Where political agents have extensive control rights over firms, private economic agents will construct linkages with the state to stabilize the property rights environment so that firms can expand and prosper. In other words, political capital investments will be visible where relations with the government are important determinants of firm success.

3. As firms make larger political capital investments to adapt to their property rights environments, their governance structures will become more rigid. By definition, political capital investments presume long-term, repeated interactions between specific groups of public and private actors. These investments are sunk costs that cannot be easily redeployed to other uses. Thus, adaptive efficiency in governance systems – the ability to change direction in response to changes in the economic environment[27] – will be inversely proportional to the magnitude of political capital investments made by firms.

4. Since governments are crucial to property rights and by extension to corporate governance, the political economy of property rights will be a critical determinant of the convergence of corporate governance mechanisms. Powerful economic forces notwithstanding, we should expect convergence to occur only where institutional inertia grounded in politics can be overcome. Contrary to the predictions of some theorists, therefore, convergence will be weak,[28] limited, and episodic.

---

[26] See, e.g., Sung Hee Jwa, "Property Rights and Economic Behaviors: Lessons for Korea's Economic Reform," pp. 9–12 (June 1997) (unpublished manuscript) (arguing that firms will be relatively small where formal property rights protections are not firmly established); J. Mark Ramseyer, "Does Corporate Governance Converge? The A-contextual Logic to the Japanese *Keiretsu*," in this volume (arguing that firms will be family-owned and -controlled in insecure property rights environments).

[27] See Douglass C. North, *Institutions, Institutional Change and Economic Performance*, pp. 80–82 (1990).

[28] "Weak convergence" is the movement of one system closer to another. "Strong convergence" is the movement of two systems toward one another. Brigitte Unger & Frans van Waarden, eds., *Convergence or Diversity? Internationalization and Economic Policy Response*, p. 3 (1995).

II. (Non)Convergence in three countries

Although it is difficult to test the property rights theory of corporate governance assembled above, I will attempt to do so by examining a natural corporate governance experiment in three countries. The United States, Japan, and South Korea are well placed to illustrate the likelihood of convergence in corporate governance: an intricate web of mutually reinforcing influences evolving over the past century might have moved the corporate control structures of the three countries together. Instead, three distinct forms of industrial organization emerged and persist.

Consider the potential for convergence. Korea was a Japanese colony from 1910 to 1945. Japan had itself just attained a relatively high level of economic success through the *zaibatsu*, family-owned and -managed conglomerates, and expanded the potential for success by establishing a viable property rights framework in the late nineteenth century. With the introduction of a stable legal regime, contracts could be enforced, so nonfamily investors and managers could be recruited to fund and run the *zaibatsu* groups.[29]

During the colonial period, Japan transplanted its property rights framework onto the institutional landscape of pre-modern Korea. Japanese legal codes, including the Japanese company law, were enacted in Korea. Korean state investment under Japanese colonial authority, private investment by the *zaibatsu*, and the interactions of Japanese elites in Korean business associations all served to mold colonial institutions in the Japanese likeness.[30] The *zaibatsu* provided the model for Korean industrial organization, as the government used a coterie of entrepreneurs as catalysts for economic modernization. Patterns of close, cooperative interaction between the public and private sectors prevalent in early modern Japan were also replicated in the Korean colony.[31] Favored entrepreneurs utilized the new property rights setup to their advantage, giving rise to the family-run conglomerates known as *chaebol* which remain central to Korean corporate governance. The colonial period thus set Korea on

---

[29] See Ramseyer, note 26 above.

[30] See Dennis L. McNamara, *The Colonial Origins of Korean Enterprise 1919–1945*, pp. 34–65 (1990).

[31] One commentator argues that "Japanese colonial influence on Korea, in 1905–45, was decisive in shaping a political economy that later evolved into the high-growth South Korean path to development." Atul Kohli, "Where do High Growth Political Economies Come from? The Japanese Lineage of Korea's 'Developmental State,'" 22 *World Development* 1269, 1270 (1994). For similar conclusions, see McNamara, note 30 above, pp. 34–65.

the Japanese path to industrial organization. As one commentator put it, "[p]rewar Japanese business organization and business-state ties provided a format for capitalism on the [Korean] peninsula."[32]

The prospects for convergence would appear to increase even further in view of the influence of the United States on both Japan and South Korea. It is not necessary to recount the familiar history to recognize the major role of the United States in the economic and institutional reconstruction of both countries after their devastation in separate wars. The explicit goal of the American Occupation authorities was to reshape the Japanese economy in America's image. Although their goals were somewhat less ambitious with respect to South Korea, American policymakers also had vast plans for the economic reconstruction of that country. Signs of American influence on the two countries range from antitrust laws banning holding companies to corporate, securities, and banking laws that share many American traits.

Economic competition and intellectual arbitrage have extended and sometimes reversed the flow of this corporate cross-pollination. As the vitality of the comparative corporate governance debate itself attests, Japanese economic success in the 1980s prompted a thorough reexamination of American governance mechanisms. Both Japan and, to a lesser extent, South Korea were once held up by American commentators as attractive alternative models of economic and social organization. At the same time, American economic successes, including most recently those associated with Silicon Valley, have prompted extensive soul searching in Japan and South Korea, leading to the importation of governance technologies perfected on this side of the Pacific.[33]

Yet for all of these potentially homogenizing influences, patterns of industrial organization and corporate governance in the three countries look very different. The United States epitomizes a stock market-centered governance system, revolving around the one-dimensional relationship between shareholders and corporate managers. Since shareholders are relatively dispersed and financial intermediaries are relatively weak, managers are held in check principally by external forces of competition in the markets for control, capital, and products. This system appears to

---

[32] McNamara, note 30 above, p. 51.
[33] See, e.g., Curtis J. Milhaupt, "The Market for Innovation in the United States and Japan: Venture Capital and the Comparative Corporate Governance Debate," 91 *Nw. U. L. Rev.* 865, 866 (1997) (discussing the Japanese desire to emulate the US-style venture capital market); "Luring Foreign Venture Capitals Vital," *Korea Herald*, Apr. 22, 1998, available in LEXIS, News Library, Non-US File (discussing the same desire in South Korea).

promote adaptive efficiency at the expense of stable, long-term commitments to the firm by banks, employees, and trade partners.

Superficially, Japan and South Korea appear to share basic governance traits, at least in contrast to the United States. In both systems, bank finance and corporate cross-shareholding are prominent characteristics of the organizational landscape. In neither country has the capital market traditionally played a significant role in finance or governance. Beyond these basic commonalities, however, the two governance systems exhibit significant differences.

The main features of Japanese corporate governance in its heyday have been extensively discussed elsewhere and can be quickly summarized. Central actors in this system are main banks and *keiretsu* corporate groups. A firm's main bank supplies debt capital and serves as a major shareholder, providing incentives to engage in state-contingent monitoring of the firm.[34] The bank's long-term, multiplex relationship with the firm supports a host of other stable commitments. *Keiretsu* cross-shareholding patterns, centered around a common main bank, raise the cost of hostile takeovers and encourage firm-specific investments by corporate constituents. Employees, for example, safeguarded from the threat of takeovers, make career-long investments of human capital in the firm. Thus, the main bank system contributes to the governance of the Japanese firm both through its monitoring role and by supporting an extensive set of relationships that constrain managerial conduct.

Other important features of Japanese corporate governance, however, are less well-developed in the legal literature. To an unusual extent by American standards, Japanese firms operate within a web of industry associations and regulatory requirements (both formal and informal) that constrain managerial decisionmaking. In many sectors of the economy, decisionmaking in firms is coordinated within an elaborate institutional environment for public–private sector cooperation which operates according to well-understood norms governing intra- and inter-industry dispute resolution and policy formation.[35]

---

[34] State-contingent monitoring refers to the fact that Japanese banks become involved in management only in "bad" states – times of borrower financial distress. The *ex ante* threat of bank intervention is thought to serve as a constraint on managerial incompetence or shirking.

[35] For a discussion of the procedural and substantive norms governing Japanese finance, see Curtis J. Milhaupt & Geoffrey P. Miller, "Cooperation, Conflict, and Convergence in Japanese Finance: Evidence from the 'Jusen' Problem," 29 *Law & Pol'y Int'l Bus.* 1–24 (1997).

Table 6.1 *Ownership of the thirty largest* chaebol

	1983	1987	1989	1990	1991	1992	1993	1994
Family share	17.2	15.1	14.8	14.3	14.1	12.6	10.3	9.7
Other firms in the group	40.0	41.1	30.0	31.3	32.9	33.5	33.1	33.1
Total in-group ownership	57.2	56.2	44.8	45.7	47.0	46.0	43.4	42.7
Outside ownership	42.8	43.8	55.2	54.3	53.0	54.0	56.6	57.3

Source: OECD Economic Surveys 1995–1996: Korea (1996), p. 114, table 40.

South Korea provides a third vision of successful industrial organiza-tion and control. Although the level of economic concentration in Korea is not particularly high compared to major industrial countries,[36] Korean industrial structure is dominated by the *chaebol* groups.[37] A number of characteristics set these groups apart from their counterparts in Japan and make Korean corporate governance distinctive on any comparative scale. First, in contrast to governance systems in virtually all other indus-trialized countries, the defining characteristic of Korean corporate gover-nance is the concentration of ownership and management in the *chaebol's* founding entrepreneur and his family.[38] Although their ownership inter-ests have been falling over time, as of 1994 the families of the *chaebol* founders still directly held about 10 percent of the shares in the thirty largest *chaebol*. Through cross-shareholding, these ownership interests increase by an additional 33 percent. Table 6.1 shows the family-based ownership structure of the *chaebol*.

Family ties are also an important determinant of participation in corpo-rate management. Many *chaebol* are still under the control of the founding entrepreneur or second and third generation family members. In most

---

[36] See Organisation for Economic Co-operation and Development, *OECD Economic Surveys 1995–1996: Korea*, pp. 114–15 & table 41 (1996) [hereinafter *OECD Economic Surveys*]. The thirty largest *chaebol* account for about one-third of the total value added and fixed assets in the mining and manufacturing sector.

[37] The Korean Fair Trade Commission defines a *chaebol* as any enterprise with total assets of 400 billion won (about $533 million at $1=750 won). As of 1992, seventy-eight *chaebol* groups controlled over one thousand Korean corporations. Chan Sup Chang & Nahn Joo Chang, *The Korean Management System: Cultural, Political, Economic Foundations*, p. 60 (1994).

[38] See Sung Hee Jwa, "Globalization and New Industrial Organization: Implications for Structural Adjustment Policies," in Takatoshi Ito & Anne O. Krueger, eds., 6 *NBER-East Asia Seminar on Economics: Regionalism vs. Multilateral Trade Arrangements*, pp. 313, 322 (1997).

chaebol, children of the founder hold key roles in management, and the eldest son is expected to succeed the founding father upon death or retirement.[39] Not surprisingly, however, the *chaebol* have had to recruit nonfamily managers as their business holdings expanded. Today, about 10 percent of the high-level managers of the largest *chaebol* groups are related to the founder.[40]

In addition to family ownership and control, the Korean *chaebol* differ from the *keiretsu* in their hierarchical, rather than network-based organizational structure. For example, each major *chaebol* has a planning and control office which serves as the intelligence-gathering and long-term planning center for the group.[41] These units make significant decisions about overall resource allocation and strategic plans for constituent group companies. Because of their importance, these offices are often under the direct control of the *chaebol* patriarch and are staffed with the most capable managers in the group. Again, superficially, it may appear that this organ has a Japanese counterpart in the form of the *keiretsu* presidents' councils. The presidents' councils, however, are not separately staffed offices but informal gatherings of top management. No evidence suggests that the councils exert centralized influence over the constituent *keiretsu* firms. In addition to central planning, the more hierarchical structure of the *chaebol* is also reflected in a more authoritarian management style and somewhat less employment security as compared to Japanese practices.[42]

The *chaebol* are also characterized by a large number of relatively small and extraordinarily diverse firms. On average, each of the five largest *chaebol* owns forty-two subsidiaries, operates businesses in thirty nonfinancial industries, and owns four nonbank financial institutions.[43] Individual companies within the *chaebol* are small by international standards. For example, on a sales basis, Hyundai Motor, Korea's largest auto manufacturer, is only about 7 percent as large as General Motors, and Samsung Electronics is only 14 percent as large as Matsushita Electronics.[44] Moreover, compared to large firms in major industrial countries, the *chaebol* exhibit an extraordinarily high degree of diversification in technologically unrelated fields.[45]

---

[39] See Yeon-ho Lee, *The State, Society and Big Business in South Korea*, p. 36 (1997).
[40] Chang & Chang, note 37 above, p. 72, table 6.9.   [41] See ibid., pp. 121–28.
[42] See Richard Whitley, *Business Systems in East Asia: Firms, Markets and Societies*, pp. 44–51 (1992).
[43] *OECD Economic Surveys*, note 36 above, p. 114.   [44] Ibid.
[45] Jwa, note 38 above, pp. 324–25 & table 11.4.

As in Japan, Korean firms have historically been heavily dependent on debt finance, and the government has utilized the banking system as its chief tool of economic management. In Korea, however, government intervention in the banking system was far more direct than in Japan. The Korean banking industry was nationalized from the early 1960s until the late 1970s, and priority industries were provided credit in the form of "policy loans." These loans consisted of both explicitly earmarked credit programs for specific industrial sectors and loans that were allocated by discretionary government intervention based on the assessed needs and progress of potential recipients of credit.[46] Because the government owned the banks, in one sense *all* loans during this period were policy loans.[47] The use of directed credit further concentrated economic power in the hands of the *chaebol*. Firms in disfavored industries found it difficult to obtain credit, while the typical recipient of a policy loan was a strong, well-established – and therefore almost by definition, *chaebol*-affiliated – enterprise.[48]

In contrast to the Japanese *keiretsu*, however, banks do not lie at the center of the *chaebol* conglomerates. As noted previously, the banking sector was state-owned during the formative period in Korea's industrialization. Despite substantial privatization of the banking sector since the mid-1980s, however, significant government intervention in lending has not been eliminated. A number of banks are still state-run or state-owned, and the government is still the single largest shareholder of many commercial banks. Moreover, the government continued to nominate the presidents of private commercial banks until recently.[49] *Chaebol* connections with the source of their financing have therefore been more attenuated than in Japan. Thus, while credit in both countries provided a mechanism for government intervention in the economy and formed the basis of close business–government relations, the *chaebol* were more subservient to the government than their *keiretsu* counterparts.

In summary, despite potential homogenizing influences, three successful economies have developed along very different organizational

---

[46] Yoon Je Cho & Joon-Kyung Kim, "Credit Policies and the Industrialization of Korea," pp. 40–45 (World Bank Discussion Paper no. 286, 1995).

[47] The percent of domestic credit consisting of policy loans obviously depends on the definition of that term. If defined as loans with preferential interest rates and availability, policy loans comprised about 40% of all domestic credit in the 1970s. Ibid., pp. 40–41.

[48] Ibid., p. 5; Roger L. Janelli, *Making Capitalism: The Social and Cultural Construction of a South Korean Conglomerate*, p. 63 (1993). More recently, policy loans have been directed toward small and medium-sized enterprises.

[49] *OECD Economic Surveys*, note 36 above, p. 43.

paths: external, market-oriented governance in the United States; internal, bank-oriented governance in Japan; and family-oriented, political governance in South Korea.

III. A property rights spectrum

Property rights analysis helps account for the emergence of these different control structures. While the characterization of national property rights regimes is an imprecise endeavor, it is nonetheless possible to distinguish among the property rights institutions of the three countries to account for the observed governance differences.[50] This section uses empirical evidence and brief sketches of regulatory politics to place the United States, Japan, and South Korea along a property rights spectrum. The United States is at one end of the spectrum, with comparatively little political control over firms and extensive legal enforcement of private control rights. South Korea lies at the other end of the spectrum, with extensive political control and less certain legal enforcement. Japan is roughly at the midpoint, although its property rights institutions place it closer to South Korea than to the United States.

Some empirical evidence

A number of recent attempts to measure various aspects of economic exchange and governmental intervention across countries provide useful insight into the way that institutions affect economic activity. Drawing partially on this work, I use six sets of empirical data to build a property rights spectrum featuring the three sample countries.

First and most ambitiously, researchers have attempted to measure "economic freedom" across countries in ways that dovetail nicely with the concept of property rights developed in section I of this chapter.[51] The theoretical predicate of the best of these works is that economic freedom consists of personal choice, protection of private property, and freedom of exchange. Governments secure economic freedom for their

---

[50] The point is not to make normative evaluations; none of the sample countries could have achieved the high level of economic success that they now enjoy without the benefit of a relatively efficient property rights structure. Rather, the point is to illustrate that a variety of control rights induce a variety of governance systems.

[51] See James Gwartney *et al.*, *Economic Freedom of the World 1975–1995* (1996); Kim R. Holmes *et al.*, *1997 Index of Economic Freedom* (1997).

Table 6.2 *Economic freedom in the United States, Japan, and South Korea, 1975–1995*[a]

	United States	Japan	South Korea
1975	6.0	5.2	4.3
1980	6.2	5.9	4.0
1985	6.5	6.5	5.1
1990	7.4	6.9	5.2
1993–95	7.7	6.9	6.7

Note: [a] Higher ratings indicate greater economic freedom
Source: James Gwartney *et al.*, *Economic Freedom of the World 1975–1995* (1996).

citizens when they enforce contracts, protect private property, and steer clear of restrictions that limit voluntary exchange.

Table 6.2 presents summary index ratings of economic freedom in the United States, Japan, and South Korea over the past twenty years. These ratings are composite scores for seventeen components of economic freedom allocated to four major areas: (1) money and inflation; (2) government operations and regulation; (3) takings and discriminatory taxation; and (4) international exchange. As Table 6.2 indicates, the United States is consistently the most economically "free" of the three countries, and indeed typically ranks among the most economically free countries in the world.[52] Japan is somewhat less free, with South Korea third, although the difference between the two countries has narrowed substantially in recent years. Given the theoretical predicate of the index, this data can serve as a rough proxy for measurements of allocation and enforcement of property rights in the three countries.

At first glance, Table 6.2 appears to indicate the absence of a close correlation between changes in economic freedom and corporate governance over time. In other words, if the degree of economic freedom were a precise predictor of industrial organization and control, Korean corporate governance today (with an economic freedom score of 6.7) should resemble American corporate governance around 1985 (when the US score was 6.5). Similarly, Japanese and Korean corporate governance systems (with 1993–95 scores of 6.9 and 6.7, respectively) should now be nearly identical. For

---

[52] The United States was ranked fourth, Japan ninth, and South Korea twelfth overall in the 1993–1995 index. Gwartney *et al.*, note 51 above, p. xxi.

example, we might expect to observe similar levels of kin-based owner-ship and equivalent numbers of public companies in the relevant systems, adjusted for the size differential between the economies. Yet close corre-lations of this type over time do not appear to exist.

There are, however, a number of plausible explanations that undercut the reliability of this conclusion. First, the simple data presented in Table 6.2 are only suggestive proxies for complex phenomena; it is no surprise that they fail to predict corporate governance patterns with scien-tific accuracy. Significantly, however, the general trend toward greater economic freedom reflected in Table 6.2 is consistent with corporate governance trends in the three countries over time. Each country has witnessed, to varying degrees, small firms growing more rapidly into large, public firms; falling kin-based ownership in large firms; and increasing numbers of firms going public at an accelerated rate. Second, since we lack the most useful data – economic freedom at the time the core insti-tutions of corporate governance in the three systems were formed – we have no base score that correlates with the emergence of a particular governance system. The three countries obviously had quite different governance systems in 1975, the first year for which data are avail-able – differences which are loosely suggested by their respective scores. Subsequent Japanese and Korean score movements may reflect a catch-up phenomenon, so that economic freedom in Korea and Japan would have to outstrip that in the United States in order for convergence to occur.

Aside from economic freedom, corruption levels in a given community provide signals about the allocation of property rights between political and private agents. From a Coasian perspective, corruption can be viewed as an efficiency-enhancing, albeit illicit sale of property rights from polit-ical to private agents.[53] Higher levels of corruption suggest concentrations of property rights in the hands of political agents, who sell those rights for cash or favors. As shown in Table 6.3, international polling data reveal that the United States is consistently perceived to be the least corrupt of the sample countries, followed by Japan, with South Korea perceived as the most corrupt of the three by a considerable margin.

Efficient property rights structures not only minimize corruption, they also reduce transaction costs generally in the economy. Thus, transaction

[53] See Pranab Bardhan, "Corruption and Development: A Review of Issues," 35 *J. Econ. Lit.* 1320 (1997); see also Shleifer, note 20 above (analyzing the causes of corruption in the new market-oriented economies of Eastern Europe).

Table 6.3 *International Corruption Perception Index, 1995–1997*

Country	Score[a]	Variance	No. of surveys on which score is based
1997			
United States	7.61	1.15	5
Japan	6.57	1.09	7
South Korea	4.29	2.76	7
1996			
United States	7.66	0.19	7
Japan	7.05	2.61	9
South Korea	5.02	2.30	9
1995			
United States	7.79	1.67	4
Japan	6.72	2.73	7
South Korea	4.29	1.29	7

Note: [a]Scale from 0–10, with 0 meaning highly corrupt, 10 meaning clean.
Source: The data were drawn from the Internet Center for Corruption Research (visited May 14, 1998) <http://www.GWDG.DE/~uwvw/rank-97.htm>.

costs will be lower where political agents exercise fewer discretionary control rights, legal means are available to enforce contracts, or levels of social capital investments are high. While there is no direct way to measure transaction costs across countries, a substitute is available. Researchers have adopted cash ratios in M2 as a proxy for transaction costs on the theory that highly liquid forms of money such as currency will be preferred in insecure property rights environments, while deposits and other transactions with financial intermediaries will take place where contracts are enforced and institutions are stable.[54] By this measure, the United States has the lowest transaction costs and correspondingly the most secure property rights of the three countries, followed by Japan, with South Korea having the highest transaction costs and weakest property rights by a considerable margin.[55]

---

[54] See Jwa, "Property Rights," note 26 above, p. 16; for a definition of M2 see note 55 below.
[55] Ibid., p. 17, table 2 (showing average cash ratio from 1970–1994 (defined as C/M2, where C is currency outside banks and M2 is a broad definition of money including currency plus time and savings deposits) of 7.02 for the United States, 8.36 for Japan and 13.14 for South Korea).

Property rights protections are not only closely related to low trans-action costs, they are also associated with the rule of law.[56] Indeed, the "rule of law" is often a shorthand for the principle that private contracts and property rights may only be impaired by legislatures proscribing generally applicable rules of conduct, and the expectation that courts will enforce private bargains. The rule of law is thus generally inconsistent with a concentration of discretionary control rights in the hands of political agents and enforcement of control rights through extra-legal mechanisms. While objective rule-of-law measurements are extraordinarily difficult to make, existing data suggest that the United States has the most secure rule of law; Japan is a close second; and South Korea is a distant third.[57]

All else being equal, the risk of doing business will be higher in countries where more control rights are in the hands of political agents, or where private property is subject to impairment due to regime instability, which may itself be a function of inequitable allocations of control in society. Indeed, the main components of "political risk" are the threat of asset seizure and the loss of property in war or insurrection. Consistent with the other findings, South Korea has by far the highest level of political risk, followed by Japan and the United States.[58]

Finally, since the corporate laws of the United States, Japan, and South Korea all contain provisions for shareholder derivative suits, control right enforcement patterns in the corporate setting should be at least weakly reflected in the extent to which this mechanism is used in the three coun-tries. While precise data are not available, by all accounts the number of derivative suits in the United States swamps those in Japan and South Korea.[59] To be sure, raw numbers of derivative suits filed are not very

---

[56] See, e.g., Harry Sheiber, "Public Rights and the Rule of Law in American Legal History," 71 *Calif. L. Rev.* 217, 218 (1984).

[57] See Rafael La Porta *et al.*, "Legal Determinants," note 19 above, tables 1 & 2 (citing International Country Risk Guide data) (Rule of Law ranking of 10.0 for United States; 8.98 for Japan; and 5.35 for South Korea on scale from 0–10, with lower scores for less tradition of law and order).

[58] See Campbell R. Harvey, "Political Risk, Economic Risk and Financial Risk" (visited May 14, 1998), <http://www.duke.edu/~charvey/Country_risk/pol/poltab7a.htm>> (showing a political risk score of 95.0 for the United States; 92.0 for Japan; 63.0 for South Korea on scale from 0–100, with lower scores for greater risk).

[59] A total of 50 derivative suits were publicly reported in Japan from 1950 to 1994. Research revealed precisely one (recently settled) derivative suit in South Korea. By contrast, each of several US studies conducted at various times in the past sixty years revealed hundreds of derivative suits, despite the fact that these studies were not intended to be exhaustive. See John C. Coffee, Jr., "Understanding the Plaintiff's Attorney: The Implications of Economic Theory for Private Actions and Derivative Actions," 86 *Colum. L. Rev.* 669, 673 & n.10, 699 & n.83 (1986) (citing empirical studies).

instructive because settlements are unreported. Moreover, differing rates of utilization of this enforcement mechanism in the three countries could reflect systemic differences such as the number and compensation of attorneys and the cost of initiating a suit in the three countries. But these systemic differences amplify, rather than diminish, the significance of the disparities. Societies that predominantly use legal mechanisms to enforce control rights are likely to erect a supportive cast of complementary institutions to facilitate that undertaking. Societies that predominantly use extra-legal enforcement mechanisms will develop substitutes for legal devices. In place of shareholder derivative suits, the property rights environments of both Japan and South Korea have generated identical, extra-legal monitoring institutions: shareholder-extortionists who use nonpublic information to monitor corporate management.[60] Putting aside the effectiveness of either derivative litigation or extortion as a tool of corporate governance, existing techniques reinforce the pattern of control right enforcement we have already seen: legal mechanisms are extensively utilized in the United States, while extra-legal enforcement mechanisms prevail in Japan and South Korea.

These empirical observations obviously do not pinpoint with scientific accuracy the property rights differences among the United States, Japan, and South Korea. However, they do suggest, albeit imperfectly, that in relative terms political agents in the United States have fewer control rights over firms than in Japan and South Korea, and that control rights in the United States are enforced more often by resort to formal means supplied by the legal system than in the other two countries.

Regulatory politics

For an alternative and supportive perspective on comparative property rights, consider regulatory politics in the three countries. Regulation is a chief form of political control over firms and a major cause of the attenuation of property rights in any market economy. Note also that there is likely to be an inverse correlation between the magnitude of political control and the frequency of resort to legal enforcement of control rights.

---

[60] On the Japanese extortionists, see Mark D. West, "Information, Institutions, and Extortion in Japan and the United States," 93 *Nw. U. L. Rev.* 767 (1999). On the Korean extortionists, see Janelli, note 48 above, pp. 132–33. Like the shareholder derivative suit, the effectiveness of this peculiar institution as an enforcement device for the benefit of shareholders is open to question.

A review of regulatory politics in the United States supports the empirical evidence that control rights over American firms are allocated largely to private agents. Political agents, of course, maintain significant levers of control over firms in this country through regulation, taxation, and subsidization. Indeed, the American corporate governance system is often viewed as a product of politically charged regulation of financial intermediaries. Yet American firms, including financial firms, appear to be constrained by political agents far less than in most other economically developed countries. In the words of political scientist David Vogel, "American business is still 'freer' than in any other major industrial nation."[61]

The origins of this freedom are both historical and institutional. Distrust of public authority, like the property rights structure, was inherited from England and runs deep in US history.[62] From the beginning, there was a perceived tension between the power of the state and the security of property rights. At the same time, the Framers feared that the viability of the political system would be undermined if it were used by factions to redistribute wealth. The political structure erected by the Framers and reinforced in the early years of the Supreme Court was aimed at strengthening the institutions of private property by "legally limiting the power of government. The objective was to embody a set of comprehensive rules in an impersonal legal structure – rules that would not be subject to political whim and change by legislative bodies."[63]

The federal structure of governmental institutions in the United States helps to ensure that political agents must compete for control rights over private assets. Regulatory competition in the United States is often framed in a race-to-the top/bottom debate. This debate, however, misses the point that regardless of whether regulatory competition is efficiency enhancing or an exercise in rent-seeking, it is a competition that benefits *private sector groups* (investors or managers, depending on one's view) at the expense of political agents. If competition in charters for commercial firms or banks is a race to the top, it is a race to permit private agents to bargain free of transaction costs imposed by an inefficient regulatory control structure. If it is a race to the bottom, it is a race to relinquish political control rights to the highest bidder. Either way, political control rights are dissipated in the competition.

---

[61] David J. Vogel, "The Study of Business and Politics," 38 *Cal. Mgmt. Rev.* 146, 152 (1996).

[62] Ibid.; see also North, note 27 above, pp. 187–90.

[63] North, note 27 above, pp. 189–90. For a discussion of early constitutional history from a property rights perspective, see *ibid.* pp. 188–93.

Not only must political agents in the United States compete for control rights over firms, they are also subject to severe limitations on their ability to unilaterally assert such rights as are allocated to them. Bureaucrats in the United States are bound by highly formalistic procedural rules which minimize administrative discretion, the principal manifestation of political control rights in all states save regimes of terror. The degree to which the decisions of political agents in the United States are formally circumscribed and exposed to review is exceptional. Indeed, "[t]he defining political feature of contemporary government regulation in the United States is the lack of administrative discretion."[64]

Constrained government set the stage for the emergence of Anglo-American capital markets,[65] which can only be sustained in a delicately balanced institutional environment.[66] Political agents must be willing to make infrastructure investments in information public goods and monitor market activities without extending the reach of their control to substantive investment decisions. Clear accounting standards and disclosure requirements that facilitate comparative analysis of individual firms, for example, provide vital support to a system in which markets collect and transmit the information by which private investment decisions allocate and price credit. At the same time, the credibility of the market itself must be maintained. This requires a sophisticated approach to financial regulation capable of maintaining systemic safety and soundness in a world based on exposure to risk.[67] In short, the capital markets model simultaneously requires governmental support of market infrastructure and minimal political intervention into the substantive issues of credit allocation and pricing.

In a pattern of mutual reinforcement, capital markets served to further disperse and privatize control over firms in the United States, by encouraging corporations to raise capital by issuing shares to an increasingly vast investing public. Capital markets substitute massive numbers of individual trades for centralized decisionmaking about capital allocation. Well-developed secondary trading markets for securities existed in

---

[64] Vogel, note 61 above, p. 153. This assertion must be understood in comparative context. It is not meant to imply that US regulators are subject to perfect supervision and completely lacking in open-ended policymaking authority.

[65] See, e.g., Douglass C. North & Barry R. Weingast, "Constitutions and Commitment: The Evolution of Institutions Governing Public Choice in Seventeenth Century England," 49 J. Econ. Hist. 803 (1989).

[66] See Smith & Walter, note 7 above, p. 10.   [67] See ibid., pp. 10–11.

the United States by the late eighteenth century.[68] Thus, the institutional fundamentals of American corporate governance – limited government, a highly developed legal system that enforces contracts, and well-developed capital markets – were in place long before the specific pieces of financial legislation that are sometimes credited with shaping the distinctive features of American corporate governance, and before the enactment of "good" corporate law that is currently popular as an explanation for dispersed ownership.

By contrast, a brief review of Korean regulatory politics suggests that control rights over firms and their financing options are extensively allocated to political agents, and legal enforcement is uncertain. For much of its history, Korea has been ruled by strong, bureaucratic regimes with extensive military backing.[69] Over four decades, a series of economic growth-minded strongmen used state-owned banks and directed credit in the form of policy loans as their main instruments of economic management. Thus, while the banks served as intermediaries, in reality, Korean industry was financed by the government. Lack of access to independent sources of credit increased the susceptibility of the *chaebol* to government control.

Korean political regimes have used both informal guidance (sometimes initiated by the president himself) as well as formal commands to achieve its economic objectives. For example, from 1968 to 1975 the government enacted a series of increasingly stringent measures to encourage the *chaebol* to make public offerings of their shares. When the early statutes providing incentives to firms going public proved ineffective, legislation was passed imposing severe tax penalties and restricting access to bank credit to large firms that refused to go public. When even these measures failed to achieve the desired results, special presidential directives imposing severe sanctions on privately held *chaebol* were promulgated.[70]

In many cases, however, political control over Korean firms was even more direct. One of the first acts of growth-minded strongman Park Chung Hee, president from 1961 until his assassination in 1979, provides

---

[68] See Stuart Banner, *Anglo-American Securities Regulation: Cultural and Political Roots, 1690–1860*, pp. 131–45 (1998); see also Smith & Walter, note 7 above, p. 13 (arguing that capital markets have dominated industrial development in the United States for well over a century).

[69] See Jwa, note 26 above, pp. 26–30.

[70] For a discussion of this episode, see Leroy P. Jones & Il Sakong, *Government, Business, and Entrepreneurship in Economic Development: The Korean Case*, pp. 120–22 (1980).

an example. In 1961, his regime enacted a statute – a "Law for Dealing with Illicit Wealth Accumulation" – subjecting leading businessmen to criminal prosecution and confiscation of their assets for engaging in what his government viewed as unproductive rent-seeking activities under the prior regime. The businessmen escaped with their freedom and their assets (except for shares of banks, which were confiscated in a move to nationalize the banking sector) only after agreeing to establish new industrial firms in areas deemed desirable by the regime and donating the shares to the government.[71]

Another example is the fate suffered by Korean entrepreneurs unfortunate enough to fall out of favor with the government. Take Yang Jung Mo, for example. Yang successfully presided over the Kukje Group, one of Korea's leading *chaebol*, until the conglomerate ran into serious financial difficulties in the 1980s. In what amounted to a hostile takeover by the presidential Blue House, President Chun Doo Hwan dried up sources of new bank financing for the Kukje Group and Yang's empire was dismantled under government supervision, on the grounds that his *chaebol* was poorly managed and could be run more efficiently by other groups.[72] Or consider the fate of Chung Ju Yung, the founder of the Hyundai Group. In an interesting parallel to Ross Perot, Chung formed his own political party and ran for president in 1992. Chung lost, but the victors were not amused. Hyundai suddenly had difficulty obtaining loans, the Korean IRS decided it was time for an extensive audit, and prosecutors charged senior executives with forgery.[73]

These anecdotes are not meant to suggest, and certainly do not prove, that Korean industry was dominated by the government. Rather, these episodes suggest high concentrations of control rights in the hands of political agents, along with extraordinarily intensive relationships between key political agents and selected entrepreneurs, relatively unconstrained by formal legal processes.

The Japanese regulatory system represents an intermediate level of control rights allocation to political agents. In Japan, as in South Korea, business–government ties are close; as in South Korea, the government used the banking sector (heavily regulated in Japan as opposed to state-run

---

[71] Ibid., pp. 69–70.
[72] Chang & Chang, note 37 above, pp. 42–43; John Burton, "South Korea's Chaebol Get Protection from the State," *Fin. Times*, Aug. 5, 1993, at 3. Reports indicated that Kukje assets were transferred to groups with ties to the Chun government. Many years later, the Constitutional Court of South Korea ruled the dissolution unconstitutional (ibid.).
[73] Chang & Chang, note 37 above, pp. 75–76.

in Korea) as a wedge with which to insert political agents into economic decisionmaking processes. Yet significant differences are apparent. Regulatory oversight of the banking sector is an integral part of the Japanese system of corporate governance, at least as it operated in its heyday. In effect, the financial regulators serve as monitors and partners of the main banks, which in turn monitor corporate borrowers. For example, informal reorganizations of failing firms are often undertaken at the behest of Ministry of Finance banking regulators. In return, the banks have been the clear beneficiaries of post-war financial policies, under which they were protected against failure and, through limited competition from the securities sector, were guaranteed a stream of rents that could be used to compensate for their delegated monitoring and restructuring operations.

Elsewhere, Geoffrey Miller and I have argued that Japanese finance is governed by a "regulatory cartel" that operates according to a well-understood set of informal procedural and substantive norms.[74] We labeled it a *regulatory* cartel because in contrast to the rule-making, enforcement, and dispute resolution activities conducted privately by a typical industrial cartel in standard economic theory, those functions are shared by both governmental authorities and the private sector in Japan. The central feature of the regulatory cartel is a series of inter-linked institutions including industry associations, employment patterns, and consultative committees attached to the Ministry of Finance that facilitate coordinated decisionmaking between the public and private sectors.

In contrast to both the formal procedures of the United States and the governmental directives in Korea, regulatory control rights over Japanese firms, in finance and elsewhere, are shared between political and private agents, and enforced pervasively through *ex ante* consultation and dispute resolution mechanisms. [75] Administrative discretion (captured by the term "administrative guidance"), informality, and a blurring of the boundary between governmental policy and private decisionmaking are thus the hallmarks of Japanese regulatory activity. These assertions, while consistent with the weight of scholarly commentary, are difficult to

---

[74] See Milhaupt & Miller, note 35 above.

[75] To assert that enforcement of control rights over Japanese firms is largely nonlegal is not to suggest that law is irrelevant in this system of industrial organization. On the contrary, institutions central to Japanese corporate governance, such as the main bank system, have been shaped by legal constraints. See Curtis J. Milhaupt, "A Relational Theory of Japanese Corporate Governance: Contract, Culture, and the Rule of Law," 37 *Harv. Int'l L.J.* (3): 35–47 (1996).

"prove" in any formal sense.[76] I offer a recent incident to illustrate the way in which Japanese regulatory activity contrasts with both the adversarial legalism of the United States and the *dirigisme* of South Korean economic management.

In the 1990s, the Japanese home mortgage-lending industry failed on a scale roughly parallel to America's savings and loan debacle. The problem arose in part because this segment of the financial industry was left virtually unregulated due to close ties between the firm managers and the Ministry of Finance regulators. With explosion in 1995 into a full-fledged crisis involving $130 billion in potentially unrecoverable debt held by every sector of the Japanese financial industry, losses were allocated and the problem was defused almost entirely through Ministry of Finance-orchestrated informal consultations among the principals.[77] While the process was neither smooth nor free of conflict – in fact, the episode is one of the most contentious in post-war Japanese economic and political history – the creation and resolution of the problem bore the signature qualities of informality, administrative discretion, and extensive private sector input into regulatory policy.

IV.   A corporate governance spectrum from property rights

Governance diversity among the United States, Japan, and South Korea can be explained as the result of rational adaptations to the different property rights environments we have seen in the three countries. Recall the two principal ways in which property rights institutions will affect economic exchange: by shaping the firms that emerge in response to the resulting opportunity sets, and by determining the governance technology that is available to these firms. Both effects are nicely illustrated in our sample.

Corporate ownership and structure in the three countries is consistent with the implications from property rights theory. In the United States, a property rights setup of limited political control and extensive legal enforcement has permitted the proliferation of contracts among corporate constituents standing at arm's length, producing large firms with dispersed, nonfamily ownership. Simultaneously, it has created an

---

[76] Readers desiring more complete accounts consistent with the text can consult a large body of literature. See, e.g., Frank K. Upham, "Privatizing Regulation: Japanese Regulatory Style in Comparative and International Perspective," 20 *Fordham Int'l L.J.* 396 (1996).

[77] For a detailed account, see Milhaupt & Miller, note 35 above.

environment conducive to the rapid transformation of small, privately held firms into large public firms.

In South Korea, a less secure property rights arrangement has generated firms that are relatively small and clustered into highly diversified groups, with ownership and management concentrated in the family. Successive Korean governments were at once a motivating force for Korean entrepreneurs and a continuing source of uncertainty about property rights protections. Thus, founding families remain in control of the *chaebol*, and their high degree of technologically unrelated diversification can be viewed as a means of reducing the political risk that particular industries will fall out of favor with the government.[78]

Corporate structure in Japan is generally consistent with its intermediate property rights position. Japanese industrial organization was first dominated by the family-owned and -managed *zaibatsu* groups in the uncertain property rights environment of nineteenth-century Japan. The *zaibatsu* gradually opened up to non-kin investors and professional managers as property rights institutions became more secure in the early part of this century.[79] Post-war economic reforms attempted to dismantle the *zaibatsu* and implement an Anglo-American style system of capital market-oriented corporate governance by dispersing control rights and eliminating the hierarchical *zaibatsu* organizational structure.[80] But given both the uncertain economic environment of the immediate post-war period and the legacy of regulatory relations between political and private economic agents in Japan, the bank-centered *keiretsu* emerged as an intermediate form of network-based joint production: neither market nor hierarchy.

Firms are shaped by property rights institutions not only in terms of ownership, management, and organizational structure, but also by the magnitude and design of the political capital investments they make. Political contracting in a given community again follows from the property rights set-up. The more control rights are allocated to political agents, the more private agents will invest in structures to stabilize their environment and reallocate those rights to themselves. Indeed, property rights analysis would predict that political capital investments to secure property rights against discretionary bureaucratic intervention are essential

[78] See Jwa, note 26 above. [79] See Ramseyer, note 26 above.
[80] Hideaki Miyajima, "The Privatization of Ex-Zaibatsu Holding Stocks and the Emergence of Bank-Centered Corporate Groups in Japan," in Masahiko Aoki & Hyung-Ki Kim, eds., *Corporate Governance in Transitional Economies*, pp. 361, 362–68 (1995).

to firm growth where resort to formal legal structures is unavailable or costly. This is evident in the contrast between the political strategies of US firms on the one hand and Japanese and South Korean firms on the other.

Firms everywhere engage in some form of political contracting, of course; regulatory capture is not a culture- or state-specific phenomenon. US firms and their industry associations engage in lobbying and campaign finance. And yet, as a consequence of the relative impotence of political control rights over firms in the United States, it would be difficult to argue that the need to engage in political activities meaningfully affects the design of internal or external corporate structures in this country.

The relative lack of pervasive political contracting in the United States stands in sharp contrast to practices in South Korea and Japan. As noted in section II, cash payments are obviously the most direct means of reallocating control rights from political to private agents. The *chaebol*, for example, have long paid a substantial quasi-corporate tax in the form of political contributions.[81] Illicit side payments from the private sector to political leaders have a long history in Japan as well.[82] Aside from corruption, more prosaic and identical systemic mechanisms of political contracting also exist in Japan and South Korea. In both countries, retired bureaucrats parachute into lucrative private-sector jobs, where they typically assume high-level managerial positions in their new host firms.[83] The principal function of these new managers is to serve as a conduit for information and contacts between the host firm and the ministry. This practice can be seen as a means of reducing uncertainty and political risk by purchasing regulatory control rights from political agents. The currency used for these purchases is attractive post-retirement employment opportunities in the regulated sector. The practice affects corporate governance by changing the regulatory environment for firms that engage in the practice.[84]

In both countries, cross-industry ("peak") associations and industry organizations provide a forum for negotiations with political agents and constrain the actions of individual member firms. In Japan, for example,

---

[81] Chang & Chang note 37 above, p. 71.
[82] See generally Richard H. Mitchell, *Political Bribery in Japan* (1996).
[83] On the Japanese practice, see Kent E. Calder, "Elites in an Equalizing Role: Ex-bureaucrats as Coordinators and Intermediaries in the Japanese Government–Business Relationship," 21 *Com. Pol.* 379 (1989); on the Korean practice, see Chang & Chang, note 37 above, p. 70.
[84] See Milhaupt & Miller, note 35 above.

regulatory policy is often worked out informally between bureaucrats and leaders of an industry association, in consultation with member firms. Once consensus on a policy is reached, it is never legally challenged by affected firms. This *ex ante* bargaining and enforcement process is facilitated in part by the retirement practices of public officials discussed immediately above. Japanese law generally imposes a two-year waiting period before an ex-civil servant may be employed by a private firm.[85] Peak associations and industry organizations provide an ideal means of complying with the law while making the transition from the public to the private sector.[86] While employed in these organizations, ex-officials are perfectly situated to facilitate coordination of policies between political and private agents. Similarly in South Korea, industry associations and the complementary career patterns of government elites play important roles in forging a bargaining space for business that is neither wholly public nor entirely private.[87]

Social capital is the glue that binds these political contracts, contributing to the extra-legal character of control right enforcement in both Japan and South Korea. Alumni connections are crucial in both countries; most government and business leaders in either country are graduates of just one or two elite universities. Educational background not only determines professional attainment, it also shapes employment practices designed to bolster contacts between the public and private sectors.[88] In South Korea, marriage is also used to strengthen *chaebol* family ties to the political establishment.[89] Thus, through these assorted practices, private firms in both countries have established devices to stabilize their property rights environment to facilitate the growth and financing of their firms.

Property rights institutions not only give shape to firms, they also circumscribe the universe of mechanisms available to perform essential corporate governance functions such as responding to failure and

---

[85] Kokka komuin ho [National Civil Servant Law], Law No. 120 of 1947, art. 103.

[86] For example, a recent survey showed that approximately one-fourth of the Japanese Finance Ministry retirees working in private firms had entered the private sector by way of industry associations or affiliated research institutes. Kazuma Tsutsumi & Jiro Yamaguchi, *Kanryo amakudari hakusho* [White Paper on the Bureaucrats' Descent from Heaven], p. 17 (1996).

[87] See Kihwan Kim & Danny M. Leipziger, "Korea: A Case of Government-Led Development," p. 34 (World Bank Lessons of East Asia Series, 1993).

[88] Alumni of the top universities working for large firms are assigned to remain in daily contact with their classmates at the relevant ministry.

[89] Chang & Chang, note 37 above, p. 63.

adapting to changed circumstances. The property rights environments in the three countries have shaped monitoring mechanisms and adaptive efficiency in their respective governance systems.

Market- and law-based mechanisms of corporate governance in the United States provide a good institutional fit with limited political control rights over private firms. Because a market-centered financial system expands opportunities for exit and increases the number of discrete exchanges among corporate constituents, explicit contracts and other formal legal mechanisms of corporate accountability predominate. Where contracts cannot be efficiently specified in advance, general gap-filling standards which invite judicial review are employed.[90] Thus, external actors such as hostile takeover bidders and the courts obtain control rights in this form of governance. The result is a largely private, market- and law-oriented monitoring system in the United States. Similarly, external mechanisms are used to enhance the adaptive qualities of economic organizations. The venture capital and IPO markets – both of which rely extensively on private control mechanisms – are endogenously derived complementaries to the American institutional framework.[91]

At the other end of the governance spectrum, Korean firms are, in a very meaningful sense, monitored and disciplined politically.[92] The government has traditionally substituted for the market for corporate control in South Korea. Political agents have responded to failure by staging both hostile and negotiated takeovers of unsuccessful firms.[93] Consistent with this control structure, adaptation in this system takes place internally, by creating new subsidiaries within the protective confines of the *chaebol* structure. As would be expected in a system of extensive political control rights, external mechanisms of adaptive efficiency such as the venture capital and IPO markets are relatively underdeveloped.[94]

---

[90] William Carney refers to this as a "litigation model of corporate governance." See William J. Carney, "The ALI's Corporate Governance Project: The Death of Property Rights?" 61 *Geo. Wash. L. Rev.* 898, 929 (1993).

[91] See Milhaupt, note 33 above.

[92] Numerous observers view the authoritarian and discretionary nature of the South Korean government's relations with the private sector as a major constraint on corporate conduct. See, e.g., Kwon, note 45 above, pp. 183–86.

[93] An example of the former is the Kukje Group dissolution discussed in section III; an example of the latter is the government's recent acquisition of a controlling stake in Kia Motors, Korea's third largest auto manufacturer. See "Stocks Soar in Seoul on Kia Takeover Plan," *N.Y. Times*, Oct. 23, 1997, at D7.

[94] For example, until the mid-1990s the government set quarterly quotas on the number of IPOs, and actually determined the initial offering price of shares. See Katherine Bruce,

In Japan, internal monitoring mechanisms reflect the allocation and enforcement of control rights over firms. Shared in roughly equal parts between the public and private sectors, control rights over firms remain with the banks, bureaucrats, and corporate group managers who formed the nucleus of Japan's early modern property rights order. Main banks perform their monitoring roles without the benefit of legally enforceable contracts,[95] but find protection in the way that political control rights have historically been exercised to restrain competition in banking and constrain the development of capital markets. Since control rights over firms are concentrated in friendly hands, corporate managers and other long-term employees have been safeguarded in the post-war period from external monitoring mechanisms that could upset firm-specific investments. As a result, employees hold considerable legally and nonlegally enforceable control rights in large firms. As in South Korea, the institutional framework internalizes adaptation within corporate groups. New firms lack the political and social capital needed to expand rapidly in the Japanese property rights environment and face concomitant institutional obstacles such as an illiquid labor market and a heavily regulated IPO market.

V. Convergence?

Are diverse national systems of corporate governance converging? On one level, recent events around the world indicate that the answer is clearly yes. But careful analysis suggests that convergence will be limited, because while competitive pressures drive firms strongly, the mechanisms of convergence operate only weakly on the political and property rights structures that account for diversity in corporate governance. Thus, the political economy of property rights institutions will render corporate governance convergence slow, sporadic, and uncertain. Since we lack a unified vision of an optimal corporate governance system, however, whether convergence occurs or not may be less important than what we learn by observing the process of (non)convergence.

"Seoul Announces Market Reform to Ease Stock Trading," *Reuter Asia-Pacific Business Report*, Aug. 22, 1996, available in LEXIS, News Library, Non-US file.

[95] Cf. J. Mark Ramseyer, "Explicit Reasons for Implicit Contracts: The Legal Logic to the Japanese Main Bank System," in Masahiko Aoki & Hugh Patrick, eds., *The Japanese Main Bank System*, p. 231(1994) (arguing that main bank contracts to monitor and rescue firms are unenforceable).

The potential for convergence

Convergence of diverse corporate governance systems could occur as a result of several interrelated forces now at work across countries. One prevalent convergence hypothesis is that globalization of product markets will lead to similar patterns of corporate organization. This hypothesis predicts that:

> Every economy will increasingly face identical potential market size and an identical set of available production technologies as the borderless economy emerges. Therefore, as the world economy becomes more integrated and globalized, the optimal structures of industrial organization will converge among individual economies . . .
>
> Of course, individual firms may use their own business strategies, diverging from the optimal structure implied by and consistent with potential as well as existing market and technological opportunities, but those firms will ultimately be defeated by market conformists.[96]

A related hypothesis is that certain governance strategies predominate in any system; competition in product, capital, and corporate control markets will therefore cause the dominant governance strategies to emerge everywhere.[97] A frequently cited example is the replacement of chief executive officers of poorly performing companies, which seems to occur in all major governance systems.[98] In essence, both claims (together, call them the convergence-from-competition hypothesis) assert that the logic of the product and capital markets dictates convergent governance outcomes.

A distinct convergence hypothesis is advanced by sociologists rather than economic-oriented theorists. Rooted in the asserted vulnerability of distinctive national institutions in the face of global economic pressures, this argument holds that as the public interest is increasingly equated with market outcomes around the world, political will to sustain involvement in the economy in defense of nonmarket-oriented visions of the public interest will crumble. Once this occurs, national institutional diversity will give way to market conformity.[99]

Fortunately for distinctive national institutions, this sociological perspective on convergence is demonstrably flawed. At bottom, it assumes that political agents everywhere are willing to relinquish control rights

---

[96] Jwa, note 38 above, pp. 320–21.   [97] See Ramseyer, note 26 above.

[98] See Steven N. Kaplan & J. Mark Ramseyer, "Those Japanese Firms with their Disdain for Shareholders: Another Fable for the Academy," 74 *Wash. U. L. Q.* 403 (1996).

[99] See Berger, note 9 above, p. 18; Ronald Dore, "Convergence in Whose Interest?" in *Diversity and Capitalism*, note 9 above, p. 366.

over firms and permit unfettered operation of the market. The developments in Asia and the transition economies of Eastern Europe, however, convincingly demonstrate that, on the contrary, politicians and bureaucrats will remain very much in business despite even radical shifts in political philosophy and social values toward market-oriented democracy.[100] From Mahathir's Malaysia to Jiang's China, markets coincide uneasily with the nationalistic and ideological tendencies of political leaders.

By contrast, the convergence-from-competition hypothesis is persuasive on a theoretical level. The potential homogenizing effects of market globalization are at least threefold. First, market size will expand in step with globalization; firms will thus be encouraged to specialize in large-scale production. Second, rapid technological innovation will create larger economies of scope, encouraging diversification and flexible production. While these two forces are in tension, all firms in a given industry will settle on either a large-scale production model or a small-scale production model, depending on the size of the market and the nature of the technologies involved.[101] Moreover, at least implicit in the convergence-from-competition hypothesis is the plausible assumption that technological advances will themselves accelerate and intensify the effects of global market forces. Third, as financial markets are globalized, access to capital will increasingly be decoupled from national regulatory requirements. Firms will need to conform to the rules of the international markets if they wish to access the deepest and widest pools of capital. As they do, idiosyncratic domestic rules will fall away, and financial regulatory regimes will converge.[102] Uniform financial rules will hasten the convergence of corporate governance mechanisms.

The convergence-from-competition hypothesis also finds anecdotal support in recent events. Consider recent developments in South Korea and Japan. The currency and debt crises in South Korea exposed firms in that country to an unprecedented degree of international corporate governance scrutiny and intervention. The IMF's policy response to the financial crisis was explicitly tied to sweeping, market-oriented

---

[100] See *World Bank Policy Research Report, Bureaucrats in Business: The Economics and Politics of Government Ownership* (1995) (analyzing the political obstacles to divestiture of state-owned enterprises despite compelling economic evidence in support of privatization).

[101] Jwa, note 38 above.

[102] This process has already taken place in the context of capital controls. See John B. Goodman & Louis W. Pauly, "The Obsolescence of Capital Controls? Economic Management in an Age of Global Markets," 46 *World Pol.* 50 (1993) (arguing that development of international financial markets brought about convergence of national capital controls).

corporate governance and financial sector forms.[103] An IMF policy memorandum emphasizes the "urgent need to improve corporate governance and the corporate structure."[104] The policy program supported by the IMF consisted of improved transparency, involving accounting and disclosure reforms, and "creating a level playing field for all private enterprises . . . [which will] involve the prompt elimination of directed lending as well as avoidance of government intervention in lending decisions or subsidies and tax privileges to bail out individual corporations."[105]

Less dramatic, but equally significant developments are under way in Japanese corporate governance. In the past few years, international market pressures, trade negotiations, and shifts in public attitudes have resulted in amendments to corporate and financial laws, outwardly bringing Japanese incentive and monitoring devices closer to those used in the United States – a weak form of convergence.[106] Stock options and shareholder derivative suits are two high-profile examples. Stock options were virtually unknown in Japan until recently due to cumbersome legal restrictions on stock issuance; now they are both legally viable and gaining currency as a managerial incentive tool. This development, which occurred overnight by Japanese standards, was clearly prompted by international competitive pressures. The lack of stock options in the Japanese universe of governance technology had created an increasingly visible obstacle for start-up firms and the venture capital industry in comparison to the United States.[107] The obvious solution was to remove the obstacle by changing the law.

Like stock options, derivative litigation in Japan was once rare, but not today. Approximately five times more shareholder derivative suits have been brought against Japanese managers in the past five years than in the preceding forty. The rapid increase in use of this monitoring device is the result of legal changes in 1993 lowering the cost of filing such suits (a direct result of bilateral trade negotiations), as well as a rash of imprudent conduct by Japanese managers in an easy money environment which bank-oriented monitoring was not well designed to prevent. Today, Japanese managers are painfully aware of their legal duties to shareholders. Heightened awareness of these duties and the threat of derivative litigation have even altered negotiations between industries and their regulators.[108]

---

[103] See International Monetary Fund, "Korea Request for Stand-By Arrangement," Dec. 3, 1997.
[104] Ibid., p. 15.   [105] Ibid.   [106] See note 28 above.
[107] See Milhaupt, note 33 above.   [108] See Milhaupt & Miller, note 35 above.

Constraints on convergence

Powerful as they may be, the forces for convergence are also subject to powerful constraints. The persuasiveness of the convergence-from-competition hypothesis diminishes if the focus is shifted from the possible causes of convergence to two related questions: *should* corporate governance systems converge? and *how* do they converge? As to the first question, showing that some governance techniques are common to most successful economies is not the same as proving the existence of a single, optimal governance system. In fact, existing theoretical and empirical research appears to suggest the contrary conclusion: there are a variety of ways to successfully organize, monitor, and control large firms. What constitutes the most efficient governance practices will therefore depend upon the institutional setting in which a given firm operates. If there is no one "best way," it is unclear exactly what should be converging.

This suggests that policymakers and private actors should tread carefully before importing foreign governance technology into their own institutional framework. Without a clear understanding of alternative systems, let alone a vision of a "model" system, intellectual arbitrage has its limitations. For example, no sooner had observers identified a number of plausible advantages of Japanese and German bank-oriented monitoring systems than other commentators began to identify serious drawbacks in comparison to the Anglo-American stock market system.[109] To take a second example, recent scholarship finds no conclusive evidence that board composition relates to firm performance,[110] and suggests that boards are structured in response to the idiosyncratic economic needs and circumstances of individual firms.[111] If this research is accurate, worldwide convergence around a legal or extra-legal norm requiring that a majority of outside directors be unaffiliated with management, while intuitively appealing, would actually be *inefficient*.[112] This risk is particularly salient since "convergence" is often taken to mean

---

[109] See, e.g., Jonathan R. Macey & Geoffrey P. Miller, "Corporate Governance and Commercial Banking: A Comparative Examination of Germany, Japan, and the United States," 48 *Stan. L. Rev.* 73 (1996); Milhaupt, note 33 above.

[110] See Sanjai Bhagat & Bernard Black, "The Uncertain Relationship between Board Composition and Firm Performance," in Klaus Hopt *et al.*, eds., *Corporate Governance: The State of the Art and Emerging Research* (1998).

[111] See April Klein, "Affiliated Directors: Puppets of Management or Effective Directors?" (Jan. 1998) (unpublished paper).

[112] Jill Fisch makes a similar cautionary argument about board reform. See Jill E. Fisch, "Taking Boards Seriously," 19 *Cardozo L. Rev.* 265 (1977).

movement by organizations in other countries toward US standards and practices.

Even assuming the existence of a "model" corporate governance system, numerous forces can throw sand into the mechanisms of convergence. From the analytical perspective outlined in section I, we see that changes in national corporate governance systems require changes in property rights institutions. To be sure, property rights institutions change when the old rules are poorly attuned to new cost–benefit structures brought about through technological advances, the development of new markets, or a change in values.[113] Globalization of product and financial markets offers an ideal setting for such a shift; it is no coincidence that changes in control structures around the world are accompanying these market developments. Institutional change, however, is far stickier than the convergence-from-competition hypothesis acknowledges.

It is the political nature of institutional change that imposes fundamental limitations on the potential for convergence. As this chapter has shown, political agents currently do not hold uniform control rights over firms in all systems, a substantial cause of governance diversity. Convergence would thus require standardizing political control structures to ensure uniformity in the exercise of control rights over firms. Increasingly global and efficient markets for capital and products may compel firm managers to act rationally or die, but to date there are no analogous market forces in operation in the political realm.[114] Thus, political agents across countries can be expected to respond very imperfectly to the logic of the global product, capital, and control markets. As the demise of the Soviet Union and the socialist regimes of Eastern Europe attest, competition ultimately appears to work for political governance as well as for products and firms, but the process is time consuming and unpredictable. As a result, the allocation and enforcement of control over corporate assets will continue to vary substantially across countries.

National differences in the political power of corporate constituents will similarly obstruct convergence. Indeed, if national political markets are efficient in the sense that organized interest groups get what they want from government, convergence will be slowed even further. Managers, labor, and institutional investors are not similarly organized and do not exert identical influence on the political process across countries. Any consciously imitated "model" or "spontaneously evolving" corporate

---

[113] See Demsetz, note 16 above, at 350–53.
[114] See Edward Rubin, "Rational States?" 83 *Va. L. Rev.* 1433, 1441–42 (1997) (noting that "the idiosyncratic, the venal, and the stupid can all flourish in a political regime").

governance system is likely to crash headlong into the conflicting political preferences of various organized groups in different countries before it reaches fruition. Even if it miraculously avoided these obstacles, disparities in the bargaining power of organized groups from one country to the next would prevent the highly choreographed institutional adjustments required to put the ideal system in place everywhere. By the time the spontaneous institutional reengineering is complete, the economic environment may be entirely different, requiring new adjustments. In short, because property rights systems are designed and maintained with political realities as well as economic efficiency in mind, we can expect continued diversity in control structures despite powerful market forces in favor of conformity. The dictum that "[i]n many circumstances, political ties are more important to survival than efficiency"[115] will be as accurate tomorrow as it is today.

Finally, even if we are witnessing formal convergence toward an optimal set of corporate and financial laws and accounting standards, enforcement patterns will continue to differ. Enforcement implicates a host of domestic institutions, including judicial systems, business practices, and social norms, that will be highly resistant to change. Without convergence of enforcement, standardization of formal rules is unlikely to be meaningful.[116]

The foregoing analysis should not be taken to suggest that convergence will be completely impeded by political constraints. Rather, it suggests that limited convergence will occur where institutional inertia grounded in political and related social constraints can be overcome to alter existing property rights structures. That process, however, is likely to be more piecemeal than pervasive, leading to weak as opposed to strong form convergence. Indeed, that is the conclusion suggested by the greatest natural convergence experiments to date – economic reform in the transition economies of Eastern Europe, and the merger of East and West Germany. There has been no Darwinian process of natural selection among corporate governance systems in the privatization of enterprises in Eastern Europe, only mechanisms selected on the basis of political feasibility.[117] There was no attempt to create an "optimal" corporate governance structure in the process of unifying the two Germanies, only a pragmatic plan to integrate a dysfunctional system of political control

---

[115] Michael T. Hannan & John Freeman, *Organizational Ecology*, p. 37 (1989).

[116] See Gérard Hertig, chapter 10, this volume.

[117] See, e.g., Suzanna Fluck, *et al.*, "Privatization with Political Constraints: Auctions versus Private Negotiations," New York University Salomon Center Working Paper no. S-96-26 (1996) and sources cited therein.

rights over firms into a relatively successful existing system. Institutional inertia ensures that it could not be otherwise.

Does (non)convergence matter?

We can expect increased borrowing to occur within the slowly evolving confines of national institutional frameworks. Therefore, convergence will occur, if convergence means an ongoing process of incremental change rather than the arrival of diverse systems at some ideal destination. No matter how much borrowing takes place, however, diversity is likely to remain the stock-in-trade of the scholar of comparative corporate governance. As Albert Hirschman has noted, "convergence in one area will be paralleled by renewed divergence in another: New problems continually arise and they will presumably again result in initially quite different probing and search patterns [so that] . . . any lasting convergence . . . is not to be expected."[118]

Ultimately, it matters little whether corporate governance systems are converging. The goals of corporate governance have already converged. All systems need to produce some measure of commitment and some measure of adaptability; all systems need to respond to problems related to failure and to problems related to success.[119] The techniques currently used to attain these goals across systems diverge here and converge there. Given the uncertainty over the components of an optimal corporate governance system, the task is to gather accurate information and permit experimentation to occur. In short, what matters is that we continue to refine our understanding of the attributes of successful and unsuccessful governance systems, and the potential for reform within a given system. For that, we need to unpack the black box of property rights and explore the political dynamics of institutional change across countries.

Conclusion

This chapter has argued that all firms are adaptations to property rights institutions. In every economy, control rights over firms are allocated between political and private actors. The structures different societies

---

[118] Albert Hirschman, "Ideology: Mask, or Nessus Shirt?," in Alexander Eckstein, ed., *Comparison of Economic Systems: Theoretical and Methodological Approaches*, pp. 289, 294 (1971).

[119] See Ronald J. Gilson," Reflections in a Distant Mirror: Japanese Corporate Governance through American Eyes," 1998 *Colum. Bus. L. Rev.* 203.

erect to allocate and enforce these rights determine how firms are organized and governed, and account for the diversity observable in corporate
monitoring and control across countries. Because initial allocations and
subsequent changes in control rights are worked out largely through political processes, corporate governance cannot be separated from political
governance.

Property rights institutions not only distinguish national corporate
governance systems, they also obstruct their convergence. The competitive efficiency concerns that drive the mechanisms of convergence operate
far more powerfully on firms than on political agents and organizations.
Thus, convergence will occur only where the political and social structures that account for institutional inertia can be overcome. In the end,
however, limited convergence may not matter. As with property rights
structures, there appears to be no optimal corporate governance system,
only collections of complementary mechanisms that fit or fail within a
country's institutional framework. Just as property rights cannot simply
be put in place to promote economic exchange, successful corporate governance mechanisms cannot simply be imported into diverse institutional
frameworks.

We should not anticipate the convergence of diverse national corporate
governance systems toward one "best way," but we can expect global
economic forces to be filtered through evolving national institutions with
increasing frequency and dramatic effect. Properly understood, the logic
of property provides a powerful means of analyzing these developments.

7

Modern politics and ownership separation

MARK J. ROE[*]

Introduction: why do only some nations have public firms?

The public firm, with dispersed stockholders in deep liquid securities markets, dominates business in the United States. Despite its pervasiveness, it has well-known infirmities, namely in the fragile ties that bind managers to shareholders. If shareholders strongly fear managers' disloyalty or incompetence, they will invest warily; if sufficiently fearful, they will not invest at all, and other ownership structures will prevail. But the core problems of binding managers to shareholders in the United States have shrunk to acceptable levels; investors are not so afraid of managers that they refuse to invest. Indeed, these problems have been handled so well that we fail to recognize the political prerequisites to resolving them and tying American managers to dispersed stockholders.

I argue here that the core problems of the public firm cannot be resolved readily, or at all, in a strong social democracy. Social democracies press managers to "defect" from loyalty to shareholders and make it harder to align managers with shareholders. When we see how social democracies weaken shareholders' ties to managers, we shall thereby discover a key political prerequisite to the rise and persistence of the public firm in the United States, namely the absence of a social democracy and its concomitant powerful pressures on the business firm.

* * *

In contrast to the American-style public firm, the family firm, or the public firm with concentrated ownership, has dominated business in France, Germany, Italy, and Scandinavia. A main bank system with significant bank stockholdings was historically important in Japan, and may

---

[*] A further presentation of the argument in this chapter, along with further supporting data, is in *Political Determinants of Corporate Governance* (Oxford University Press, 2003).

still have some strength left to it. How do we explain this difference between the US and most of the rest of the developed world, and its persistence?

Diffusely owned public firms must make managers loyal to share-holders. Agency costs arise when managers' agendas differ from share-holders' agendas. Diffuse shareholders want the firm to maximize profits; unconstrained managers often prefer to maximize the firm's size, prefer not to take severe risks with the firm even if the risks would maximize profits, and often prefer to defer hard, disruptive actions. When block-holders and private ownership (as opposed to state ownership) persist, they may persist because they serve a function for shareholders. Block-holders and private owners have the means and the motivation to monitor managers, a motivation and an authority that dispersed shareholders in the Berle-Means corporation often lack. Hence, blockholding may have persisted on the European continent because managerial agency costs were potentially higher there and stockholders lack good alternative means of keeping managers loyal.

Most corporate governance analyses ignore employees, and when we put them back into the governance inquiry, we get a richer understanding of how a society organizes its corporate institutions: social democracies and the American-style public firm mix badly because public firm agency costs in social democracies are higher *and* the mechanisms that would control the agency costs are harder to implement.

A tension always exists between current employees and invested capital, and a great deal of American corporate governance mitigates this tension. It does so by inducing managers to act in shareholders' interests, and, oftentimes, against the immediate interests of employees with jobs in place. When economic realities change, employees could be laid off. When technologies change, managers must alter the firm's structure and day-to-day working environment in ways that make incumbent employees and often the managers themselves unhappy. Employees' and managers' jobs must be restructured or put at risk. Work, if the excitement of change is unattractive, becomes disruptive, difficult, and risky; workers and managers may resist change. Managers, for their own reasons, not only frequently delay these restructurings, but also have a long-known propensity to expand the firm's ongoing operations, even at the cost of shareholder profits; their expanding the firm down a known path usually favors themselves and current employees, but it often fails to maximize shareholder profits.

In social democracies – nations committed to private property, whose governments play a large role in the economy, emphasize distributional considerations, and favor employees over capital-owners when the two conflict[1] – public policy emphasizes managers' natural agenda and demeans shareholders' natural agenda. The pressure on the firm for low-risk expansion is high, the pressure to avoid risky organizational change is substantial, and the tools that would induce managers to work in favor of invested capital – high incentive compensation, hostile takeovers, transparent accounting, acculturation to shareholder wealth maximization norms – are weak. Unconstrained managers may well go along, but shareholders would prefer to go slow in, say, expanding the firm, because expansion is harder to reverse later than it would be in another political environment. Life may well be better for more people, but the internal structure of public firms must necessarily be weaker for shareholders.

Hence, managerial agency costs are higher in social democracies than elsewhere, and we have just found a deeper, richer social and political explanation not only for the history of family ownership in France, Germany, Italy, and Scandinavia, and possibly for the Japanese main banks, but also for the rise of the public firm in the United States. Social democracies – like corporatist polities – do not strongly control public firm agency costs well, because they do *not* want unbridled shareholder wealth maximization, and, hence, by weakening shareholder wealth maximization institutions, they widen the gap. When the gap is wide enough, the large American-style public firm is rendered unstable without subsidy, making it compatible with neither corporatist polities nor social democracy. Social democracies may improve aggregate welfare, but they do so with fewer public firms.

* * *

A road-map for this chapter: in section I, I first set out the structural contrast in ownership around the world and next show how social democracy (a) wedges open the gap between managers and shareholders and (b) raises the costs of closing the gap. In section II, I show some fundamental correlations: if we array the world's richest nations along a left–right spectrum, this spectrum correlates powerfully with ownership concentration. I also briefly discuss the reasons for American exceptionalism. In section

---

[1] Adam Przeworski, "Socialism and Social Democracy," in Joel Krieger *et al.*, eds., *The Oxford Companion to Politics of the World*, pp. 832, 835, 837 (1993) (social democracies seek "to implement 'functional socialism', even if ownership of productive resources remains private").

III, I discuss stronger tests and provide alternative formulations of the thesis. In section IV, I describe some reservations. In section V, I explicitly draw out the implications for understanding the American public firm. Finally, I conclude.

I.   Social democracies' pressures on the public firm

Some nations' large firms are diffusely held, while others have historically been closely held, because many never go public, and big blockholders persist even in those that do. In Germany in the 1990s, nearly every large firm has had a large blockholder, usually from a family, but for some firms from a bank, an insurance company, or another corporation. In France, the family or entrepreneurially controlled sector was large, growing, and highly competitive. In Italy family firms have persisted and few firms are truly public. In Japan, the largest firms have had four or five banks and insurers that each own about 5 percent of each firm's stock. Most such differences thus far persist, despite converging living standards and business technology.

No single factor can fully explain every difference and I discuss the conventional explanations elsewhere.[2] I do not wish to displace the other explanations completely, but rather to make a large space for the unrecognized political explanation and show why it is as important for the world's richer nations (or more so) as any current explanation.

Agency costs and the public firm

The United States has a rich literature on agency costs of the disjunction between managers' goals and shareholders' goals. Shareholders, particularly diversified shareholders who are distant from the corporation, want their firm's profits maximized. Managers historically preferred to expand their firms, as expansion yielded them more power, prestige, and pay. Managers, with their own human capital tied up in the firm, often wanted to avoid many profit-maximizing risks; shareholders, who can diversify better than managers, have usually preferred their firms to maximize expected value, without respect to risk. Managers often used up capital in place rather than restructure a firm, because restructuring can be painful.

---

[2] See Mark J. Roe, *Political Determinants of Corporate Governance* (Oxford University Press, 2003; Mark J. Roe, "Political Preconditions to Separating Ownership from Corporate Control," 53 *Stan. L. Rev.* 539 (2000).

And in simple terms managers may not have wanted to work as hard and as long as shareholders would prefer.

Corporate governance is traditionally seen in the United States as a principal–agent problem. Principals cannot get agents to perform perfectly. The principals often are less well-informed than their agents about the tasks to be performed and, afterwards, about how well the agents performed them. The principals usually are more time-constrained than the agents in the activity involved. Stockholders as principals cannot automatically get their agents, the firm's managers, to pursue stockholders' interests. In the United States, the public firm principal–agent problem is layered over a free-rider problem because the stockholders are fragmented and distant from the firm, with each unwilling to invest heavily in monitoring their managerial agents and in making those agents toe the line to perform for shareholders. This much is not new.

That is, when stockholding is diffuse, these agency cost problems for shareholders increase, because diffuse, free-riding shareholders lack the motivation to monitor managers. Moreover, their small holdings deny them the means to monitor effectively – managers have little reason to pay attention to a small shareholder acting alone – and deny them the information base they would need to be effective. Yet, *despite* these problems, the US has many public firms, whose shares are diffusely owned. Part of the reason this is so is well known: diffuse ownership yields risk-bearing advantages that partly offset the agency cost disadvantages of large firms. Part of the reason is that professional managers despite their debilities are often better at their job than the second or third generation of family managers.[3]

And part of the reason that the US has so many public firms is that it developed tools to constrain managerial agency costs. These institutions have been the independent and active board, incentive compensation, hostile takeovers and proxy contests, securities markets signaling from securities analysts, competitive capital and product markets, and socialization in business schools and on-the-job to a shareholder wealth maximization norm. I hardly argue that these devices perfectly align managers with stockholders; but since the US has so many Berle-Means firms with diffuse ownership, (i) we will see more agency cost failures in the United States in the aggregate, and (ii) corporate law academics and finance

[3] Alfred P. Chandler, *The Visible Hand: The Managerial Revolution in American Business* (1977); cf. Harold Demsetz, "The Structure of Ownership and the Theory of the Firm," 26 *J.L. & Econ.* 375–90 (1983) (sole owner maximizes personal utility, not firm value).

economists, because they correctly focus their attention on improving or understanding the core American corporate governance institutions, are susceptible to incorrectly believing that the US controls agency costs badly, when the prevalence in the US of the Berle-Means firm more likely shows an institution whose costs, even if not trivial and even if still susceptible to improvement, are sufficiently contained to be viable for all of its key players.

Social democracies and agency costs: raising the stakes

Social democracies raise agency costs for shareholders in the public firm, and, to the extent they do so, shareholders' natural reaction would then be to find an alternative organizational form. German codetermination – by which labor gets one-half of the supervisory board of Germany's largest firms – is an explicit manifestation of social democracy, one that well illustrates the effects on corporate organization of social democracy. We first look at social democracy's effects through codetermination, seeing the dilemma a family-owned firm faces when considering whether to take their firm public, and then we generalize to look at social democracy's effects on agency costs and ownership structure without codetermination. The formal social democratic institution of codetermination is not needed for social democracy to affect the public firm's internal workings, but the formal institution boldly illustrates the political effects.

Social democracy's effects through codetermination

Germany has had a long ideological and political encounter with codetermination. It first arose after World War I when revolutionary leaders established workers' councils (counterparts to the better-known soviets arising elsewhere), which evolved into employee representation on the supervisory council of the larger firms. After World War II, labor leaders sought to be represented on the boards, partly to convince the Allies not to dismantle Germany's coal and steel industry, by asserting that they, labor, would constrain the wartime industrialists via positions on the firms' supervisory boards. From this "deal" came full-parity codetermination of labor and shareholders in the coal and steel industry. Codetermination also had its capitalist promoters, who sought a "middle way" between the raw capitalism of the marketplace and the extreme socialism of state-ownership. Later political events expanded this codetermination, to one-third of the supervisory board of most other industrial firms, and in 1976 to one-half of the board of Germany's larger firms.

Consider how codetermination affects agency costs – and thereby affects German corporate ownership structure and securities markets – by observing how the family owning a successful firm would think about doing an initial public offering and withdrawing from managing and owning the company, in light of codetermination. Their supervisory board has never been strong. It has met for the statutory minimum of (until recently) twice annually. The meetings are formal, without serious give and take. The accounting reports that the board gets are not very good, the board gets them at the very beginning of a semi-annual meeting, and then the reports are whisked away from them at its end. The board is not a serious monitoring mechanism inside the firm. This is the typical traditional picture painted of the German boardroom.

Board-level monitoring has not in the late twentieth century been critical to the firm for two reasons. First, many family owners were also the firm's managers; hence, the disjunction between ownership and management was weaker than in the public firm, and agency costs lower. Second, even if the family did not manage the firm directly but hired professional managers, the family members met monthly with managers to review results and performance. In effect, the monitoring role of the active board was fulfilled apart from the supervisory board, whose meetings were stale, formal, and ineffective.

The family may have considered moving more of the monitoring into the boardroom, partly to get ready for a public offering, partly to formalize the informal monthly meetings with managers. But they concluded not to move it inside the boardroom, because they preferred not to give more information and authority to the labor members of the supervisory board.

The family, as we've hypothesized, is hoping to leave the firm. They want to sell their stock and diversify their investments. The firm has been returning $50 million in earnings to them annually, and they accord a capitalization rate of 10 to those earnings, valuing the firm at $500 million.

The underwriters with whom they speak confirm that the firm would be worth $500 million if the average annual earnings of $50 million were expected to persist. But the underwriters, thinking about selling the stock to the potential diffuse public stockholders, say that they fear the earnings will not persist if the board remains weak, meeting only twice annually and receiving such poor information. Eventually there will be an external crisis in the firm's markets or an internal one in the firm's organization, and a weak, poorly informed board is likely to respond more slowly and less effectively than a stronger one. Eventually current managers will retire or be unable to manage the firm well, and a weak board will resolve a succession crisis less effectively than a strong one. Thus far, the underwriters say, the family has fulfilled the role that a strong board would play. But if the family leaves, the firm will at times be rudderless.

The underwriters put a value on the weak board if the firm lacks direction from the family owners, saying that over time they'd expect that earnings would be $40 million, not $50 million, if the board is weak and ineffective. They accord those earnings the same capitalization rate of 10, valuing the firm at $400 million, not $500 million.

The family and underwriters then consider charging up the board: they consider making the board meet monthly; they consider improving the information flow to the board; they consider adopting more transparent accounting, with statements going to the board well before the meetings; they consider instilling in the board an ethic of involvement; and they consider building aggressive audit, executive, and compensation committees. These improvements to the board, the family tells the underwriters, will reduce the monitoring and weak board problems, the expected earnings should then be re-pegged to $50 million, and the firm should be valued at the original $500 million in the initial public offer, not $400 million.

The underwriters respond that, yes, the board would be better. But, they ask, in whose interest would the board run the firm? With the supervisory board codetermined, the charged-up board would tilt more to labor when labor's and shareholders' interests conflict than would a purely shareholder-dominated board. Managers would be monitored more, but they would not necessarily be monitored in shareholders' interests. The enhanced board would create value, but some of that value will go to labor not stockholders. The underwriters conclude that the firm will indeed be worth $500 million, but $100 million of that value will go to labor. These numbers are not out-of-line with the current empirical work on the effect of the 1976 codetermination law, the one that expanded labor's representation from one-third of the supervisory boards of large firms to one-half. The data available show a 10 to 20 percent effect on shareholder value.[4]

---

[4] Felix R. FitzRoy & Kornelius Kraft, "Economic Effects of Codetermination," 95 *Scand. J. Econ.* 365 (1993); Frank A. Schmid & Frank Seger, "Arbeitnehmer Mitbestimmung, Allokation von Entscheidungsrechten und Shareholder Value," 5 *Zeitschrift für Betriebswirtschaft* 453 (1998); but see Theodor Baums & Bernd Frick, "The Market Value of the Codetermined Firm," in Margaret Blair & Mark J. Roe, eds., *Employees' Role in Corporate Governance*, p. 206 (1999) (finding no impact); Bernd Frick, Gerhard Speckbacker, & Paul Wentges, *Arbeitnehmermitbestimmung und moderne Theories der Unternehmung, Zeitschrift für Betriebswirtschaft*, pp. 745–63 (1998-V) (critiquing studies that showed codetermination as negatively affecting stock price).

The family wants to keep that $100 million. They can re-visit whether they should sell out completely. They may decide to keep the firm private and reexamine whether they can find an heir who will run it. Or they may hire professional managers to run the firm, if they have not done so already. Or they may sell the firm, but sell it not to diffuse stockholders who will discount the price because they would fear agency costs, but to another dominant owner, who need not discount the price because he or she can overcome those costs. Such block sales are common in Germany. To keep that $100 million difference, the family does *not* launch an IPO; hence there is one less public firm in Germany and one less family interested in seeing Germany developing a strong securities market.

And thus German social democracy, institutionalized in corporate governance via codetermination, induces this firm to stay private, so as to avoid the costs to shareholders of enhanced labor voice inside the firm. Social democracy in the form of supervisory board codetermination, hence, mixes badly with the public firm.

Social democracy's effects without codetermination

Social democracy's pressure on the public firm persists *even if we remove the formal institution of German supervisory board codetermination.*

(*a*) *General effects: favoring employees over shareholders* – Recall the basic agency costs to shareholders: unconstrained managers, unlike shareholders, prefer to expand their firms for more satisfaction, power, prestige, and pay. Managers want to avoid many profit-maximizing risks that would risk their careers. Managers prefer to use up capital in place rather than to restructure a firm, because restructuring is painful. And managers may be more willing to tolerate slack than would shareholders.

These managerial tendencies fit well with employees' goals, and a second basic corporate governance problem – for employees and capital-providers – is the persistent tension between invested capital and current employees, a tension muted in the US, but not muted everywhere. Employees *also* are averse to risks to the firm, as their human capital is tied up in the firm and they are not fully diversified. Employees *also* prefer that the firm expand, not downsize, because expanding often yields them promotion opportunities while downsizing risks leaving them unemployed.

(And institutional creditors, who loom larger in European firms than in their American counterparts, prefer to avoid risk and to maintain stability. Incompletely diversified family stockholders, the last key player in large continental European firms, also prefer stability more strongly than diversified American public firm stockholders. The key risk-avoiding pieces all fit together in continental Europe. The fit here may not be accidental. European history may have created a craving for stability, to overcome an unstable past. Corporate institutions that facilitate that stability survived. An American analyst (such as myself) sees the lack of a key corporate structure as a failing, but social democracy may not only have satisfied a European demand for stability but also produced a sense of solidarity that may have increased social welfare.)

On a simple level, employees prefer higher wages, shareholders prefer lower wages (at the same level of productivity). Because wages are not precisely determined, managers hold some discretion in setting wages; weakly monitored managers will not fight as strongly for shareholders as strongly monitored managers. Even in the US, slight differences in shareholder control of managers affect wage rates, with less-monitored managers, in states where anti-takeover laws are strong, conceding higher salaries to employees than where the laws are weak. On a more complex level, American managers of firms in declining industries tended in the 1980s to use up their equity capital before shrinking their firms unless corporate governance controls induced them not to use up equity first; this is the strategy that incumbent employees would prefer.

(b) Direct effects: softening change and raising agency costs – Social democracies favor incumbent employees. They act directly by insisting that firms not lay off employees; managers not tied tightly to shareholders will resist such efforts only weakly (because they do not pay for going along, but take a great deal of heat for resisting the government). Such governments will also seek to stabilize employment in firms with dominant stockholders, but dominant stockholders, with their own money on the line, can oftentimes resist the government's actions more vigorously.

(c) Indirect effects: rigid labor markets as raising agency costs – Even when social democratic employment policies affect diffusely held and closely held firms equally, these policies ought to affect ownership structure. Social democratic policies often make it hard to lay off workers, even during economic adversity.[5] True, *when* the firm faces adversity and seeks to downsize, each ownership structure faces the same constraints. Hence, one might (mistakenly) conclude that social democracies will not affect

---

[5] See "Des réactions politiques et syndicales sévères," *Le Monde*, Sept. 11, 1999, at 16, quoting the leader of the governing French party: "It's unacceptable that a large firm can decide to reduce employment simply to enhance shareholder profits."

the choice between ownership structures. But dominant stockholders would be more averse to expanding *ex ante* when labor markets are rigid than if employment rules were looser. Unconstrained managers often prefer to expand their firm, as is quite well developed in the managerial literature. Since they gain from expansion, but do not always pay the price if expansion turns out to be unprofitable, they may well (unless constrained) expand, their firms may deteriorate more, and in anticipation of this risk, stock has diffused into public markets less in social democracies than in more conservative nations, because in such nations the stock would have been worth less to diffuse stockholders than to close owners.

Government policies wedge open the gap between shareholders and employees, by creating laws and a social climate that make it harder for managers to downsize when technology demands downsizing or harder for managers to take risks with the enterprise when markets warrant it (from a shareholder perspective). They give employees more rights to resist change.[6] They construct nationwide bargaining platforms that favor employees, platforms in which "coalition costs" among shareholders are lower, and hence shareholders ought to be more successful, by acting cohesively. They see managers and employees as allied, and opposed to distant institutional shareholders,[7] who, because they merely seek financial gain, must be constrained.[8] Managers, already disposed for their own reasons to expand unnecessarily, to go slow when revamping the firm, to avoid risk,

---

[6] Cf. Arnaud Leparmentier, "L'Allemagne industrielle de nouveau conquérante," *Le Monde*, Nov. 28, 1998, at 1, 17 (Gerhard Schröder, when minister of Lower Saxony – he is now the German Prime Minister – had a steel mill nationalized rather than see it taken over by a foreign firm, because he did not want a restructuring that would affect the German employees); Alain Faujas, "Allemands et Italiens n'attendent rien de bon des entreprises," *Le Monde Economie*, June 1, 1999, at IV ("60 percent [of the French] feel that government regulation and taxes handicap French firms, but [they applaud this result] as 51 percent also say the State must more severely control firms to prevent them from degrading social conditions"); *ibid.* (a majority in each of Germany, Italy, and France believe "the firms' interests and the people's interest are not the same," while in Britain a majority thought the contrary).

[7] From a book well known in European business circles: "is the firm a simple piece of merchandise? Or is it a community *in which the stockholders' power is balanced by managerial power, which is in turn co-opted by the employees?*" Michel Albert, *Capitalisme contre Capitalisme*, p. 19 (1991) (translated from the French) (emphasis added); cf. David Charny, "Workers and Corporate Governance: The Role of Political Culture," in Margaret Blair & Mark Roe, eds., *Employees and Corporate Governance*, p. 91 (1999) (distinguishing labor/corporate governance regimes, as "hard," "soft," and "mixed").

[8] Frédéric Lemaître, "Le Succès de l'actionnariat salarié bouleverse le capitalisme français," *Le Monde*, Mar. 2, 1999, at 15, col. 1.

and to refuse to downsize, feel pressured to slow down further and face social opprobrium if they move too quickly. Managers who excessively expanded their enterprises in a strong social democracy would especially burden their shareholders, as reversing a mistaken expansion is hard to accomplish in a social democracy.

Strong social democracies raise the pressures on managers to abandon their shareholders and side with employees to do what managers want to do all along: expand, avoid risk, and avoid rapid change.

Social democracies, in short, raise managerial agency costs.

Social democracies and agency costs: shareholders' control of managers

Moreover, social democracies hinder, or break, the mechanisms that could control agency costs. When the gap separating managers from shareholders is small, some of the tools may not be worth their cost. Nations with lower agency costs may not need all of them. But as agency costs rise – as the gap between managers and shareholders widens – or as intense competition makes even a moderate gap harder to tolerate, the demand for gap-closing tools will rise. Social democracies not only widen the gap as we saw in the prior section, but make the gap-closing tools – shareholder wealth maximization norms, transparent accounting, incentive compensation, and hostile takeovers and proxy fights – harder to employ.[9]

That is, in the US, much corporate governance has the effect, and often the intention, of breaking managers' preference for continuance, excessive risk reduction, and over-expansion, the goals employees also prefer. When these governance devices succeed, they align managers more closely with shareholders than they would otherwise be aligned. They reduce the overlap between managers' goals and employees' goals, and enhance the overlap between managers' goals and distant stockholders' goals. Managers become stockholders themselves and get stock options that are valuable if their firm's stock price rises. Managers see their results "posted" daily in liquid stock markets. Managers are monitored by outside

---

[9] The US historically lacked some but not all of these tools, but its gap was smaller than elsewhere because American firms felt only weak social democratic pressures. In recent decades, intensified competition and technological change have called forth stronger tools than American shareholders previously needed. And, when American industries were less competitive, large firm oligopolies lost something from managerial agency costs, but gained oligopoly profits to spread around to shareholders, managers, and employees.

directors, whose lawyers tell them that they, the directors, work primarily for shareholders. Managers and directors are socialized in business school and at work to believe that shareholder wealth maximization is a valid norm, one that they should pursue. These tools are usually weaker, and sometimes denigrated, in a social democracy.[10]

Consider, for example, a soft control: a belief in shareholder wealth maximization. This norm, widespread in American business circles, surely affects what managers think about their tasks.[11] But it is not self-evident outside of American business circles that business be organized around a shareholder wealth maximization norm, a norm that does not inherently and directly derive from even a utilitarian norm: why *shareholders'* wealth, when shareholders make up such a small and already-favored part of society?[12] One answer is that this is the distributional "price" for getting good capital allocation. Another is that shareholder wealth roughly proxies for total wealth and no other norm is, right now, plausible to implement in diffusely owned firms: managers need, in this analysis, a measurable guide and *total* wealth maximization is too hard to measure and implement. But this "proxy" justification is theoretically contestable and widely disbelieved in social democracies. Managers there see more newscasts, read more articles, and have more conversations disparaging shareholder wealth maximization than their counterparts see, read, and have in a nonsocial democracy. Political leaders sympathize with employees more there than elsewhere. American labor has tolerated a corporate focus on profitability more willingly than has labor abroad.

Social atmosphere is important when managers have discretion, as they must have; the social pressures they feel affect how they exercise that

---

[10] For a detailed discussion, see Roe, *Political Determinants*, note 2 above.

[11] See, e.g., the famous essay by Milton Friedman, "The Social Responsibility of Business is to Increase its Profits," *N.Y. Times Magazine*, Sept. 13, 1970, at 33. Although aggressive when it appeared, in the US Friedman's perspective is now mainstream in business circles and not unthinkable then (as it may be in some social democracies now). Cf. Andrew Graham, "The UK 1979–95: Myths and Realities of Conservative Capitalism," in Colin Crouch & Wolfgang Streeck, eds., *The Political Economy of Modern Capitalism: Mapping Convergence and Diversity*, pp. 117, 119 (1997) (cultural primacy of profit in Margaret Thatcher's Britain); Michael E. Porter, "The Microeconomic Foundations of Economic Development," in *World Economic Forum, The Global Competitiveness Report* [1999], pp. 38, 42 ("In western Europe . . . the inability to place profitability as the central goal is . . . the greatest constraint to economic development.").

[12] Cf. Robert Kuttner, "Soaring Stocks: Are Only the Rich Getting Richer?" *Bus. Wk.*, Apr. 22, 1996, at 28 (wealthiest 20 percent own 98 percent of American stocks).

discretion. Weakly monitored public firm managers in social democracies find it psychologically hard to work primarily for shareholders. They believe themselves to be somewhat evil, or at least not wholly good, if they maximize shareholder value and tighten up the workplace.[13] Hence, they will do so only reluctantly, and sometimes not at all.

Incentives and techniques that would otherwise control and align managers with public shareholders are weak and used only sporadically. Labor market rigidities are more costly to shareholders of diffusely owned firm's than closely owned firms. The Berle-Means firm's higher relative cost to shareholders in social democracies reduces its incidence, and shareholders would seek another means of control, namely, direct control via block ownership.

II.   The data

Regressing ownership concentration on politics

We now have a simple, powerful theory that social democracies open up a gap between managers and distant stockholders, and that they impede firms from developing the tools that would close up that gap. What correlations should flow from the theory, and do the data confirm or contradict the predictions? We could compare political orientation with ownership structure, expecting that left nations would correlate with lower diffuse ownership and right nations with higher diffuse ownership.

So they do. Table 7.1 lists nations' politics from most left to most right, based on a poll of political scientists around the world.[14] Table 7.2 lists the nations' incidence of block ownership in their larger firms; those with the highest score have the fewest firms with concentrated ownership and, hence, their largest firms have the most diffuse ownership.[15] Table 7.3 shows the correlations' statistical significance, which is high.

---

[13] This antishareholder sentiment is hardly absent in the United States. It ebbs and flows, stronger during the years of Ralph Nader's 1970s Campaign GM, say, and weaker during the Reagan 1980s, but surely it is much weaker in the US than in continental Europe.

[14] The political data is from Thomas R. Cusack, "Partisan Politics and Public Finance: Changes in Public Spending in the Industrialized Democracies, 1955–1989," 91 *Public Choice* 375, 383–84 (1997), which arrays a survey from Francis G. Castles & Peter Mair, "Left-Right Political Scales: Some 'Expert' Judgments," 12 *European J. Pol. Sci.* 73 (1984).

[15] The ownership data and judgment are from Rafael La Porta, Florencio Lopez-de-Silanes, & Andrei Shleifer, "Corporate Ownership around the World," 54 *J. Fin.* 471, 492 (1999), who sought to show something else: that failure to protect minority stockholders is the primary determinant of a nation's inability to get diffusely held firms.

Table 7.1 *Political placement of richest nations' governments in 1980s*

Sweden	2.22
Austria	2.37
Australia	2.50
Norway	2.63
Finland	2.68
Italy	2.76
France	2.83
Netherlands	3.14
Belgium	3.16
Denmark	3.40
Switzerland	3.43
Canada	3.67
Germany	3.82
United States	3.92
Japan	4.00
United Kingdom	4.00

Table 7.2 *Percentage of widely held firms among twenty largest public firms*

Austria	0.05
Belgium	0.05
Italy	0.20
Norway	0.25
Sweden	0.25
Netherlands	0.30
Finland	0.35
Denmark	0.40
Germany	0.50
Canada	0.60
Switzerland	0.60
France	0.60
Australia	0.65
United States	0.80
Japan	0.90
United Kingdom	1.00

Table 7.3 *Regressing diffusion on politics*

	Regression coefficient (t-statistic)	Adjusted R-squared
Index of diffusion v. 1980–1991 political index (Table 7.2 v. Table 7.1)	0.33 (3.66*)	0.45
Index of diffusion v. four-decade political index (four-decade index available from author)	0.45 (5.23**)	0.63

*Significant at 0.005 level.
**Significant at 0.0005 level.

Discussion of data

Again, these results are statistically significant; the R-squared value suggests that political orientation explains quite a bit of the variation. The reader need not be reminded that correlation need not imply causation; the facts here though comport with the theory that social democracies drive a wedge between shareholders and managers, and thereby raise agency costs.

One should be cautious in interpreting these statistical results. True, they are strikingly strong in that the indices are only partly tuned to the political hypothesis I've set out here. But first, the ownership index does not include privately held firms that have never gone public. European accounts say these are many, but systematic, comparable data for these nations is unavailable. (It's not surprising, based on the political thesis here, that such financial data for the strongest social democracies is not easy to uncover; some owners keep their firms private to keep their profile low.) The twenty largest US firms are nearly all public firms; the twenty largest firms in each European country may include several fully private firms. If so, better data here should strengthen the political hypothesis.

Second, the ownership index uses each nation's twenty largest firms. Perhaps there is a size beyond which *only* public firms can exist, because, for example, private parties lack the wealth to take on a major ownership interest. If only the US economy has historically been big enough to generate twenty of these very big firms, then size not politics might be the underlying determinant. But one can correct for size, by using the twenty largest firms in each economy worth just over $500 million. Elsewhere I do so and find that the powerful political correlation persists.[16] Size is not the primary determinant.

Third, the political indices are based on the averaging of a poll of political scientists who rated political parties from left to right on a numerical scale[17]; characteristics beyond economic issues, such as nuclear disarmament, race, and other non-economic issues surely figured into the judgment. These characteristics only roughly correlate with the economic left–right scale that would be the best foundation for this study. For example, the French conservative parties were consistently rated as more conservative than the American Democratic Party,[18] although on economic issues I see them as to the left of the Democratic Party. Despite the "noise," politics correlates with ownership concentration.

We can reduce this third problem by looking at another measure of the strength of a nation's social democracy, the extent it compresses incomes and reduces inequality. A standard measure of income inequality, the Gini coefficient, can relate the richest nations' relative tolerance for inequality and, hence, the relative strength of social democracy. Elsewhere I report correlations between income inequality to diffuse ownership: nations that refuse to tolerate much inequality have fewer diffusely owned public firms and much more concentrated ownership.[19] A second rough measure of social democracy could be government spending as a percentage of gross domestic product; this also yields a statistically strong correlation. And the OECD has comparative measures of legally mandated employment protection. Stronger protection persistently predicts weaker ownership diffusion, as Figure 7.1 shows. And on the ownership side, one would want an alternative to the concentration indices prevailing in the finance literature, because these indices include government ownership blocks (a social democratic factor to be sure, but not one that is the focus of this chapter) and do not include privately held firms that never have gone public. An alternative index measures the size of each nation's stock market in proportion to the size of its economy, data that the OECD puts together. I substituted this for the concentration index, re-ran the regressions, and the statistical strength persisted, as I show elsewhere.[20] We thus have several measures of concentration and several proxies for social democracy; all the correlations between social democracy and ownership concentration and weak securities markets were strong.

---

[16] See Roe, *Political Determinants*, note 2 above.
[17] Castles & Mair, "Left-Right Political Scales," note 14 above.
[18] Ibid., at 78, 83.   [19] See Roe, *Political Determinants*, note 2 above.   [20] See ibid.

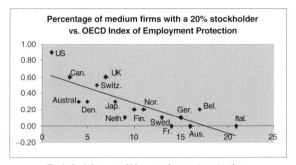

Figure 7.1 Employment protection as predicting ownership separation in the wealthy west

But while the correlations are strong, a sample of the world's sixteen richest nations isn't big enough to readily test out the comparative power of *other* explanations. But we cannot extend the sample, because the poorer nations are not economically "ripe" for large public firms. So, the nature of legal systems (common law vs. civil law) has been advanced as helping to explain ownership concentration, with French and German systems protecting minority stockholders badly.[21] We would want to test out the comparative explanatory power of politics and law, by, say, finding those nations that protect minority stockholders well, *but* are strong social democracies, and then see the density of public firms there. If such nations regularly had diffuse ownership, the legal theory would seem stronger; but if they had concentrated ownership, the political explanation would seem to trump the law-based one. A few nations fit this category: good law, strong social democracy, but few public firms.[22] The theory is not that corporate law is unimportant: transition economies that fail to produce satisfactory legal institutions may never get public firms, regardless of whether social democratic policies are strong; rather the argument here

---

[21] La Porta *et al.*, note 15 above.

[22] Data suggests that Denmark, Germany, Norway, and Sweden have good minority shareholder protections but weak ownership diffusion. They have all been social democratic nations. See Mark J. Roe, "Corporate Law's Limits," 31 *J. Legal Studies* 233 (2002).

is that *in Europe and the wealthy west,* legal differences are joined, and perhaps overshadowed by, political differences.

Thus the correlations here make for, in a lawyer's rhetoric, a *prima facie* case that political placement affects structure, but doesn't give us a clear sense how heavily to weight the political explanation against the prevailing more standard ones. Hence, the discussion of competing theories needs also to be qualitative, not quantitative, and I offer that discussion next, by looking behind the numbers at several of the nations, such as France, Germany, Italy, Sweden, the United Kingdom, and the United States. Such a qualitative, nation-by-nation look tends to buttress the political theory.

Qualitative discussion of selected nations

France

Qualitative French business histories are consistent with the social democracy thesis. Consider Charles Kindleberger's perhaps hyperbolic description in a standard work of European economic history:

> [The French family firm] is said to have sinned against economic efficiency . . . by failing . . . to extend into new markets . . . Public sale of stock was avoided . . . Recruiting was undertaken from within the family, except for faithful retainers who assisted the firm against the revolutionary working force.[23]

Profitable French firms that sought to downsize have been excoriated in the press by political leaders, with political threats made to deny them discretionary government benefits if they persisted.[24] Employee stock ownership was promoted as a means to resist takeovers,[25] presumably especially those that would have led to lay-offs and downsizing. Reports to the French Prime Minister extolled employee stock ownership not for the perhaps denigrated Anglo-Saxon reasons of promoting employee loyalty and motivation, but to shift the balance of power inside the firm

---

[23] Charles P. Kindleberger, *Economic Growth in France and Britain*, p. 115 (1964).

[24] "Michelin," *Le Monde*, Sept. 23, 1999; David Owen, "Provision Put Brakes on Michelin," *Fin. Times*, Mar. 15, 2000, at 20 (the Prime Minister's "remarks were seen as a warning that there were limits to the extent to which big French companies should adopt aggressive Anglo-American style profits-oriented tactics.").

[25] Laurent Mauduit, "M. Jospin ouvre avec précaution le dossier de l'épargne salariale," *Le Monde*, Jan. 29, 2000, at 6.

away from owners and to employees.[26] Modern French managers have been socialized in two elite schools – two small state schools, l'Ecole nationale d'administration and l'Ecole polytechnique, account for half of the managers and directors of France's leading firms[27] – to think more of national progress than of shareholder profit maximization.[28]

One might believe that the "real" reason for low separation in France is its statist, dirigiste political orientation. If the bureaucrats disrupt the stock market, then innovations that make such markets work will be undermined and investors will go elsewhere. The difficulty with this view is that a statist government that is *conservative and pro-investor* could *promote* the stock market. Indeed, before World War I, the best current data show,[29] French stock markets were developing nicely, better by some measures than the American markets. France *was* statist and dirigiste back then, *but* it was much more conservative. A statist but *conservative* regime can copy another nation's legal and institutions innovations, save on the expense of innovation, and promote stock markets. It might be late, but it won't *suppress* the securities markets. The question is not whether the nation is statist, but whether it's inclined to be friendly to stock markets. When France was friendly, stock markets flourished. When it wasn't, they didn't.

By mid-twentieth century (after the French economy was essentially re-set to ground zero during World War II), France was still statist but it was no longer reliably conservative. Left-oriented parties were popular, won elections, and induced the whole political spectrum to move leftwards, a move that has only halted and reversed quite recently. Before the spectrum started to shift back, it was true that French policy tended to undermine, or not support stock markets, but the cause wasn't pure dirigisme. It was due to the politicians (and those who elected them) having little sympathy with capitalism, stock markets, and securities institutions. Those who point to the French governments' hostility or indifference here are (merely?)

---

[26] Ministère de l'Economie, des Finances et de l'Industrie, *Rapport au Premier Ministre sur l'epargne salariale*, Jan. 2000, at 2, Pt II, pp. 8–10, 15.

[27] Cf. Michel Bauer, *Administrateurs et Dirigeants du CAC 40* (Report of CNRS Observatoire des Dirigeants, Sept. 1997).

[28] Cf. François Hollande, "Pour une extension des stock-options à l'ensemble du personnel," *Le Monde*, Oct. 7, 1999, at 6 (leader of France's governing socialist party says that "although our goal is not to socialize the means of production, one can neither leave the private sector without rules . . . nor allow stockholders alone to decide, without any input from employees, what to do solely due to shareholders' purely financial interests").

[29] Rahhuram G. Rajan & Luigi Zingales, "The Politics of Financial Development" (Aug. 1999) (University of Chicago Working Paper).

pointing to one manifestation of their social democracy and one of the mechanisms by which social democracy undermined stock markets and the separation of ownership from control.

Germany

Germany's formal board structure strongly illustrates the "social democracy" effect, as we saw in section II. German boards for large firms *must* have half of the directors from labor. This codetermination affected boardrooms. Meetings were infrequent, the information background was weak, and the meetings were quite formal; codetermination made it hard for shareholders and managers to charge up the boardrooms with frequent, substantive, well-informed meetings, because to do so would have enhanced labor's voice and authority inside the firm. Managers and shareholders preferred not to further empower labor, so they weakened (or failed to strengthen) the boardroom.

Shareholders control managers otherwise. Dominant blockholders meet managers informally outside of the boardroom. Were ownership diffuse, shareholders would lose this means of monitoring managers, and shareholder value would presumably decline. With the board codetermined, shareholders could find the alternative of a more powerful boardroom unattractive: if they charged up the boardroom to better monitor managers, they'd make labor more powerful. The trade-off for shareholders – better monitoring of managers versus more powerful labor influence – might be tough to make; shareholding might therefore remain concentrated so that shareholders can avoid making the trade-off.[30]

This trade-off helps to explain the resistance Germany has had to changing corporate and securities laws, accounting practice, and other institutions to better support diffuse ownership. Germany has had little problem in writing and passing good laws in other areas, or in building effective bureaucracies. True, public choice pressures could explain the result – banks prefer not to see good securities markets develop and family owners want their perquisites to persist. But public choice resistance can sometimes be overcome, and it's plausible that when it isn't, it's because countervailing pressures for reform do not come from shareholders, managers, and policymakers. The countervailing pressures might not come because these players cannot profit from going public in Germany's social democracy, with Germany's boardroom structure.

[30] Mark J. Roe, "German Codetermination and German Securities Markets," 1998 *Col. Bus. L. Rev.* 167.

Italy

Italy has many small family-owned firms and few public firms. A simple legal theory, one based solely on poor minority stockholder protection, is plausible for Italy, which is reputed to have a slow and inefficient court system.[31] Indeed, the direction in the statistics supports the idea that a factor beyond politics is at play in Italy: its firms are even less diffusely owned than political placement would predict. Weak corporate law though may be only part of the story even in Italy. Players dissatisfied with basic corporate law have not been unable to use contract to give themselves the private law rules that they want.[32] Economic-based social conflict has been historically high, labor-influenced political parties powerful, and a communist party that for several decades was supported by a quarter of the Italian electorate. Italian Christian Democratic governments fostered small closely held businesses, because they thought employees would identify with owners in small firms, but oppose them, especially distant owners, in large firms. Large firms provoked more social tension than smaller closely held ones.[33]

Japan

Japan doesn't fit as a traditional social democracy, but post-World War II Japanese social history might be consistent with the thesis. As is well known to Japanese economic historians, the Japanese main bank system was not a traditional element of Japanese corporate structure, but one that developed strongly after World War II.

Labor history in Japan also suggests the importance of post-World War II developments. Lifetime employment was not a key Japanese labor institution before the war. Rather, it developed after the war, partly in response to vicious labor conflict,[34] as managers and other leaders sought to bring enough peace to Japanese factories to allow production to go forward. At roughly the same time, the main bank system, by which banks

---

[31] Cf. Luigi Zingales, "The Value of the Voting Right: A Study of the Milan Stock Exchange Experience," 7 *Rev. Fin. Stud.* 125 (1994).

[32] Minority stockholders in Mediaset, Silvio Berlusconi's principal corporate vehicle – Berlusconi is the former Prime Minister and has a wheeler-dealer reputation – insisted on a corporate charter term super-majority board approval for any related-party transaction. (They expected board representation and, hence, veto power. Board approval for such transactions is not required under Italian corporate law, but contract could fill the gap.)

[33] Linda Weiss, *Creating Capitalism: The State and Small Business since 1945*, pp. 104–05, 127–37 (1988).

[34] Ronald J. Gilson & Mark J. Roe, "Lifetime Employment: Labor Peace and the Evolution of Japanese Corporate Governance," 99 *Colum. L. Rev.* 508 (1999).

owned noticeable blocks of stock of large industrial firms and had a say in their governance, independently expanded.

The labor institution did not have to induce the ownership institution for the political theory here to be confirmed. All that is needed is for the two to have been stable complements once each arose, even if one did not induce the other. Some leading commentators on the Japanese firm say that they indeed do operate as complements.[35]

Sweden

The world's first democratically elected socialist government took power in Sweden in 1920. It has been for quite some time the paradigm of the social welfare state, with cradle-to-grave social coverage.

Sweden presents variants of the political theory here. First, Sweden is reputed to have a good corporate law that protects minority stockholders. That is, a leading explanation for why concentrated ownership persists is that if minority stockholder protection is poor, outsiders buy stock only reluctantly, or only at a steep discount. Their reluctance translates into heavy ownership concentration and few public firms. But by conventional measures Swedish institutions protect minority stockholders well: not only are there no anecdotes of insider blockholders diverting value to themselves,[36] but the premium for voting stock, a measure of the value of control (and the opportunity to divert value into the controllers' pockets) is low, approaching that prevailing in the United States, at about 7 percent.[37] Outsiders could buy without gross fear of expropriation

---

[35] Masahiko Aoki, "Unintended Fit," in Masahiko Aoki, ed., *The Role of Government in East Asian Economic Development* (1997).

[36] Jonas Agnblad, Erik Berglöf, Peter Högfeldt, & Helena Svancar, "Ownership and Control in Sweden: Strong Owners, Weak Minorities, and Social Control," in Fabrizio Barca & Marco Becht, eds., *The Control of Corporate Europe*, p. 228 (2001).

[37] See Zingales, note 31 above, at 146–47 (1994); cf. Clas Bergström & Kristian Rydqvist, "Ownership of Equity in Dual-Class Firms," 14 *J. Banking & Fin.* 255, 267 (1990) ("data do not support the argument that dual classes are used [in Sweden] for wealth expropriation by holding control with little equity"); Clas Bergström & Kristian Rydqvist, "The Determinants of Corporate Ownership: An Empirical Study on Swedish Data," 14 *J. Banking & Fin.* 237 (1990) ("the value of control does not derive from the possibility to expropriate the fringe of minority shareholders . . . *[but] has to be motivated by some other economic motives*") (emphasis supplied); Martin Holmén & Peter Högfeldt, "Corporate Control and Security Design in Initial Public Offerings," pp. 38, 39 (Stockholm School of Economics working paper, Dec. 15, 1999) ("Outside shareholders do not refrain f[ro]m investing on the Stockholm Stock Exchange since 55 percent of the Swedish population own shares . . . and 33 percent of outstanding shares are owned by foreign investors . . . [T]he ratio of the stock market capitalization held by minority shareholders in relation to GDP . . . is

from insiders; and insiders could sell and diversify without taking a gross discount. Yet they do not.[38]

Second, closely related to the legal theory is a theory based on trust. In mistrustful cultures, outsiders will greatly fear the depredations of insiders. But if trust is high and insiders will no more steal from outside stockholders than would citizens steal an unlocked bicycle, outsiders will entrust their investments to insiders. Sweden is a high trust society. Yet ownership remains concentrated, despite the high level of trust. Outsiders feel protected, but public securities markets are poorly developed.

Third, Swedish ownership has a high disjunction between cash flow rights and control rights. That is, the controlling family, often the Wallenberg family, has, say, 51 percent of the company's votes, but gets a smaller fraction of the company's profits. It does so by building ownership pyramids (by which it owns 51 percent of the "top" holding company, which in turn owns 51 percent of an intermediate company, which in turn owns 51 percent of other intermediate companies, until finally a lower-level company owns 51 percent of the operating company) or by using dual-class common stock (in which one class of stock gets 10 votes per share and another 1 vote per share).

Complex and intricate theories have arisen to explain the use of pyramids, dual-class structures, and nonvoting stock. The most sophisticated rely on the owner seeking to protect the rents it gets from controlling the firm. That is, the controller is reluctant to leave control "up for grabs" because if the controller dips below 51 percent control of the operating company, an outsider could grab a majority and then reap the benefits of control.[39] The theory is plausible. However, in its current stark form, it cannot explain the Swedish situation well, or at all, because Sweden is said to protect minority stockholders well. Hence, in Sweden, little of value would be left "up for grabs" by controlling shareholders who exited and diversified.

0.51 for Sweden compared to 0.58 for the US . . . Thus, *it is not likely that weak investor protection has hampered financial market development in Sweden*") (emphasis supplied).

[38] German results are similar. When a block is sold, the sales premium reflects the benefit to the blockholder of diverting value from the outside stockholders. But the premium is only 10 percent, about that of the control premium in the United States, and not much different than the 7 percent voting premium in dual-class companies. Julian Franks & Colin Mayer, 14 *Review of Financial Studies* 943 (2001). Blockholders seem not to be diverting much more value *from minority stockholders* in Germany than in the US.

[39] See Lucian Arye Bebchuk, "A Rent Protection Theory of Corporate Ownership and Control" (Working Paper, 1999).

Adding employees and social democratic pressures back into the Swedish equation lets us explain the Swedish ownership concentration. Social democracy affects ownership in two ways here. First, the concentrated owner has stronger incentives than the Berle-Means managers to avoid giving up too much in shareholder value to social pressures. Although an owner whose 51 percent in control rights corresponded to equal cash flow rights would have even greater incentives to retain shareholder value, the issue here is one of relative strength. The pyramid, dual-class, or nonvoting structure is less than ideal in providing incentives, but it still motivates a focused owner to deflect some social pressures: (a) a lot of the controller's wealth is still on the line, and (b) the structure preserves the controller's authority even while cash flow rights decline.

Moreover, if the concentrated owner is progressive, has a social conscience, and is not a thirsty shareholder-wealth-maximizer, then the political authorities and voters may prefer the incumbent over someone else who might grab control. That is, the authorities may prefer to avoid government ownership for its well-known inefficiencies, but not want the crass, cold market as the alternative. If the Swedish incumbents, such as the Wallenbergs, are "soft" players, who can cooperate with a social democratic ethos, then it may well be the social democratic forces who want to stop control from going "up for grabs." If control were "up for grabs," an American-style shareholder-wealth-maximizer might grab control, tighten the workplace, and undermine the social democratic program.[40]

Rents are to be protected, but they're not the ordinary owner's rents from control (because the evidence is that value diversions in Sweden are low), but the *political* rents that a social democracy produces for the firm's employees and political players.

Second, social democracies level wealth and income. While they raise the "incentive" to focus control, they constrict the "supply" of rich people with the wealth to own very large industrial companies. *When technology and scale economies demand very large industrial firms, and when social democratic pressures demand focused ownership but reduce the number of wealthy people, then tools to yield control without vast wealth will be demanded.* Pyramids, dual-class structures, and non-voting stock are the typical such tools. Sweden, like several of the other social democracies, has them.

---

[40] Cf. Almar Latour & Greg Steinmetz, "Swedish Giant: Barnevik Set about Task of Preserving Wallenberg Empire," *Wall St. J.*, May 18, 1998, at A1 (Wallenbergs resist outside shareholders' wealth maximization goals as "not [necessarily] serving society's best interests").

United Kingdom

The United Kingdom would seem the hardest case for the political theory here, in that by reputation Britain has had a deep securities market for quite some time, but has been on both sides of the fence politically, having been a strong social democracy for a good part of this century, and having been one of the planet's economically most conservative nations since 1979.

But the UK *also* seems to fit badly with a law-driven theory. A competing theory to the political theory is that law protecting minority stockholders is the key to creating diffuse ownership, with family-founders turning their firms over to professional managers by selling out into the stock market. British common law judges are said to have protected minority stockholders well. Yet, leading business historians, such as Alfred Chandler, say flatly that the largest British firms were family-dominated as late as World War II, and that family influence and control persisted well after then as well.[41] Chandler blames family control for Britain's industrial decline in the mid-twentieth century.

This persistent family ownership during Britain's social democratic era seems consistent with the political theory, but not with a legal theory: if law protected the minority stockholders, why didn't the families sell out and diversify quickly (as some eventually started to do in the 1970s, and many did in the conservative 1980s[42])? Many of these families were still block-owners in the 1970s. (The "managerial revolution heralded by Berle and Means in 1932 has probably not yet happened [here] . . . : over 55 percent of the largest 250 UK industrial companies [are] under owner control" said one authority in 1980, and, not anticipating the results in the subsequent two decades, concluded: "most [British] firms are unlikely ever to become controlled by their own professional

---

[41] Alfred P. Chandler, *Scale and Scope* 242 (1990); Alfred D. Chandler, Jr. and Herman Daems, "Introduction," in Alfred D. Chandler, Jr. & Herman Daems, eds., *Managerial Hierarchies: Comparative Perspectives on the Rise of the Modern Industrial Enterprise*, p. 6 (1980) ("Until World War II, the British economy was for the most part an example of family capitalism."); Leslie Hannah, "Visible and Invisible Hands in Great Britain," in Chandler & Daems, eds., *Managerial Hierarchies*, pp. 41, 53 ("The separation of ownership and control . . . had not progressed far enough to displace founding or family directors from company boards[;] . . . 119 [out of the 200 largest firms in Britain], or 59.5 percent, [had founding or family directors] in 1948").

[42] Cf. Michael J. Brennan & Julian Franks, "Underpricing, Ownership and Control in Initial Public Offerings of Equity Securities in the UK," 45 *J. Fin. Econ.* 391, 407 at table 7 (1997) (nondirector family stockholders exit, going from 44 percent of the stock pre-IPO to 3 percent seven years later; insiders who remain as directors do not exit as rapidly).

managers".[43]) But within several years, by the mid-1980s, many of these families were in fact gone from the largest British firms[44]; Britain's revolution from the right in 1979 made, on the theory presented here, the fully public, diffusely owned firm a more viable entity.

Yet, Britain by many measures had deeper securities markets and more public firms than much of the rest of the world, *earlier in the twentieth century*, even though families held on to blocks and managerial positions until quite late in the century. To explain this pattern, a synthesis of the minority-protection theory and the political theory works well. That is, British institutions protected minority stockholders, so that family owners could sell much stock even in the early twentieth century without too severe a discount. Yet during that time, class conflict was often severe.[45] The potential for high agency costs in the managerial firm was there and, hence, the family owners had reason to retain concentrated ownership. This hybrid theory seems to explain the British facts: (a) a long history of firms going public; (b) family retention of control in many public firms until well after World War II (when good law arguably protected the minority stockholders and politics made concentration desirable for shareholders); and (c) a sell-off by the family owners in the late 1970s and in the 1980s (when Britain's lurch to the economic right made diffuse ownership more stable).[46]

---

[43] Arthur Francis, "Families, Firms and Financial Capital: The Development of UK Industrial Firms with Particular Reference to their Ownership and Control," 14 *Brit. J. Sociology* 29 (1980); cf. Steven Nyman & Aubrey Silberston, "The Ownership and Control of Industry," 30 *Oxford Econ. Papers* (74): 74, 85–86 (1978) (our "evidence . . . of [British industrial ownership in 1975, with at least 40 percent of the 250 largest firms having a dominant blockholder, and would show more if nominee shares were identifiable] shows that the extent of managerial control is more limited than has been thought and may not have an inexorable tendency to increase."

[44] John Scott, "Corporate Control and Corporate Rule: Britain in an International Perspective," 41 *Brit. J. Sociology* 351, 366–67 (1990) ("decline of family control" from 1976 to 1988).

[45] Neville Kirk, *Change, Continuity and Class: Labour in British Society* 159, 166 (1998).

[46] On another note, I earlier argued that America's populist financial politics precluded a hand-off early in the twentieth century from the family owners to financial institution which might have taken large blocks of stock, were they permitted to do so. Some have posed Britain's history as a counter-example. The facts, however, are not really supportive of this critique. Britain's financial institutions didn't take the blocks, *but the families did not fully sell out until later in the twentieth century*. By contrast the drive in the United States to build tremendous enterprises in the much larger American economy at the beginning of the twentieth century induced a demand for size and a demand for a new ownership form (apart from family ownership). Britain didn't have this impulse, because it was smaller.

This political interaction with ownership structure helps to explain Chandler's conundrum: if the British families held on to control (as Chandler reports), and ran many firms into the ground (as he argues), why didn't they sell out when they got bored with running their firms? Many offer cultural accounts to explain the result. But perhaps more was at work. Family owners may have run their firms badly, but when class conflict was rife, perhaps the alternative to family control was *worse* for owners.

* * *

Timing and path dependence are important in understanding Britain: Britain's social democracy arose well *after* its basic securities markets were well developed. Had investors and companies tried to develop stock markets *for the first time in, say, the 1950s*, they would have had a much rougher time than they did earlier in the century. But when Britain lurched to the left, *stock markets already were in place*, and the institutions had more than a little staying power.[47] British political authorities could implement their goals by nationalizing target industrial firms; they didn't need to undermine all stock market institutions (although they might not have supported them were they first emerging then). I suspect that one would find that neither stock markets nor ownership separation grew much during this political period; they trod water and survived, and then only because *other* changes were higher on the political authorities' agenda.

Path dependence can mean that an institution could persist even if the environment would not call it forth at that time.[48] British securities markets and the initial, modest steps toward separation arose when Britain was conservative and laissez-faire. Later, when British politics alternated between social democracy and mainstream conservatism (and then stepped toward strong conservatism in 1979), the institutions in

---

[47] Brian Cheffins and John Coffee believe that this British example fully undermines the social democracy thesis. But they exaggerate its importance. Had strong British securities markets and ownership separation arisen *at the time of the social democracy, instead of well before*, then the example – the best they have – would be more telling. Or, for it to be useful, they need to show that British securities markets and ownership separation were proceeding at the same rate as before Britain became social democratic, and after it became social democratic. This they don't do. Those data are not readily available, so they should hardly be faulted here for not spending two years of research uncovering the data, but the secondary indications (size of the security market – it wasn't growing – and Chandler's and others' qualitative observations of persistent family domination even of public companies), both point in the *opposite* direction from the one they need. Separation was slow, or perhaps nonexistent, during that era.

[48] See Mark J. Roe, "Chaos and Evolution in Law and Economics," 109 *Harv. L. Rev.* 641 (1996); Lucian A. Bebchuk & Mark J. Roe, "A Theory of Path Dependence in Corporate Ownership and Governance," 52 *Stan. L. Rev.* 127 (1999).

place persisted, but didn't seem to grow. The City's institutions presented an interest group that could resist some change. They also were a source of revenue (from trading in international securities) that even social democratic governments might not have wanted to demolish. Moreover, even here one wouldn't want to dismiss the possibility of there having been moderate social democratic effects: the City had reason to fear nationalization during Britain's social democratic era, and this social democratic fear accounts for some of their passivity in corporate governance: if they took the lead in rationalizing an industry, and the disruption engendered salience and opposition, nationalization (the result for French financial institutions) would have been more likely. This they understood. And, hence, better to be quiet.

United States

Why has the United States had fewer social conflicts of the type that would debilitate the public firm? The reasons why it has had less conflict, and hence more diffuse ownership, correspond to the reasons why a strong socialist movement did not arise in the United States.

Mobility, both geographic and economic, has been high, or at least the average person has believed it high.[49] Dissatisfied people have blamed their local circumstances (which they thought they could change, by heading out West or by getting another job) more than their class position. Hence, class conflict was less likely. And incipient conflicts were violently suppressed.[50]

The US has also had a long and deep antigovernment bias, so citizens have not looked as longingly to government to resolve problems as Europeans did. Economic conflict was not absent in the US, but manifested itself differently than in Europe, often leading politicians to break up concentrations of economic power, a result that further propelled the public firm, because there were fewer financial institutions that could build up large American firms at the end of the nineteenth century than there otherwise would have been.[51]

In the nineteenth century, America systematically destroyed strong financial institutions: American voters historically tended to be intolerant

---

[49] Frederick Jackson Turner, *The Frontier in American History* (1920).

[50] See, e.g., John R. Commons, "Is Class Conflict in America Growing and is it Inevitable?" 13 *Am. J. Soc.* 756 (1908), reprinted in Malcolm Rutherford & Warren J. Samuels, eds., *III Classics in Institutional Economics*, pp. 112, 120 (1997).

[51] Mark J. Roe, *Strong Managers, Weak Owners: The Political Roots of American Corporate Finance* (1994).

of big government *and* of big private finance. This fragmenting of finance may also have later diluted other social conflict, *by removing the visible targets of a strong social democracy movement*; and, with the visible targets gone, norms like shareholder-wealth-maximization flourished more easily than they otherwise would have. (Similarly, destroying family control in continental Europe could reduce subsequent social conflict sufficiently so that managerial agency cost control institutions could emerge in the newly created public firms.) Political packages might be complementary: American politics can tolerate pro-shareholder institutions, if the typical shareholder is CalPERS, not J.P. Morgan. European politics can tolerate large, influential stockholders, banks and families, as long as it also stabilizes employment and circumscribes the range of actions of the stockholders, bankers, and the family owners.

Moreover, ethnic conflict in the US has been deep, at times vicious. For some of the social conflict that would affect the Berle-Means firm to express itself in the political arena, employees would have had to act together or politicians would have had to appeal to all employees to elect them to enact a common program.[52] But if ethnic divisions – principally based on race – made it historically hard for American politicians to make an economic appeal across racial lines, then the kinds of conflicts that increased agency costs in public firms on the European continent became rarer in the US.[53]

Extending the sample?

One could extend the "sample" to include more nations outside of western Europe, developed Asia, and North America, adding, say, Thailand, Malaysia, Nigeria, and Argentina. But extension would reveal little, because too many of these nations have not yet arrived economically at the point where their economies demand many large firms. And some lack the basic institutions needed for a very advanced economy, such as a capacity to enforce contract and to define property rights effectively. More telling is to look at those nations that have already developed many

---

[52] See, e.g., Commons, note 50 above at 118–19; John R. Commons, "History of Labor in the United States: 1896–1932," (1935), reprinted in Rutherford and Samuels, eds., *III Classics in Institutional Economics*, pp. 438, 455.

[53] Cf. E. E. Schattschneider, *The Semi-sovereign People: A Realist's View of Democracy in America* (1960) (politicians seek to divide the electorate on issues in which the divider will be allied with a majority of the division). I hardly mean that only the US has had ethnic conflict, but that America's long simmering race and ethnic divisions stymied economic-based coalitions that arose in many other nations.

of the needed institutions, and have a high demand for large economic units, but for which politics in some of them makes some institutions function poorly or not worth building.

III. Alternative formulations of the thesis

Political change and time-series data

As politics changes, ownership structure could also change. Thus one could try to measure political change and see if ownership changes. But this kind of longitudinal study is not technically possible right now – the multination historical ownership data are either unavailable or unreliable. Moreover, there are surely lags, of uncertain length, in economic reaction to political change. And, most importantly, one would need to hold the *other* conditions constant. Economic, technological, and institutional conditions have changed greatly during the past decades. Economies used to be less competitive – American industry tended toward oligopoly, European firms were small and largely confined to their national economy, and globalization was an idea then for the future. Weaker competition produced more organizational slack, some of which was "spent" in looser ownership and organizational arrangements.[54] It will be hard, or impossible, to do a time-series test that holds these other conditions constant and measures only politics' effects on ownership structure.

But in gross, the recent shifts in Europe are consistent with the social democracy thesis. Economic policy has moved rightward in recent decades in Europe. One cannot simply measure "social democracy" by the name of the political parties in power, as their programs have changed, with social democratic parties becoming less interventionist and less hostile to shareholders. This shift could lead to other predictions: as economic politics has moved rightward, diffuse ownership has become more feasible in Europe. As it becomes more feasible, the demand from policymakers and investors could increase (as it has) for institutions that better support diffuse ownership.

Political change and alternative formulations of the thesis

I have thus far looked on the political players as public-regarding actors with sincerely held views seeking to build the good society, and in social

---

[54] Mark J. Roe, "Rents and their Corporate Consequences," 53 *Stan. L. Rev.* 1463 (2001).

democracies that vision differs from the one prevailing in the US. Those holding these ideologies might seek to maximize social well-being, but in doing so they reduce the incidence of public firms, securities markets, and diffuse ownership. One can, however, look more crudely at the phenomena, as simple rent-seeking.

Social democracy as rent-seeking

Interest groups seek laws and structures that benefit themselves. So, one could see social democracies as labor's crude but successful rent-seeking. (Or see conservative nations as financial interests' crude but successful rent-seeking.) Ideology may help or retard success of one group or another, but in this public choice view it is raw self-seeking that is at stake. Labor wins in the name of stability in some nations; shareholders win in the name of fluid capital markets in other nations. Concerted arrangements via tripartite corporatist bargaining characterize some nations, as the three players – labor, owners, and the government – negotiate corporatist deals. This is not exactly social democracy, but it is government (often) taking labor's side in negotiations inside the firm.

Or simple micro-economic foundations

We could begin without using social democracy, by viewing the firm as having three inputs: capital, management, and labor. We could begin the abstraction with labor institutions determined first, with capital and management variable. If labor markets are rigid, with employees "owning" their jobs, then management and capital structures will evolve differently there than in economies with fluid labor markets, where employees have few "property" rights in their jobs. Capital, but not management, would be reluctant to expand.

Concentrated ownership as facilitating social democratic politics

I have thus far relentlessly viewed politics as independent of business structure, with social democracy inducing, or strengthening, concentrated ownership structures. But causation may run the other way, at least at times.

German codetermination again provides a concrete example. Earlier in this century, the visible power of Germany's large banks, people's envy and resentment of rich industrialists, and the disorientation and anomie induced by Germany's rapid transformation from an agricultural nation to an industrial one helped call forth codetermination to tame the bankers and industrialists, and to give the workers a voice in the strange new industrial enterprises. Corporate structure may have *induced* politics then, as much as it was induced by politics. Not all productive arrangements are equally stable politically; some induce political opposition, some a democratic polity finds more acceptable.[55] Social democracy and concentrated ownership mutually reinforce one another.

Rent-seeking in small national economies

Business structure may induce social democratic politics in another way. Many of the strongest social democracies have been small nations, in which product markets have been less competitive, because only a few firms can reach efficient economies of scale. Weaker competition produces rents – profits above those needed by capital to invest – and these rents can be captured not just by the capital-owners but shared with managers and employees. There is thus more "give" and more of a possibility of successful rent-seeking through government and social action when there are supra-competitive profits. These rents may also strengthen social democracy by increasing envy and perceived unfairness. And they may provide more to fight over. Rent-seeking employees may win more often in small economies, especially those whose oligopolistic firms are not fully exposed to world markets.[56]

When product market competition is fierce, rents are reduced and excess profits competed away. One reason for American exceptionalism is that the American economy has been more competitive, making rents in the US smaller and more fragile (i.e., more easily lost as they will be competed away and therefore less worth seeking).[57] In the smaller national economies, rent-seeking below the surface and social democratic ideologies above it could have produced concentrated economies unable to strongly support diffuse stockholders. The parallel here between corporate results and James Madison's famous analysis in the Federalist No. 10 is obvious.

And concentrated ownership in such nations can persist because the concentrated owner must be represented generally on the national scene

---

[55] See generally Mark J. Roe, "Backlash," 98 *Colum. L. Rev.* 217 (1998).

[56] I develop this theory and supporting data in Roe, "Rents," note 54 above.

[57] Even modest rents create indeterminacy in corporate ownership and governance. Rents allow different players to get value out of the firm, and different players may win by chance in some political environments and lose in others. When competition in the American economy was weaker, and oligopoly stronger, mild pressures to soften the workplace and make managers socially responsible to employee constituencies may have been more effective than they would be today. See Roe, "From Antitrust to Corporate Governance," *The American Corporation Today*, Carl Kaysen, ed. (1996), 102–27.

when sectors negotiate decisions and allocations. This is not left–right politics, but it is concentrated ownership being induced, or supported, by the political framework.

As the small economies integrate into free-trade zones, the potential for local rent-seeking will diminish, enhanced product market competition will make traditional social democratic corporate governance harder to maintain, and the demand for securities institutions will rise.[58] Governments whose firms face intense competition that renders them unable to implement a social democratic program through firms or labor markets may either abandon their goals or implement them via social insurance that leaves firms out of the picture.

Craving stability

Social democracy may not fully capture the ideological metric here. Some nations may crave stability more than do others. Histories of war, devastation, social instability, market collapse, or starvation can drive this craving. If voters crave stability, they may insist on rules and a business atmosphere that make change harder than it would otherwise be. The core cause though may then not be social democratic ideology, or employee rent-seeking, but a society seeking stability.[59]

Indeed, before World War I's start to Europe's self-destruction and economic instability, securities markets were *stronger on the continent than they are today*, and not that much weaker than they were in the United States.[60] Politics was more conservative, and social democratic movements were on the political fringe.

Managers' utility functions

Another way to look at this issue could be through managers' utility functions. Human nature does not demand that managers maximize, say, firm size or profitability. In cultures that emphasize other values, and inculcate them through schooling and other means, managers may

---

[58] Whether path dependence diminishes the demand for corporate change is analyzed in Bebchuk & Roe, "A Theory of Path Dependence," note 48 above.

[59] Karl Polanyi, *The Great Transformation* (1944).

[60] See Rahhuram G. Rajan & Luigi Zingales, "The Politics of Financial Development" (total securities issuances as a percentage of GNP were higher in France in 1913 than in the US and only slightly lower in Germany). In the 1900–1913 period, French and Japanese firms sold *more* stock in their nations than American firms did in the US. Cf. Yoshiro Miwa & J. Mark Ramseyer, "Corporate Governance in Transitional Economies: Lessons from the Pre-war Japanese Cotton Textile Industry," 29 *J. Legal Stud.* 171 (2000) (surprisingly strong equity market in end-of-nineteenth-century Japan).

maximize something else, and that something else may make them less able, or less willing, to do shareholders' bidding.

Technological change

As technology evolves, the underlying organizational forms may evolve as well. Movement away from heavy smoke-stack manufacturing toward rapidly moving service industries could affect corporate governance in two ways. First, the new industries may be less susceptible to the social and economic conflicts that raise agency costs. Second, further empowering employees in service industries may be efficient from capital's perspective. Even if agency problems arise due to continuing conflict there, these agency problems may not be as costly to invested capital because the ratio of invested capital to human capital is often less in the new service and high-tech industries than in the old heavy manufacturing industries. Stock options for managers *and* employees are common in high-tech firms, where commitment and human capital are important. When technology renders the old-style smoke-stack factory less important, social conflict cannot lead to it being expropriated. More simply, when a firm is expanding, fewer conflicts irritate the relationship between social democracy and the public firm.

IV. Reservations and refinements

I hardly mean here that we have discovered the single cause that explains why some nations gets deep securities markets and strong ownership separation and other nations do not. There are other foundations, both economic and institutional, and they too can affect the results. A nation must be at a level technologically and economically to demand very large enterprises and wide capital-gathering. It must have basic legal institutions that enforce contracts and corporate obligations (or substitutes for these institutions). I only mean here to add politics as a key foundation, one that is missing from the current literature, which I do not intend here to challenge but to extend.

So, one could find some non-social democracies that are poor and not yet technologically ready for a variety of reasons for large public firms and ownership separation. (Those kinds of firms just wouldn't add value.) This observation would be important for many purposes, but it wouldn't contradict the thesis here, since there are several preconditions, political, economic, and institutional. Similarly, one might find a rich, nonsocial democracy but one whose institutional structure – say, via weak corporate or contract law enforcement – doesn't yield strong securities markets and ownership separation. For the same reason, this wouldn't contradict the political theory.

Moreover, I have focused in this article on one feature: the strength of pro-labor social democracy in a nation. It is an important political feature in the modern west, but it is not the only political feature. Thus other political institutions can affect the corporation: if a nation is populist and uncomfortable with strong financial institutions, then we should see fewer such strong financial institutions (and, hence, one big block player would have been removed from the scene).

Or, if a nation has an extremely strong leveling culture, then we might see fortunes taxed away after a single generation or conceivably even taxed away during the first generation (by a high and effective income tax and wealth tax); this could have corporate ownership implications as well. (Presumably it would propel means to maintain control via pyramids and dual-class stock that require little invested capital to maintain control.) One might point out these features as alternative or additional political influences. They do not undermine a political theory, but enrich it.

Counter-examples would be important in undermining a monocausal theory. But they don't directly undermine a theory that promotes a contributing, even a strongly contributing, cause. That is why one must look to general trends, with tools such as regression analysis, however crude that might be.

Moreover, the strongest counter-examples in the literature do not even seem to be strong counter-examples. That is, as I've previously noted, Britain has had good securities markets, but has been on both sides of the fence politically. But it is telling that Britain's social democratic era came *after* the laissez-faire era in which its securities markets first developed. Britain's securities markets did not *first* arise *during* Britain's social democratic era. They arose before. Strong securities markets survived the social democratic era, but may well have not arisen during it.

Moreover, ownership separation seems, according to Chandler and others, to have gone much more slowly in Britain than in the United States. Families may well have hung on longer there than in the United States because when they were ready to sell and turn the firm over to professional managers, the political environment wasn't conducive.

France is also said to be a counter-example, in that it is said that French statism undermined its securities markets. It is true that France was statist and hostile or indifferent to securities markets. It is also true that French securities markets have been weaker relative to similarly wealthy nations during the modern post-World War II era.

But France also was *not* a conservative nation during this era. Commentators who point out that the government was either indifferent to, or hostile to, the development of the French stock market may only be telling us *one* of the manifestations of French social democracy, i.e., a hostility to capital and its supporting institutions.

In an earlier era, before World War I, France – statist then as well, having licensed stockbrokers in a way that made them state agents – *nevertheless* had a powerful stock market that rivaled that of London and surpassed that of New York in many dimensions. How could it have done so if statism was the key relevant variable? It couldn't have. But statism alone wasn't the relevant variable. Rather, it's that the government then was conservative and tolerated stock markets and capitalist institutions' development.

V.   Political preconditions in the United States

While I have thus far primarily analyzed the political realities around the world, I need not remind the reader that this chapter is as much about the United States as it is about the rest of the world. The American Berle-Means firm is usually seen by American analysts as an economic institution that evolved because of the technological and financial problems of large size, learned how to feed its concomitant voracious demand for capital, and developed means to control the loosely supervised managerial agents at the top of the firm.

But substantial political prerequisites existed to the rise, evolution, and business domination of the large public firm. Economic-based social conflict in the US was lower than it was elsewhere. With conflict lower, shareholders could remove themselves from overseeing the firm day-to-day without fearing that managers would be "captured" by social democratic pressures. In time, ways to tie managers to shareholders arose, and they could not easily have arisen were the United States more of a social democracy.

Conclusion on political preconditions to separating ownership from control

The American-style public corporation is a fragile contraption, filled with contradictions, one easy to destabilize and destroy. It dominates American business, due to its ability to agglomerate capital and to spread private risk efficiently, but it needs multiple preconditions to arise, survive, and prosper. One powerful precondition is the institutional ability to control agency costs, an ability that a social democracy reduces, or destroys.

True, the benefits with which the public firm is associated – innovation, competition, and high tech, for example – might be obtained without Berle-Means firms. The American-centered view that the public firm is the pinnacle of business organization may be incorrect. Innovation, competition, and efficient production can be reached in different organizations. Nations that deny themselves one organizational form do not condemn themselves to economic backwardness, but leave themselves without one tool in the organizational toolkit. (And, similarly, nations that overly fragment institutional shareholding and financial voice inside the corporate boardroom deny themselves a different tool.)

Moreover, this is hardly a reason to condemn social democracies. What gets lost in shareholder tools may be gained on the shop-floor; net efficiency effects may be zero. And the solidarity and equality in these nations may make more citizens happier, and those societies may in the long run be more stable and productive. Many European players, even managerial players, believe this to be so.[61] Citizens in nations with a yearning for stability, perhaps one created by gloomy destructive histories, may get special value from the stability of a social democracy.

But productivity effects and the overall value of a social democracy are not the principal lines of thought here. The key point here is that a nation's creating of many public firms and deep securities markets in social democracies is more than just a technical problem of its creating the right legal institutions, but a problem that goes to the core of the social and political organization of that society. As such, reformers will find technical solutions frustrating or impossible to implement; and even if implemented, the technical reforms will have little effect unless and until the underlying political reality changes. One may see little demand for the institutions that support securities markets until a social democracy has softened enough to lay the political foundation for making public firms viable.

Capital markets and institutions, managerial markets and institutions, and labor markets and institutions interrelate. Some types fit well together, complementing one other, and some do not. Politics can determine one type of the three and thereby indirectly determine the other two, because sometimes only a restricted set of the others will fit the one that politics determined. America's historical antipathy to private institutional

---

[61] See Albert, note 7 above.

power overemphasized one kind of capital market, and thereby affected the managerial institutions of the public firm.[62] Foreign politics affected labor institutions and these in turn affected managerial institutions and capital structure. Had American labor institutions differed – had the US been more of a social democracy – the public firm would have had rougher going in the US and may have been a minor, not a major American business institution.

This result is not merely technical, and, hence, any change will not be purely technical either. The result maps back to a society's political condition: social democracies raise the agency costs to shareholders in the Berle-Means public firm. They exacerbate managerial tendencies to expand unprofitably, to avoid risk, and to avoid biting the bullet and forcing organizational change when markets and technologies have shifted. In each case incumbent employees tend to prefer that these changes not go forward, incumbent employees have a strong political voice in social democracies, and managers have a rougher time bringing about organizational change in the social democracies. Oftentimes they do not want to bring about these organizational changes anyway.

Aligning managers with shareholders is harder in social democracies than elsewhere: owners dislike transparent accounting, which would give employees more information than many owners would be happy with their employees having, but transparent accounting is necessary for distant securities holders. Hence, the demand for accounting transparency has been weaker in the social democracies and, as long as accounting was opaque, close owners (who can privately extract information from the firm and its managers) persisted. Shareholder-wealth-maximization norms have been weaker in the social democracies. The strong control mechanisms of the hostile takeover and publicly known incentive compensation have been harder or impossible to implement in the social democracies.

The political theory here is that social democracies wedge open the gap between shareholders and managers in public firms, by raising agency costs and reducing the efficacy of the techniques that would control them. This wedge has been small in the United States, and we have thereby uncovered the critical precondition to ownership separating from control and, hence, to the rise and persistence of the dominant form of business organization in the United States, namely the historical absence of a strong social democracy.

---

[62] Roe, *Strong Managers*, note 51 above, pp. xiii–xvi, 283–87.

PART III

Specific institutions

8

The politics of corporate convergence

DAVID CHARNY*

I. Background and motivation: types of convergence theory

Convergence theories come in several varieties. One account discovers a tendency towards the rules that are, in fact, objectively best, by some efficiency standard. This account identifies the main purpose of corporate law – to minimize the costs of raising capital – and discovers the optimal rules to achieve this purpose. On this view, once one stipulates to certain basic features of capitalist social organization (private property, dispersed wealth for investment), there is no reason in the end to doubt that one can identify the single set of most desirable rules.[1] Recent work comparing national corporate systems casts some doubt on the most sweeping form of this functionalist claim. On the basis of this work, it is arguable that there are multiple sets of efficient corporate governance institutions, each set supported by a different set of underlying legal rules (or by the different practices produced by the interaction of laws and various nonlegal norms and sanctions). Given multiple efficient systems, there is no *prima facie* functionalist reason for convergence to occur. The existence of these multiple sets seems to fall out of the debates over the past decade about the relative effectiveness of the very different systems of the various advanced industrial countries and from more recent data pointing to substantial similarities in corporate performance, by various measures, such as executive turnover and acquisition rates.

Of course, it can still be argued that there is a single most efficient system among the multiple possibilities observed. Despite similarities

---

* Chapter prepared for the Conference on Convergence in Corporate Governance, Columbia Law School, Sloan Project on Corporate Governance (Dec. 5, 1997). Research for this chapter was done in part while I was Olin Fellow at Columbia Law School, for whose hospitality I am grateful. I am also indebted to Jeff Gordon, Reinier Kraakman, Katharina Pistor, Mark Roe, Chuck Sabel, and Roberto Unger for helpful discussions and suggestions.
    This piece reflects developments through August 1999.
[1] E.g., Robert Clark, *Corporate Law* (1986) (Appendix).

in performance measures, there may be hidden costs to some types of systems; or it may be that some systems have functioned well because they faced unique or transient economic environments. (For example, the Japanese system may have been uniquely well suited to a post-war industrial strategy featuring a high domestic savings rate, and massive capital investment in export-oriented, high-growth, second-tier technologies.) On this view, the future convergence of corporate systems, despite past diversity, would be projected on the basis of the gradual convergence of the economic and social circumstances of the advanced industrial economies, either through parallel national developments or through the opening up of global markets. In particular, "globalization" apparently changes the economic environment – by increasing the size of markets and correspondingly the efficient scale of production, by rapidly diffusing new technologies, and by creating a common global capital market which subjects national investment opportunities to similar standards – in a way that seems to put pressure for convergence on the different corporate governance systems.

An alternative approach to the convergence problem abandons the functionalist claim to have discovered a single "best practice," and instead emphasizes the advantages of compliance with a uniform norm. It might be that, even though a number of corporate governance systems are equally efficient, corporations and their economies derive advantages, when dealing with a single larger or "global" economy, in having the same systems as other participants in the larger market. Convergence would be driven by this efficiency advantage. Thus, "transplantation" arguments claim that it is important for nations who wish to enter the international arena – as exporters of goods or importers of capital – to adopt commercial and corporate rules similar to those of the leading players. Having adopted the common rules provides a familiar legal environment to wary foreign investors, certifies the reliability and seriousness of the nation's attempt to attract foreign investment, and reduces the transaction costs of structuring deals by permitting use of a formulaic set of transactional templates.

In a sense, it would be futile to quarrel in broad terms with the fundamental premises of either of these accounts of convergence. After all, one cannot contemplate any substantial chunk of human history without remarking the tendencies to learn from observing one's neighbors what practices work well, and to imitate practices that are familiar, whether they work well or not. In either case, the notion of "convergence" is simply the antechamber onto a more interesting and substantive debate about what the rules should be, or about what the extant rules actually are. From the legal perspective, the question of convergence becomes interesting because of the problems it raises about what effects laws have and about how laws change. As to the effect of law, debates about legal convergence raise the refreshing, or at least reassuring, possibility that the content of legal rules actually does matter. As to change, claims about convergence as a positive matter would seem to imply an account about how legal rules adapt to changed economic circumstances – i.e., what mechanisms actually bring convergence about.

The difficulty is that our understanding of both questions is primitive. In the recent corporate literature, the emergent, and paradoxical, conclusion seems to be that substantially different rules and different institutional practices lead to very similar results on such crucial matters as the standards of conduct to which managers are held accountable.[2] This recent evidence joins in spirit a venerable legal literature, which emphasizes that the primary sources of standards for commercial conduct are not legal rules, but extant social norms as enforced by various nonlegal sanctions, such as reputation and repeat dealings. On this account, convergence of legal rules should be a matter of indifference.

Similar difficulties confront those who would offer theories about mechanisms of convergence. If the rules do not matter, of course, it is difficult to get much traction at all on the question of how they change.[3] If the rules do matter, then claims about convergence towards an optimum must discover a beneficent and enlightened lawgiver who will adopt the optimal rule, or a more subtle social mechanism which achieves the same result. Of course, history does provide a few salient examples of the wise and beneficent legislator: one thinks of Rousseau invited to draft the constitution of Poland, or Bernie Black drafting the Russian corporate code. More commonly, however, lawmakers approach their tasks with

[2] E.g., Steven Kaplan, "Top Executive Turnover and Firm Performance in Germany," 10 *J.L.Econ. & Org.* 142 (1994); Steven Kaplan, "Top Executive Rewards and Firm Performance: A Comparison of Japan and the US," 102 *J. Pol. Econ.* 510 (1994); Jun-koo Keang & Amil Shirdasani, "Firm Performance, Corporate Governance, and Top Executive Turnover in Japan," 38 *J. Fin. Econ* 29 (1995).

[3] The implications for convergence of this view might be interesting to work out, because one would have to search for accounts of legal evolution that did not depend on law's factual effects, stipulated to be nil. Presumably, matters such as ideology, symbolism, and mere historical inertia would emerge as important factors. Cf. Alan Hyde, "A Theory of Labor Legislation," 38 *Buffalo L. Rev.* 383 (1990). These factors may also play a role in an eclectic theory, in which the law's effects still leave a substantial flexibility in an economically deterministic account.

distinctive biases introduced by their own interests (and those of their backers), and by ideological commitments. There is no assurance that legislators so motivated will enact an efficient body of rules, and every reason to suspect that they will not.

Within this broad sketch of the intellectual setting for convergence theories, I shall confine myself here to two aspects of convergence theory. For the purposes of this analysis, take as given one big controversial premise of convergence theory – that there is a single set of most efficient rules, or "best practices" for corporate legal regulation, at least when viewed from the perceptive of minimizing the costs of capital investment in enterprise. The rules' advantages may reflect comparative efficiency of the rules' content, or it may arise simply from the desirability of uniformity or compliance with norms that govern in the global market generally, even if these represent only one among a number of efficient structures.

Even making this controversial stipulation, the analysis here will suggest that there is still reason to be skeptical about any short-run tendency towards convergence in the direction of a single set of effective legal rules. The basis of the argument is the "public good" aspect of corporate rules. To account for convergence, one requires a political theory of the formulation and effect of corporate rules; conversely, obstacles to convergence that arise from the fact that corporate law rules are the products of collective action.

These political obstacles should be distinguished from a distinct, albeit closely related, normative conception of political obstacles to convergence. In the normative conception, rules of corporate design are modified to serve political goals that supplement, without displacing (or necessarily conflicting with) the goal of reducing capital costs. Promoting a cooperative style of labor relations, and facilitating national economic coordination, are two goals that, as I and others have argued, apparently loom large in most industrial countries.[4] I do not wish to reenter the normative debate here. Rather, the claim here is that political forces, as a positive matter, will hinder convergence; and that these political forces represent not only actors, such as workers or consumers, who are in a sense "outside" of the system for raising capital, but also entrepreneurs, managers, financiers, and capital suppliers. Even within this more narrow frame – narrow in reducing the spectrum of relevant actors and considering only their positive motivations – political barriers to convergence loom large.

[4] David Charny, "Workers and Corporate Governance: The role of Political Culture," in Margaret M. Blair & Mark J. Roe, eds., *Employee and Corporate Governance* (1999). David Charny, "The German Corporate Governance System," *Colum. Bus. L. Rev.* 145 (1998).

II. Interest groups and corporate lawmaking

The analytic difficulty with functionalist accounts is to specify the causal link between a social system's performance of certain functions with its stability or survival.[5] The mere efficiency or desirability of a legal regime is *ipso facto*, no guarantee of its emergence or survival. In the present context, the most plausible explanation for the emergence of efficient rules to govern corporate organization would extend the familiar view, and, from what one can tell, widely held account of the choice of optimal capital structures. On this account, the entrepreneurs or firm founders who determine capital structure internalize all of the costs of suboptimal or inefficient choices: inefficient choices impose costs on investors who enter into a contractual relationship with the entrepreneur; in turn, investors demand compensation *ex ante* for any costs imposed on them *ex post* by inefficient contract terms, or, more generally, by inefficient governance or capital structure arrangements.

This observation readily extends to legal rules governing the relationship between investors and the firm. If the law permits them to do so, investors and the entrepreneur are likely to contract around, or opt out of, inefficient rules promulgated by law; even if the rules are purportedly mandatory, they may be thwarted by "implicit" agreements to depart from the legally established rule.[6] Finally, in federal or international settings, it may be possible to opt out of a body of inefficient rules by the firm's choice of the jurisdiction of incorporation.

These basic claims from the "contractualist" debates carry implications for the legislative process itself. Presumably entrepreneurs who bear the cost of inefficient rules have an incentive to seek to change those rules that they cannot get around by the various opt-out strategies: after all, if inefficient rules are not changed, it will be the entrepreneurs themselves who bear a substantial portion of the costs. Investors would have similar incentives, because they may lose potentially profitable investment opportunities altogether if entrepreneurs find the inefficiencies of the legally mandated investment contract so costly that they must forgo raising capital altogether. As a class of entrepreneurs and financiers emerges, therefore, it should form, on this account, a powerful political force for movement towards more efficient rules. The force is strengthened as a jurisdiction enters the international capital markets: foreign as well as

---

[5] Jon Elster, *Making Sense of Marx* (1985), provides a useful discussion.
[6] That is, one party violates the legal rule, while the other party commits itself, through some nonlegal mechanism, not to use whatever power it has to enforce the legal rule.

domestic investors would then have an incentive to impose efficient rules, and these foreign investors may have additional clout because of their enormous wealth and alliance with foreign sovereigns (the paradigm, of course, is the World Bank).[7]

For clarity, it is perhaps worth contrasting this situation with the dynamics of public choice in other regulatory areas. The characteristic feature of the more general setting is that the various interest groups are not in contractual or market relationships with each other, and so the attempt of one group to impose costs on others does not redound to losses for the cost-imposing group, as it does win a case where entrepreneurs would try to impose costs of investors. In the standard case, the public arena is used by one powerful group of actors to impose costs on others; under the contractualist view, an attempt by entrepreneurs to impose costs on other investors would be self-defeating, as these costs, in the end, would fall back on the entrepreneurs themselves.

Are there problems with this contractualist story? Consider again the basic premise: internalization to entrepreneurs of the costs of suboptimal governance structures. The literature has identified at least two glitches in this account – mechanisms by which the private incentives of entrepreneurs, managers, and controlling shareholders are severed from the socially desirable incentives. Both are relevant to the lawmaking processes needed for convergence.

First, entrepreneurs and controlling shareholders may prefer rules about capital structure different from those that would be socially optimal. Consider recent work on control transactions and optimal capital structure.[8] This remarkably deep and elegant work demonstrates that, even *ex ante* (at the time of incorporation, or more generally, the design of the firm's capital structure) entrepreneurs may profit by departing from the social optimum. A suboptimal capital structure may enable the founder and controlling shareholder to extract greater surplus when he sells control. Further, there is a single set of legal rules that realign managerial incentives with the social optimum: rules that provide for payment to all shareholders, at the shift of control, of an appraised value of their shares.

---

[7] The intervention by foreign actors to impose rules efficient by their lights was once referred to as "imperialism," though the term is now to be avoided as tainted with unsavory associations.

[8] Lucian A. Bebchuk & Luigi Zingales, "Corporate Ownership and the Decision to Go Public: Private versus Social Optimality" in Randall K. Morck, ed., *Concentrated Corporate Ownership* (2000); Lucian A. Bebchuk, "Efficient and Inefficient Sales of Corporate Control," 109 *Q. J. Econ.* 957 (1994).

For our purposes, the important corollary is that entrepreneurs no longer have incentives to push for the optimal set of legal rules in legislative fora.[9] They would prefer rules that would permit them to extract the maximum gain for themselves. Though the analysis at first cut seems to pertain to a narrow set of the vast range of corporate rules, the consequence of the discrepancy could be considerably broader. Contrast two economies: an economy in which controlling shareholders can gain from controlling shareholder structures that they design to maximize the premium upon sale of control; and, on the other hand, an economy in which the advantages of this situation are minimized by appropriate legal rules. Corporate rules and practice will differ in many other respects as well. A small elite of controlling shareholders will have little reason to develop an extensive system of disclosure, to encourage changes of control through hostile takeovers, or give outside shareholders the power vigorously to enforce the duties of managers to maximize share value. The point is not that the single rule will generate these consequences directly, but rather that the system of shareholdings that developed is one that, as a political matter, will sustain the development of management-protective rules and remove impetus for development of shareholder-protective ones. Other types of inefficient value-extraction rules may also be favored by managers. High-level managers may wish to preserve opportunities for taking of perks and excessive compensation, even though these distort effort incentives, and so reduce the value of investments *ex ante*.[10] Consequently, the corpus of corporate rules that emerges under the influence of these groups may depart substantially from the optimum.

More generally, subgroups of investors, entrepreneurs, or managers who have interest-group power will benefit from pushing for suboptimal rules. Once an economy becomes sufficiently wealthy and diverse, social roles will be subdivided, and so not all of costs of *ex ante* governance inefficiencies will be borne by groups with a decisive influence of the making of the law. This balance of influence has obviously differed among the wealthy industrial nations. For example, in the United States, financiers and lawyers may benefit from excessive disclosure requirements, which make work for them and may raise barriers to entry.[11] Indeed, once one

---

[9] Note: this "corollary" is not in the Bebchuk and Zingales paper, and so they shouldn't be held responsible for it.

[10] Lucian A. Bebchuk & Christine Jolls, "Managerial Value Diversion and Shareholder Wealth," 15 *J. L. Econ. & Org.* 487 (1999).

[11] This might account for the defects of securities regulation analyzed in Roberta Romano, "Empowering Investors: A Market Approach to Securities Regulation," 107 *Yale L.J.* 2359 (1998).

stipulates that entrepreneurs, managers or controlling shareholders may benefit from suboptimal rules, moves towards the optimum will occur under a very fragile set of circumstances. Particularly, economies may get stuck in a "low shareholder protection" trap. The lack of vigorous shareholder protection discourages the widely dispersed shareholdings and market trading; the absence of these practices prevents, in turn, the development of a group with interests to press for more effective protections. Further, even if the practice of dispersed shareholdings emerges, this may not confer interest-group clout. The shareholders would fit the classic pattern of a dispersed group, each member of which has too attenuated an interest to lobby directly for improvements.[12]

Generally, neither jurisdictional competition, nor, more generally, competition among economic systems can be relied upon to align managerial incentives with social interests with regard to formulation of corporate rules. With regard to jurisdictional competition, the important data for America show that reincorporations (generally to Delaware) are accompanied by abnormal returns, a pattern which has been interpreted to suggest that these reincorporations represent moves towards shareholder value-enhancing rules, or at that these moves are not part of a race to the bottom. Correspondingly, jurisdictions would have an incentive to adopt efficient rules to attract incorporations. Unfortunately, the data do not remove the prospect that the jurisdiction of incorporation may provide managerialist rules. The basic arguments here are familiar. Reincorporation may signal some highly profitable transactions are coming, but the abnormal increase in share value which reflects this then does not also imply that the rules of the new jurisdiction are really better. In fact, the new jurisdiction may be chosen precisely because managers see that the jurisdiction has rules loose enough to let them divert to themselves substantial amounts of the transactional surplus. In the present context, the force of these arguments is that even a federal system, which might be thought to reduce the interest-group distortions on corporate lawmaking, may not push towards the set of optimal rules.[13]

---

[12] Of course, this is the classic formulation of Mancur Olson, *The Rise and Decline of Nations: Economic Growth, Stagflation, and Social Rigidities* (1982).

[13] Compare Roberta Romano, *The Genius of American Corporate Law* (1993). It is notable as well that for some transactions, such as tender offers, competing jurisdictions in a federal system have provided rules that reduce shareholder value in order to protect managers. Indeed, Geoff Miller persuasively argues, contrasting the American and British rules to takeovers, that the British rules are superior precisely because the British system for corporate regulation is unitary rather than federal. This hardly bodes well for federal systems as guarantors of convergence towards best-practice rules.

The same is true for economic competition among different national corporate systems. Note that, at first cut, many inefficient corporate rules are basically redistributive in form: they permit entrepreneurs, managers or controlling shareholders to divert to themselves wealth that optimal rules would allocate to shareholders as a group. There is no direct net loss of wealth from these transactions; and the resultant enrichment of those who are already among the wealthiest members of society, though of political concern on grounds of redistributive justice,[14] does not reduce total wealth. Rather, the economic losses from inefficient corporate governance rules take several indirect forms. First, as we have noted, the prospect of managerial diversion causes investors to demand a higher *ex ante* return on their investment; this increase in the cost of capital may cause some profitable investment opportunities to be lost, because they do not generate the additional return needed to compensate investors for expropriation risk. Further, managerial effort that would be put to socially productive purposes is instead diverted towards value expropriation.[15] Finally, inefficient corporate rules may induce shareholders to expend greater costs to protect themselves by their own monitoring of managers than would be expended by a legal system that monitored efficiently.

These costs may prove to be a drag on economic development. Concretely, for example, certain profitable sectors that require high-risk capital investment – such as new technologies – may not emerge because current managers are not focused on creation of new value, and entrepreneurs who would develop these opportunities cannot raise the capital because of the high risk of appropriation seen by relatively poorly informed shareholders. The need for careful monitoring of managers by other shareholders may also prevent firms from achieving optimal size; firms remain too small because they cannot raise capital for further growth, or particularly because only with small firms can outside shareholders get enough information (or information simple enough for them to analyze) to assure themselves that they are not the victim of managerial expropriation.

---

[14] Political controversies have been spurred, for example, by high executive salaries and particularly stock options and gains from trading. Theories of distributive justice that condemn these are not easy to develop; one might argue that the wealth is acquired arbitrarily rather than earned.

[15] Also, it may be that skill at value creation in firms and skill at value appropriation are distinct and to some extent mutually exclusive; so the types of managers who emerge as successful in a system that favors value appropriation are not those who ought to be managing the economy, from the perspective of value enhancement. Cf. George A. Akerlof, "Loyalty Filters," 73 *Am. Econ. Rev.* 54 (1983).

Again, the key point is that these costs are not borne by extant controlling shareholders and managers. In fact, controllers may benefit, not only by direct expropriation, but also by the indirect effects of the current rules in stymieing development of new firms or sectors. (With new enterprises thwarted, capital investment will continue to flow towards extant firms.) The drag on macro-development is experienced mainly by a dispersed group of economic actors – workers who might be employed by new firms, investors who might lose investment opportunities, consumers who would buy products that are cheaper or of higher quality. Again, these social actors form dispersed groups, each member of which has only a very small stake in corporate rules: consequently, they may not effectively mobilize for reform.

Internationalization of capital markets mitigates this grim picture to some extent. Firms who wish to escape the inefficiencies of local rules may be able to do so by going onto global markets, and, correlatively, subjecting themselves on some matters (such as disclosure requirements) to the more efficient rules imposed by the sovereigns who regulate these markets. But there are apparent restrictions to this escape hatch: for example, local firms may not be able to evade unduly restrictive mandatory local rules by "going global." Perhaps more importantly, there may be no way for the local firms to commit themselves to remain subject to the more efficient global rules: investors may fear that, at some later date, the firm may find a way to withdraw from efficient global governance to take advantage of the opportunities for expropriation created by the local rules.[16] Overcoming these barriers may require changing local rules; and, by hypothesis, the extant managers, who benefit from the current, inefficient local rules, have no reason to change the local rules to permit potential competitors to take advantage of the more efficient rules in other markets or jurisdictions.

Finally, and perhaps most familiarly, pressures from product market competition have only an attenuated effect on managers' preference between optimal and suboptimal rules. This is another lesson of the "contractualism" debates that has direct application to the question of convergence. Even if inefficient corporate rules reduce not only the economic competitiveness of the *economy* but also the competitiveness of the manager's *own firm*, managers still may not have sufficient incentives to seek the better rule. Managers and controlling shareholders may bear only a small proportion, or none at all, of the economic losses from

---

[16] Cf. Jeffrey Gordon, "The Mandatory Structure of Corporate Law," 89 *Colum. L. Rev.* 1549 (1989) (making this argument in the context of the mandatory-rules/opt-out debate).

reduced competitiveness. As long as a firm remains solvent, the ability to extract value may appeal more than the ability to create value, some of which is shared with other shareholders, or with employers, suppliers or other firm participants. Of course, at some point the pie will have shrunk so much that managers' share, even if large, is worth little; as the firm approaches that point, managers' concern with the firm's well-being correspondingly increases. But inefficiencies in legal rules alone are unlikely to bring the firm even close to that point; and before then, managers may tolerate substantial inefficiencies in legal rules in order to increase their own ability to expropriate gains.

III.   Social norms: "embeddedness" of institutions

So far we have focused on the processes that go into forming legal rules. A second type of doubt about convergence refers instead to rules' effects. The theoretical underpinnings are found in the literature on nonlegal sanctioning systems and norms. It is sufficiently banal that the conduct of parties to commercial relationships is predominantly determined, not by legal rules, but by various background social standards of conduct enforced by nonlegal sanctions, such as concern with market reputation, the renewal of the relationship in future dealings, and general social approval. These supplement or trump the commands for formal legal rules or explicit contracts.[17] The law may play an important role in creating or supporting these nonlegal normative systems: e.g, by requiring disclosure that provides information for monitoring of reputations, or by legally enforcing implicit norms when relied upon in the face of informational deficiencies or mistakes.

These basic lessons extend to the more complex forms of social interaction that characterize firms and inter-firm cooperation. For example, in the "learning by monitoring" interactions that characterize some manufacturer–supplier relationships, an embedded sequence of tournaments, with increasing payoffs as players move through succeeding

---

[17] I draw here, for example, on Charny, "Nonlegal Sanctions in Commercial Transactions," 102 *Harv. L. Rev.* (1990); Eric E. Poser, "Law, Economics and Inefficient Norms," 144 *U. Pa. L. Rev.* 1697 (1996); Lisa Bernstein, "Private Commercial Law in the Cotton Industry: Creating Cooperation through Rules, Norms, and Institutions," 99 *Mich. L. Rev.* 1724 (2001); Lisa Bernstein, "Merchant Law in a Merchant Court: Rethinking the Code's Search for Immanent Business Norms," 144 *U. Pa. L. Rev.* 1765 (1996). An admirable development of some of these themes in the context of corporate organization is Curtis J. Milhaupt, "A Relational Theory of Japanese Corporate Governance: Contract, Culture and the Rule of Law," 37 *Harv. Int'l L. J.* 3 (1996).

rounds, provides noncontractual incentives for cooperation. In this set-up, reputational monitoring is accomplished, through certification of competence and more informal measures, as suppliers deal with multiple manufacturing firms in a given industry. A cognate example is found in the biotech industry, where reputation for successful cooperation is developed as collaborators move through successive projects, with competence measured by project turns, publications, and patents.[18]

What is the bearing of these social phenomena on the positive claims for convergence? Suppose, first, the arguments of the previous section are unconvincing, and that in fact there remains at least a tendency for jurisdictions to converge to a single "best practice" standard. This tendency would not mean that explicit *legal* rules will converge: if a given norm can be enforced, with roughly equal efficiency, by either a legal standard or a nonlegal one, convergence in norms may be accomplished despite the persistence of wide variations in what the realists somewhat quaintly called the "law on the books." Perhaps more strikingly, the costs of apparently inefficient legal rules might be sharply reduced by nonlegal mechanisms. Finally, legal rules perhaps should differ because of the way they support the operation of nonlegal sanctioning mechanisms.

Consider again the question of ownership structure. The analysis in the previous section was premised on the observation that owners may choose suboptimal shareholding structure in order to maximize their gains upon sale of control. Similar adjustments in capital structure may permit increased extraction of gains during the controlling shareholder's managerial incumbency as well. This analysis can be developed further by embedding these shareholding structures (and the background legal rules) in a set of contextual specifications about how various groups of shareholders, as well as other corporate participants, transact among or cooperate with each other. The contextual specifications will often reveal social norms and sanctioning systems that temper the inefficiencies of the ownership structures that appear inefficient when considered abstractly. Indeed, in the most halcyon accounts, an apparently inefficient ownership structure may achieve a net efficiency gain, and any residual distortion in distribution of payouts can be understood as a reasonable bribe to managers for maintaining, or at least acquiescing in, a set of transactional arrangements. In the larger structure, shareholding plays a role in stabilizing the complex interactions among various participants in the firm. Legal forms may appear as opportunistic (here, in the biological sense, not

---

[18] Henry Hansmann, "What Determines Firm Boundaries in Biotech?" 152 *JITE* 220 (1996).

the Williamsonian one) adaptation, forming part of a strategy by which participants attempt to create new commercial ties.

Illustrative is the variety of forms which have accommodated emergent collaborative production methods. In the German system legal rules revising the Konzern doctrines (rules governing the relations of affiliated companies) permitted the emergence of the new form of the management holding company, under which a strategic planning parent used partial share-owning ties as the form basis for coordination of production among the numerous subsidiaries.[19] In this setting, the partial share-ownership structure is not primarily opportunistic or redistributive, but rather provides the formal basis for cooperation between parent and subsidiaries. What directs the exercise of the parent's formal power towards benign rather than redistributive uses was the balance of informational advantage between parent and subsidiary. Workers at the subsidiary firms possess crucial information about production processes and market demand needed for coordination of activities with other subsidiary firms, and for strategic planning by the parent. (Strategic planning is the parent's crucial, if not sole, function.) In these circumstances, opportunistic conduct by the parent provokes retaliation in the form of information-withholding by the subsidiary stakeholders (who may also be minority shareholders in the firms, or indeed, may have been sole shareholders before the control was sold upon entry of the firm as a subsidiary in the Konzern structure). This tit-for-tat relationship fosters cooperation and precludes the purely opportunistic use of the controlling shareholder structure. The controlling shareholder structure performs better than other, contractual means of arranging cooperation: the share investment bonds the participants to the prosperity of the firm, and it obtains tax and regulatory advantages of single-firm treatment for the entire set of the parent and the various cooperating subsidiaries.

Of course, similar modes of cooperation can be obtained under very different legal structures, again reflecting the influence of the background social and regulatory environment. Perhaps the starkest contrast to the German model is found in the apparently Hobbesian regime of post-Soviet Russia, in which cooperation emerged under the dark shadow, as it were, of drastically ambiguous or underdefined property and firm rights. In this setting, effective control of the productive units devolved to the

---

[19] This discussion draws on John Griffin, "The Politics of Ownership and the Transformation of Corporate Governance in Germany, 1973–1995" (1997), unpublished Ph.D dissertation, Massachusetts Institute of Technology.

workers and managers on the scene; possession conferred control. This control was eventually ratified by a system of privatization which assured that control in the form of share-ownership and board seats as well would pass to current managers and workers.[20] Correspondingly, it appears that the legal basis for the complex forms of legal cooperation – either though share-ownership or through control-contracts – provided in Germany, were entirely absent in Russia, either as a matter of the law on the books or because of the lack of effective contract enforcement. Nonetheless, at least on some accounts, cooperation among "firms" emerged through informal ties among groups of managers and workers. Again, the tit-for-tat basis in information sharing was sufficient to sustain cooperation, here on the foundation of a much more primitive construction of firm property rights.[21]

Thus, the valence of a controlling ownership structure may vary substantially depending upon background norms of commercial conduct. One possibility – perhaps to be associated with Berle and Means – sees the minority/dispersed shareholder as simply the victim of the controller's opportunistic conduct; hence the almost comic obsession, in the American case law and literature, with the fiduciary duties of the controlling shareholder and the "equal opportunity" rule. Under a different set of social norms, the claims or interests of various minority shareholders may receive substantial deference, whether protected by legal rules or not.

The lesson of these contrasts is not the relatively crude assertion that legal structures do not matter. Certainly no particular ownership or governance structure is the *sine qua non* for a any stipulated type of production process or corporate culture. The lesson of these examples is that social and commercial norms may modify the effect of legal rules – here, the rules which determine ownership structures – in ways which would pretermit any simple identification of a "best practice" legal rule. Even if we could prescind from political factors identified in section II and assume convergence of a demonstrable "best practice" rule, there would be no such rule towards which systems would converge.

Initially, these observations would simply require convergence theorists to widen their scope of inquiry. Rather than simply look at the "law

---

[20] Katherina Pistor, "Company Law and Corporate Governance in Russia," in Jeffrey D. Sachs, ed., *The Rule of Law and Economic Reform* (1997).

[21] Charles F. Sabel & Jane E. Prokop, "Stabilization Through Reorganization? Some Preliminary Implications of Russia's Entry into World Markets in the Age of Discussive Quality Standards," in Roman Frydman *et al.*, eds., *Corporate Governance in Central Europe and Russia, Volume 2: Insiders and the State* (1996).

on the books" or the "law in action," they would have to delve into actual corporate practices, and try to trace them back to the legal or nonlegal mechanisms that induced the conduct at issue. This in itself raises substantial conceptual difficulties, because one must be able to prescind from apparent cultural influences which are in fact extraneous or artifactual; the danger is that, when the complexity of the problem is displayed, it is easy to see why theorists of norms are so tempted to have recourse to tendentious or vacuous appeals to culture or "social construction," as was the case particularly in the early literature comparing Japanese, American, and European forms of enterprise organization.

More puzzlingly, however, the influence of norms – as to content and sanctions for commercial conduct – raises public choice problems as pressing as those discussed above for legal rules, although very different in structure. Fundamentally, norms display the basic problems of collective action: everyone benefits from having them, but no particular actor can garner all of the advantages from sustaining them. The constant temptation to renege, therefore, must be deterred by some enforcement mechanism built into the structure of the interaction governed by the norm. If norms are to converge, then one must have an account – analogous in structure to the one required for explicit legal rules – of how the content of the norms will converge to the supposedly efficient or best-practice form. For example, the cooperative inter-firm structures that constrain controlling shareholder abuse in German management holding companies arguably depend upon the technical sophistication of German workers and small-firm managers in the Mittelstand and a historical pattern of dense networks for firm interchange of information: a social structure that rests upon public action in such matters as education, worker organization, and property rights in information.

Public choice interacts with norms in two other respects. First, the social coordination upon which norms depend, and which they facilitate, may have harmful as well as beneficent consequences. For example, the ability of firms to coordinate production decisions may be used to fix prices, restrict output, or retaliate against current competitors and potential market entrants. Second, the interaction of emergent legal rules with background transactional norms may generate institutional coalitions to sustain the current. For example, in Germany, despite widespread recognition of the relative ineffectualness of the current dual-board structures and of the numerous impediments to markets in corporate control and IPOs, efforts for substantial reform have so far been stymied. Entrenched groups seek to maintain certain key features, such as codetermination, the bank proxy system (as a source of income for banks, banks have widely opposed change even though the proxy system has played an ever-diminishing role in corporate governance over all), and the accounting rules. Efforts at reform have shifted over to seemingly trivial changes in legal capital requirements. This political paralysis, achieved by conflicts among a divergent set of powerful interest groups, set the stage for the development of the management holding form. Judicial adaptation of rules in the face of legislative paralysis fostered, or at least ratified *ex post facto*, the new collaborative relations among parents and subsidiaries which this structure required. But, while the political paralysis set the stage for local adjustments (by contract, ownership transfers, and court decisions) that established the new forms, the very success of these arrangements dulls impetus for the governance changes that these new collaborative relationships would otherwise require.

IV. Permanent disequilibrium?

We are very far from having a dynamic model for the development of corporate rules. Despite the obstacles erected by expropriative corporate interest groups and recalcitrant norms, the groups who are broadly interested in securing efficient corporate governance – a group including present and prospective shareholders, entrepreneurs, and other enterprise participants – may be sufficiently effective to push corporate rules in the direction of efficiency. Local groups may be strengthened by the intervention of well-organized supra-national or global interest groups, such as the groups behind harmonization in the EU, or the World Bank. At some point, if there were a single set of efficient corporate rules for advanced industrial economies, we would see convergence.

For now, though, we have sparse evidence to make a judgment of the relative balance of political forces. What often is striking in discussion of the evidence is what I think of as the trope of "exceptionalism": each counter-example to convergence is dismissed as reflecting some peculiar feature of the counter-example, not a problem with convergence theory itself. Germany is stuck with codetermination, supported by seemingly insuperable labor and corporate interests and in turn a powerful blockage to takeovers and IPO markets; Britain either benefits or suffers from a strong unitary system of lawmaking; France has an exceptionally powerful administrative elite and is, well . . . French. At some point, in good Kuhnian fashion, the accumulation of anomalies has to perturb the theoretical superstructure. In particular, convergence theorists offer no reason to think that the factors that produce each exception are likely to disappear in some convergent process. It is at least equally likely that, even if one obstacle to convergence – say, German codetermination – were removed, it would be replaced, because of historical or political factors, with another structure equally exceptional, not with some bland new global norm. As corporate rules, and their economic background, become more labile, exceptions would not disappear; they would proliferate in a sort of corporate Cambrian age. We would see, not the "end of history," but its perpetual acceleration.[22]

---

[22] This last contrast was suggested to me in a conversation about this chapter with Reinier Kraakman.

9

Ungoverned production: an American view of the novel universalism of Japanese production methods and their awkward fit with current forms of corporate governance

CHARLES F. SABEL*

I

The debate about convergence is at bottom, of course, a debate about the competitive viability of two species or flavors of capitalism. The first might be called the neoclassical synthesis, to underscore its reliance on coordination through market exchange, or shareholder capitalism, to underscore the related idea that the corporation exists for the benefit of its equity owners. It is best represented, in intellectual spirit if not in fact, by the United States. The second form is sometimes referred to as stakeholder capitalism, to emphasize its assumption that the corporation is a community (like the larger society of which it is a part), and should therefore be jointly controlled and in that sense "owned" by all those – suppliers of labor as well as of capital or components – who collaborate in production. Its exemplars are Germany and most especially Japan. In this brief chapter I argue that the world's economies are not converging on either shareholder or stakeholder capitalism, nor again on a hybrid of the two or their ecological coexistence. The claim is, rather, that competitive pressures are driving firms towards a novel form of production organization based on collaborative problem-solving techniques pioneered by the Japanese but elaborated elsewhere in ways with crucial elements of the Japanese system within which they were originally housed. Whether the discipline imposed on firms by the diffusion of these new methods

* This chapter was originally prepared for the Conference on Socio-economic Systems of the Twenty-First Century sponsored by the Institute of Fiscal and Monetary Policy of the Japanese Ministry of Finance. With the usual disclaimer, I would like to acknowledge helpful discussions with my Columbia colleagues, especially Mark Roe.

produces convergence on "the one best way" in the sense supposed by the framing debate is a question reserved to the conclusion.

An American familiar with the evolution of the organization of production (narrowly understood as the procedures by which goods and services are designed and produced) and governance (the way, and to whose benefit, corporations are monitored) in the US in the last decade has, for starters, reason to be wary of dichotomies like shareholder and stakeholder capitalism. On the one hand, organization of production in the US has become in that time substantially more collaborative or team-like: in a word, more "Japanese," and, for reasons touched on below, less "neoclassical" or "American." But on the other, during this same period there has been surprisingly little change in the basic pattern of US corporate governance. Indeed, if it has changed at all, the US governance system has become more "American" in the sense of treating the corporation as an instrument to be used exclusively for the benefit of its equity owners. Assuming, to avoid obvious circularity, that the US governance system will not automatically become "Japanese" just because the production system is, and, conversely, that the US version of Japanese production methods will not fail simply because the governance system remains American, an informed American could well doubt that we have *any* production system in the way the question about convergence intends.

This unsystematic "convergence" – of production systems but little else – has, in fact been widely noted in the US. Michael Porter, for example, commenting on Fukao's[1] comparison of governance regimes, observes that the Japanese system is portrayed as "supportive" of lean production, while the American system is said to be "not supportive." This, Porter continues, is "clearly too simple," because "many US companies have adopted lean production and closer partnerships with suppliers in recent years."[2] The comment is ungenerous because Porter forgets to add that he, too, has portrayed the US financial and governance systems as hostile to such cooperation. But the truncated remark, coming from a past partisan of the notion of systematic differences among forms of capitalism, also reflects the absence of a conceptual vocabulary suited to analysis of the patchwork of actual adjustment.

---

[1] Mitsuhiro Fukao, *Financial Integration, Corporate Governance, and the Performance of Multinational Companies* (Washington, DC: The Brookings Institution, 1995).
[2] Michael E. Porter, "Comments on Mitsuhiro Fukao," in *Financial Integration, Corporate Governance, and the Performance of Multinational Companies* (Washington, DC: The Brookings Institution, 1995), 92–95.

Informed observers in societies as different as, say, Brazil and Germany could, moreover, reasonably respond on the same lines as their American counterparts. For in these countries too production is becoming more Japanese, but governance is not. To my knowledge there is no systematic change of governance in Brazil; and in Germany the well-documented central development is the withdrawal of banks from corporate monitoring[3,4]: a move towards "Americanization." By the same token, some Japanese observers, looking at the confusion of main-bank governance (and its drift, perhaps, towards "Americanization"), but noting the stability of many other, crucial features of the Japanese production system, may wonder whether it is judicious to class their own country as *either* Japanese *or* neoclassical? Nor are these impressions simply arti-facts of an arbitrarily narrow comparison of the production and gover-nance elements of the respective national bundles. While production was becoming more Japanese in the US, for instance, industrial relations were becoming so much more "American" in their disregard for unions and company or internal labor markets (and, conversely, their increasingly strict dependence on the operation of open or external ones) that many US industrial-relations experts have trouble recognizing what country they are now in.

The infirmities of the shareholder/stakeholder dichotomy bring me to the possibility of novel developments beyond the reach of the familiar cate-gories. This alternative view is that Japan has pioneered a distinct form of decentralized production organization that is universal, in the strict sense that its core features facilitate adoption in the most diverse settings, regardless of cultural preconditions. But, the general argument continues, the new form of organization, derived from Japanese experience and now developing independently of it, is not neoclassical: for this new decentral-ization depends on the continuous, disciplined exchange of information among all those collaborating in production, not the contractual relations among autonomous agents, each presumed to know by itself what needs to be done to meet its obligations to the others, which is, of course, the neoclassical view. Finally, the very same features of the Japanese-derived system that allow it to diffuse independent of cultural preconditions and that distinguish it from the neoclassical synthesis render ineffective the

---

[3] J. S. S. Edwards & Klaus Fischer, "Banks, Finance and Investment in West Germany since 1970" (Center for Economic Policy Research, 1991).

[4] John Griffin, "The Politics of Ownership and the Transformation of Corporate Governance in Germany, 1973–1995," unpublished Ph.D. dissertation, MIT (1996).

current governance structures – all of them, including the Japanese main-bank system – which permitted the emergence of the novel type of decentralization in the first place.

Thus, where the convergence debate asks us to consider the meaning of governance patterns (taken to be "ideas of the corporation" or particular institutions) as parts of coherent bundles including production, political, educational, and, cultural systems as well, this alternative view suggests that the bundles are not presently coherent at all, and that the parts, particularly the production-organization piece, may even be in tension with each other. If that is so, we ought to be thinking hard about how to harmonize the pieces – perhaps in many, nationally or culturally specific ways – and not trying to determine whether the bundles are the same or different, and, if the latter, which differences are best.

A brief presentation is of course not the place to attempt a full examination of the theoretical underpinnings and practical implications of this alternative view.[5] Instead, I focus on the puzzle of how Japanese production methods can be diffusing to the US and elsewhere even though the other institutions of the Japanese bundle – especially main-bank or *keiretsu* governance – are not. Then I suggest how an answer to that question throws light on new forms of governance that are emerging in the US, and why these latter may have relevance to unsolved problems elsewhere. The starting point is a crucial change in US production organization that is at the center of what makes the puzzle puzzling.

II

That crucial change is the diffusion in the United States of Japanese customer–supplier relations, often taken to be the core of the Japanese production system as a whole. In these new supply relations a small number of top-tier contractors assume responsibility for co-developing crucial modules or subsystems with the final producer, coordinating the production of low-tier suppliers producing parts for subassemblies for their module, delivering the components just-in-time, and meeting targets for incremental improvement of production according to targets agreed with the customer. Benchmarking, simultaneous and value engineering, as well as target pricing are the familiar disciplines by which this collaboration is coordinated.

---

[5] Susan Helper *et al.*, "Pragmatic Collaborations: Advancing Knowledge while Controlling Opportunism", 9 *Industrial and Corporate Change* 3 (2000).

Indeed, production itself is in some sense jointly managed by the collaborators: with inventory buffers removed (just-in-time-production) defective parts or components quickly disrupt the flow of operations. To resume production it is necessary to eliminate the source of the initial disturbance. This is accomplished through a set of disciplines that trace problems back to root causes, wherever they may lie in the organization of the customer or supplier. An example of one of these disciplines is an insistent series of questions sometimes called the five whys: why is machine A broken? Because no preventive maintenance was performed; why was the maintenance crew derelict? Because it is always repairing machine B; why is machine B always broken? Because the part it machines always jams; why does the jam recur? Because the part is warped from heat stress; why does the part overheat? A design flaw. Thus error-detection and correction, like benchmarking and simultaneous engineering, reveals possibilities for improvement in unexpected (mis-) connections among the parts of apparently distinct organizations.[6]

The exact extent of the diffusion of these methods is hard to measure; but the combination of anecdote and survey results is compelling. In the auto industry, to take the most familiar example, there are well-documented stories of spectacularly successful implementation of the collaborative system, of which the development of the Chrysler LH cars is one of the best known. It is an open secret of the automotive trade press that Chrysler (now Daimler-Chrysler), in general, is better at the new methods than General Motors, and Ford is in between. Chrysler was, at the time it developed the LH car, the weakest of the big three American auto manufacturers. Its success therefore casts substantial doubt on the thesis still sometimes heard in the US – and often advanced five years ago to explain *Japanese* achievements – that the true "innovation" of the new methods is nothing more than the use of market power by the strong to shift the costs of adjustment to the weak. Nor are the new methods restricted to "advanced" sectors of the economy such as semiconductor manufacturing and a rejuvenated automobile industry: the same practices are now widespread in the production of textiles and garments, as well as footwear.[7]

---

[6] John Paul MacDuffie, "The Road to 'Root Cause': Shop-Floor Problem-Solving at Three Auto Assembly Plants," 43 *Management Science* 4 (April 1997), at 494–5.

[7] Frederick H. Abernathy *et al.*, *A Stitch in Time: Lean Retailing and the Transformation of Manufacturing: Lessons from the Apparel and Textile Industries* (New York: Oxford University Press, 1999).

Academic surveys of relations in the industry show accordingly that the length of contracts between customers and suppliers is increasing (again with company-specific differences)[8] – so much so, in fact, that suppliers report that they would undertake no further investment in equipment for particular projects if the contracts were further lengthened. Similarly, the proportion of parts which the customer regards as "black boxes" because the supplier's know-how was indispensable to its realization has increased rapidly in the US and is reaching Japanese levels.[9]

There are, to be sure, still differences between the two countries in this regard. Japanese customer firms are apparently better at conceptualizing the phases of the design process so that, for example, the periods in which innovations in component design with repercussions on adjacent components or on the specification of the product as a whole are clearly separated from periods in which suppliers must devote themselves to improving their products within established parameters; and the clarity of the distinction avoids the disruption that results from blurring this distinction in the US. But this plainly is a difference of degree, not of kind.[10] As of the mid-1980s, moreover, the same difference existed in Japan between Toyota, which was, of course, the more "Japanese" in the precision of its indications, and Nissan, which was the more "American." Once Nissan (now Renault-Nissan) noticed the difference – long hidden because its suppliers did not traditionally work for the Toyota group and vice versa – it switched to the "Japanese" system. US firms, if they come to the same conclusion, can presumably do the same.[11]

There are many other examples of the spread of aspects of the Japanese production system. But innovations in customer–supplier relations, in addition to being a precondition of the rest, is important because it sheds light on our puzzle: the disjuncture or divergence between production and governance systems, and more generally the strange incoherence of

---

[8] Susan Helper, John Paul MacDuffie, & Charles F. Sabel, "Pragmatic Collaborations: Advancing Knowledge while Controlling Opportunism" in 9 *Industrial and Corporate Change* 3 (2002).

[9] Takahiro Fujimoto, "The Origin and Evolution of the 'Black Box Parts' Practice in the Japanese Auto Industry" (Discussion paper 94-F-1 presented at Fuji Conference, Tokyo University, Faculty of Economics, January 1994).

[10] Jeffrey K. Liker, R. R. Kamath, S. N. Wasti, and M. Nagamachi, "Supplier Involvement in Automotive Component Design: Are There Really Large U.S. – Japan Differences?," 25 *Research Policy* 1: 59–89 (1996).

[11] Takahiro Fujimoto, "Organizations for Effective Product Development: The Case of the Global Motor Industry" (unpublished Ph.D dissertation, Harvard University, Graduate School of Business Administration, 1989).

the bundles of features that are supposed to form types of capitalism. The new (to us in America) supplier relations, after all, seem to suppose not only long-term relations between customer and supplier – at least as long as it takes to design and build a whole model generation – but also and above all assurances, for both sides, that the relations will in fact be long-term. Unless customer and supplier have some sort of commitment to each other, it seems, the customer will not make itself vulnerable to the supplier by making it the sole source of a crucial subsystem. Nor will the supplier make itself vulnerable to the customer by dedicating resources to a project that will be worthless if the latter cancels the order. (This is just a variation of the well-known argument that it is necessary to offer the workforce lifetime employment, or some equivalent, to secure participation in continuous improvement activities that lead eventually, through cumulative reorganization, to the displacement of every worker from his or her current job.) Whatever the precise form of those assurances, moreover, they all have as *their* precondition the justifiable expectation on both sides that the relation between us can be stable if we want it to be. If someone – a shareholder, perhaps – can tell the customer to cancel its order with the supplier simply because of disappointment with the *customer's* performance, the supplier will look elsewhere for business, and the customer's response will be the same if the prospects are reversed. So, if the bundle view is correct, whatever else we may imagine has or has not happened in the organization of corporate governance in the US we should be safe in assuming that nothing has happened in governance (or any other institutions) during the period in which the new supplier relations were being introduced, to increase the likelihood of such paralyzing disruptions. If anything, on this view, the governance should have become more hospitable to long-term cooperation, for example, by favoring finance through "patient" capital which is indifferent to short-term turbulence because of its dedication to long-term results.

But, as already suggested repeatedly, the change, if any, has been in the opposite direction: to render firms more answerable to shareholders with a keen eye for short-term results, and thus less reliable as long-term partners. I say "if any" because it is not clear, on inspection, that much has changed at the level of institutional design, despite familiar talk of the shareholder revolution and the like. But recall that a finding of no change would leave us just as puzzled as before, since the old – pre-revolutionary – institutions of corporate governance already were supposed to give impatient capital so much control of affairs that Japanese production relations were excluded. Let me say briefly, in any case, what the evidence suggests has happened as a result of all the churning of US governance institutions, and use the conclusions from this quick review to reformulate the puzzle.

III

Take first what has changed. As a result of shareholder suits and other legal developments, boards of directors certainly take more seriously today their formal obligations as representatives of the corporation's equity owners than they did a decade ago. This is particularly true in the case of mergers and acquisitions, where recent decisions obligate the board to seek the best price for the company they monitor if it has been put up for sale. But it is also generally agreed that boards play a larger role than before in the selection, or at least the review of the selection, of the CEO, in scrutinizing corporate strategy, and in establishing goals and procedures for selecting members of and assessing the performance of the board itself. It is also true that the board of directors is widely perceived as having greatly increased its power, as demonstrated in the spectacular dethronement of the CEO with the help of the board and institutional shareholders at such corporations as General Motors, IBM, Kodak, AMEX, Westinghouse, and Apple.

But beneath this surface, most everything is as before, where before refers to situations where boards of directors could hardly be thought of as loyal representatives of vigilant and demanding shareholders. Recall that from the 1930s through the late 1970s US boards were widely regarded as abject creatures of the managers who appointed and remunerated them. From the circumstance that the boards are not the abject creatures of management does not necessarily follow that they are its equals, and still less that they exercise mastery over it in the name of the shareholders. The most current evidence suggests strongly, in fact, that they are not and do not. Thus a recent representative survey of some 100 directors of major US corporations commissioned by the Institutional Investor Project of Columbia University (which has close ties to the institutional shareholder activists) found that the "vast majority" of those interviewed dismissed the idea of formally separating the office of CEO from the office of chairman of the board of directors, and reserving the latter for an outsider, who would presumably be a better representative of share-holders than the inside CEO.[12] The study found further that the directors were reluctant even to (and infrequently did) *meet* with representatives

---

[12] Elizabeth Neiva, "The Current State of American Corporate Governance" (New York: Institutional Investor Project, Columbia Law School, 1996).

of institutional investors, and that this reluctance was "tame relative to their aversion to inviting investors to serve on corporate boards." The ideal director for the directors interviewed – the same kind of people who presumably say that the corporation should be managed in the interest of the shareholders – is, correspondingly, a person like themselves: the CEO (or, increasingly, the division president) of a large corporation. A recent econometric study of the relation between board composition and corporate performance reinforces the conclusion that the inside managers are still very much in charge. This study finds that many boards now have investment, strategic development, and finance committees whose purpose is to evaluate long-term investment and finance decisions. But, crucially, membership on these committees is disproportionately left to inside or management directors, presumably the same people who formulated the plans in the first place, and the higher the percentage of insiders in these bodies the (marginally) better the corporate performance.[13] So a crucial result of all the academic and institutional agitation for increased participation of outsiders friendly to shareholders on corporate boards is reorganization that puts inside managers in charge of reviewing their own work, and, for good measure, a study that shows, theory aside, that this is not obviously a bad thing.[14]

Others can try to sort out the complex relations between public perception and reality, and the even greater gap, perhaps, between the latter and certain academic reform projects. For present purposes the relevant conclusions are the ones anticipated above: at a minimum, changes in governance have not been a cause of the introduction of the new production methods in the sense of providing assurances of stability that were lacking before. It is simply not clear whether anything of relevance to production organization in this sense has changed. If the governance churning has had any effect on reorganization, it should have been to obstruct "Japanization," for whatever change has taken place is so ambiguous that it has made an uncertain situation more uncertain still, and so less conducive to long-term relations. Because, however, confused and complex as the governance structures were or are, they plainly have not blocked the introduction of the Japanese supplier relations, the plausible upshot of all this is that formal governance institutions in the US

[13] April Klein, "Firm Performance and Board Committee Structure," 41 *J. L. & Econ.* 1: 137–65 (1998).

[14] Sanjai Bhagat & Bernard Black, "The Non-correlation between Board Independence and Long-Term Firm Performance" *J. Corporation L.* 27: 231–74 (2002).

(and by extension elsewhere) have neither helped nor hindered the reorganization of production very much, at least not in any way we can grasp with the help of current theories of the corporation.

(It might be objected, parenthetically, that the introduction of new methods would have been faster had the governance institutions been more hospitable. But recall that according to the standard view of the difference between stakeholder and shareholder capitalism Germany and France have more patient capital and more hospitable governance structures than the US. Yet they lag behind the Americans, substantially, in the adoption of the new methods. This observation might be parried by arguing that "Japanese"-type governance will produce Japanese production relations only in the presence of other features of the Japanese bundle. But then we are back where we started, for how do we explain the diffusion of those methods in the US, where not much seems Japanese?)

All this leads to a reformation of our original puzzle: what is it about the Japanese production system that allows its diffusion given some minimum *de facto* level of stability, but in the *absence* of the kind of governance assurances of stability that seem to be its precondition? Or, put in a way that points towards the alternative thesis, could it be that the construction of Japanese production systems does not suppose the existence of long-term relations, because the system somehow in the course of its operation is able to *produce* them?

This is, in my view, just the innovative and potentially universalizing property of the Japanese system, and it is achieved through the disciplines and institutions the collaborators use to assess continuously one another's capacities while they are solving problems jointly. These disciplines link discussion of actual performance by the cooperating parties – monitoring – to discussion of how to improve operations given that performance – learning; hence I refer to the whole process as learning by monitoring. Just-in-time production, where parts are produced one at a time as needed, is an extreme example: a defect introduced at one workstation literally stops the flow of production, so discussion of improving the production set-up by identifying and eliminating the disruption becomes a precondition for continuing production at all. Strictly analogous disciplines such as value-added engineering and target pricing allow suppliers and customers to set goals and metrics for assessing progress in achieving them in relation first to design, then to production projects. Think of this as an information-symmetricizing machine, which works to ensure that the parties come to share the same understanding of their situation, and to redefine their purposes and interests accordingly, in the very process of exploring the ambiguities they encounter in pursuit of their initial goals. With some additional argument that would be a distraction here this mutual exploration of unknown states of the world can be shown to be distinct from the neoclassical view of coordination of independent actors through formal contracts – whose very purpose is to fix *ex ante* the conditions of exchange, with at most a few exceptions, in the case of relational contracts, for foreseeable "unforeseeable" contingencies such as fluctuations in the price of raw materials or labor.

Notice that in this setting partners do not need equivalent levels of sophistication, nor do they need to depend on a history of prior – social? economic? – relations as an assurance of mutual liability. A subcontractor with rudimentary production skills, for instance, can start as a low-tier supplier, and move up the hierarchy of suppliers as it is able to demonstrate greater capacity and reliability. Or both parties can increase in sophistication together, the customer delegating more responsibility to the supplier, to conserve resources for more and more complex design and coordination tasks, and the supplier becoming an increasingly equal partner, providing not just black boxes but whole new technologies. If either partner is unable to achieve the stability and discipline needed to maintain the flow of information required to work with the other, this will be evident in disruptions in the information exchange early enough for the more capable collaborator to help correct the problem or seek an alternate partner.

Another, more general way to put the same point is to say that skills (of individuals) and capacities (of firms) in the Japanese system are general-purpose, not firm-specific or dedicated in the sense of suited to transactions only with particular, known partners. Indeed, diversification among many clients or employers should actually result in efficient gains: if problem-solving or co-development is the master skill or capacity, then the more different problems solved, the easier it becomes to solve the incremental problem at the margin of experience. Diversification should, in other words, yield economies of scope. The risk of this open, diversified strategy is clearly the possibility of encountering an unreliable partner, and investing so much in the partnership that failure is ruinous when it is finally detected. Learning by monitoring reduces this risk. Given the general-purpose character of the activities and the associated economies of scope, learning by monitoring explains how the world over, in giant, state-owned Chinese steel mills, in Brazilian automobile firms, and in the US, parties with no tradition of collaboration, or rather, long histories of mistrust or negligent indifference to one another are successfully adopting "Japanese" methods.

None of this has much to do with any straightforward understanding of stakeholder capitalism. Where is trust in the sense of the sentiment of mutual obligation said to be characteristic of such systems?

By way of response consider three observations. The first is that the more American observers learn about the Japanese system, the modern archetype of stakeholder capitalism, the more struck they are, too, by how very un-Japanese it appears. The idea that even first-tier subcontractors compete with each other in the design stage of major projects, each sending its own engineers to work with the potential customer; the notion that rates of improvement are carefully negotiated and recorded in agreements – this and much more of the measurement and constant comparison of performance with goals does not comport with the picture of the Japanese as relying on mutual dedication to common tasks to carry the burden of intimate relations.[15] Second, the more Japanese scholars focus on the Japanese system, the more they, too, come to doubt cultural explanations. Wada, for instance, in an excellent study of the history of supplier relations at Toyota, criticizes two Americans, Monteverde and Teece, for arguing that there was less vertical integration in Japan than in the US because "close cooperative relationships between assemblers and suppliers" reduced the danger of opportunism in Japan.[16] From his study of Toyota, "reputed to be the assembler with the closest cooperative relationships with its suppliers," Wada draws the contrary conclusion that "these close cooperative relationships were realized under a system of evaluations of suppliers by Toyota, which stimulated a competitive spirit among suppliers. It is not that Toyota was not liable to opportunistic exploitation, but that close cooperative relationships in themselves contain the means for preventing the occurrence of opportunism. The evaluation system brought into the close cooperative relationships is the important factor that raised the percentage of Toyota's reliance on external production and that brought about the tiered inter-firm relationships."[17]

Koike, moreover, makes a second and related argument against the culturalist view in stressing the role in promotion decisions of

---

[15] Charles F. Sabel, "Learning by Monitoring: The Institutions of Economic Development," in Neil Smelser & Richard Swedberg, eds., *Handbook of Economic Sociology* (Princeton, NJ: Princeton-Sage, 1994), pp. 137–65.

[16] Kirk Monteverde & David J. Teece, "Supplier Switching Costs and Vertical Integration in the Automobile Industry," 13 *Bell Journal of Economics* (1): 206–13 (1982).

[17] Kazuo Wada, "The Development of Tiered Inter-firm Relationships in the Automobile Industry: A Case Study of Toyota Motor Corporation," in *Japanese Yearbook on Business History*, pp. 23–47 (1991).

evaluations of the ability to respond to unusual circumstances and encourage problem-solving by groups. His position is, however, significantly different from the one urged here, for instance, in stressing the role of tacit knowledge in production where I am emphasizing the importance of explicating tacit knowledge when necessary through learning by monitoring.[18] I refer to his views, and the others from the Japanese debate as well[19], not to suggest, improbably, that my position turns out to be the "Japanese," one, but rather to indicate only that there are authoritative voices in the Japanese debate – at least the part accessible to a nonspecialist – which can be construed in favor of the notion that Japanese innovations are of potentially general significance.

IV

Where does all this leave the problem of governance? More precisely, what is the relation between the kind of monitoring that goes on in Japanese production systems in connection with project selection, design, and the like, and the kind of higher-level monitoring – of the viability of whole lines of business or divisions, or how to choose among very different but plausible long-term development goals, of how to respond to threats or opportunities facing the corporation as a whole – that is rightly the province of corporate governance. From the point of view of the report under discussion, the answer is that the relation already is, or will soon be, harmonious: either "Japanese"-style main-bank monitoring will, after a period of turbulence, return to its "natural" role of monitoring "Japanese" corporations, or, after (substantially?) more turbulence, a neoclassical synthesis, more American in its outlook, will solve the problem. But the empirical remarks and theoretical thrust of the argument so far suggest a different, much less harmonious conclusion.

Empirically, neither the main bank nor the US shareholder system has given evidence of doing a good job at monitoring the new kinds of decentralized production when they need to be monitored: in times of trouble. As contingent corporate monitors, the Japanese main banks are

---

[18] For problem-solving see Kazuo Koike & Takenori Inoki, eds., *Skill Formation in Japan and Southeast Asia*, pp. 8–10 (Tokyo: University of Tokyo Press, 1990); for tacit knowledge of skills, see pp. 10–15.

[19] Especially, Ikujiro Nonaka & Hirotaka Takeuchi, *The Knowledge-Creating Company: How Japanese Companies Created the Dynamics of Innovation* (New York, Oxford: Oxford University Press, 1995), which emphasizes the process by which Japanese firms partially explicate tacit knowledge.

supposed to take control of corporations when sitting managers demonstrate incapacity; in practice, during the current recession, the banks have not themselves demonstrated much capacity to act on such contingencies. Firms under their supervision have wasted free cash flow in American style. Moreover, current developments have probably accelerated the trend away from bank lending to corporations that began when large Japanese firms were allowed to issue securities directly. For its part, the US shareholder system of monitoring has never failed at the supervision of Japanese-style corporations for the simple reason that it has not yet had a chance to: allowing decentralization to proceed produces improved performance insofar as there are gains from decentralization, but such improvement is no guarantee that the permissive governance conditions are also suited to early detection of errors in the emergent system. On the contrary: if the foregoing is not too far off the mark, the US system as currently constituted might fail too, and for reasons related to the deep-seated difficulties of main-bank monitoring.

The problem is that the information generated by the Japanese or learning by monitoring system for its day-to-day and medium-term needs is presumably also necessary to understand how to correct large errors when they occur, yet is not available to the "contingent" monitors – main banks or shareholders – who intervene when such emergencies occur. The paradox is that only agents monitoring the (new) corporation day-to-day – which is to say participating in its routine project selection and evaluation procedures – could know enough of its highly decentralized operations to correct large errors in an effective way; but just such agents are discredited when the errors come to light; and outsiders, whatever bundle of interests they are trying to maximize, simply can not learn enough fast enough to be useful. From this perspective, therefore, the differences between main banks with their view of the corporation as a community and shareholders with their vengeful selfishness are less important than the similarities in their limitations. Doing badly in the name of the good cause is presumably better than doing badly in the name of the bad, but this not much of a consolation for the victims of incompetence.

But of course there is a way out. There *are* in both systems providers of capital who also supply efficiency-increasing information – ideas about co-investment possibilities, about alternate managerial strategies, and the like. In this their relation to the "Japanese" corporation is like the relation of its suppliers of components or skill. In the US these are the venture capitalists, who operate not only in high-tech industries but, increasingly, in the restructuring of mature sectors through "leveraged build-ups" and other novel devices that allow for profound restructuring of the firm's relation to its customers, use of information, and organization of production. Their Japanese counterparts are the managers in the large corporations who decide on the internal diversification strategy. Both know how to combine managerial advice and guidance, rooted in deep knowledge of the decentralized corporation, with expertise in finance. Neither is a shareholder or a stakeholder in the standard sense, for they are too much like managers (or employees or suppliers) to count as the former, and too much like owners – but of what kind? – to count as the latter. Perhaps the next round of research, dedicated more to the joint exploration of the unknown than to evaluation of what exists, will explore the lessons these groups have to teach for constructing a general governance system that makes the best of the "Japanese" production system as it spreads through the world.

V

What, finally, are the implications of the foregoing for the debate about convergence? First and most directly, the story I have been telling about the diffusion of a new, problem-solving production system and the emergence, perhaps, of a coordinate form of governance cast doubt on the validity, in the current context, of two arguments frequently marshaled against the proposition that convergence on any one model is a likely outcome. The first, ecological, thesis asserts simply that organizations are adapted to their environments, and, as environments differ, so too will organizations. Globalization in the sense of the spread of new customer–supplier relations across many previous disjoint sections of the world economy is not equivalent to the homogenization of production relations the world over. But it does take the self-evidence off the ecological claim that environments are manifestly different and, perhaps, shifts the burden of proof from those arguing for some broad convergence of setting to those disputing it. In any case, the world's economies seem more "global" than before in the aspects canvassed above, and the ecological argument correspondingly less forceful.

The success of the new organizational forms poses a more direct challenge to the second, path-dependency thesis against the possibilities of convergence. According to this thesis systems or societies become path-dependent, or locked into their initial choices when the unrecoverable or sunk costs of those choices are high, and the returns to proceeding down the chosen path are positive or increasing. (Think of economies of scale, where production costs per unit decrease with volume, or network externalities, where the value of attachment to a network increases with the number of other users attached.) The burden of the characterization of the learning-by-monitoring systems discussed above is that economies of scope are becoming more important than they were in relation to economies of scale, if not absolutely more important than the latter. If true, this cuts against the path-dependency view in two ways. First, it shows that the pursuit of efficiency does not require progress down one, ever narrower path. Exploration of alternatives is an efficiency-increasing alternative. Second, it casts doubt on the assumption, buried deep in the path-dependency claim, that systems and societies come in tightly integrated bundles. There would not be much scope for economies of scope if many pieces of apparently discrete bundles could not be recombined into new hybrids.[20]

At the limit, indeed, learning-by-monitoring organizations can be thought of as designed to detect and correct inefficient path dependency by obligating the actors continuously to examine their initial assumptions in the light of current experience. The fact that they can in some measure do this by using benchmarking and new kinds of problem-solving to disentrench routines and survey choices otherwise obscured by habit suggests that the path-dependency view seriously underestimates both our capacities for organized self-reflection and the plasticity of the human world, and least in current settings.

But the arguments against the plausibility of the divergence thesis do not immediately buttress the case for convergence on a single model, at least not in anything like its familiar form. First, as the example of the five whys shows, learning-by-monitoring directs attention at least as much to the particulars of local problems, and local means for solving them, as to general principles of problem-solving. In this sense it is more a lingua franca of problem-solving than a fully specified model for organizing design and production. Many subtleties aside, the diffusion of a lingua franca for characterizing a process for adapting to local particularities is plainly not the same thing as, and surely need not lead to convergent adoption of, a single outcome – a model of the one best way of doing things. Indeed, as Herbert Simon noted long ago, if any method of organization were a perfect "adapter," allowing actors to adjust effortlessly and

[20] Charles Sabel, "Intelligible Differences: On Deliberate Strategy and the Exploration of Possibility in Economic Life," 1 *Rivista Italiana degli Economisti* (1): 55–80 (1996).

perfectly to their respective environments, we could afford to ignore the organizational machinery altogether (as economists normally ignore the working of the firm) the better to focus on the relation between changes in the setting and changes in behavior.[21] So if learning-by-monitoring were such a perfect adapter, all we would "see" would be the differences its invisibly uniform processes produced.

But of course learning-by-monitoring is no such perfect adapter, and its intrinsic limitations suggest a second reason that convergence in the sense of diffusion of the one best way is highly unlikely. Flexible, learning-by-monitoring organizations are designed to solve high-dimensional problems – those that must satisfy many unrelated criteria at once. High-dimensional problems typically yield optimal designs – solutions that are best on all the relevant dimensions – only by rare accident. These systems, we saw, aim to produce an increasing variety of product at higher and higher levels of quality and ever lower prices and shorter intervals between models. Their marvel is that they reveal pursuit of at least some of these goals to be compatible in the sense that gains in, say, variety, do not come at the price of steep penalties in quality or speed of development. But this kind of compatibility does not imply that there are no trade-offs in the rate of improvement along various dimensions: on the contrary, it is reasonable to expect that improving quality comes, at least after a time, at the cost of a slow-down in improvements in variety or vice versa. To assume otherwise is to expect both a miraculous harmony among apparently disjoint ends, and a miraculous ability to discover this harmony beneath the veil of experience. Given this limit, we are likely to have many variants of flexible, economy-of-scope production systems because each will be better than the others in reconciling some of the many dimensions of improvement that such systems will have to satisfy. And in fact, while there does appear to be convergence on learning-by-monitoring methods in design and production, there is no sign in the literature of convergence on the best ways of implementing even a discipline as apparently narrow as the five whys. Some companies create *ad hoc* problem-solving teams; others maintain standing groups dedicated to particular types of problems (trim, electrical, leaks, in assembly plants, for example).[22] All have advantages and disadvantages, and each may in time give rise to wholly

---

[21] Simon, Herbert, *The Sciences of the Artificial* (Cambridge, MA: MIT Press, 1969).

[22] See the contrasting problem-solving strategies of Ford, Honda and General Motors described in MacDuffie, note 6 above, at 483–495.

new ways of viewing problem-solving in general. *Mutatis mutandis*, the same is true of customer–supplier relations.[23]

Finally, there is the possibility that the loose connections between governance and production systems that I portrayed as transitional may turn out to be persistent. Put another way, maybe the lesson of the long transition of the last twenty years is that economies are (nearly) always in transition, and simply lack the coherence that convergence theory in any version, including the attenuated one advanced here, supposes. Thus we might get learning-by-monitoring in production, along with the persistence of different but workable governance systems. But regardless of whether and eventually how these tensions are resolved, on the facts of the 1990s, corporate governance is most definitely in transition from categories and debates we know all too well to categories that will have to be invented through new disputes. At the very least, as I read the situation, those who think the old controversies are about to be decided (and they know how) are in for a surprise.

---

[23] Gary Herrigel, "Emerging Strategies and Forms of Governance in the Components Industry in High Wage Regions," and Josh Whitford & Jonathan Zeitlin "Governing Decentralized Production: Institutions, Public Policy, and the Prospects for Inter-firm Cooperation in the United States," both forthcoming in 11 *Industry and Innovation* (1–2) (2004).

10

Convergence of substantive law and convergence of enforcement: a comparison

GÉRARD HERTIG*

Despite many similarities among the corporate governance systems of the leading industrial countries, there are also many important differences, including the basic level of investor protection.[1] The question, of course, is whether these differences will prove durable in the face of the global-ization of trade and investment. These forces jointly favor some degree of convergence, either because they are accompanied by statutory harmo-nization or because they reduce barriers to extra-jurisdictional influence.

The purpose of this chapter is to point out that "convergence" is not simply a feature of substantive law – of the expression of rights and duties that is characteristic of law. Rather, convergence also depends upon whether those legal rights and duties are enforced to comparable effect.[2] In other words, convergence of law on the books does not necessarily correlate positively with convergence in enforcement – there might be even trade-offs between them. My goal is not to focus on the theoret-ical aspects of the relations between substantive law and enforcement in the corporate governance area, but rather to show the "volatility" of the convergence correlation and to explore its implications.

Section I describes my analytic approach. Subsequent sections (II–VII) compare convergence of substantive law and convergence in enforcement in six areas which are important for corporate governance: transparency; voting rights; fiduciary duties; insider trading; takeovers; and bankruptcy.

---

* I would like to thank Jeffrey Gordon, Hideki Kanda, and the participants at the "Conver-gence in Corporate Governance" conference organized by the Columbia Law School Sloan Project on Corporate Governance for their valuable comments and suggestions.
[1] See Mark J. Roe, "Comparative Corporate Governance," in P. Newman, ed., *The New Palgrave Dictionary of Economics and the Law*, p. 342 (1998); Klaus J. Hopt, *et al.*, eds., *Comparative Corporate Governance: The State of the Art and Emerging Research* (1998).
[2] See, e.g., Rafael La Porta, Florencio Lopez-de-Silanes, Andrei Shleifer, & Robert W. Vishny, "Investor Protection and Corporate Governance," 58 *J. Fin. Econ.* 3 (2000).

The comparison will permit me to draw some preliminary conclusions regarding the nature and timing of the correlation, as well as to sketch out some of the reasons why enforcement might affect the convergence of substantive law, and vice versa (section VIII).

I. Simplifying the approach

Generally speaking, substantive legal frameworks can be deemed to converge when substantive rules and standards[3] have become or are becoming similar. Enforcement systems converge when compliance with substantive law has become or is becoming more similar.

Unfortunately, these propositions are rather amorphous, which brings me to make a limited number of simplifications.

1. As far as substantive law is concerned, the first issue is to determine the *level* of the convergence analysis. Given that market-driven functional convergence should come first,[4] neither the legal framework as a whole nor legal details will serve as a benchmark. The relevant level will be convergence of core rules or standards in areas that are essential for corporate governance, e.g., transparency or takeovers. For example, if a jurisdiction forbids insider trading, the ban on taking advantage of "material non-public information" will be considered relevant for comparison purposes, and possible differences in the definition of "materiality" will be ignored.

While variations in that definition may have significant practical consequences, there are two good reasons for ignoring them. First, it is difficult to see how substantive law can converge unless core rules and standards are similar. For example, a court decision on "materiality" will presuppose that trading on the basis of material nonpublic information is prohibited. Second, convergence of "non core" substantive law could well be largely a function of enforcement. For example, when two jurisdictions start with the same broad statutory definition of "insider trading", the jurisdiction in which available remedies make it more profitable to sue the offender could end up with a different definition of "materiality" simply because its courts have to decide on a broader range of issues – not because of diverging legislative intent or differences in judicial approaches.

---

[3] See Louis Kaplow, "Rules versus Standards: An Economic Analysis," 42 *Duke L. Rev.* 557 (1992).

[4] See Ronald J. Gilson, chapter 4, this volume; John C. Coffee, "The Future as History: The Prospects for Global Convergence in Corporate Governance and its Implications," 93 *Nw. U. L. Rev.* 641 (1999).

It is more difficult to simplify a second issue, the *degree* of similarity needed to conclude that substantive law is converging. For example, when one jurisdiction limits the prohibition of insider trading to insiders and another extends it to tippees, does the difference in scope have relevance? This chapter will assume that it does not. Convergence being a dynamic process, it is trends and general similarities that are important, not the fact that one jurisdiction mirrors the other.

2. Convergence in enforcement can be very hard to measure. Hence, comparative enforcement analyses often make use of proxies, for example by referring to estimates of "law and order" compiled by credit risk agencies.[5] This chapter will distinguish between enforcement systems and compliance levels.

The comparison of *enforcement systems* will be based on their two core variables, enforcement agents and sanctions.[6] For example, when analyzing fiduciary duties, my comparison of enforcement systems will boil down to comparing the role of attorneys and the available remedies.

However, comparing enforcement systems is an approach that does not always permit conclusions about the *degree of compliance* with substantive law. Indeed, compliance is not merely a function of enforcement systems. Market pressures, the self-enforcing nature of substantive law, ownership structures, politics, social norms and/or culture all affect compliance levels.[7] Thus, whenever the available data allows, convergence in compliance will also be taken into account.

3. There are additional complications when convergence of substantive law is compared to convergence of enforcement. A first simplification will be to focus on *correlation* rather than causation. For example, this chapter will analyze whether there is convergence of both substance and enforcement, not whether convergence of substance leads to convergence of enforcement. Causation will only be considered to the extent

---

[5]   See Rafael La Porta, Florencio Lopez-de-Silanes, Andrei Shleifer, & Robert W. Vishny, "Law and Finance", 106 *J. Pol. Econ.* 1113 (1998); Katharina Pistor, Martin Raiser, & Stanislaw Gelfer, "Law and Finance in Transition Economies," 8 *Econ. Trans.* 325 (2000).

[6]   The approach has a long tradition and remains in use. See Rafael La Porta, Florencio Lopez-de-Silanes, & Andrei Shleifer, "What Works in Securities Laws?" (Working Paper, 2002) (comparing public and private enforcement in forty-nine jurisdictions).

[7]   On these issues, see Rafael La Porta, Florencio Lopez-de-Silanes, & Andrei Shleifer, "Corporate Ownership around the World," 54 *J. Fin* 471 (1999); Mark J. Roe, *Political Determinants of Corporate Governance* (2003); Symposium Issue, "Norms and Corporate Law," 149 *U. Penn. L. Rev.* 1607 (2001); Amir N. Licht, "The Mother of All Path Dependencies: Toward a Cross-Cultural Theory of Corporate Governance Systems," 26 *Del. J. Corp. L.* 147 (2001).

that convergence in substantive law prevents or limits convergence in enforcement (or vice versa).

A second simplification concerns the *timing* of convergence. Obviously, both types of convergence need not be simultaneous, as time is often needed for change to occur. On the other hand, if convergence of substantive law and convergence of enforcement occur far apart, it is difficult to argue that they are correlated. This chapter will generally keep the comparison within what should be a broadly acceptable time-frame, i.e., two to three decades.

4. The analysis will be limited to the *US*, the *EU* and, to some extent, *Japan*. This is mainly a quantitative simplification. However, comparable industrial development, the growing recognition of the importance of shareholder value in all these jurisdictions,[8] and the existence of reliable courts also justify the limitation.

5. The comparative corporate governance debate has tended to focus on *large publicly traded* corporations. Given the differences in the distribution of large, medium-sized and small firms across jurisdictions,[9] neglecting small to medium-sized firms may lead to biased conclusions. It would be wrong to allege that smaller firms necessarily face a fundamentally different set of corporate governance issues. For example, the fact that a firm is small and closely held does not prevent complex decision-making issues from arising, in particular when the firm is family owned or attempts to overcome size disadvantages by cooperating (formally or informally) with other firms.[10]

That having been said, publicly traded corporations are generally subject to more extensive legal requirements, in particular through securities regulation. If a given jurisdiction has a greater proportion of publicly traded firms, an undiscriminating comparison with a jurisdiction that has few publicly traded firms may be flawed. This possible bias will be ignored, but my chapter will try as much as possible to distinguish between large (often publicly traded) and small to medium-sized (often closely held) firms.

---

[8] See for Europe, Eddy Wymeersch, "Gesellschaftsrecht im Wandel: Ursachen und Entwicklungslinien," 30 *ZGR* 294 (2001); for Japan, Takeo Hoshi & Anil K. Kashyap, *Corporate Financing and Governance in Japan: The Road to the Future* (2001).

[9] See, e.g., European Commission, *Enterprises in Europe*, Fourth Report (1996).

[10] See also Joseph A. McCahery & Erik P. M. Vermeulen, "The Evolution of Closely Held Business Forms in Europe," 26 *J. Corp. L.* 855 (2001).

Summarizing, I will conclude that the correlation between convergence in substantive law and enforcement is *positive* when convergence in core rules or standards is accompanied by parallel changes affecting enforcement agents, sanctions and compliance levels – or vice versa. When convergence in substantive law is not accompanied by convergence in enforcement, this chapter will consider that there is *no correlation*. Finally, the conclusion will be that there is a *trade-off* when convergence of substantive law prevents or limits convergence of enforcement – or vice versa.

II. Transparency

Convergence in the transparency area will be analyzed both in general and from a more specific point of view.

In general

Securities regulations aimed at enhancing issuer and capital market transparency were adopted decades ago in both the US and, under US influence, Japan. Until recently, most EU member states refrained from adopting statutes that could be considered similar to US securities regulation. EU integration has brought major changes in the European landscape. There is now an EU law framework with transparency requirements that are becoming increasingly similar to those in the US – a trend that should be reinforced by post-Enron regulatory reforms.[11]

There are signs that convergence will not remain limited to substantive law. Japan and the EU jurisdictions have been, or are, setting up a public regulatory system that is inspired by the SEC model – essentially because mandating transparency is considered to be ineffective if enforcement is left to private parties.

To be sure, enforcement systems remain significantly different. In the US, the power to bring public action is centralized and private suits are favored by attractive collective action possibilities, e.g., class actions. The EU, on the other hand, still follows a less powerful decentralized enforcement approach and private enforcement faces many barriers. However, despite remaining objections to establishing a European SEC, the idea can no longer be considered as heresy and public enforcement should gather

---

[11] See Klaus J. Hopt, "Modern Company and Capital Market Problems: Improving European Corporate Governance after Enron," 3 *J. Corp. L. Stud.* 211 (2003).

speed in the coming years.[12] Similarly, common approaches towards collective actions seem to be emerging. Various EU member states are considering fostering private suits by introducing some sort of class action while the US is trying to curb class action abuses.[13]

In short, there is currently no correlation between convergence in substantive law and convergence in enforcement, but this may change in the near future.

Accounting and disclosure requirements

Developments in two areas of great importance for corporate governance, namely accounting and disclosure requirements, generally confirm this big picture assessment.

Substantive requirements for *publicly traded* firms are converging towards the Anglo-Saxon model, not least because of the major role played by US capital markets and financial intermediaries.[14] For accounting standards, the issue is merely whether the end result will be closer to US-GAAP or to IAS.[15] Anglo-Saxon prospectus requirements are being transplanted to continental Europe and Japan. Rules requiring listed companies to inform investors in a timely way about events that have a material impact have spread to civil law jurisdictions, which also increasingly require significant shareholders to disclose their holdings when they reach given thresholds.

Admittedly, the degree of past divergence or current convergence is debatable. Some studies show significant divergence in the accounting area, especially between common law jurisdictions (notably the US and the UK) and civil law jurisdictions (especially Germany and France).[16] Other commentators downplay the impact on continental European firms

---

[12] See Gérard Hertig & Ruben Lee, "Four Predictions about the Future of EU Securities Regulation" 3 *J. Corp. L. Stud.* 359 (2003).

[13] Klaus J. Hopt, "Company Law in the European Union: Harmonization and/or Subsidiarity?" 1 *Int. & Comp. Corp. L. J.* 41 (1999); Private Securities Litigation Reform Act, 109 Stat. 737.

[14] Klaus J. Hopt, "Common Principles of Corporate Governance in Europe," in Basil S. Markensinis, ed., *The Clifford Chance Millennium Lectures: The Coming Together of the Common Law and the Civil Law*, p. 105 (2000); Werner F. Ebke, "Accounting, Auditing and Global Capital Markets," in Theodor Baums *et al.*, eds., *Corporations, Capital Markets and Business in the Law*, p. 113 (2000).

[15] For the EU, see Regulation 1606/2002 requiring listed companies to use International Accounting Standards by 2005, *OJL* 243/1 (2002).

[16] See La Porta *et al.*, note 5 above.

of a shift from EU standards to IAS or US-GAAP – implying that any significant divergence may have more to do with creative accounting than with accounting standards themselves.[17] Similarly, one can argue that the content of U. S. disclosure requirement remains more stringent, in particular when it comes to nonfinancial and forward-looking data.[18] There is, however, a clearly recognizable convergence trend.

For the reasons mentioned when discussing transparency in general, convergence in substantive law does not correlate with convergence in enforcement. On the other hand, convergence in substantive law does correlate positively with convergence in compliance.

Publicly traded firms have been increasingly opting into transparency regimes that are more demanding than the one which applies to them. Most notably, non-US firms are increasingly seeking listings on US exchanges. For example, the New York Stock Exchange (NYSE) has experienced significant growth in foreign company listings, with 472 non-US companies listed in 2002, compared to fewer than 50 at the beginning of the 1990s.[19] The obvious purpose of such a listing is to facilitate access to US capital markets. However, more often than not, the main value of a US listing is to credibly signal to investors worldwide a commitment to continued voluntary compliance with (stringent) US accounting and disclosure standards.

This puts pressure on large continental European and Japanese firms that are not listed in the US. As a minimum, it encourages them to comply fully with the (less stringent) accounting and disclosure requirements applicable to them. Actually, there is growing evidence that major EU firms are going beyond that minimum to please investors and that Japanese firms are joining the bandwagon.[20] To be sure, US firms' transparency remains superior, but recent studies and scandals show that the gap may

---

[17] Jörg Baetge & Stefan Thiele, "Disclosure and Auditing as Affecting Corporate Governance," in Hopt *et al.*, note 1 above, p. 719; Steven J. Huddart, John S. Hughes, & Markus Burnnermeier, "Disclosure Requirements and Stock Exchange Listing Choice in an International Context," 26 *J. Acc. & Econ.* 237 (1999).

[18] See Gérard Hertig, Reinier Kraakman, & Edward Rock, *Issuers and Investor Protection*, in Kraakman *et al.*, *The Anatomy of Corporate Law, A Comparative and Functional Approach* (2004); La Porta *et al.*, note 6 above (discussing IPOs).

[19] Source: NYSE, www.nyse.com (as of November 23, 2003). European exchanges and the Tokyo Stock Exchange have also experienced growth in foreign listings, but the NYSE is the only exchange that has not seen a decline over recent years.

[20] Hideki Kanda, "Japan's Financial Big Bang: Its Impact on the Legal System and Corporate Governance," in Takeo Hoshi & Hugh Patrick, eds., *Crisis and Change in the Japanese Financial System* p. 277 (2000).

have mattered less in the past decade and, in any event, is not what it used to be.[21]

A more open question is whether the positive correlation holds when *closely held* firms are taken into account. Substantive convergence developments mainly concern publicly traded firms. For example, US corporate law generally does not subject closely held firms to disclosure requirements or accounting standards. EU law, on the other hand, requires closely held firms to disclose their financial statements to the public and to obey minimum accounting standards. The extent of this divergence can be disputed, however.[22] EU accounting law allows for partial exemptions for smaller firms, bringing the regime closer to the US one. The reverse applies to the US: a substantial number of small US firms are being traded over the counter, which makes them "public" companies subject to mandatory disclosure and stringent accounting standards. Nevertheless, it is safe to say that substantive law has yet to converge as far as closely held firms are concerned.

By contrast, there are similarities in enforcement systems. None of the jurisdictions under consideration here has or is likely to institute public enforcement for closely held firms, and the lack of listing generally makes transparency-related private actions rather difficult. This means that, as for publicly traded firms, there is no correlation in convergence – the difference being that in this case there are few signs of convergence one way or the other.

Interestingly, this does not prevent convergence in compliance by closely held firms as well. Despite harmonization, EU closely held firms have succeeded in limiting public access to their financial statements.[23] US closely held corporations, for their part, are generally obliged to provide credit agencies with detailed financial and accounting data if they are

---

[21] See Standard & Poor's, *Transparency and Disclosure Study* (October 2002), available at www.standardandpoors.com (the annual reports of US companies provide less information than those of many non-US companies, but overall disclosure is equal to that of top-ranked UK companies); Jeffrey N. Gordon, "What Enron Means for the Management and Control of the Modern Business Corporation: Some Initial Reflections," 69 *U. Chi. L. Rev.* 1233 (2002).

[22] See Gérard Hertig & Hideki Kanda, "Creditor Protection," in Kraakman *et al.*, note 18 above.

[23] Some 30 percent of French SARLs and nonlisted SAs as well as 80–95 percent of Germany's closely held corporations are reportedly not disclosing their financial statements: see Maurice Cozian, Alian Viandier, & Florence Deboissy, *Droit des Sociétés*, no. 413 (15th edn, 2002); Mathias Habersack, *Europäisches Gesellschaftsrecht*, p. 68 (2nd edn, 2003). Germany, however, has recently adopted legislation to address the issue.

seeking external finance. In other words, weak enforcement systems allow EU firms to comply less than they should, whereas the market forces US firms to comply more than the applicable regime requires.

Summing up, there generally is convergence in compliance. For publicly traded firms, this goes hand in hand with convergence in substantive law, and convergence in enforcement is likely to follow. For closely held firms, compliance and enforcement levels are similar, but substantive law is not converging.

III.   Shareholders' voting rights

The corporate governance role of shareholders is also largely a function of their voting rights.

From a substantive point of view, shareholders' right to vote on fundamental issues such as elections to the board, charter amendments, mergers and dissolution is recognized by law in virtually all OECD jurisdictions. Differences remain regarding other powers of the shareholders' meeting, but their importance should not be overestimated. First, jurisdiction-specific provisions are normally merely applicable by default.

Second, those differences in voting rights that are due to mandatory provisions are likely to be of diminishing importance. Jurisdictions that constrain the powers of the shareholders' meeting do so either to favor managers (especially when they are a powerful interest group) or to protect other stakeholders such as employees, local suppliers and customers, etc. Should jurisdictions converge on the respective importance of shareholder and stakeholder value, differences in voting rights will be reduced. There are strong indications that such a trend is in the making. For example, whereas stakeholder value used to play a comparatively more important role in continental Europe and Japan, the importance of shareholder value has increased.[24] At the opposite end of the spectrum, shareholder value is less dominant in the US; stakeholders' interests have been getting an increased amount of attention in recent years, especially when it comes to takeover bids and fiduciary duties.[25]

Voting rights are essentially self-enforcing, as their effectiveness is more a function of voting than of enforcement systems. The main comparative issue is whether jurisdictions diverge in the way they deal with the collective action problems faced by shareholders of public companies.

When there is a *controlling shareholder*, free riding by minority shareholders will not deter him from monitoring management. His discretion

---

[24] See Wymeersch, note 8 above.   [25] See below, sections IV and VI.

in forcing management to do what he wants may vary depending upon how well a given jurisdiction protects minority shareholders, but this is unlikely to influence his activism or to affect management's compliance with the resolutions of the shareholders' meeting.

To the extent there is no controlling shareholder, the effectiveness of voting rights depends upon institutional shareholder activism and the role of individual investor representatives.

In recent years, *institutional investors* around the world have been able to increase their influence and to use their voting power to make management more accountable. Of course, cost issues, free-riding, and other problems make the level of shareholder activism subject to debate, even in the US. However, there is both empirical[26] and anecdotal evidence that pension and mutual funds, in particular, are getting increased managerial attention and results.

It is true that continental European institutional investors are not yet playing as active a role as (at least some) American or British institutional investors.[27] (However, lack of investor activism may be offset by controlling shareholder activism, as many public continental European firms still have a concentrated shareholder structure.[28]) But US institutional investors are increasingly investing in continental European companies, due to their need for geographically diversified investments. The involvement of US players should increase activism both directly and by providing leadership to their European counterparts.

Even in Japan, where perfunctory general meetings and passive institutional shareholders have long been the rule, there are clear signs that cross-shareholdings are no longer sufficient to prevent institutional shareholders from using their voting powers to play a real corporate governance role.[29]

Information and other transaction costs will often result in *individual investors* not attending the general meeting. This is why corporate laws

---

[26] Willard T. Carleton, James M. Nelson, & Michael S. Weisbach, "The Influence of Institutions on Corporate Governance through Private Negotiations: Evidence from TIAA-CREF," 53 *J. Fin.* 1335 (1998); Michael P. Smith, "Shareholder Activism by Institutional Investors: Evidence from CalPERS," 51 *J. Fin.* 227 (1996).

[27] Alexander Bassen, "Einflussnahme institutioneller Anleger auf Corporate Governance und Unternehmungsführung – Ergebnisse einer empirischen Untersuchung," 14 *ZBB* 430 (2002); Klaus J. Hopt, "Shareholder Rights and Remedies: A View from Germany and the Continent," 2 *Company Financial and Insolvency L. Rev.* 261 (1997).

[28] See Marco Becht & Fabrizio Barca, eds., *The Control of Corporate Europe* (2002).

[29] See Mitsuaki Okabe, *Cross Shareholdings in Japan: A New Unified Perspective of the Economic System* (2002) (concluding that cross-shareholdings are declining and the shares thus made available have been acquired by foreign investors and institutional investors).

allow for shareholders to be represented. Proxy voting through depository institutions plays an important role in continental Europe, whereas proxy solicitation is well established in the US.

It is generally considered that voting through European depository institutions has not allowed for an effective representation of shareholder interests. For custodians, representing shareholders is either an unprofitable business or an activity that conflicts with their interests as lenders or financial advisers.[30] As a result, voting power has often shifted away from shareholders, to the benefit of lenders or managers. Nevertheless, a divergence with the US is less easy to establish than is often believed. First, despite (or because of) proxy regulation, the level of shareholder involvement has historically been low in the US.[31] Second, it is not clear whether recent increases in US shareholders' use of the proxy process have prevented managers from influencing shareholder voting.[32] Third, individual European investors are increasingly investing through mutual funds, which (competition *oblige*) are tending more and more to choose representatives other than banks, or to give specific instructions to the latter.

To summarize, voting rights used to be much more effective in continental Europe because the ownership of public companies was highly concentrated. Now that shares in public companies are becoming more widely held, global convergence is likely. Firms around the world are facing increasingly similar levels of institutional investor activism and diversity in proxy systems is unlikely to significantly affect the (overall) effectiveness of voting rights.

IV. Fiduciary duties

Basically, managers everywhere have two general substantive duties (referred to as "fiduciary duties" in common law jurisdictions): a duty of care and a duty of loyalty.

The *duty of care* implies that managers must exercise the degree of skill, diligence and care that a reasonably prudent person would exercise in similar circumstances. It is well known that US courts are reluctant to

---

[30] See Theodor Baums & Eddy Wymeersch, eds., *Shareholder Voting Rights and Practices in Europe and the United States* (1999).

[31] See Frank H. Easterbrook & Daniel R. Fischel, *The Economic Structure of Corporate Law*, pp. 81–89 (1991).

[32] See Jennifer E. Bethel & Stuart L. Gillan, "The Impact of the Institutional and Regulatory Environment on Shareholder Voting" 31 *Fin. Mngmnt* 29 (2002).

second-guess managerial decisions (business judgment rule). Civil law courts (German courts in particular)[33] are increasingly adopting similar approaches (albeit less explicitly), and protect management against interference in its business decisions.

The purpose of the *duty of loyalty* is to protect shareholders against opportunistic behavior on the part of managers and controlling shareholders. It is exaggerated to believe, as common law scholars sometimes do, that the duty of loyalty as conceived in continental European jurisdictions is significantly less protective of minority shareholders. Those who put the emphasis on differences in the duty of loyalty often fail to take proper account of the protection offered by criminal law provisions (e.g., the French provisions on *abus des biens sociaux*).[34] More importantly, civil law jurisdictions are showing some "common law creativeness" in protecting minority shareholders, especially when dealing with groups of companies.[35]

Convergence in substantive law does not correlate with convergence in enforcement. There is no denying that case law is much richer in the US than in the EU (especially continental Europe) or Japan, even taking into account recent increases in litigation and public action outside the US.[36] Disparities in standing to sue are unlikely to cause the divergence. There are no great differences in the right of bankruptcy receivers to sue managers who have violated their fiduciary duties or in the standing to sue of shareholders directly injured by breaches of fiduciary duties. The same is true of the right of shareholders to sue managers on behalf of the corporation, since US-type derivative actions are available in the EU or Japan. To be sure, EU or Japanese shareholders may face significant procedural hurdles, but this is also the case for US shareholders.[37]

---

[33] Theodor Baums, "Personal Liabilities of Company Directors in German Law," 7 *Int. Company and Commercial L. Rev.* 318 (1996).

[34] Regarding similarities between French and US case law, see François Vincke, "La Relation actionnariat et Conseil d'administration," 61 *Revue de la Banque* 435 (1997).

[35] Klaus J. Hopt, "Legal Issues and Questions of Policy in the Comparative Regulation of Groups," in P. Balzarini *et al.*, eds., *I Gruppi di Società* (1996), p. 45.

[36] See Deborah Steinborn, "Getting Legal, Lawsuits are the Latest Trend for European Shareholders," *Wall St. J.*, June 11, 2001 (European edn); Paul Davies, *Introduction to Company Law* (2002), p. 690 (UK directors are increasingly subject to disqualification procedures for violation of their fiduciary duties in the vicinity of insolvency); Mark D. West, "Why Shareholders Sue: The Evidence from Japan," 30 *J. Legal Stud.* 351 (2001).

[37] See, e.g., James A. Fanto, *Corporate Governance in American and French Law* (1997); Theodor Baums, "Company Law Reform in Germany", 3 *J. Corp. L. Stud.* 181 (2003).

In my opinion, the main reason for the divergence to remain significant is the institutionalized availability of contingent fees for US attorneys.[38] This fee system, which awards the attorney a significant percentage of any recovery, including settlement, makes litigation much more profitable in the case of either derivative actions or collective actions.

On the other hand, from a compliance perspective, one cannot fail to notice that directors worldwide are paying an increasingly similar degree of attention to their fiduciary duties. This is partly because US directors, the most exposed to litigation, are now able to reduce their risks by ensuring that the corporation's charter excludes liability for most breaches of the duty of care.[39] However, factors other than enforcement systems are influencing directors' attitudes.[40] In particular, directors in civil law countries seem increasingly concerned about their fiduciary duties, despite the low risk of sanctions and the availability of insurance against most of them. This should mean that being considered competent and trustworthy is the main concern, not the enforcement risk.[41]

If that is the case, we can conclude that convergence in substantive law does correlate with convergence in compliance, but that convergence in substantive law is not correlated with convergence in enforcement.

V. Insider trading

Under US influence, both the EU and Japan have adopted substantive provisions on insider trading, namely a prohibition of trading on the basis of material nonpublic information. As in the US, the aim is to force insiders to "disclose or abstain," and the provisions enacted in the EU and Japan are basically comparable.[42]

Differences remain regarding the scope and content of the prohibition.[43] For example, it applies only to insiders in listed companies in

---

[38] Note that resistance to contingent fees is diminishing in the EU and Japan, as litigation becomes a more acceptable part of the business environment.

[39] See, e.g., Section 102(b)(7) Delaware General Corporation Law, adopted in response to *Smith* v. *Van Gorkom* (Del. Supr. 1985, 488 A 2d 858).

[40] See Gérard Hertig & Hideki Kanda, "Related Party Transactions," in Kraakman *et al.*, note 18 above.

[41] See Melvin A. Eisenberg, "Corporate Law and Social Norms," 99 *Colum. L. Rev.* 1253 (1999); Margaret M. Blair & Lynn A. Stout, "Trust, Trustworthiness and the Behavioral Foundations of Corporate Law," 149 *U. Penn. L. Rev.* 1735 (2001).

[42] See for the EU: *OJL* 16/96 (2003) Directive Market Abuse; for Japan: Sections 166 and 167 Securities and Exchange Law; for the US: Rule 10b-5.

[43] Ongoing EU regulatory reforms should reduce differences with the US. See Michael Leppert & Florian Stürwald, "Die insiderrechtlichen Regelungen des Vorschlages für eine

Japan and the EU, whereas in the US it applies even if the company is not traded on a national exchange. However, the main difference is that US case law is significantly richer and more complex than in the EU or Japan.[44]

That difference cannot be explained in the same way as for fiduciary duties, that is, by a different incentive structure for enforcement agents. Acknowledging the importance of public action to enforce prohibitions on insider trading, Japan and EU member states have set up generally well-funded SEC-like enforcement agencies. Nevertheless, their activity has been decidedly unimpressive in many jurisdictions, including Japan and Germany.[45]

One could consider this quite a predictable development. US pressure left Japan and EU member states with no other choice than to harmonize substantive law. That having been done, more concentrated shareholding structures provided reasons for Japan and continental Europe to undermine substantive convergence by lack of enforcement.[46] On the one hand, some degree of insider trading had to be tolerated to ensure that controlling shareholders could be compensated for bearing nondiversifiable risk. On the other hand, state ownership and political connections generally gave rent-driven insiders the power to hamper enforcement efforts.

I believe that differences in shareholder structures cannot be the only explanation for enforcement deficiencies, as the latter do not always vary according to whether ownership is dispersed or not. For example, while there are very few (if any) jurisdictions other than the US and the UK where listed companies are widely held, a substantial 38 of the 103 jurisdictions that have adopted insider trading provisions are considered as engaging in prosecution activity.[47] Or, to take another example, Japanese and European public enforcers have not become any more active following Japanese firms' recent unwinding of cross-shareholdings, or the increase in widely held firms in continental Europe.

Marktmissbrauchsrichtlinie und der Stand der Umsetzung im deutschen Wertpapierhandelsrecht," 14 *ZBB* 90 (2002).

[44] For a recent discussion of US insider trading law, see Donald C. Langevoort, "Reading Cady, Roberts: The Ideology and Practice of Insider Trading Regulation," 99 *Colum. L. J.* 1319 (1999).

[45] Anita Raghavan *et al.*, "Europe's Police are Out of Luck on Insider Cases," *Wall St. J.*, (Aug. 17, 2000) (US edn), at C1.

[46] On differences in shareholder structures, see La Porta *et al.*, note 7 above, and Becht & Barca, note 28 above.

[47] See Utpal Bhattacharya & Hazem Daouk, "The World Price of Insider Trading," 57 *J. Fin.* 75 (2002)

A final example is even more telling. Although UK enforcement agents initially adopted the aggressive approach that was in line with the UK's dispersed shareholder structure, results have not matched expectations. Admittedly, the fact that UK prosecutors sought criminal sanctions rather than the administrative or civil sanctions favored by the SEC had something to do with this.[48] The approach meant facing a high burden of proof, and as a result, the number of convictions was virtually zero,[49] leading to embarrassing public setbacks that had a negative effect on prosecutors' activism. However, if lack of enforcement had simply been the result of adopting the wrong enforcement mechanism, necessary reforms would have long ago been undertaken. In my opinion, there is a more fundamental explanation for the lack of enforcement in the UK, viz. resistance to the heavy hand of the state.

In other words, there is evidence that divergence in enforcement has a "leave the markets alone" next to the shareholder structure explanation.[50] There are reasons to believe that enforcement failures in both Japan and the EU are the *result* of convergence in substantive law. Jurisdictions agreed to adopt more stringent substantive provisions, but made sure that their enforcement systems would insure for the law to remain "on the books". Paradoxically, it might well be that, in the absence of harmonization, (less convergent) substantive prohibitions would be accompanied by (less divergent) enforcement.

VI. Takeover defenses

In the US, the takeover wave of the 1980s resulted in many states adjusting their company laws to restrain hostile bidders. For example, statutes were amended to require "disinterested shareholder" approval of a hostile takeover, to give minority shareholders the right to sell their shares to a hostile bidder at a fair price, or to restrain post-takeover business combinations by a hostile bidder. Moreover, state courts construed board authority as broadly as possible so as to give managers wide latitude to

---

[48] See La Porta *et al.*, note 6 above (no evidence that criminal sanctions work); Richard S. Biegen, Lionel E. Pashkoff, & Paul G. Roche, "Countries Strengthen Insider Trading Laws," *Nat'l L. J.*, C 19 (November 13, 1995) (prevalence of enforcement through criminal, rather than civil or administrative, processes in G-7 countries).

[49] There were three convictions between 1995 and 1999 (compared to 162 civil case successes for the US SEC) – see Raghavan *et al.*, note 45 above.

[50] The debatable effectiveness of US enforcement efforts may also have contributed to this attitude. See Hasan Seyhun, "The Effectiveness of Insider Trading Sanctions," 35 *J. L. & Econ.* 149 (1992).

engage in defensive tactics without having to consult shareholders.[51] Such protection for incumbent management often operated under the pretense of protecting the workforce against out-of-state predators.

Although hostile takeovers used to be a rare occurrence, the past decade has seen takeover legislation blossoming in continental Europe, with statutes or self-regulatory codes in force in all major jurisdictions. Under UK influence, the general purpose is more oriented towards market transparency and shareholder protection than in US reforms. Thus, the proposed EU Takeover Bids Directive is likely to provide that the board of the target company should abstain from any action which may result in the frustration of the offer, unless it has the prior authorization of the general meeting of shareholders.[52]

This prohibition on defensive tactics unless shareholder consent is obtained could be considered a major divergence in substantive law. In my opinion, it is more likely to indicate that substantive law is mutually converging from two opposite sides.[53] US reforms are aimed at putting some constraint on an active market for corporate control, by increasing management's latitude to oppose hostile takeovers while still permitting tactics that should favor the bidder rather than management – for example, partial bids. European legislation, on the other hand, is aimed at creating a less dormant market for corporate control, while introducing features that should protect management by making takeovers more expensive – for example, mandatory full bid provisions.[54]

The "convergence from opposite sides" view seems to be supported by a comparison of the success rate of hostile takeover bids during the past decade. In the US, the use of poison pills and other defensive measures has quite often thwarted hostile bids. Targets of hostile bids between 1994 and 1997 have managed to remain independent 35 percent of the time (up from 22 percent between 1988 and 1993) and, because of the intervention

---

[51] Compare Lucian Arye Bebchuk & Allen Ferrell, "Federalism and Corporate Law: The Race to Protect Managers from Takeovers," 99 *Colum. L. Rev.* 1168 (1999).

[52] See Report of the High Level Group of Company Law Experts, *Issues Related to Takeover Bids* (2002), available at www.europa.eu.int.

[53] See Richard W. Painter & Christian Kirchner, "Takeover Defenses under Delaware Law, the Proposed Thirteenth EU Directive and the New German Takeover Law: Comparison and Recommendation for Reform," 50 *Am. J. Comp. L.* 45 (2002) (Delaware's approach lies somewhere between the German and UK approaches); Bernard S. Black, "The First International Merger Wave (and the Fifth and Last US Wave)," 54 *U. Miami L. Rev.* 799 (2000) (discussing the similarity of US and EU legal barriers to hostile takeovers).

[54] For a recent discussion of European provisions, see Paul Davies & Klaus J. Hopt, "Control Transactions," in Kraakmann *et al.*, note 18 above.

of white knights and other parties, targets have been acquired by the hostile bidder only 38 percent of the time.[55] In continental Europe, where the delay in the adoption of the Takeover Bids Directive has generally been used by EU member states to bring their legislation closer to expected minimum standards, the image is a reverse one. Long unknown, hostile bids have mushroomed.[56] Nevertheless hostile bidders had to withdraw 47 percent of the time between 1990 and 1999.[57]

It is true that these data do not necessarily reflect convergence in substantive law. Similarities in the success rates of hostile takeovers can be misleading. When ownership is concentrated, the ratio of defeated hostile takeovers does not say much about the effectiveness of defensive measures: controlling shareholders can accept a takeover bid regardless of management hostility.[58] Moreover, success rates may reflect converging changes in the economic or social environment rather than regulatory convergence.

However, the point is not that substantive convergence has led to similar rates of success for hostile bids. What counts is the interplay between substantive convergence and divergence in the enforcement area.

The main US jurisdiction, Delaware, has been keen to maintain a legal regime that encourages litigation by maintaining uncertainty.[59] By contrast, the adoption of the EU Takeover Bids Directive has been delayed for years because of UK fears that harmonization would result in bids becoming bogged down in litigation, if its nonbinding code had to be enshrined in a statute. Recent compromises make it likely that the Takeover Bids Directive will be adopted in the near future, but it is indisputable that disagreement at the enforcement level has significantly reduced the pace of convergence in substantive law.

Takeover legislation is therefore a good example of the way convergence in substantive law can be slowed down by a willingness to simultaneously harmonize enforcement. This convergence trade-off contrasts with the insider trading situation. There, jurisdictions readily yielded to pressures to harmonize substantive law, but were able to prevent unwanted consequences by avoiding convergence in enforcement. Here, the willingness

---

[55] Data reported by Steven Lipin, "Takeover Defenses Increasingly Thwart Hostile Bids," *Wall St. J.* (July 1, 1997) (European edn) at 11.

[56] See "Mariage à la Mode," *Economist*, April 29, 2000, at 10 (European Business Survey).

[57] See *Corporate Control Alert*, April 2000, at 13.

[58] A good example is provided by the increase in takeover activity in Japan, following the unwinding of cross-shareholdings: see Dean Yoost & Shin Nakanishi, "Defenses against Takeovers Weaken," *The Nikkei Weekly*, September 4, 2000, at 7.

[59] Ehud Kamar, "A Regulatory Competition Theory of Indeterminacy in Corporate Law," 98 *Colum. L. Rev.* 1908 (1998).

to ensure the effectiveness of substantive convergence by harmonizing enforcement backfired, delaying the whole process by many years.

VII. Reorganization and bankruptcy

Reorganization and bankruptcy procedures are an essential part of any corporate governance convergence analysis.[60]

Despite globalization and the increase in cross-border investments, reorganization and bankruptcy laws remain very territorial. International efforts to reduce diversity have accomplished very little. Nevertheless, there are signs that some degree of harmonization is now perceived as necessary.

A United Nations Commission on International Trade Law (UNCITRAL) Model Law on Cross-Border Insolvency was adopted in 1997.[61] It aims at promoting "modern and fair" legislation on cases where the insolvent debtor has assets in more than one state. However, the Model Law relates essentially to the international enforcement of domestic decisions. It implies almost no harmonization of substantive law and thus leaves room for a variety of national approaches.

As a result, convergence of substantive law is not to be expected in the foreseeable future.[62] This is not very surprising. By definition, reorganization and bankruptcy laws apply to most firms, regardless of their size. Differences across countries in firm-size structures and in access to finance make substantive harmonization extremely difficult (and probably undesirable).

On the other hand, there are signs that some degree of international cooperation in the enforcement area is deemed necessary. As I have already mentioned, the main purpose of the Model Law on Cross-Border Insolvency is to promote mutual recognition of decisions based on domestic law when the debtor has assets in more than one state. A similar approach is adopted by the EU Regulation on Insolvency Proceedings.[63] US courts, for their part, are showing some willingness to let US creditors choose

---

[60] See David A. Skeel, "An Evolutionary Theory of Corporate Law and Corporate Bankruptcy," 51 *Vand. L. Rev.* 1325 (1998).

[61] The Model Law is available at www.uncitral.org; see also R. Harwer, "UNCITRAL Model Law on Cross-Border Insolvency," 1997 *Int'l Insolv. Rev.* 146.

[62] See also Paul B. Stephan III, "The Futility of Unification and Harmonization in International Commercial Law," 39 *Va. J. Int'l L.* 743 (1999).

[63] *OJL* 160/1 (2000). See also Axel Flessner, "The Future German International Insolvency Law and its Relationship to the European Convention on Insolvency Proceedings," 1999 *Eur. Bus. L. Rev.* 2.

between US and foreign insolvency regimes in international bankruptcy situations.[64]

In the short term, these developments are of rather secondary importance from a corporate governance perspective. It is difficult to predict whether harmonization efforts will have an impact in the longer term and, if so, whether they will bring convergence of domestic substantive law or convergence in the domestic enforcement area. Nevertheless, one point can be made about international harmonization efforts. Mutual recognition of insolvency decisions required convergence in enforcement. It did not require convergence of substantive rules beyond a vague plea for "modern and fair" legislation.

In sum, convergence in substantive rules does not correlate with convergence in enforcement.

VIII.   The nature and "volatility" of the correlation

In the above six sections I have shown that the correlation between convergence of substantive rules and convergence of enforcement is complex and may change quite rapidly.

A positive correlation between convergence in both substantive law and enforcement systems seems to be rather the exception. It is much easier to find areas where there is no such correlation in convergence. This applies, for example, to transparency, fiduciary duties and bankruptcy. Transparency requirements and fiduciary duties are converging, but enforcement has yet to converge. The reverse is true in the reorganization and bankruptcy area: enforcement seems to be converging, whereas substantive laws remain quite far apart.

However, while correct at the present time, conclusions about the lack of correlation may have to be revised in the near future. In the areas just mentioned, transparency and fiduciary duties, the correlation is likely to become positive because most jurisdictions are adopting a favorable attitude towards litigation.

There is also evidence pointing to the existence of trade-offs between convergence in substantive law and convergence in enforcement systems. Harmonization of insider trading laws has been followed by highly divergent enforcement – implying that a lower degree of substantive convergence would have been accompanied by more comparable enforcement.

---

[64] See Lucian A. Bebchuk & Andrew T. Guzman, "An Economic Analysis of Transnational Bankruptcies," 42 *J. Law & Econ.* 775 (1999).

In the takeover area, on the other hand, the willingness to ensure that substantive law was effectively enforced delayed substantive convergence by many years.

I have also shown that a correlation analysis is more complex than a mere comparison between substantive law and enforcement systems. Substantive convergence may be accompanied by convergence "in practice," independently of convergence in enforcement. This is the case when substantive law is self-enforcing: the effectiveness of voting rights has much less to do with enforcement systems than with shareholder structure and the ability of investors to overcome collective action problems. This is also the case when reputation makes compliance essential. For example, market pressures force publicly traded firms to comply with transparency requirements that go beyond those resulting from applicable laws. Similarly, directors' concerns for their reputation induce them to comply with their fiduciary duties independently of the applicable enforcement regime.

In short, there is a need to develop an overall theory from an agnostic starting point. Further studies will most probably show that any specific convergence or divergence situation is likely to have multiple origins. In particular, differences in ownership structures and divergence regarding the social value of litigation are certainly influential. Moreover, it is likely that interactions between substantive law and enforcement will be identified. Among other things, the cost of enforcement is likely to be one of the factors determining the convergence – or divergence – of substantive law.[65]

---

[65] See Gérard Hertig & Hideki Kanda, "Rules, Enforcement and Corporate Governance" (Working Paper, 1998).

11

Cross-shareholding in the Japanese *keiretsu*

J. MARK RAMSEYER*

The Japanese corporate "groups" (popularly called the *keiretsu*) present something of a puzzle.[1] At least as usually recounted, the firms in the group both invest heavily in and trade heavily with each other. The puzzle is why.

In the US, we cite these intra-group trades and investments for a variety of propositions. Implicitly comparing them to spot-market transactions, some observers claim they reflect a distinctively Japanese preference for keeping social contacts within closed groups (Gerlach, 1992). Others tie them to the current debates over path dependence, and claim they prove history matters. For a time, some even called the groups nontariff trade barriers (Lawrence, 1993).

Yet in many ways, group firms invest and trade in ways that reflect straightforward economic calculations. I first describe the groups themselves (section I). I then advance two propositions. First, when group banks trade on member stock, they sometimes (not always) trade on inside information (section II). If US banks do not do the same, in part it is simply because they cannot legally hold stock. Second, the higher cross-holdings before World War II reflected the role that the wealthy

---

* This chapter was written in 1997, and does not reflect the results of more recent work on the subject by Miwa & Ramseyer (2000, 2002a, 2002b, 2002c). To the extent that these more recent studies are inconsistent with this chapter, readers should rely on Miwa & Ramseyer.

   I gratefully acknowledge the advice and assistance of Stephen Choi, John Coates, Mark Fisher, Andrew Guzman, Shinsaku Iwahara, William Klein, Lewis Kornhauser, John Lott, Curtis Milhaupt, Geoffrey Miller, Tom Roehl, Roberta Romano, Arthur Rosett, Richard Samuels, Eric Talley, Mark Tilton, Mark West, and participants in workshops at Columbia University, Cornell University, Harvard University, University of Illinois, New York University, and the University of Southern California. I received financial assistance from the Lynde and Harry Bradley Foundation, the Sarah Scaife Foundation, the Sloan Foundation, and the John M. Olin Foundation.

[1] As noted in the introductory footnote, this chapter was written in 1997, and does not reflect subsequent research, most relevantly Miwa & Ramseyer (2002c).

families at the center of the groups played as venture capitalists (section III). Group firms no longer play such a role, but only because the wealthy families at their core disappeared in the wake of World War II.

I. Introduction[2]

The keiretsu

The *keiretsu* groups are a diverse lot. Depending on the definition used, observers offer widely varied lists (see Sheard, 1996: 23 for the standard taxonomy). Most everyone names six central groups, even if they offer widely varied lists of who is in each: the Mitsui, Mitsubishi, Sumitomo, Fuji, Daiichi-Kangyo Bank (DKB), and Sanwa. The presidents of some of the firms do regularly meet for lunch, and in this chapter I focus on the resulting lunch clubs.

Typically, the lunch clubs include twenty-odd members – from forty-five at DKB to nineteen at Sumitomo. They cross a wide range of industry lines. The Mitsui group includes two banks, for example, two insurance companies, a trading company, a construction firm, a paper company, an oil company, a steel company, Toshiba, Toyota, and even a real estate firm.

The shareholdings

Keiretsu members often do invest in each other. Note, however, three qualifications. First, the cross-shareholdings are often quite small. Where some scholars place *keiretsu* cross-holdings at upwards of 70 percent,[3] among the six lunch clubs the intra-group cross-shareholding (the mean of the amount of any firm's shares held by all other group members combined) instead averages 18 percent. It ranges from a low of 11.7 percent among the forty-five DKB group firms to a high of 27.5 percent among the twenty-six Mitsubishi firms.

Second, these cross-holdings are largely reciprocal pairings. Within a group, firm A will tend to buy stock only in those firms that have in

---

[2] The figures in this section are calculated from the data given in Toyo keizai (1996: 28–45).
[3] Gerlach (1992: 74) quotes sources putting the percentage of shares held by "stable" shareholders at 70 percent. Although he does not refer to this as the *keiretsu* cross-holding figure, he does elsewhere characterize the *keiretsu* as providing group members with "a stable core of long-term shareholders" (*id.*, 4–5). Other observers conflate the 70 percent figure with *keiretsu* cross-holdings. In fact, the 70 percent figure usually just reflects the percentage of stock held by corporations rather than individuals.

turn bought stock in A. If there is any broader "groupism" within the *keiretsu*, the cross-shareholdings do not show it. Take the Mitsui. The average Mitsui group member invested in 10.04 other Mitsui firms. If the twenty-five group members[4] had invested in each other randomly, the odds that any two firms would invest in each other would be $(10.04/25)^2 = 0.161$. That figure, in turn, would predict reciprocal cross-holdings in $(325)(0.161) = 52$ of the 325 possible pairings among the 25 firms. In fact, reciprocal investments appear in ninety-five.

Furthermore, when these Mitsui firms invest in each other, they invest close to the same amount of funds. In a fifth of the reciprocal shareholdings, the economic value of the smaller investment was within 25 percent of the larger. In over half, it was within 50 percent.

Third, within each lunch club, several financial firms and a few other outliers own most of the cross-held stock.[5] For example, the two banks and two insurance firms own almost all of the cross-held Mitsui stock. Although the cross-holding within the Mitsui group averages 16.5 percent, if I drop the four financial firms the combined ownership of the other Mitsui firms in each other averages 5.81 percent. Within each group, there remain a few other outliers: Mitsui Real Estate owns nearly 16 percent of Mitsui Construction, for instance, Sumitomo Metals owns 23 percent of Sumitomo Light Metals, and Hitachi Assembly owns over half of Hitachi Chemicals, Hitachi Metals, and Hitachi Electric Wire. If I drop the six Mitsui firms with the highest percentage of shares held by other nonfinancial members, the *total* cross-holding among Mitsui firms drops to an average of 2.29 percent.[6] Among the other lunch clubs, it drops to a figure ranging from 1.84 and 1.87 at Sanwa and Fuyo to 7.98 and 9.14 at Sumitomo and Mitsubishi.

These cross-held shares do not make group members major shareholders in each other. Indeed, the nonfinancial firms rarely buy enough stock even to place among a firm's twenty largest shareholders. Consider the Mitsui again. The twenty-six Mitsui firms invested in each other 271 times, and the twenty-two nonfinancial firms invested 177 times. The four financial firms placed in the top-twenty list with every investment. The rest placed in that list less than a quarter of the time.

---

[4] Actually twenty-six, but one is a mutual insurance company.
[5] By law, banks can hold only 5 percent of the stock of any given firm (Antimonopoly Act, Law No. 54 of 1947, § 11), but they often own close to that amount.
[6] I.e., the average of the *total* percentage of any member firm's stock that is held by all other members of the group combined.

Whether a given investment is large or small obviously depends on the benchmark – and perhaps even these shareholdings will strike some readers as large. Note, however, that for most of the post-war years, for regulatory reasons Japan had no commercial paper market and extremely low bank deposit interest rates (Ramseyer, 1994; Litt *et al.*, 1990). Given the limited alternative investment opportunities, these corporate shareholdings become less mysterious than they might otherwise seem.

II.   The financial firms

Why they hold

One reason banks hold stock in their debtors seems straightforward: to constrain moral hazard. Once a firm borrows money, it has an incentive to raise the risk level on the projects it undertakes. By holding a borrower's voting stock, Japanese banks can sometimes mitigate this problem. Nineteenth-century US banks mitigated moral hazard by loaning primarily to insiders (i.e., other directors) over whom they had other formal and informal controls (Lamoreaux, 1991). Modern US banks neither buy stock nor limit loans to insiders – but only because the law prevents them from buying stock and their sheer size prevents them from lending only to directors. To mitigate moral hazard, they negotiate elaborate contractual limits on debtor discretion instead (Smith & Warner, 1979).

Although Japanese antitrust law stops banks from holding more than 5 percent of any debtors' stock (Antimonopoly Act, Law No. 54 of 1947, § 11), lunch-club banks often still place among their debtors' largest shareholders. Obviously, a 5 percent interest will not give a bank legal control over its debtor. As Black (1992: 815–16) points out, however, it may give a shareholder both the means and the incentive to assemble a shareholder coalition large enough to influence managerial direction when necessary. In essence, a 5 percent stake helps make credible a shareholder's threat to intervene if the managers perform at substandard levels.

Those commentators who insist that Japanese cross-holdings serve primarily a culturally embedded symbolic role usually argue that the cross-held shares reflect and cement the trades between the two firms (e.g., Gerlach, 1992: 76–77; 1989: 157). That reflective symbolism, they imply, stems from the way changes in cross-holdings correlate with changes in the underlying trades. In fact, for the lunch-club banks, shareholding changes and debt-level changes show no such correlation. With the Sakura bank (the main Mitsui bank) and the Mitsui group members, for example, the correlation between shareholding changes and debt-level changes during 1986–1994 was a mere 0.011.

Why they trade

Introduction

If the need to mitigate moral hazard helps explain why banks hold stock, it does not explain why they sometimes trade that stock. Although (as noted above) they do not trade in a way that correlates with changes in debt levels, they do trade. Take the intra-group shareholdings at the six lunch-club money-center banks (i.e., not trust banks) from 1986 to 1994. During those years, the banks shifted shareholding levels at a firm about 38 percent of the time (541 of the 1432 firm-years involved). In the years with such shifts, the change averaged 13.8 percent.

Consider, therefore, a straightforward explanation: banks trade in debtor stock when they learn undisclosed information in the course of monitoring their loans.[7] Because banks regularly monitor debtors, they sometimes have access to more accurate and timely information than other firms. Based on that information, they could potentially trade and profit. If they did, the debtor shareholders would suffer no loss from this. Given inter-bank competition, these stock market gains would instead lead to offsetting cuts in the interest rate banks charge.

To test this insider-trading hypothesis, one would ideally examine stock prices immediately before and shortly after a bank traded. Unfortunately, although I know the stocks a bank owned each March (the end of each fiscal year), I do not know when during the year it traded on any stock. As a cruder alternative, therefore, I test whether the direction and magnitude of a bank's trades during any given year contain information that helps explain the direction of stock price movements during that year (holding constant general market shifts). Absent any reason to think banks would *systematically* buy stock *after* a price increase or sell after a price fall (absent

---

[7] Insider trading has been illegal during most of the post-war years, but public enforcement has been weak. See Ramseyer & Nakazato (1999: 115). The absence of a well-organized options market in Japan meant that for most of the post-war period insider trading would generally have had to take the form of direct trades in equity.

any reason to think banks invest stupidly *as a rule*), an affirmative result would suggest that the bank traded on undisclosed information.

Accordingly, as the dependent variable I use the price of each lunch-club firm's stock in March (Year 2; EndPr). As explanatory variables, I use: (i) the price of the same stock a year earlier (Year 1; StartPr); (ii) the fractional change in the Tokyo Stock Exchange composite index from Year 1 to Year 2 (Index); and (iii) [(the shares the lunch-club bank owned in the firm in Year 2) – (the shares it owned in the firm in Year 1)]/(the shares it owned in the firm in Year 1) (BkInvDec). Using ordinary least squares, I then calculate the equations reported in Tables 5 and 6. Although I investigate trades only for the lead lunch-club banks, I have no reason to think that the trades by other banks with large investments at stake would be any different.

The Mitsui *keiretsu*

For tractability, consider first the Mitsui data in Table 11.1. Most importantly, the coefficient on the Sakura Bank's (the successor to the Mitsui Bank) investment decisions (BkInvDec) is positive. With a t-statistic greater than 2, it is significant at more than the 95 percent level. Apparently, the Sakura Bank's investment decisions did contain information that correlated with the direction the stock price moved that year. Necessarily, the results suggest (tentatively to be sure) that the bank earned modest profits trading on nonpublic information it acquired in the course of monitoring its loans.

In Equation I, I treated StartPr and Index as separate variables. As one would expect, the coefficient on StartPr is close to 1, and the coefficient on the Index is an approximate average of the stock prices involved. Because the relationship between the two is multiplicative rather than additive, in Equation III, I used the product of the two as the independent variable. The coefficient on the product is positive and statistically significant, again at the 95 percent level.

Several readers of a prior draft suggested that the positive correlation between a bank's trades and debtor stock price changes might reflect the impact of a new loan rather than insider trading. Suppose, they argued, that the bank bought stock when it loaned additional funds, and sold that stock when the firm repaid the loan. Because a large new loan might signal positive information about the firm's prospects, the firm's stock price would then rise when the bank bought the firm's stock. Crucially, however,

Table 11.1 *Trading profits by* keiretsu *banks: the Mitsui case*

	I	II	III	IV
BkInvDec	61.36 (2.19)	61.68 (2.20)	54.03 (2.05)	54.34 (2.06)
BkLoanDec		−10.92 (−0.93)		−10.22 (−0.93)
StartPr	0.90 (25.24)	0.90 (25.23)		
Index	946.74 (10.77)	942.79 (10.71)		
StartPr*Index			0.87 (27.59)	0.86 (27.56)
Intercept	−887.104	−880.60	136.47	138.82
	(−8.09)	(−8.01)	(4.03)	(4.09)
R^2	0.78	0.78	0.81	0.81
No. of observations	192	192	192	192

Notes:

- Dependent variable = the price of each *keiretsu* firm's stock in March of Year 2 (EndPr).
- BkInvDec = [(the shares the bank owned in the firm in Year 2) − (the shares it owned in the firm in Year 1)]/(the shares it owned in the firm in Year 1)
- BkLoanDec = [(the loans Sakura had outstanding to the firm in Year 2) − (the loans it had outstanding to the firm in Year 1)]/(the loans it had outstanding to the firm in Year 1)
- StartPr = the price of the stock in March of Year 1.
- Index = the fractional change in the Tokyo Stock Exchange composite index from Year 1 to Year 2.
- The regression is ordinary least squares.
- The table gives the coefficient, followed by the *t*-statistic.
- The sample includes all Sakura Bank shareholdings in the stock of the core Mitsui *keiretsu* members from 1986 to 1994.

Sources: Toyo keizai, ed., *Kigyo keiretsu soran* [Overview of Firm *Keiretsu*] (Tokyo: Toyo keizai shimpo sha, various years); Toyo keizai, ed., *Kabuka soran* [Stock Price Overview] (Tokyo: Toyo keizai shimpo sha, various years).

it would not rise because the bank was trading on inside information. It would rise because the bank provided new credit.

In fact, this counter-hypothesis does not work. To test it, in equations II and IV, I add changes in the Sakura Bank's outstanding loans at a firm (BkLoanDec). As Table 11.1 illustrates, the coefficient on BkLoanDec shows no statistical significance, while the coefficient on BkInvDec remains positive and significant.

wealthy individuals – and rather than invest separately these family members pooled their wealth in a family partnership. They then hired professional managers to invest that pooled wealth in industrial ventures.

Although historians sometimes dismiss them as "conservative," the *zaibatsu* families invested heavily in new and (within Japan) untried technologies. Black & Gilson (1998) describe venture capital firms as those that invest in "high-growth, high-risk, often high-technology firms that need[ed] capital to finance product development or growth." So too the pre-war *zaibatsu*.

To take new and untried technology to the market, the *zaibatsu* families supplied extensive and expensive technical and managerial expertise (again as the venture capital firms often do – see Sahlman, 1990; Gompers, 1995: 1464–65). Because they did so single-handedly, they had little incentive to share the returns with anyone else. Because they provided most of the skills that mattered, they demanded near-total equity stakes.

Granted, modern venture capitalists use securities other than stock to adjust the relative incentives of the venture capitalists and the start-up's managers. Typically, for example, venture capital firms today will prefer convertible securities for the advantages they offer in solving the various agency and informational problems the new venture presents (see Gompers, 1998). Lacking the markets necessary for such tactics, Japanese *zaibatsu* investors in the late nineteenth century instead took much of the equity. Presumably, they then motivated the start-up's managers through a heavily performance-based compensation contract.

As investors specializing in high-risk, high-return projects (and exactly as Black & Gilson predict), the *zaibatsu* often moved much of their money out of a firm once it succeeded. At that point, they earned only market returns on the shadow price of the stock. Rather than earn market returns on nondiversified investments, they sold the stock. Then, they either moved the funds into new high-risk ventures or parked it in diversified portfolio investments.

Exceptions notwithstanding,[10] the *zaibatsu* story is thus one of rich investors (i) pooling their assets within family-based partnerships, (ii) hiring professional managers who used this pooled wealth to take big stakes in and to transform high-risk, high-technology ventures, and then

---

[10] Obviously, there were exceptions. The *zaibatsu* invested heavily in some industries where they took only modest fractional interests. Although both the Mitsubishi and the Mitsui invested in railroads, for instance, they usually bought only minor equity percentages (Ramseyer & Rosenbluth, 1995: 127). Although the Mitsui dominated the giant Kanebo cotton-spinning firm, as of the late 1920s the Mitsui held less than 10 percent of Kanebo stock (*id.*, at 146).

(iii) moving their assets to new ventures once a firm succeeded. When the Mitsui bought the Miike coal mines in 1888, the mines were inefficient and dangerous affairs tied to traditional technologies and convict and outcast labor. The Mitsui placed the mines under a young MIT-trained engineer named Takuma Dan. Dan bought lavishly expensive western technology. In the process, he cost the Mitsui huge amounts of money, but it was money well spent. Within a few years Miike earned massive returns: profits rose from ¥80,782 in 1889 to ¥310,310 for the second half of 1893, to ¥733,704 in the second half of 1908.[11]

Once they had brought their firms to success, the *zaibatsu* firms often cashed in some of their investment. Once the Mitsui had transformed Miike into a profitable modern mine, it earned only market returns on Miike's shadow price. So long as it had more profitable places to park its money, it had an obvious incentive to sell some of its Miike interest. It did just that. In 1933 it sold two Miike subsidiaries, and by 1945 had sold a third of Mitsui Mining itself.[12]

Among the *zaibatsu*, the Mitsui and Mitsubishi most aggressively sold the firms they had built. Unfortunately, we lack extensive, annually updated data on pre-war cross-holdings. We do, however, have surveys from 1928 and 1945. Based on that data, Table 11.3 compares the Mitsui and Mitsubishi interests in several firms. The story is simple: after introducing sophisticated modern methods and earning huge returns for that risk, the Mitsui and Mitsubishi sold the stock at market prices.

Although the *zaibatsu* owned 50–60 percent interests in some firms, in many they owned 100 percent; in others they owned small portfolio interests. In effect, the average may have spanned firms at different stages along that chronological process: new firms still owned 100 percent by the *zaibatsu*, firms the *zaibatsu* had recently transformed into modern successes, and firms they had long ago transformed and partially sold to the public.

The *keiretsu* no longer play the venture-capitalist function that the pre-war *zaibatsu* played, but only because the occupation dispossessed the extraordinarily wealthy families at their core. After the war, the US-controlled occupation officers placed much of the blame for Japanese aggression on the *zaibatsu* families. In order to "democratize" the economy, they destroyed them financially.

---

[11] See Roberts (1989: 130–35); Yasuoka (1979: 198). Production at Miike went from 574,000 tons in 1891 to 1.1 million tons in 1903, 1.5 million tons in 1907, and 2.1 million tons in 1912. Takeda (1992: 65).

[12] Table 11.3; Mochikabu (1970: 29). The formally articulated reason for the sell-offs in the 1930s was to share the economic wealth of the conglomerates with the public.

Table 11.3 *Mitsui and Mitsubishi sell-offs*

	Intra-group shareholding (%)	
	1928	1945
A. Mitsui		
Mitsui Trading	100.0	53.3
Mitsui Mining	100.0	65.8
Toyo Rayon	100.0	44.9
Mitsui Trust Bank	50.8	16.0
B. Mitsubishi		
Mitsubishi Paper	100.0*	35.8
Higashiyama Agriculture	100.0*	63.8
Mitsubishi Heavy Industry (Shipbuilding)	99.4	42.2
Mitsubishi Trading	97.8	48.9
Mitsubishi Warehousing	97.4	60.6
Mitsubishi Electric	88.3	53.3
Mitsubishi Bank	64.4	39.7
Mitsubishi Mining	64.2	48.6
Mitsubishi Trust	50.4	39.7

Note: *Estimates, by Takahashi.
Sources: 1928 figures are from *Kamekichi Takahashi, Nippon zaibatsu no kaibo* [A Dissection of the Japanese Zaibatsu] (Tokyo: Chuo koron sha, 1930); 1945 figures are from *Mochikabu gaisha seiri iinkai, Nihon zaibatsu to sono kaita*i [The Japanese Zaibatsu and their Dissolution] (Tokyo: Hara shobo, 1970 [1951 edn]).

The lower contemporary shareholding levels follow straightforwardly. The *zaibatsu* families held large interests because they were heavily involved in transforming high-technology ventures. Investing most of the effort, they demanded most of the returns. With the wealthy families gone, the post-war *keiretsu* could no longer play that role. No longer playing such a role, they no longer took large equity stakes in affiliated ventures.

IV.   Conclusions

Modern *keiretsu* banks invest in the stock of their debtors to mitigate debtor moral hazard. They occasionally trade in the stock because in monitoring those debtors they obtain material nonpublic information. The nonfinancial *keiretsu* firms invest in each other only at trivial levels.

And the *zaibatsu* families held large interests in firms before the war because they were venture capital financeers. As such, they behaved much the way their silicon valley peers behave today. In many of the ways that matter, the shareholding patterns among major Japanese corporations reflect the simplest of economic calculations.

References

Aoki, Masahiko & Hugh T. Patrick, eds. (1994). *The Japanese Main Bank System: Its Relevance for Developing and Transforming Economies*, p. 231. Oxford: Oxford University Press.

Black, Bernard S. (1992). "Agents Watching Agents: The Promise of Institutional Investor Voice." *UCLA Law Review*, 39: 811.

Black, Bernard S. & Ronald J. Gilson. (1998). "Venture Capital and the Structure of Capital Markets: Banks versus Stock Markets." *Journal of Financial Economics*, 47: 243.

Gerlach, Michael (1989). "*Keiretsu* Organization in the Japanese Economy: Analysis and Trade Implications," in Chalmers Johnson, Laura D. Tyson, & John Zysman, eds., *Politics and Productivity: How Japan's Development Strategy Works.* New York: Harper Business, p. 141.

(1992). *Alliance Capitalism: The Social Organization of Japanese Business.* Berkeley: University of California Press.

Gompers, Paul A. (1995). "Optimal Investment, Monitoring, and the Staging of Venture Capital." *Journal of Finance*, 50: 1461.

(1998). "Ownership and Control in Entrepreneurial Firms: An Examination of Convertible Securities in Venture Capital Investments" (manuscript, January 1998).

Lamoreaux, Naomi R. (1991). "Information Problems and Banks' Specialization in Short-Term Commercial Lending: New England in the Nineteenth Century." In Peter Temin, ed., *Inside the Business Enterprise: Historical Perspectives on the Use of Information.* Chicago: University of Chicago Press, p. 161.

Lawrence, Robert Z. (1993). "Japan's Different Trade Regime: An Analysis with Particular Reference to *Keiretsu.*" *Journal of Economic Perspectives*, 7(3):3.

Litt, David G., Jonathan R. Macey, Geoffrey P. Miller, & Edward L. Rubin (1990). "Politics, Bureaucracies, and Financial Markets: Bank Entry into Commercial Paper Underwriting in the United States and Japan." *University of Pennsylvania Law Review*, 139: 369.

Miwa, Yoshiro (1996). *Firms and Industrial Organization in Japan.* Basingstoke, UK: Macmillan.

Miwa, Yoshiro & J. Mark Ramseyer (2000). "Rethinking Relationship-Specific Investments: Subcontracting in the Japanese Automobile Industry." *Michigan Law Review*, 98: 2636.

(2002a). "The Myth of the Main Bank: Japan and Comparative Corporate Governance." *Law & Social Inquiry*, 27: 401.

(2002b). "Banks and Economic Growth: Implications from Japanese History." *Journal of Law & Economics*, 45: 127.

(2002c). "The Fable of the Keiretsu." *Journal of Economics & Management Strategy*, 169.

Mochikabu gaisha seiri iinkai (1970). *Nihon zaibatsu to sono kaitai* [The Japanese *Zaibatsu* and their Dissolution]. Tokyo: Hara shobo (1951 edn) (principal volume).

Nihon keizai shimbun, ed. (1996). *Nikkei kaisha joho* [Nikkei Company Information]. Tokyo: Nihon keizai shimbun sha, 1996 IV.

Ramseyer, J. Mark (1994). "Explicit Reasons for Implicit Contracts: The Legal Logic to the Japanese Main Bank System," in Aoki & Patrick (1994, p. 231).

Ramseyer, J. Mark & Minoru Nakazato (1999). *Japanese Law: An Economic Approach*. Chicago: University of Chicago Press

Ramseyer, J. Mark & Frances M. Rosenbluth (1995). *The Politics of Oligarchy: Institutional Choice in Imperial Japan*. Cambridge: Cambridge University Press.

Roberts, John G. (1989). *Mitsui: Three Centuries of Japanese Business*. New York: Weatherhill, 2nd edn.

Sahlman, William A. (1990). "The Structure and Governance of Venture-Capital Organizations." 27 *Journal of Financial Economics* 473.

Sheard, Paul (1996). "*Keiretsu* and Market Access: An Economics of Organisation Approach." In P. Sheard, ed., *Japanese Firms, Finance and Markets*. Melbourne: Addison Wesley.

Smith, Clifford W., Jr. & Jerold B. Warner (1979). "On Financial Contracting: An Analysis of Bond Covenants." 7 *Journal of Financial Economics* 117.

Takahashi, Kamekichi (1930). *Nippon zaibatsu no kaibo* [A Dissection of the Japanese *Zaibatsu*]. Tokyo: Chuo koron sha.

Takeda, Haruhito (1992). "Tagakuka jigyo bumon no teichaku to kontsuerun soshiki no seibi [The Consolidation of Conglomerate Organization and the Establishment of Diversified Business Sections]." In Juro Hashimoto & Haruhito Takeda, eds., *Nihon keizai no hatten to kigyo shudan* [Japanese Economic Growth and Enterprise Groups] 53. Tokyo: University of Tokyo Press.

Toyo keizai (ed.). (various years). *Kigyo keiretsu soran* [Overview of Firm *Keiretsu*]. Tokyo: Toyo keizai shimpo sha.

Toyo keizai (ed.). (various years). *Kabuka soran* [Stock Price Overview]. Tokyo: Toyo keizai shimpo sha.

Yasuoka, Shigeaki (1979). *Mitsui zaibatsu shi: kinsei, Meiji hen* [The History of the Mitsui *Zaibatsu*: Early Modern and *Meiji*]. Tokyo: Kyoiku sha.

INDEX